The Leisy brewery, circa 1905.

Breweries of Cleveland

by Carl H. Miller

Schnitzelbank Press

Cleveland

ISBN 0-9662084-0-4
Library of Congress Catalog Card Number: 97-91334
Printed in the United States of America

Published by
Schnitzelbank Press
P. O. Box 771012
Cleveland, OH 44107-0044

On the cover...

Front: A Cleveland brewery worker, circa 1910.
Photo by Andrew L. Kraffert (1874-1958), veteran *Plain Dealer* photographer.
Courtesy of Western Reserve Historical Society.
Cover design by Steve P. Getch, GMedia.

Back: A painted glass advertising sign, circa 1905.
Author's collection.
Photo by Ed Oshaben.

End sheet photos courtesy of the Western Reserve Historical Society. Unless otherwise noted, all illustrations in this book are from the author's collection.

BREWED & BOTTLED IN CLEVELAND, OHIO

CROOKED RIVER®

GREAT BEER. RIGHT HERE.™

Crooked River is proud to have led
the rebirth of the local brewing
tradition in Cleveland, and
proud to have supported
this worthwhile project.

Descendants of Cleveland's
brewers – in toast to their proud
brewing heritage – have contributed
to the publication of this book.

Werner D. Mueller Family,
In memory of his grandfather, Ernst W. Mueller

❧

Harvey G. Oppmann Family,
In memory of Andrew W. Oppmann

❧

In loving memory of our grandfather, John T. Feighan,
founder, Standard Brewing Company

❧

In honor of Isaac, Otto and Herbert Leisy,
Amanda Leisy Cortlett and Hugo A. Leisy

❧

John Marsh Kaercher and Mary Kaercher Smith,
In memory of Jacob and Rosina Walther Mall

❧

Thomas C. Pavlik Family,
In memory of Jaro H. Pavlik

Acknowledgements

The author extends his thanks and gratitude to the following individuals, without whose aid the quality of this project would have been severely diminished:

Bill Carlisle, whose enthusiasm for the topic was unmatched, and whose massive collection of brewery photos and artifacts was graciously made available for use throughout the book's preparation.

Werner D. Mueller, whose extensive research and support of local history has contributed immeasurably to the book.

Harvey G. Oppmann, for his many suggestions and constant willingness to aid in completion of the project.

Tim Liston, for his sincere interest in preserving the history of Cleveland's breweries and for his support of the book.

Dr. Robert E. Ward, for his wisdom and guidance, and for access to his enormous collection of research on Germans in Cleveland (soon to be published under the title *History of the Cleveland Germans*).

Glenn C. Kuebeler, whose collection of research and artifacts of the Cleveland & Sandusky Brewing Company has added a distinct depth to the book's coverage of that company's history.

Glen Nekvasil, for the use of his research of Cleveland's breweries, particularly his comprehensive study of the Carling Brewing Company.

Ed Oshaben, for photographic work on pictures of bottles and other breweriana in the book, and for access to his large collection of Cleveland beer bottles.

Kathleen Webber, for her superb editing and many helpful suggestions.

And all of the people who lent their support: Christine & Robert Armstrong, Bob & Jeanette Bendula, Carl Bennett, Bob Bickford, Peter Blum, Beth & Dave Burgham, Ian Dowie, The Feighans, Steve Getch, Jeanne Goodspeed, Walter Haller, Harry Hobson, Dick Hurley, Bob Kay, Jack Keeler, Prof. Walter Leedy, Jack & Dianne Linna, Rebecca McFarland, George McGinty, Dr. Robert A. Musson, John O'Brien, Thomas C. Pavlik, Larry Pillot, Rick Porello, Terry Rancagli, Mike Sapienza, George Schneider, Anne Sindelar, Charlotte Sliger, Mary Kaercher Smith, Virginia Stief Sords, David L. Stashower, Marylou Traffis, Bill Viancourt, Richard Wright, Anthony Zappiltelli, Cathy & Nicholas Zoldak, and Lois Zverina.

In memory of my father,
whose love of history
sparked my own.

Table of Contents

Introduction   9

Chapter One: The Pioneer Brewers   13

Chapter Two: The Germans And Their Lager Beer   31

Chapter Three: Menace And Maturity   57

Chapter Four: The Beer Barons   81

Chapter Five: The Business Of Brewing   101

Chapter Six: The Saloon   125

Chapter Seven: Demise Of An Industry   143

Chapter Eight: Happy Days Are Here Again   157

Chapter Nine: An End To Depression   179

Chapter Ten: The Fatal Fifties   195

Chapter Eleven: Carling: The Quest For A National Market   217

Chapter Twelve: Coming Full Circle   247

Appendix: Histories of Selected Cleveland Breweries   257

References   263

Selected Bibliography   279

Index   285

Introduction

March 31, 1933 was a special day in Cleveland. Some 3,000 people gathered on Public Square and surrounding downtown streets to celebrate the imminent return of beer after thirteen years of National Prohibition. There were parades and fireworks, speeches and cheers. An undeniable sense of renewed hope permeated the Depression-era crowd. They knew, after all, that the re-legalization of beer signified a changing of the times. They knew that beer would mean more than just the return of the corner tavern. It would mean employment, reduced crime, and revitalization of entire neighborhoods that once bustled with brewery activity. Indeed, the brewing industry has always played an important role in the health and well-being of the city. And Clevelanders reciprocated with a special fondness for their hometown beers. It was a time when drinking a "foreign" beer – that is, a beer brewed outside Cleveland – was held in nearly the same regard as rooting for a rival ball team. Even today, bygone names like Leisy's, P.O.C., Erin Brew and Gold Bond are recalled with unusual sentiment by those who remember the post-prohibition heyday of these and many other Cleveland beers.

In the days before prohibition, as well, Cleveland's brewing trade was a source of pride for the city. Men like Isaac Leisy, Leonard Schlather, Carl Ernst Gehring and Andrew W. Oppmann – to name only a few – built enormous brewing enterprises in Cleveland. Their names came to be synonymous not only with quality beer, but with the success and prosperity of the German people in Cleveland. These were men who, in their prime, were pillars of the community. They chaired important civic committees and sat on the boards of large financial institutions. Their wealth and keen business sense won them great respect and admiration. But, most importantly, they brewed good beer. And it was the beer that was the foundation of their fortunes.

Simply stated, Cleveland has always been a beer town. But what made it so? A wide variety of circumstances contributed to the success of the city's early breweries. Ultimately, however, each of the various ingredients can be linked to one of three basic factors: the city's access to Lake Erie; its heavy industrial character; and its large German population. And, although these components are highly interrelated (i.e., the lake attracted industry, and industry attracted immigrants), each had its unique impact on the development and prosperity of the local brewing industry.

From the time of the city's founding in 1796 through the post-Civil War industrial revolution, Cleveland's major asset was Lake Erie. In every phase of the city's early commercial and industrial development, lake transportation played a crucial role. For nearly its first half-century, Cleveland was largely an agricultural center, processing grain received from Chicago and Buffalo via the Great Lakes, and from the inlands of the Midwest via the Ohio Canal. With the onset of the Civil War, Cleveland's production of iron and steel (the virtual cornerstone of the city's industrial base) began in earnest and was fed entirely by lake shipments of iron ore from the rich mines of the upper Great Lakes regions. Iron and steel, in turn, gave rise to countless metal-intensive industries – shipbuilding, machine tools, steam engines, etc. All depended on lake transportation for the receipt of production materials and delivery of goods to distant markets. Despite the undeniable importance of rail transportation to the growth of local manufacturing, Lake Erie was, as it remains today, a vital part of the city's industrial prowess.

To the brewing trade, as well, the Great Lakes offered tremendous advantages. Cleveland's position as an early hub for grain processing created an abundance of inexpensive raw materials for local brewers. And, of course, the distribution of their product via the waterways was key. Many of the same port cities that sent grain to Cleveland received lake shipments of beer made using that very grain. But, for brewers, proximity to the lake offered one very special advantage beyond mere transportation: an unlimited supply of *ice*. Before the advent of artificial refrigeration in the 1870s, brewing was very much at the mercy of the seasons. While beer-makers in most locales brewed only as long as ice supplies held out, Cleveland brewers were typically able to operate year round due to the enormous quantities of ice harvested from Lake Erie during winter. This, in turn, opened up a substantial shipping trade for local brewers, who supplied beer to inland regions where the brewing season was cut short by a lack of ice. By the 1870s, for example, a handful of Cleveland brewers had already established distribution facilities in Pittsburgh, where the scarcity and high cost of ice hindered brewing during the warm months.

It has been said that the Civil War transformed Cleveland from a commercial center into an industrial one. The explosive growth of heavy industry – and all of the economic "fallout" that came with it – provided the foundation for the city's brewing industry, and, indeed, for countless other lines of manufacture. Ever-expanding transportation and communication systems, the large immigrant labor force, a strong urban infrastructure, and economic stability all grew from Cleveland's character as an industrial center. At the heart of it all was *technology*. A wave of mechanization and improved production processes was rampant in virtually all industries, and brewing was certainly no exception. The local presence of a number of innovators in brewing equipment – among them the Arctic Ice Machine Company, the Loew Manufacturing Company, and many others – pushed Cleveland brewers to the forefront of new technologies. Bolstered first by the local manufacturing boom caused by the Civil War, and later by the immense post-war industrial development, the number of breweries operating in Cleveland grew steadily throughout the late 1860s until peaking at about *thirty* in the following decade.

But the story of any industry is, in the end, the story of the *people* who comprise and patronize that industry. Cleveland's large immigrant population – particularly the German segment – was a central factor in the local beer trade. Although the various English-style brews (ale, porter, stout and the like) dominated during the early 1800s, heavy European immigration had caused a major shift in tastes by mid-century. Many cities, Cleveland among them, began turning out larger and larger quantities of the German brew, lager beer. There is no question that the working class nature of Cleveland's immigrant population was directly related to its widespread consumption of beer. However, as concerned the Germans, the issue ran much deeper. Beer was a staple within their culture, class notwithstanding. The Sunday afternoon beer garden was a fundamental institution in German life. To them, beer was an important social icon. It represented friends, family, camaraderie, and patriotism. And so, as the number of immigrants grew, so too did the brewing of lager beer. At the hands of skilled European brewers, the Cleveland brewing industry began a period of steady expansion which continued, in general terms, well into the twentieth century.

It is important to recognize that it was not the *size* of its brewing trade that made Cleveland a great beer town. The city has never ranked among the nation's top brewing centers in terms of the amount of beer produced. Most American cities or towns of any consequence supported at least one or two breweries during the eighteenth and nineteenth centuries. All of the major cities supported dozens. Although Ohio as a whole consistently ranked as the third largest beer producing state (behind New York and Pennsylvania) for much of the nineteenth century, the combined output of Cleveland's breweries can only be described as *moderate* when compared to that of other major Midwestern cities. Unquestionably, Cincinnati contributed more to Ohio's status as a leading brewing state than any other single city. During the 1890s, the output of Cincinnati's breweries rivaled that of great brewing cities like Philadelphia, New York and Milwaukee.

Nevertheless, Cleveland boasted a healthy brewing industry for much of its history, and brewing was always an important part of the city's makeup. Although a variety of strictly local characteristics certainly shaped the way the brewing industry developed, Cleveland's brewers were subject to the same fundamental evolutionary path which prevailed for brewers in most American cities. Once the hand-powered era of the early 1800s gave way to heavy mechanization during the 1870s and 80s, the brewing industry experienced a tremendous surge in production capacity. With expanded brewing capacity came increased competition. The last decade of the nineteenth century was fraught with price wars and brewery consolidations. In the new century, however, attention turned to the growing momentum of the prohibitionists. Due largely to a sort of widespread denial that National Prohibition was a real possibility, brewers did not mount much of a battle against the "dry" movement. By the time prohibition became a clear eventuality, little had been done by the brewers in their own defense. In 1920, the nation was thrust into a thirteen-year ban on the manufacture and sale of alcoholic beverages.

The repeal of National Prohibition in 1933 was met with great fervor. Breweries across the country were refurbished and hurriedly put back into operation (though many of the old time brewing families had faded away or become involved in pursuits too far remove from brewing to warrant their return to beer). Early growth was slow. It would be several years before the production of beer would again reach pre-prohibition levels. The outbreak of war in 1941 brought conflicting influences on the brewing industry. Although a strong war-time economy bolstered beer sales, raw materials for brewing were scarce throughout the war years. The post-war prosperity, however, brought with it some of the best years brewers had ever witnessed. Beer consumption rose and the expansion of brewing facilities was widespread. But, it was not long before the small, regional brewer began to fall behind in the competitive race for business. Advances in brewing technology, development of the interstate highway system, and the birth of mass media communications all spurred emergence of "national" brewers. By the mid-1950s, regional brewers everywhere had begun to watch their sales erode under competition from heavily-capitalized and vigorously-promoted national brands like Budweiser, Schlitz and Pabst. As the dominance of the national brewers continued through the next several decades, nearly the entire nation's beer production was in the hands of a few colossal brewing companies. The era of the locally-brewed, locally-consumed beer had all but completely disappeared.

By the mid-1980s, a faint glimmer of hope began to sparkle for those lamenting the loss of their hometown beers. In regions where brewing had been idle for years, a rash of small startup "brewpubs" and "microbreweries" began to appear. A virtual regeneration of brewing in America was soon in progress. Making beer in a style reminiscent of an earlier era, beer drinkers-turned-entrepreneurs had sprouted up in nearly every major U.S. city by 1995. While the product of these affectionately-dubbed "craft brewers" represents only a minuscule portion of the country's beer production, it is clear that America's taste for beer is changing. A new generation is longing for the beer drinking traditions of an earlier time – a time when every town had its own complement of breweries, and each brewery had its own unique product.

Be that as it may, the nickel beer, the clip-clop of the horse-drawn beer wagons, and the grand old architecture of the typical nineteenth century brewery are gone forever. That fact is poignantly underscored by the words of one old timer, whose simple but near-poetic recollections of the early days of Schmidt & Hoffmann's brewery on Cleveland's east side were preserved in a 1920s newspaper article:

> *Well, sir, maybe you came by on a real hot day, and you wanted to inspect the brewery. First of all you went to the office and told 'em you'd kinda like to look over the plant. Then the man in the office would give you a brass check and in you'd go.*
>
> *The brewmasters were always glad to have people inspecting the plant because they took great pride in their work. They'd take 'em around and finally end up in a room to sample the beer. They'd draw it off in a big copper ladle and it had the prettiest collar you ever saw.*
>
> *But of course the beer was cold – awful cold – so cold that it would pretty near freeze your mouth. So the brewmaster would get an iron poker and heat it until it was red hot, and then plunge it into the beer. You could hear the hiss across the street, and this took off the worst of the cold.*
>
> *You'd be standing around there with your lips watering, not feeling very wicked either, and he'd pour out the beer in mugs, and when everybody had a glass you'd raise 'em together in kindness and bring 'em up to your lips, and before they quite got there you'd smell the beer and maybe a lively little bubble would jump out and land on your nose, and you could smell the coldness of it. And then you got it to your mouth and took a long pull on it. Boy, it tasted just like cream.*

It is this sort of timeless affinity for Cleveland's historic beers and breweries that gives importance to the preservation of their memory.

Chapter One

The Pioneer Brewers

The last two decades of the nineteenth century have been called the "golden age" of brewing in America. On the streets of nearly every city or town of any consequence rattled the mighty beer wagons of a nearby brewery, from which came brew that enjoyed the support and strict loyalty of the community. The local brewery was, in a sense, a source of pride for its area. It was a fixture in the neighborhood, and nearly every resident was affected by its presence in some way. All could hear the brewery's obligatory steam whistle, which blared like clockwork morning till night and set each day's pace for the entire vicinity. Many made the daily trip past the brewery, studying its splendid architecture and admiring the brewery owner's well-appointed mansion, which traditionally sat just adjacent to the brewery itself. And perhaps others simply harbored a childhood memory of being sent to fetch beer for the dinner table right from the brewery tap room. Indeed, the typical brewery of the late nineteenth century was closely tied to its community, and brewing was entirely a local endeavor. Brewers carved out strong regional markets and, as the century came to a close, the majority of such neighborhood breweries had grown into magnificent enterprises, monuments to a burgeoning industry.

But the commercial brewing of beer in America began long before the heyday of the late nineteenth century. Efforts to stimulate brewing in America date to the nation's very beginnings, when settlers urged experienced English brewers to travel to the new land and supply colonists with quality beer. And, of course, ultimately they came. By the start of the eighteenth century, signs of a tangible brewing industry had emerged within the American colonies. Pennsylvania's was perhaps the most active. Philadelphia, in particular, boasted a handful of rather sizable early breweries, and their products were held comparable to the

13

best brews imported from England.[1] As settlers spread west, the development of commercial brewing followed close behind. Towns like Pittsburgh, Cincinnati and Cleveland began to accumulate significant populations after 1800, and each witnessed the slow but steady rise of a number of industries, brewing most certainly among them. Although conditions were often difficult for brewers of the new frontier, many nevertheless managed to cultivate a respectable trade.

Hubach's Tavern at the corner of Kinsman and Lee was a typical establishment of its day. In early nineteenth century Cleveland, beer was dispensed almost exclusively at taverns and inns.

The typical pioneer brewer sold his product mainly to taverns and inns, where the great majority of beer was dispensed in the early days. Some brewers, after having made their handful of daily deliveries to tavernkeepers and innkeepers, simply peddled the remainder of their beer in the town center – mug by mug – off the back of a small cart. Three cents bought any parched passerby a seidel of freshly-tapped beer, drawn right from the keg. Others took their excess beer to market, in hopes of selling it to merchants or bartering it for other necessities. Selling beer directly to households, though surely of interest to early brewers, presented certain problems. Virtually all beer was packaged in wood kegs during the pioneer days (and throughout much of the nineteenth century), and even the smallest of such vessels tended to contain a quantity of beer much in excess of the typical family's needs. Affluent families sometimes kept beer cellars, in which they stored casks of "stock ale" for personal use. But the great majority of families could not afford expensive stock ales, and necessarily opted for the more common "present use ales" which, if not consumed quickly, tended to sour.

The bottling of beer (that is, the packaging of beer in a crude stoneware container) was engaged in by some early brewers who undoubtedly recognized its benefit for households. However, bottling was a highly troublesome task for brewers. In particular, the lack of an effective bottle enclosure throughout much of the nineteenth century was a constant menace to brewers who attempted to bottle a portion of their product. Leakage often resulted in flat or spoiled beer, a pitfall that few brewers were willing to accept. By and large, bottled beer was not something which could be found in any great abundance until late in the century.

In the early days, "take home" beer was obtained at the local tavern with the use of a *growler*.

14

Inside a typical nineteenth century saloon.

In general, households were left to their own devices in obtaining the family beer. Some simply made daily trips to a nearby tavern with a small tin pail, called a "growler," which the tavernkeeper placed on a scale and filled with beer until it weighed the proper amount. Some neighborhoods pooled their resources, periodically buying a keg of beer and having each family draw off its respective share.[2] This was particularly common within early German enclaves. Many housewives brewed some type of rudimentary beer themselves, the tools for which often consisted of little more than a couple of copper pots and an open hearth. And the ingredients were limited to whatever happened to be close at hand. Such household creations undoubtedly took a variety of forms, and probably were often of questionable fitness for consumption.

Indeed, the term "beer" has been used to encompass a vast array of beverages throughout its history. Generally speaking, beer might be defined as any beverage made with some type of malted grain as its base ingredient, then fermented through the introduction of yeast. But, of course, there is virtually no end to the list of ingredients that can be added to the process to achieve a desired taste or quality. The use of hops has been perhaps the most common additive over the centuries. Beer as we know it today, mostly lager beer, was not known to the pioneer brewers. Instead, brewing reflected the thoroughly Anglo-Saxon nature of early America. The popular brews of England – mainly ale, porter and stout – were the norm in pioneer days, and for many years remained the common drinks. Ale is typically heavier in body and more bitter-tasting than lager beer, and usually has a higher alcohol content. Although traditional ale was always strictly unhopped, the addition of hops had become common in ale brewing by the mid-1800s. Porter, originally a concoction made simply by mixing ales of differing strengths and types, is darker and heavier than most ales, and often has an almost sweet taste. Stout is heavier still than both ale and porter, and is usually the darkest and sweetest-tasting of the English brews.

In addition to ale, porter and stout, there was a number of somewhat vaguely-defined brews in popular consumption throughout the early 1800s. Among them were small beer, strong beer, table beer and common beer. Distinctions between them were largely based on alcoholic content and, accordingly, on their ability to keep without spoiling. Small beer, for example, soured much more quickly than did strong beer because of the former's lower alcohol content. Table beer and common beer were apparently intended for household consumption, and most probably were relatively low in alcohol content. Each of these brews is presumed to have been made using hops, thus distinguishing them from the traditional unhopped ales.

Inside The Early Brewery

Although a wide variety of different brews existed during the pioneer days, the basic processes involved in brewing were the same for all. However, the exact nature of the various chemical reactions which took place in the brewery were a complete mystery to the pioneer brewer. Scientific knowledge not being among his tools, the early brewer relied heavily upon "empirical means." Gauges and control panels, after all, were not the tools of his trade, as they are for brewers today. Rather, brewing was necessarily more of a hands-on affair, and the amount of physical labor involved was staggering:

> *The work required for the production of one brew of beer was exceedingly protracted and difficult. The hauling, dipping, pumping, breaking, stirring and boiling were tiresome work for the laborer, indeed requiring from fifteen to seventeen working hours every day, and making the brewers' occupation one of hard toil and of almost unbearable labor.*[3]

The making of beer entailed a number of different steps and stages, and the entire process could take several weeks to complete. The brewer's first task was known as "malting" – the conversion of some type of cereal grain (usually barley) into malt. This was accomplished by first steeping the grain in water. For some, steeping was continued "till the water be of a light reddish color." Others tested an individual kernel of the grain by pinching it between thumb and forefinger: "When it sheds its flour upon the fingers it is ready."[4]

Fermenting beer inside a Cleveland brewery.

The grain, having absorbed the proper amount of moisture, was next spread out on a stone floor and allowed to germinate. During this process, the grain's natural starches were converted to soluble sugars necessary for brewing. Frequent shoveling and turning of the grain was necessary to assure uniformity. Once germinated sufficiently, the grain was dried to halt the process, then roasted to acquire the desired darkness and consistency. Thoroughly roasted malt was what gave porter, stout, and the darker ales their color and body. Likewise, pale malt (slightly roasted) was used for lighter ales and table beer.

The finished malt was then ground to the proper texture by the brewer. The resulting grist was mixed thoroughly with hot water in a large wooden vessel. During this step, the sugars in the grist were communicated to the liquid, which was then called "mash." Particularly in the brewing of early lager beer, a portion of the mash was sometimes transferred to a kettle where it was boiled, then poured back into the mash tub, and repeated a number of times. The goal of this extra step was to extract as much of the grain's sugars and other substances as possible. Once the mashing process was complete, the grain was strained off. The syrupy liquid which remained was known as the "wort."

The wort was then transferred to the brew kettle, where hops were added and the liquid was boiled for a length of time. Often, more than one different type of beer would be made from a single brewing, and it was at this stage that the wort was sometimes divided into separate batches for differing treatments throughout the remainder of the process. It is suspected, however, that the earliest pioneer brewers rarely had more than a single kettle, making this practice difficult. And, beyond that, tending to more than one brew at a time, particularly at the boiling stage, would certainly have required extra brewery hands; one of the more challenging and intensive tasks of the early brewer was to maintain the very specific temperatures required for a successful hopping. His tools for doing so often included only his sense of touch and constant manipulation of the open flame beneath the kettle.[5] Too much heat, of course, would burn the wort and render it useless, while not enough heat would result in unsuccessful extraction of the desired qualities and flavor from the hops.

The mixture next passed into cooling vessels – large, flat tubs in which the wort sat at a depth of about two inches in order for rapid cooling. Manually-powered fans were sometimes hung over the tubs to quicken the process.[6] Cooling was necessary to prepare the wort for what was perhaps the most crucial stage in brewing: the fermentation stage. Fermentation was begun by transferring the wort into large, open casks and adding yeast. During this stage, the yeast "fed" on the sugars in the wort and produced alcohol and carbon dioxide. The early brewer had little understanding of the chemical reactions at work during fermentation. He knew only that this was

Top: One early method of roasting malt involved placing it in rotating drums and passing it over hot coals.

Middle: The early brew kettle, usually of copper construction, rarely held more than a few barrels of beer.

Left: A pair of early fermenting casks. The fermentation stage was perhaps the most crucial of the brewing process.

the point in the process where his creation was transformed – almost magically – into what could properly be called beer. In order to provide himself with a constant supply of yeast, the brewer recouped a portion of the excess yeast from each brewing for use in the next. This recycling of yeast, although probably unbeknownst to the early brewer, contributed significantly to achieving consistency from brew to brew.

     A variety of final treatments was undertaken by the brewer just prior to kegging. Nearly all brewers took measures to clarify their beer, and remove all remaining yeast particles and other substances. The most popular method for clarifying was to add wood chips or shavings, which would attract the floating particles and sink to the bottom of the vat. Many brewers also found it beneficial to the quality and characteristics of their product to briefly reintroduce hops into the brew, which was supposed to have helped guard against souring. Other brewers added a small portion of fresh wort to the finished beer – a process known as "krausening."[7] The goal, again, was to achieve some particular quality or characteristic desired by the brewer. Finally, the beer was packaged in wood kegs.

     Obviously, the making of beer by the pioneer brewer was something quite tenuously accomplished. With the help of virtually no mechanical aids or scientific knowledge, much in the early brewery was left to chance. At each stage of the brewing process, the variables were many: the type and quantity of malt used; the fashion in which the mashing process was undertaken; the amount of hops added, the intermittence of their addition during boiling, and the length of the boiling period; the type of yeast used in fermentation, and the length and nature of that entire process; and, of course, the wide range of last minute additives and treatments employed by the brewer. Indeed, trial and error played a major role in the whole endeavor. But it was exactly this type of variation in means and methods that allowed each brewer to craft a beer which was uniquely his own.

Beer In Early Cleveland

Cleveland's first brewers of beer must have been its tavern owners. The typical tavernkeeper, after all, was well accustomed to making much of his own purveyance himself, particularly in sparsely developed regions where there was often little alternative. That being the case, Lorenzo Carter, who built the first tavern in Cleveland in 1802, may very likely have been the first to brew beer in the small village. Carter, in fact, was sort of Cleveland's inaugural pioneer, having been responsible for a number of the village's "firsts," such as erecting the first frame dwelling, hosting the first wedding, arranging the first social dance, and building the first log

warehouse. In 1800, Carter and his family were the only non-Indian inhabitants living in Cleveland proper.[8]

In addition to the back room concoctions of tavernkeepers, early villagers could expect an occasional shipment of beer from outside sources. As late as 1829, for example, the arrival of twenty-five barrels of beer from Detroit was worthy of significant attention in the *Cleveland Herald*.[9] Such shipments of "foreign" beer, though unpredictable, were undoubtedly much anticipated by tavern owners and beer drinkers alike.

By the 1830s, however, interest in commercial brewing in Cleveland had sprouted. An early settler of Cleveland recalled, "The Rev. Elijah F. Willey, a Baptist clergyman, put in operation on a small creek, now and for many years known as Walworth Run, near Willey Street*, a brewery, the first in Cuyahoga County."[10] Land records show that Reverend Willey first acquired properties in the Walworth Run area beginning in 1835, the brewery property most probably among them.[11] However, it is important to note that, by 1832, Cleveland had already counted among its commercial developments a well-established brewery doing business in the Flats as The Cleveland Brewery. It is likely, therefore, that although Reverend Willey's operation certainly qualifies as one of the village's earliest commercial breweries, it may not have actually been the first.

Furthermore, the likelihood that the small village may have witnessed one or two earlier

The "Flats" – a half-mile wide valley which cradles the winding Cuyahoga River – had developed as Cleveland's industrial center by the mid-1800s. A majority of the city's earliest breweries were located in the Flats.

---

*Willey street, incidentally, was named not for the Reverend, but for his brother, John W. Willey, whose extensive land holdings in the Walworth Run area earned it the name "Willeyville" for a time. John W. Willey also held the distinction of being Cleveland's first mayor, serving from 1836 to 1838.[12]

failed attempts at commercial brewing establishments is very high. In fact, in 1823, Dutch immigrants set up a distillery which was allegedly "followed by a series of breweries."[13] Despite a scarcity of evidence to corroborate that claim, the notion that the commercial brewing of beer had made its start in Cleveland as early as 1823 is not at all difficult to believe. After all, dozens of different lines of manufacture were already well represented in Cleveland by this time, among them paper making, book binding, gun making, wagon manufacturing, ship building, and all types of garment manufacturing, to name just a few.[14]

Although it certainly seems reasonable that local entrepreneurs might have recognized a demand for Cleveland-brewed beer already in the 1820s, it is nevertheless easy to see why any such ventures would have found it difficult to survive for any significant length of time. A village of only about 600 inhabitants in 1820, Cleveland simply did not yet offer a wide enough market for non-essential goods to sustain its own brewery on a long term basis.[15] Taverns and inns were still few in number and, anyway, whiskey and other distilled spirits were often the favored custom in the earliest of those establishments. As for households, means for the brewing of beer in the home were quite common in developing regions, and Cleveland was certainly no exception. In the summer of 1819, a local newspaper printed the following articles for the home brewer: "To Fine or Clarify Beer in 24 Hours," "To Feed And Give Flavor to a Barrel of Beer," and "To Cure a Butt of Ropy Beer." Also published were recipes for "Spruce Beer," "Molasses Beer," and "A Good Household Beer." Indeed, "self-reliance and resourcefulness," as one historian commented, "were man's greatest assets."[16]

The completion of the Ohio Canal in 1832 stimulated Cleveland's industrial development immensely. Beer was sent into the Ohio interior on canal vessels like this one.

Not until about 1825 did the small village begin to offer a more attractive environment for entrepreneurial activity. The opening of the Erie Canal through to the Hudson River in October of that year meant that Cleveland would become a natural "gathering place" for farm produce and textiles destined for Buffalo, Albany, and other eastern points. Already in November, the *Cleveland Herald* proudly reported that wares sent from Cleveland were being sold on the streets of New York City.[17] Conversely, merchant warehouses began to appear in the Flats along the Cuyahoga River, prepared for the dispersal of goods arriving from the east.

The announcement in 1825 that Cleveland had been selected as the northern terminus of the Ohio Canal brought a virtual onslaught of outside investment. Completed in 1832, the canal connected Lake Erie to the Ohio River, thus opening trade with Cincinnati, New Orleans, and the entire Mississippi Valley. Merchant vessels traveling between the east coast and the south often chose the canal route over the Ohio River, exchanging cargo as they went and stimulating commercial development at each stop. Naturally, Cleveland was a mandatory stop for such vessels. One historian painted the following picture of the canal's boomtown effects on the village of Cleveland:

> The little town woke up one morning to discover itself a crossroads of commerce, with a traffic jam rapidly developing. Thus quickly did Cleveland feel the impact of the new water route; new wharves were built along the riverfront to accommodate the swarm of sailing ships that converged on the village, but the demand was such that most of the time there were ships anchored in the harbor, awaiting their turn for unloading. Cargo piled up on the docks and spilled on to the wooden sidewalks, blocking the path of the throngs that filled the waterfront – the sailors, longshoreman, merchants, and passengers.[18]

As early as 1834, Cleveland was shipping ten million pounds of merchandise annually via the canal. By 1838, that figure had almost doubled.[19] Owing almost exclusively to the prosperity brought by the Ohio Canal, Cleveland's future as a major commercial and industrial center began to take shape.

It was, therefore, probably no coincidence that Cleveland's first substantially successful brewery was founded during the same year as the completion of the Ohio Canal.

The Cleveland Brewery

In the spring of 1832, entrepreneur Robert Bennett and local physician Dr. Samuel J. Weldon announced the establishment of The Cleveland Brewery and invited villagers to partake in the brewery's supply of ale and table beer.[20] The new brewery was located in the Flats on Canal Street near Champlain, just along the Ohio Canal. Frontage on the canal was undoubtedly key in the selection of a site, facilitating the brewery's reception of raw materials as well as its shipping of beer both into the Ohio interior and to points accessible from Lake Erie. Later advertisements invariably noted that the brewery's products were not only consumed locally, but also manufactured for "export use."[21]

Given that alcoholic beverages were widely used in the practice of medicine throughout the nineteenth century, one might speculate that Dr. Weldon's involvement in the brewery was motivated by his need for a reliable supply of medicinal substances. Regardless, Dr. Weldon, who was one of only nine members of the Cleveland Board of Health,

The Cleveland Brewery,

BEING now in operation, the subscribers will deliver to order ALE and TABLE BEER, in barrels, halves or quarters, to suit the convenience of purchasers.

Ale per bbl.	$6 00
" half do.	3 00
" qr. do.	1 50
Table Beer per bbl.	3 00
" " half do	1 50
" " qur do.	1 00

ROBERT BENNETT.
SAML. J. WELDON

P. S. Bakers and their families supplied with Yeast. The Grains will make excellent feed for cattle or hogs; and merit the attention of those families in the village who keep cows.

To the Farmers we would say, that we shall in the ensuing falll be prepared to furnish them with Seed Barley, for the produce of which we will give them a good price.

WANTED—Immediately, 1000 bushels of Barley, delivered at the Brewery, for which the highest price in Cash will be paid.

May 29, 1832.   4-3m

This advertisement appeared in the May 29, 1832 edition of the *Cleveland Herald*.

certainly must have drawn upon the output of the brewery when the infamous cholera epidemic of 1832 reached Cleveland just weeks after the brewery's establishment.[22]

Be that as it may, Dr. Weldon appears to have relinquished his interest in the brewery by February of 1833, when Robert Bennett placed the following notice in the *Cleveland Herald*:

> *CLEVELAND BREWERY – The proprietor, in acknowledging the past favors of his friends, takes this opportunity of informing them that he has added to his establishment, the Malting Business, which he flatters himself will enable him to offer to the public, Beer of a superior quality, viz. Ale, Strong Beer, Bottled Porter, Brown Stout, Etc. Rectified Cordials of various flavors, and of the best quality, prepared by the proprietor. Distillers can be supplied with Malt, or have their grain malted on reasonable terms. Yeast for sale at the residence of the subscriber, in Euclid street.*
>
> R. BENNETT.
>
> *N.B. – The highest market price will be paid for barley.*[23]

If the above advertisement is to serve as any indication, it would appear that Bennett entertained high expectations for his business. For that reason, it is somewhat surprising to find that he, like Weldon, had left the business by early in 1834. It is surmised that Bennett's addition of the malting operations – which certainly must have required at least a minimal capital outlay – may have left him overextended. After all, the local demand for malt could not have been exceedingly strong given the city's limited number of distilleries and the complete absence of breweries other than Bennett's.

The Cleveland Brewery spent the next several years passing through a somewhat complicated series of management changes. It came into the possession of brothers Joseph and Richard Hawley who, in the spring of 1834, announced that a constant supply of beer would be kept on hand throughout the following summer.[24] In 1837, Joseph was replaced in the partnership by brewer Herrick Childs, a recent arrival from Massachusetts. The firm of Hawley & Childs lasted only a short time, though, and by December of 1839 Childs was alone in the business. Both ale and beer were his products and it was reported that the output of the brewery was about 1,600 barrels* annually.[25] However, the Hawley family had apparently kept ties with the brewery. Thomas Hawley and his son-in-law, John Hawley Cooke, were leasing it from Childs by the end of 1840. Offering bottled ale and porter as their products, the new Hawley & Company pledged to use "unremitting exertions to please all who may favor them with their custom."[26] Nevertheless, notification was made in 1843 that Childs was "again in the old establishment." Two years later, it was announced in the *Cleveland Herald* that the brewery was once again available for lease.[27]

At some point not long after the publication of that last notice, the original Cleveland Brewery was replaced by an entirely new structure. It is possible – even likely – that a fire may have necessitated the new brewery. Fires were virtually routine in most early industrial settings and especially in breweries, where open flames were used in various stages of the brewing process. Whatever the case, construction of the new Cleveland Brewery – "a fine superstructure of brick" – was completed in 1847 and sold as soon as finished to Samuel C. Ives.[28] The new proprietor had been involved with brewing in Cleveland for several years, starting as a brewer with Herrick Childs.

---

*The production of beer is universally measured in "barrel" units. According to brewing industry measurements, a full barrel contains exactly thirty-one gallons of beer.

He later gained control of the old City Brewery near the canal, and operated it in partnership with brewer Henry Lloyd throughout the 1840s. Now having purchased the newly-constructed Cleveland Brewery, Ives was assured success by his "ten thousand customers through the West."[29]

As exaggerated as that estimate may have been, the Cleveland Brewery did, in fact, enjoy great prosperity under Ives' ownership, and the plant was frequently expanded. The original capacity of twenty barrels at each brewing was soon increased to forty-five barrels. Just a few years later, in 1852, a mammoth new four-story brewhouse was constructed. The new facility reported a capacity of one hundred barrels at each brewing, totaling between 7,000 and 8,000 barrels annually. A local newspaper called the brewery "the largest, and most complete in machinery and apparatus, of any in the city," and further claimed that there were "few in the country superior to it."[30] Indeed, in just a few short years, Samuel C. Ives had built what can rightfully be called Cleveland's first visibly auspicious brewing enterprise. The beginnings of a soon-to-be burgeoning industry were clearly apparent.

In the early days, the financial success of a brewery often depended as much as anything on the personal reputation of the brewmaster. John C. Brewer, who was regarded as "one of the best brewers in the country," was hired by Ives in 1849. It might be reasonably assumed that Brewer's long involvement in the brewery was largely responsible for the enduring prosperity of the business.

For more than fifteen years, John C. Brewer oversaw the manufacture of the Cleveland Brewery's products, including the colorfully-titled Old Bee's Wing Ale, the feature brand. Interestingly, Brewer provided his services to at least one other local brewery during his employment with Ives. After all, a seasoned brewmaster was a rare and much-sought commodity in early Cleveland.

Samuel C. Ives, Cleveland's first beer mogul.

At the very peak of the brewery's success, Samuel C. Ives died on August 24, 1856 at age forty-five.[31] (The cause of his death was reported as "inflamed liver," an affliction which, for obvious reasons, was not too uncommon among some early brewers.) Ives had amassed significant wealth during his years in the brewing business, such that each member of his

By the mid-1850s, Ives' Cleveland Brewery had grown into a substantial enterprise.

IVES' CLEVELAND BREWERY,
Canal Street, Cleveland, Ohio.
CONSTANTLY ON HAND FOR CITY and Export use, XX, XXX Pale, Amber and Cream Ales, Porter and Brown Stout. ☞Particular attention is called to my stock of Present Use and Cream Ales, a sound and reliable article of which can always be found on hand during the warmest weather in summer. ☞Orders addressed to F. D. STONE, Agent, will receive prompt attention.
aug7

"That Devilish Woman"

Court records concerning a dispute over Samuel C. Ives' estate provide an uncommonly personal glimpse into the colorful, if not unruly, lifestyle of this early Cleveland brewer. The records detail a series of rather unseemly goings-on with which Ives was hopelessly involved. The troubles began in 1850 when an East Indian women known only as Phoebe – rumored to be a prostitute – arrived in Cleveland. Ives, a married man, reportedly became "very friendly" with her, and, within a short time, the young lady was openly describing herself as Ives' mistress.

The illicit relationship, however, apparently soured after Ives found Phoebe in her home with a canal captain, who quickly fled through a window to escape Ives' charge. Disheartened by the incident, Ives reportedly paid Phoebe $500 "to get rid of her." Indeed, the relationship seemed finished when Phoebe gathered her belongings and departed for Toledo. She soon returned to Cleveland, however, and was discovered living in one of Ives' houses – empty at the time – and demanding another $500 to vacate the property. Phoebe was later found having purchased a fur on Ives' account with a local merchant, allegedly forging Ives' signature on a purchase order. Although admitting no guilt, Phoebe quickly paid the merchant his debt after a constable investigated the charge and threatened a visit to the local jail.

Having tired of her unfaithful husband's antics, Mrs. Ives obtained a divorce in 1855. In the meantime, Ives and his adulteress had reconciled such that, in January of 1856, the two retreated for three days to Painesville, Ohio where they were married. Ives, who observed that "this Cleveland is a great place for talk," hoped to keep the marriage a closely guarded secret in order that his young daughter Eliza would not learn of the marriage. Friction continued between Ives, his first wife, and his new wife, and the secret was not kept for long.

Throughout much of the ensuing turmoil, Ives' health was in rapid decline. At one point when Ives' illness had become life-threatening, the first Mrs. Ives informed Phoebe that she would be "kicked out of house and home" should Ives not survive. The bed-ridden Ives calmed his new bride by claiming that he had set aside $25,000 for her and their expected child, which they would receive upon Ives' death. Be that as it may, Ives' affection for his new wife began to wane. Referring to Phoebe as "that devilish woman," Ives pursued reconciliation with the first Mrs. Ives, going so far as to offer a $500 reward to anyone who succeeded in getting him and his first wife back together. And, in fact, when Ives' illness finally took his life in the summer of 1856, it was his daughter Eliza and the first Mrs. Ives who were at his bedside.[33]

Phoebe, incidentally, gave birth in 1857 to a child whom she named Samuel C. Ives, Jr. The court action for which all of the above testimony was recorded was between the guardian of little Samuel, Jr. and that of young Eliza Ives, who were dueling over rights to one of Ives' many properties.

family was left a healthy bequest. However, the Cleveland Brewery – clearly his most valuable asset – was bequeathed solely to Ives' beloved fourteen-year-old daughter, Eliza.[32]

On young Eliza's behalf, the brewery was leased to the firm of H. G. Lucas & Company, which continued the production of ale, porter and stout as before. The company was headed by local maltster Henry G. Lucas, who enlisted partners Francis Rowe and George L. Newman in the operation of the brewery. By May of 1857, however, the partnership had been dissolved. Lucas purchased his partners' shares in the company, which operated not only the brewery, but also the Forest City Malt House on the city's west side.[34] Carrying on alone in the business, Lucas also advertised himself as a dealer in "hops and highwines."

Eliza Ives, grown and married, still held title to the Cleveland Brewery in August of 1862, when management of the works was taken over by her husband, Frank D. Stone, nephew of Cleveland industrialist and railroad magnate Amasa Stone. In bidding his farewells to the brewery, Henry G. Lucas placed the following announcement in the *Plain Dealer:*

> *The subscriber having…retired from the Brewing business in the city of Cleveland, and having disposed of all of his stock and interest therein to Mr. F. D. Stone, as manager for the proprietors of "The Ives' Brewery," would now cheerfully and respectfully recommend the new management to the numerous patrons and customers of the former establishment – taking this opportunity, at the same time, of thanking all old friends and past customers for the very liberal and successful support hitherto so cordially extended to him, and now gratefully acknowledged.*
>
> *H. G. LUCAS.*[35]

Referred to as "Colonel Stone" by his friends, Frank D. Stone had just returned from service in the Union Army when he took over direction of the brewery. A local newspaper boasted that he was "a young man of energetic business qualities, and will, no doubt, conduct the business with success."[36] Indeed, under Stone's management, the brewery remained among the city's largest producers of ale until its sudden demise on New Year's Day of 1865.

On the evening of January 1st of that year, the Cleveland Brewery was completely destroyed by one of the largest fires the city had yet witnessed. The brewery had twice been the victim of attempted arsonists just within the previous two weeks. Interestingly, the final blaze was attributed to "Confederate emissaries sent North to inflict a staggering blow upon their victors."[37] The culprits had picked their night judiciously. While freezing temperatures rendered the steamers' hoses useless, the strong winter winds bolstered the fire and carried sparks and flaming debris to surrounding buildings, many of which ignited. By the time the first pail of water was thrown, nearly half the brewery had already collapsed. The *Cleveland Leader* offered its readers the following rather dramatic account of the brewery's peril:

Eliza (Ives) Stone and her husband, Frank D. Stone, operated the Ives Cleveland Brewery until it fell victim to fire in 1865.

> *The roads, hill-sides and neighboring roofs were black with spectators – men, women and children – and as the red light shone on them it burned up their dark outlines, and made them children of the fire; and as the conflagration roared, and walls fell with a*

crash, and men shouted, and the flames leaped hungry and hellish toward the sky, and clouds of smoke, sparks and cinders arose like torments, it was a spectacle sublime as any "dreadful"-minded poet could conceive of the sublimities of Tophet.[38]

In June of 1865, Stone and his wife Eliza were reported as leaving for Iowa where they intended on raising sheep and going into the wool business.[39]

The Ale Brewer's Heyday

The period between 1850 and 1870 was a prosperous time for ale brewers. Taking notice of the development of ale brewing locally, the *Cleveland Leader* wrote in 1858:

One important branch of business carried on in Cleveland is that of the manufacture of Ale. There are in the city some half dozen [ale] breweries, most of them doing a large business. It is demonstrated that Cleveland is an excellent location for the purchase of barley, as well as for the sale of its product. Both ale and beer are shipped in all directions, and the orders from abroad keep pace with the increased manufacture. The prices are low enough to compete with the best breweries of the East, and their qualities are said to be unsurpassed.[40]

The city's ale breweries produced about 18,000 barrels in 1858, a figure which continued to climb throughout the following decade.[41] The shipping of Cleveland beer to outside locales was a significant factor in the development of the city's brewing industry during this period. For example, of the 53,500 barrels of ale and beer produced in Cleveland during 1867, about 10,500 barrels were shipped out of the city. The great majority was sent via Lake Erie. A paltry fifty-two barrels were sent on canals, while 3,600 were shipped by rail, thus illustrating the dramatic demise of the canal system in the shadows of rail transport.[42]

The Lloyd & Keys Cleveland City Brewery on St. Clair Avenue between West 9th Street and Old River Road. Founded in 1859, the Cleveland City Brewery remained in operation until 1909, when Daniel H. Keys closed the brewery and retired after working for more than sixty years as a brewer in Cleveland.

Although the growing popularity of the German lager beer certainly accounted for a significant portion of Cleveland's rising malt liquor production during the 1860s, the city's largest brewing establishments were still primarily its ale breweries. Many had been in operation for a number of years, had cultivated a substantial trade, and were well-established in the community. The Forest City Brewery, at Seneca (West 3rd)

Street and Canal, was among the most popular of the city's ale breweries. Founded by Charles C. Rogers in 1839, the brewery ultimately passed into the hands of Carling & Company of London, Ontario, who renamed it the London Brewery.[43] Thomas Newman was engaged in the brewing of ale at his "old stand" on Irving (East 25th) Street near Pittsburgh Avenue, having begun around 1850.[44] The Eagle Brewery on Michigan Street was a fixture in the city for many years. It was established in the early 1840s by George W. Hamilton, but was later taken over by its brewmaster, John Quinn. The Lloyd & Keys Cleveland City Brewery commenced the manufacture of ale in 1859 on the St. Clair Avenue hill. The brewery endured until 1909, when Daniel H. Keys – due to his "advanced age and poor health" – shut down the works.[45]

Although dozens of brewers manufactured and sold ale in Cleveland over the decades, few achieved the success and prosperity of brewer John M. Hughes. The decidedly superior reputation of his ales, the proportions to which his enterprise ultimately grew, and the respect which he enjoyed within the community made Hughes a virtual paragon among Cleveland's ale brewers.

The Hughes Brewery

John M. Hughes came to Cleveland in 1847 from New York, where he had been engaged in various pursuits in Albany and New York City for a number of years. Not long after his arrival, Hughes found work as a brewer at the Spring Street Brewery. Established in 1846 by Truman Downer, the brewery sat at the base of the east bank of the Flats on Spring (West 10th) Street, between Main Street and St. Clair Avenue. Downer took on a partner, Thomas F. Wyman, not long after starting the business, and the two had developed the enterprise considerably by 1850 when Downer decided to leave Cleveland to take up brewing in Chicago. Seeing an entrepreneurial opportunity, Hughes bought the brewery from Downer and Wyman for the sum of $3,200.[46] Oddly, the brewery's adjacent malthouse was not included in Hughes' purchase. Rather, the malting facilities were sold to local maltster John B. Smith.[47]

Hughes' new venture was not initially graced with the best of luck. Just six months after its purchase by Hughes, the brewery was ravaged by a fire from which only the company's books could be rescued. All else was destroyed. The morning following the fire, the cold pages of the press stated simply, "The XX brewery was burned last evening. Loss total."[48] Nevertheless, the brewery was up and running again within a reasonable amount of time. By 1853, Hughes had moved the brewery's

An 1868 invoice for a quarter barrel of Hughes Ale.

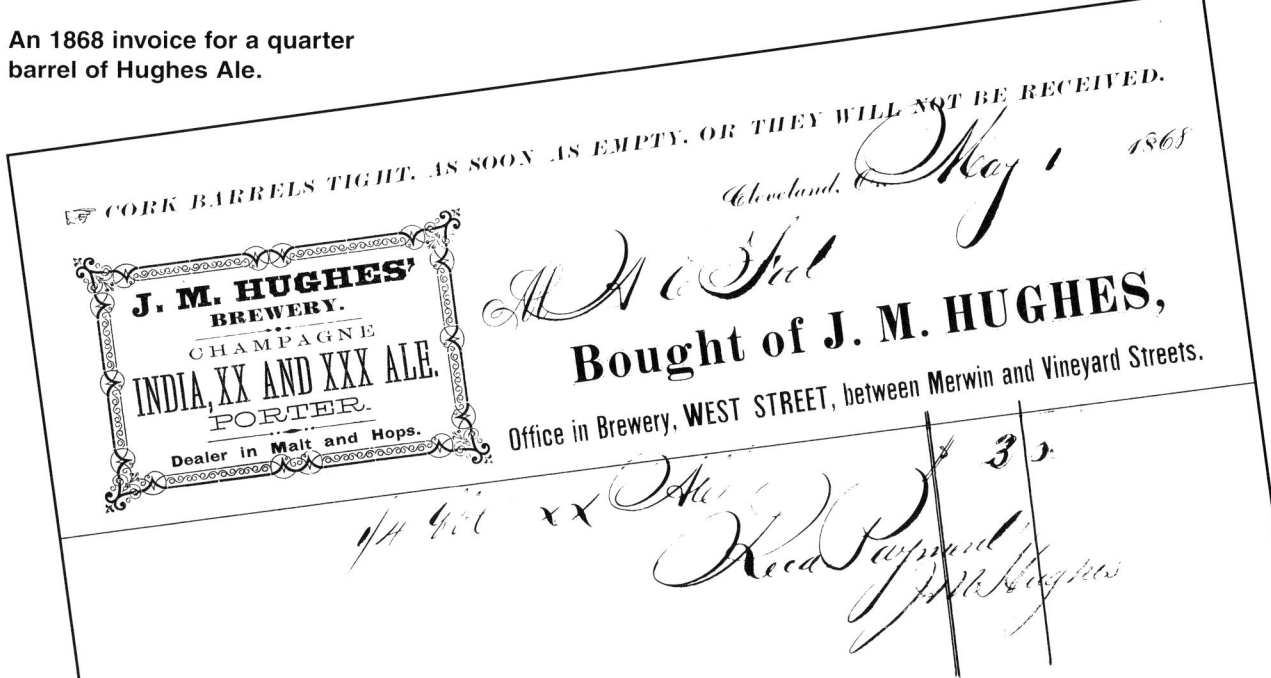

office to nearby Merwin Street, presumably due to expanding operations within the brewery.[49]

Indeed, Hughes' production of ale soon outgrew the old Spring Street Brewery. In 1857, construction began on a new, "more commodious" brewery and malt house which would cost a then impressive $15,000 to complete.[50] The new structures were located on West Street in the Flats, between Merwin and Vineyard, with valuable frontage along the Ohio Canal. Finished and fully occupied by the beginning of 1858, the new works employed twenty men (more than any other brewery in the city) and was capable of producing no less than 10,000 barrels of ale per year. When famous journalist and humorist Artemus Ward embarked on a sight-seeing tour through Cleveland in 1861, among the sites he visited was the new Hughes Brewery, "where a stop of thirty minutes was made to refresh."[51]

Like his original brewery on Spring Street, Hughes' new plant on West Street suffered a destructive dose of misfortune. Four men in Hughes' employ were going about their business in the brewery's malthouse one Sunday afternoon, when a series of loud cracking noises caused them to bolt from the building in fear. Once outside, the workers watched as the entire four-story malt house collapsed with a tremendous crash, instantly reducing the entire building to a mass of ruins. The mound of debris, which spilled across the entire width of West Street, was laced with the estimated 12,000 bushels of barley and malt which had been stored in the building. At Hughes' direction, the brewery crew was put to work immediately recovering as much of the grain as possible before foul weather rendered it worthless. After all, the value of the building's contents nearly matched that of the building itself, it was said. Recognizing the urgency of the mission, local maltsters John B. Smith and Louis Umbstaetter offered temporary storage of the recovered grain at their respective facilities.[52]

Such minor setbacks notwithstanding, the Hughes brewery enjoyed a good business over the years. John M. Hughes, clearly more so than any other brewer of ale in Cleveland, was known for the supreme quality of his products. While most brewers were undoubtedly content to target the masses of the working class, Hughes – by virtue of the superior quality of his ale – seems to have cultivated a slightly more affluent clientele over the years. It was said of Hughes' ale that "The best families in the city consider their cellars imperfectly stocked until they have a cask of it."[53] Testimonials to the high grade of Hughes' ale, such as the one which follows, are found in relatively uncommon abundance:

> *Ever since the days of that convivial and celebrated Monarch, King Cole, good ale has been regarded as a healthful and agreeable beverage by the wisest of men. It aids digestion, is conducive to portliness, warms the blood, and drank in rational quantities makes a man better generally. The extensive brewery of John M. Hughes, Esq., of this city, justly enjoys a wide reputation for turning out excellent ales. We doubt if they can be surpassed, and the large and constantly increasing demand for them sufficiently backs anything we may say in their favor. With probably the best appointed brewery in the West, and a corps of very skillful practical brewers, Mr. Hughes is enabled to produce ales which may safely challenge comparison with any in America.*[54]

Along with quality came variety. Hughes is known to have marketed as many as eight or ten different types of ale at any one time. Among the many choices were Kennett Ale, Amber Ale, Champagne Ale, India Pale Ale, Cream Ale, Burton Ale, and Bitter Ale, not to mention the standard present use and stock ales. Of course, Hughes' porter and brown stout were also regularly available.

Through the success of his brewery, Hughes and his wife Eliza enjoyed a comfortable lifestyle. Having no children, they resided at different times in the city's most prestigious (and presumably expensive) downtown hotels. Interestingly, the Hughes were living at the Weddell House in 1861 when Abraham Lincoln made his locally-famous address from the corner balcony of that establishment. Most of their time, however, was spent living instead at the American House on Superior Avenue just off Public Square.[55] While Hughes tended to the concerns of his brewery, Mrs. Hughes occupied herself with a variety of charitable activities, a pastime which was then often reserved for the well-to-do. In particular, Mrs. Hughes was active in the Cleveland Protestant Orphan Asylum. Advertisements periodically appeared in local newspapers requesting that "benevolent people living in the country" bring some small donation with them when visiting in the city, which could be dropped off at the Hughes brewery in care of the asylum.[56] It is wondered whether those "benevolent people" who appeared at the brewery with donations in hand were invited into Hughes' office to discuss more substantial contributions.

A victim of heart disease, John M. Hughes died in 1871 at age seventy-six. As a well-respected businessman, Hughes received the expected tributes in all of the local newspapers. However, it was the following accolade which was perhaps the most meaningful:

> *IN MEMORIUM – At a meeting of the employees of the late John M. Hughes, deceased, the following resolutions of respect and condolence were passed:*
>
> *WHEREAS, it has pleased an all-wise God to remove from us our beloved employer and esteemed friend, and,*
>
> *WHEREAS, We are desirous of giving expression of our deep regard for him and the loss we have sustained; therefore,*
>
> *Resolved, That in his death we have lost a friend, who had won our respect and esteem by his uniform kindness and solicitude for our welfare. That, during our long association with him we have always found him one upon whom we could rely under all circumstances, and to whom we could look not only for advice and counsel, but substantial assistance when in need. That, in his death we have sustained a loss which we deeply mourn, and that we tender to his honored widow and relatives our heartfelt sympathy in their affliction. That the Secretary of this meeting be instructed to present a copy of these resolutions to the widow, and to furnish a copy to each of the city papers for publication.*

Thomas Sholl,	*George A. Rhoades,*	*O.F. Rhoades,*
Matthew Nichols,	*William Magnam,*	*Thomas Howlett,*
Fred Nichols,	*George S. Allen,*	*Robert Madden,*
Fred Bruhler,	*A.S. Allen,*	*John Socklen,*
John O'Malia,	*Peter Wieser,*	*James E. Foley,*
James Skelly,	*Michael Halpin,*	*George Schutts.*[57]
Frank Miller,	*Richard McCurry,*	

There are numerous historical accounts which claim that the typical mid-nineteenth century brewery worker endured a life of subjugation – if not outright abuse – at the hands of his employer. Hughes, it would seem, did not have this in common with his contemporaries.

After Hughes' death, the brewery passed into the hands of his wife, Eliza. Hughes' nephew and long-time bookkeeper, Levi F. Ives (no relation to brewer Samuel C. Ives), served as superintendent.[58] By 1884, ownership of the brewery had passed from Eliza Hughes to her sister, Miss Cornelia A. Bowlsby.[59] The circumstances surrounding the change in ownership are not entirely clear, but it is suspected that some type of trusteeship may have been involved.

John M. Hughes' brother, Arthur Hughes, became president of the brewery when it was incorporated as The Hughes Brewing Company in 1888.[60] Arthur Hughes was engaged in the stone quarrying business locally, doing business for many years under the name of Wilson & Hughes Stone Company, which later evolved into the Ohio Stone Company. John H. Kirkwood, an officer of the latter company, was also involved in the brewery, replacing Arthur Hughes as the brewery's president after Hughes' death in 1890.[61] Incidentally, Levi F. Ives remained in charge of the brewery's day to day operations, and held the official positions of secretary, treasurer and general manager once the brewery was incorporated.[62]

An 1871 advertisement demonstrating the health-giving qualities of Hughes Ale.

The brewery produced its last barrel of Hughes ale in 1894 after a number of years in gradual decline. Although the 1880s represented one of the most dramatic periods of expansion for the U.S. brewing industry as a whole, the Hughes brewery exhibited few signs of growth during its last two decades of operation.[63] The likely cause of the brewery's stagnation was simply the disappearance of a strong market for ale compared to the growing popularity of lager beer. The brewery's output, which was never adapted to include lager beer, had averaged about 10,000 barrels of ale per year throughout the 1870s. By its final year, production had dwindled to 1,500 barrels annually.[64]

Valued at about $50,000 at the time of its discontinuance, the old brewery was taken over by the J. & A. McKechnie Brewing Company of Canandaigua, New York which used the buildings as a distribution facility until about 1898.[65] The following year, veteran Cleveland brewer Hugh Spencer organized the Spencer Brewing Company and began brewing ale in the plant. By 1901, however, the venture had failed. The brewery closed its doors for good, thus marking the end of an era for the manufacture of ale in Cleveland.[66]

Indeed, by the latter part of the nineteenth century, the manufacture of ale had fallen into decline not only in Cleveland, but all across the country. Anglo-Saxon tastes and customs simply no longer prevailed as they had in early America. English-style brews faced ever-shrinking demand as the steady flow of European immigration propelled lager beer into national dominance. Those brewers of ale who assimilated by adding lager beer to their product fared better, at least, than those who did not. But, by and large, the brewing industry in America had become a purely *German* industry, operated and controlled almost exclusively by German immigrants. Unquestionably, the days of prosperity for ale brewers were, as the Germans would say, "auf die Neige" – on the wane.

Chapter Two

The Germans and Their Lager Beer

Heavy European immigration into America throughout the mid-1800s brought with it the beginnings of a brewing revolution which, in little more than a few decades, completely changed the face of the U.S. brewing industry. In particular, the large volume of newly-arrived Germans – and their unperishable love of the German-originated *lager beer* – had a tremendous impact on the brewing of malt beverages in America. Lager beer was, without question, a staple in the life of the typical German. And, although the earliest German immigrants may have necessarily suffered through a temporary substitution of their lager beer with the available ales and porters, it was not long before demand forced supply. By the 1870s, lager beer had gained a clear dominance over the common English brews. A virtual *rebirth* of the brewing industry in America was under way.

The fundamental difference between lager beer and all of the various malt beverages which were already predominant in America was lager's use of *bottom fermentation* yeast – that is, a type of yeast which settles to the bottom of the vat during fermentation. First identified by German brewers during the early 1800s, this particular type of yeast resulted in a lighter, more effervescent brew with a distinct amber color.[1] Lager beer also differed from ale in that it required a lengthy aging period before it was ready for consumption; the German word "lagern" means *to store*.

From a manufacturing standpoint, perhaps the most crucial characteristic of lager beer was that it required cold temperatures throughout much of the brewing process. The bottom fermentation yeast which gave lager beer its unique characteristics simply performed better in lower temperatures. And due to lager's relatively low alcohol content, it was necessary that the brew be kept sufficiently cold throughout the entire aging process to prevent spoilage. This single requirement – this need for consistently cold temperatures – introduced a whole set of new factors into the brewing process, and represented a constant challenge to early brewers of lager beer. Most brewers accommodated themselves by digging cellars into hillsides, taking advantage of the constant underground temperature.[2] However, the cellars only provided insulation from outside elements and did not themselves sustain temperatures low enough to prevent spoilage of the beer. Therefore, large quantities of ice – harvested from lakes, ponds, and rivers – were hauled into the cellars to keep the beer cold. Ice was stockpiled each winter and made to last as long as possible into the warm months. Once the supply of ice ran out, lager brewing was finished for the season. Many early lager brewers turned to the production of ale during the warm months. Others engaged themselves in entirely different lines of business until the brewing season returned. Only after the development of ice-making machinery during the 1870s were brewers able to produce lager beer year round.[3]

There is some degree of uncertainty surrounding exactly when and where lager beer was first brewed in America. But the most often recited version of

Above: The Forest City Ice Company's ice-harvesting facility at the mouth of the Rocky River. During the late 1800s, breweries consumed a significant percentage of the natural ice supplies.

Below: Harvesting ice in Plymouth, Ohio in the nineteenth century.

history says that, in 1840, Bavarian brewer John Wagner brought a quantity of lager beer yeast with him to America, where he set up a rudimentary lager brewery on the outskirts of Philadelphia. Others, supplied with lager yeast from Wagner, soon followed. By the mid-1840s, lager breweries were in operation in several eastern cities, among them Boston, New York, and Buffalo. And even a few midwest cities, such as St. Louis and Chicago, boasted early lager beer breweries.[4]

This burst of new lager breweries around the country was paralleled by a wave of German immigration throughout the 1840s. The unsuccessful Revolution of 1848 was driving tens of thousands of Germans from their homeland in search of political freedom. Many others were motivated by America's promise of economic opportunity. By the early 1850s, Germans were entering America in numbers far greater than any other nationality, resulting in a German-born growth rate of 123 percent in this country during that decade. All told, about 1.5 million Germans emigrated to America between 1840 and 1860.[5]

Many German immigrants flocked to the cities, where work could be had or trades could be practiced. Cleveland, like most midwest cities, received a large share of such immigrants. One early Cleveland resident observed, "German immigration in 1849-50 was so sudden that soon the physiognomy of social life took on a different shape and became significantly German."[6] For much of the latter half of the nineteenth century, Germans accounted for about one-third of Cleveland's population. The largest surges occurred in 1873 and 1881, when more than half of the new immigrants arriving in Cleveland were of German origin. Until 1895, Germans remained the largest nationality to enter the city on an annual basis.[7]

However, the mere volume of German immigrants alone is not sufficient to explain the rapid and near phenomenal popularity of lager beer in America. After all, the masses of German immigrants might just as easily have *Americanized* their taste for drink (as they did in so many other respects) and adopted a liking for ale, porter, and

To Germans, lager beer was far more than just a beverage. It was a cultural mainstay. Lager beer represented patriotism, health, family, and friendship.

stout. But, to Germans, lager beer was more than simply a beverage; it was a cultural mainstay. Lager beer was inextricably woven into the fabric of German society and, for many immigrants, it represented one of the few familiar tastes of the homeland present in the new country. In fact, lager beer, in some sense, became an outright symbol of the German heritage in America. When the first serious wave of the temperance movement struck during the 1870s, Germans in several American cities took to the streets and marched with beer kegs on their shoulders, protesting what they viewed as an attack on their right to practice the customs of their homeland. In Cleveland, as in other cities, such demonstrations often erupted into violent street brawls. Public outbursts over the regulation of lager beer in Chicago were so fervent that they collectively became known as "The Lager Beer Riots."[8] The opposition in such conflicts – largely temperance advocates – appears to have succeeded only in bolstering the typical German's determination to retain the cultural practices of his native land.

The significant role that the Sunday afternoon beer garden played in German society throughout the nineteenth century was most certainly a central factor in the German attachment to lager. And it is perhaps in this context that the prevalence of lager beer in America is best understood. German immigrants, once settled in America, tended to establish a number of certain recreational institutions in imitation of those from their homeland. Among the more common of such institutions were singing societies, literary clubs, German language newspapers, gymnastic clubs ("Turnvereine"), drama societies and, of course, beer gardens.[9] In fact, the beer garden was not only one of the most commonly established German institutions in America, but often served as the place of origin or manifestation for many of the others. Beer gardens were, in many ways, the social linchpin of the German community, playing an important role in the immigrant's ability to retain and share his cultural heritage.

Beer Gardens in Cleveland

In Cleveland, the beer-loving German had many drinking establishments from which to choose. Among the very earliest to cater exclusively to the lager beer trade was William Richter's place on Ontario Street. One early German resident recalled:

> It was an event when William Richter, that good-natured Saxon, advertised to the whole of humanity in Cleveland that he was opening the first lager beer bar in a charming one-story board hut on Ontario Street. His customers saw it with cheerful faces, and the new institution was greeted by Teutons, both old and young, dedicated to good drink, particularly recent immigrants who could find no enjoyment in the usual drinks, such as "Present Use," "Stock Ale," and "Ginger Pop." To have lager beer from the tap in the land of hard liquor, what German nature friendly to drinking could not have felt the pull of home?[10]

Richter obtained his supplies of lager beer from a Pittsburgh brewer, presumably due to a lack of any which was brewed locally. Although Richter's establishment enjoyed wide popularity for its first many months, it was said that the "good-natured Saxon" eventually fell victim to his incurable habit of extending credit to his customers in a far too liberal manner.

As the number of Germans increased in Cleveland, so too did its count of lager beer saloons. The Cleveland City Directory for 1857-58 listed more than seventy-five exclusive purveyors of lager beer. Among the most frequented were Henry Barcher's Wine and Lager Beer Saloon, Fisher & Shafer's Lager Beer Hall, Kindsvater's Billiard and Beer Saloon, George Fay's Philadelphia Lager Beer Saloon, and Mathias Adams' Lager Beer Hall.[11] And, indeed, several others throughout the city presumably enjoyed a brisk business. Many such beer halls, though confined entirely to the indoors, called themselves "gardens" nonetheless. They were often decorated with an abundance of flowers and greenery in order to simulate an outdoor setting.

However, it was the genuine outdoor beer gardens which attracted the masses (season permitting, of course). Unlike the common beer halls, which were essentially little more than places for the consumption of lager beer, gardens offered a full-blown recreational family outing. Among the typical beer garden fare was live entertainment of various kinds, pavilion dancing, sporting activities, an abundance of food, and plenty of shady trees ideal for a family picnic. Particularly on Sundays (the only non-work day for most immigrants), the area beer gardens attracted throngs of Germans in search of a leisurely afternoon of relaxation and socialization with fellow countrymen.

Inside a typical nineteenth century beer hall.

Many of Cleveland's beer gardens were situated right within the congestion of the city, such as Volk's Garden on Michigan Street or Trinkner's Garden on Ontario.[12] Although such beer gardens were undoubtedly a welcome oasis, they certainly could not have been entirely free of the bustle and noise of the city. Thus, the most popular beer gardens were located in outlying areas, where patrons could enjoy the sprawling lawns and serenity of the country. In addition, when Sunday liquor ordinances became predominant during the 1870s, those gardens which were located outside the city limits enjoyed immunity to the drinking restrictions. Some of Cleveland's longest-lived and most frequented beer gardens sat along Willson (East 55th) Street, just beyond what was then the eastern edge of the city limits.

Around 1862, German immigrant Frederick Haltnorth established Haltnorth's Garden on the northeast corner of Willson Street and Woodland Avenue. The garden was perhaps the largest and most popular of Cleveland's beer gardens, and was certainly the most elaborate. In its heyday, Haltnorth's Garden included such amenities as a museum, a bowling alley, a rifle range, a photo gallery, and a large fishing pond spanned by a picturesque bridge.[13] An enormous concert hall, which housed a saloon and two restaurants, sat near the garden entrance. However, most of the summer entertainment was performed outdoors in an open-air theater which seated 800 people. Performances by the Cleveland Philharmonic Orchestra were frequent, as were presentations of comic opera by some of the day's most popular opera companies.[14] Of course, at the center of all activity was an ample supply of cold lager beer.

August Burckhardt's brewery, at the corner of Pearl Street and Monroe Avenue, was among the many small lager beer breweries doing business on Cleveland's west side during the 1870s.

Separated from Haltnorth's Garden by only a narrow alley was Lied's Garden, a 2-1/2 acre resort sometimes referred to as Union Park. The garden opened in 1862 under the proprietorship of Balthasar Lied, a German immigrant who had been involved in a variety of local drinking establishments since arriving in Cleveland in 1842. Open to the public on Sundays only, the garden was enjoyed by crowds of Germans who, "in God's free nature, in the shade of large trees, with snacks and good drink, recover from the efforts of the week." Lied and his family lived on the premises. Although the garden was leased to outside management after 1883, Lied remained the garden's "gentlemanly host" until his death in 1900.[15]

Further north along Willson Street, at the corner of St. Clair Avenue, sat Kindsvater's St. Clair Garden, established by Paul Kindsvater in 1866. For several years, Kindsvater had conducted one of Cleveland's early lager beer saloons inside town. (Much to the delight of temperance advocates, the saloon was ultimately acquired by a local clergyman for the purpose of converting it into a Sunday school.) Kindsvater had also been a partner in a pioneer Cleveland lager beer brewery. After 1871, the German entrepreneur devoted himself exclusively to the management of his Willson Street "pleasure park."[16] Like the other beer gardens along Willson Street, Kindsvater's garden was frequented on a typical Sunday by hosts of Germans seeking an afternoon of family recreation. Interestingly, Paul Kindsvater served

Haltnorth's Garden was the most popular of Cleveland's beer gardens. Shown here is the main entrance to the garden on Willson (East 55th) Street.

Paul Kindsvater's imposing residence marked the entrance to his beer garden on Willson (East 55th) Street near St. Clair Avenue. The building in the rear, obscured by trees, was the beer hall and dance pavilion. This photo was taken about 1870.

as a director of the St. Clair Street Railroad.[17] After all, the horse-drawn street cars which carried the droves of city dwellers to the outlying gardens on Sundays were of critical importance to the success of the gardens.

One of Cleveland's earliest beer gardens sat on the hillside along Forest (East 37th) Street south of Croton Avenue in what was then a remote corner of the city. The well-appointed garden and adjoining brewery were established in the early 1850s by John Dangeleisen. He continued to run it for several years in addition to operating a lager beer saloon inside town on Erie (East 9th) Street. A writer for the *Wächter und Anzeiger* recalled that a favorite pastime at Dangeleisen's was a game which the Germans called "Kind und Kegel" (skittles) and that crowds at the garden were especially large during bock beer* season.[18] By the 1870s, the resort was in the possession of German immigrant Henry Rochotte and, later, Frank Payer. However, both the brewery and the garden had closed by 1875 as the city's expanding industrial character began to encroach on the area.

Despite the typical beer garden's lazy atmosphere and the usual collective good cheer of its patrons, a day at the local garden was not always without period disquiet. Events such as the one described below in 1858 were routinely reported by local newspapers:

> *A fight took place at Daegleison's on Sunday afternoon last, which had its origin in long and frequent draughts of that enticing and highly-respectable beverage called "lager beer." The combatants, some six or eight in number, were mostly Germans, and pitched into each other, it is said, with great earnestness. Two or three were thrown into the canal and the consequent dunking considerably cooled their ardor and restored quiet. Lager beer on Sunday afternoons is not a very desirable institution.*[19]

Indeed, a good scuffle seems to have been as much a part of standard beer garden festivities as the beer itself. Haltnorth's Garden, for example, was so often the site of such altercations that efforts were made to stop the horse-drawn street cars from running to the garden on Sundays. The *Cleveland Leader,* a proponent of those efforts, wrote, "scenes are enacted there every Sabbath that should excite a blaze of indignation in the breast of every respectable citizen."[20]

That notwithstanding, the Sunday afternoon beer garden was a significant social institution in the lives of countless immigrants. And, like any city with a substantial concentration of German-born inhabitants, Cleveland saw a large number of such establishments flourish throughout much of the 1800s and early 1900s.

Lager Beer in Early Cleveland

The Germans' consumption of lager beer in Cleveland had already made a dramatic impact on the city's malt liquor production by 1870. In the *Annual Statement of Trade* for that year, it was noted that 76,610 barrels of beer had been produced in Cleveland during the year, and that "of this large amount the brewers report but a small proportion of Stock Ale. The decided preference of consumers generally is said to be for...Lager, instead of Stock Ale."[21] In 1874, an estimated two-thirds of the output of the city's breweries was comprised of lager beer. And that percentage climbed as more lager breweries emerged. Indeed, in 1878, the number

---

*Bock beer is a dark lager beer traditionally brewed only in springtime.

Weiss Beer: A German Tradition

Lager beer made its debut in Germany during the early 1800s, and soon thereafter established itself as that country's national beverage. However, beer in some form had already been an integral part of German life for centuries when lager beer began its swift ascent into widespread consumption. Prior to the 1800s, Germans quaffed a wide variety of different brews. Among the most predominant and time-honored was a top-fermented beverage made with wheat, commonly called weiss beer. ("Weiss" is the German word for *white*, reflecting weiss beer's light color.) Certain regions of Europe produced so much weiss beer that legislation had to be enacted regulating the supply of wheat; brewers consumed the grain in such quantities that not enough of it was being allocated to bakers for making bread.[24] Although the introduction of lager beer rendered many early German brews passé, weiss beer enjoyed a small yet sustaining demand well into the beginning of the twentieth century.

Naturally, that demand accompanied the throngs of Germans which emigrated to America throughout the 1800s.

Jospeh Beltz

In Cleveland, the manufacture of weiss beer was pioneered by German immigrant Joseph Beltz, who operated the city's sole weiss beer brewery for several decades. A native of Germany's Rhine Valley, Beltz emigrated to America in 1867 and came directly to Cleveland. His first job here was in the employ of John Dangeleisen, one of the city's early lager beer brewers. Later, the young Beltz established himself in business as a cooper, applying the trade he learned in Germany. He located his venture at the corner of Slater (East 61st) Street and Outhwaite Avenue, where he later added a saloon and wine shop to his enterprise. It was also at this location that Beltz set up his weiss beer brewery in 1876.[25]

The Beltz brewery made a slow start. In 1878, a paltry three barrels – about 1,000 bottles – of weiss beer were sold.[26] And by 1884, the brewery was making less than 500 barrels a year – the smallest output of any Cleveland brewery. However, in 1898, the brewery was re-equipped to manufacture ale and porter. This addition to the brewery's output represented Beltz' first venture into the production of brews other than weiss beer, and marked the beginning of a period of rapid change for the brewery.

In 1901, the brewery was incorporated as the Beltz Brewing Company with a capitalization of $100,000. Joseph Beltz was president and treasurer, Valentine Koenig was vice-president, Lawrence C. Beltz was secretary,

of breweries operating in Cleveland reached a remarkable twenty-six, due largely to a rash of new lager breweries.[22] The great majority were scattered throughout the city's west side, where the concentration of Germans was highest. Clearly, lager beer had made a place for itself in Cleveland. Before long, names like Leisy, Schlather, Gehring, Oppmann and many others would come to represent the Germans' complete dominance of beer-making in Cleveland.

Some twenty years before the uptrend of the 1870s, however, several local brewers had already been involved in the manufacture of lager beer. There is strong evidence which suggests that brothers Michael and Martin Stumpf, German immigrants, may have brewed lager beer in Cleveland as early as the mid-1840s. A 1902 commemorative edition of *Wächter und Anzeiger* newspaper, a volume dedicated to preserving the accomplishments of local Germans, names the Stumpf brothers as the city's pioneer brewers of lager beer.[23] Problems arise, however, when the volume attempts to provide further detail. For example, the date and location given by the authors

and John J. Beltz was brewmaster.[27] Perhaps more significant was the brewery's introduction of lager beer during the same year, which sparked an almost immediate surge in business. By the end of 1901, about 10,000 barrels of beer had been brewed during the year, an astounding figure given the miniscule scale of the brewery just a few years earlier.[28] The works was substantially enlarged throughout the following years, so that by 1906 the brewery was reportedly capable of producing 75,000 barrels of beer annually.[29]

The production of weiss beer had ceased at the Beltz brewery by 1905, vastly overshadowed by the sales of lager beer.[30] However, one of Beltz' sons, Carl E. Beltz, who had grown up working inside his father's weiss beer brewery, was not so quick to abandon whatever market for weiss beer still lingered. The young Beltz established his own weiss beer brewery in 1905 on East 67th Street off Woodland Avenue, and inherited the trade which his father had spent thirty years cultivating. Operating on a presumably small scale, Carl E. Beltz faithfully carried on the family weiss beer tradition until his brewery closed in 1914.[31]

Although the Beltz name was virtually synonymous with weiss beer in Cleveland, several others had engaged in its manufacture by the turn of the century. Among those who brewed weiss beer in Cleveland over the years were Wenzl Medlin, Jacob Voelker, Andrew Kress of the Kress Weiss Beer Company, and Frederick Ehle & John J. Hammer of the Buckeye Weiss Beer Company.[32]

Nevertheless, by the time statewide prohibition took effect in Ohio in 1919, the manufacture of weiss beer had all but disappeared, never again to re-emerge as a significant factor within the industry.

Above: Wire-bale bottle with porcelain stopper, embossed for Jos. Beltz & Sons Weiss Beer.

Right: A delivery wagon for Carl E. Beltz' Weiss Beer Brewery, circa 1905.

as to the establishment of a brewery by the Stumpfs are known to be inaccurate, necessarily casting a certain degree of doubt upon the reliability of the entire claim.

Having commenced business around 1846, the Stumpf brothers do seem to have preceded any other Germans in the founding of a brewery in Cleveland. It does not automatically follow, unfortunately, that the brothers *must* have brewed lager beer right from the start simply because they were German. After all, the various English brews – ale, porter, stout, etc. – faced a ready market, while the demand for lager was yet uncertain. It is known, however, that the Stumpf brothers were certainly lager brewers fairly early on, if not from the very beginning. By 1852, when lager beer was being produced by at least two other breweries in Cleveland, the Stumpfs had already been involved in their operation for a number of years. In fact, the brothers' early start, coupled with the assertion made by the German authors, is the strongest piece of evidence in their favor. And, as no other lager brewer claims to have been the city's first, there is little doubt that the

Stumpf brothers were, indeed, Cleveland's first brewers of lager beer.

The younger brother, Michael, was the first to emigrate to America from their hometown of Darmstadt, Hesse, Germany. He arrived in Cleveland prior to 1845 and worked as a laborer, possibly at one of the ale breweries in the Flats. Martin followed his brother to America in 1846 and, within a short time, the two started in the brewing business together under the name of M. Stumpf & Company.[33] Michael had purchased a small piece of land on Lake Street between Muirson & Canfield (Lakeside Avenue between East 12th and East 13th), and it was here that the Stumpf brothers set up shop and commenced to brew their first lager beer.[34] Little effort, if any, was made to advertise the brewery. The brewery's initial customers would have been the handful of German saloons or taverns doing business in the city. That being the case, the brothers undoubtedly relied solely on personal sales calls to stimulate business. Due to the absence of any other locally-brewed lager beer, sales to the German establishments were probably virtually automatic. It is even likely that the Stumpfs established their own saloon or beer garden in conjunction with the brewery, as did many early lager brewers.

Be that as it may, the partnership of M. Stumpf & Company had ended by 1850, when Martin left to pursue his own brewing venture.[35] For the rest of their years in Cleveland, the Stumpf brothers were engaged in separate brewing enterprises.

For over thirty years, Michael Stumpf remained in business at his Lake Street brewery, which operated virtually unchanged throughout that period. Production never grew much beyond early levels, and the brewery ranked among the city's smallest throughout much of its existence. In 1857, fire nearly destroyed the brewery. It was noted at the time of the fire that the brewery and its contents were valued at $4,000. Rebuilding of the works was completed by 1860, and Michael Stumpf was employing as many as three brewery hands. All were German immigrants, and all lived with Michael and his family at their residence on Muirson Street.[36] By the 1870s, sons William H. and Louis N. Stumpf had come of age and were assisting their father in the family business. (In addition to the brewery, the Stumpf family business briefly included a confectionery on Superior Avenue.[37]) The brewery's output during that decade traces the demise of the business: in 1875, the brewery produced 1,116 barrels; in 1878, 845 barrels; and in 1879, just 290 barrels.[38] Unable to survive in what had become a fiercely competitive industry, the old brewery produced its last barrel of lager beer in 1882. Michael Stumpf never again re-entered the brewing business. He spent his remaining years serving as a tax assessor for the 5th Ward. Michael died in 1886 inside one of the old brewery buildings, which had been converted into a residence for his family.[39]

Virginia Stief Sords Collection

This modest building on Lake Street (Lakeside Avenue) housed Michael Stumpf's brewery. By the time this photo was taken, the brewery had ceased operation and was converted into a dwelling. Seated in the yard are Louis and Anna Stumpf, children of Michael Stumpf.

Like his brother Michael, Martin Stumpf was active in brewing in Cleveland for many years. Soon after leaving the partnership with Michael around 1850, Martin set up a small lager beer brewery on Hamilton Street between Muirson & Canfield, just one block over from Michael's brewery on Lake Street. In fact, the rear of each of the brothers' lots was separated only by an alley.[40] It seems probable, considering the proximity of their breweries, that the brothers may have shared resources in some way. Joint acquisition of raw materials, barrels, brewing tools, delivery wagons, and possibly even brewery hands would have greatly benefited each, particularly given their small levels of production. Nevertheless, the breweries maintained a clear independence of each other in terms of their respective trade.

Although Martin remained in his Hamilton Street brewery for less than a decade, the venture appears to have developed significantly while in his possession. Additional land was acquired on nearby Davenport Avenue along the shore of Lake Erie. Most probably, the land was used for the purpose of locating additional beer cellars there. Not only was the lot crossed by a steep bluff thus facilitating the digging of cellars, but the lake frontage undoubtedly allowed for easy access to ice. (It was not at all uncommon for early lager beer brewers to locate the bulk of their lagering cellars some distance from the main brewery in order to take advantage of more practical accommodations elsewhere.[41]) In 1859, Martin sold his brewery to the firm of Kindsvater & Mall for $5,000, a sum which appears to have been significantly greater than his initial investments in the business.[42] Martin spent the next several years involved in a variety of local breweries.

Incidentally, Martin's brewery on Hamilton Street enjoyed a long and prosperous history after its sale to Kindsvater & Mall. The new proprietors were a natural combination: Jacob Mall, a German-trained brewer, had been brewmaster at one of Cleveland's earliest lager beer breweries; and Paul Kindsvater was owner of a popular lager beer saloon on nearby St. Clair Avenue.[43] By 1870, the Hamilton Street site had become too confining and the entire brewery was moved to the Davenport Avenue property, where lagering cellars had already been dug and in use for several years. Over the next half-century, the brewery thrived, first as the Jacob Mall Brewing Company, and later as the Gund Brewing Company.

An early advertising lithograph featuring the brewery on Davenport Avenue.

41

Schmidt & Hoffmann

Although it is fairly certain that brothers Martin and Michael Stumpf were the first to brew lager beer in Cleveland, two other German immigrants – C. W. Schmidt and Robert Hoffmann – have been called the city's first lager brewers "of any consequence."[44] That is, they ultimately found long-term commercial success where the Stumpf brothers, relatively speaking, did not.

C. W. Schmidt was a sort of patriarch within Cleveland's early German community. Born in Gruenstadt in the Palatinate, he played a prominent role in the German political uprisings of 1848, serving in the revolutionary parliament until its overthrow by Prussian-led forces. Schmidt then fled to France. In his absence, he was sentenced to death for his involvement in the revolution. In 1852, he traveled to America, coming straight to Cleveland. Over the years, Schmidt's extensive involvement in local German affairs (as well as his notorious past) made him a well-known and respected figure among the city's Germans.[45]

Reproduction of an 1880 advertising lithograph.

Schmidt & Hoffmann established their lager brewery in 1852 at the junction of Hough and Ansel Avenues, in what was then East Cleveland Township. Far removed from the bustle of the city, the small township was little more than a sparsely-settled forest when Schmidt & Hoffmann began their operation. However, the five-acre piece of land on which the partners commenced business was particularly well-suited to the brewing of lager beer. The lot sat atop a substantial hillside allowing for easy construction of beer cellars. A branch of Doan Brook passed directly through the brewery property, providing an ample supply of pure water, a commodity of utmost importance to any brewer. In addition, the brook fed into a small pond located on brewery grounds just across Ansel Avenue, where quantities of ice could be harvested during winter.[46] Most of the lager breweries which later sprung up inside the city had little choice but to acquire ice from independent dealers, a costly and troublesome task. Indeed, the remote location of Schmidt & Hoffmann's brewery was, in many ways, an asset. Quick access to Euclid Avenue (then the main route into Cleveland from the east) and nearby Doan's Corners prevented isolation from the masses.

During their first year of operation, Schmidt & Hoffmann brewed about 700 barrels of lager beer, a relatively small amount by the standards of most of the ale brewers located inside town. But, of course, lager beer was still in its infancy in many parts of the country, Cleveland certainly among them. It was not until the 1870s, after more than two decades of gradual escalation, that the production of lager beer had gained a strong foothold. By 1878, the Schmidt & Hoffmann brewery was producing about 7,600 barrels of lager beer annually.[47] A local publication noted during that year that

So often and extensive have been the additions built to the original building that it is almost lost in comparison with the present structure, which has grown to reach the

dimensions of sixty by one hundred and forty feet, with annexed ice houses, four in number, which have a capacity of three thousand tons. Nine great arctic cellars hold the immense deposits of beer until it becomes ready to place upon the market, and one fermenting cellar, filled with fourteen large vats of sixty barrels each capacity...turns out the clear, sparkling and refreshing beer, known throughout Cleveland, and recognized at first taste, on account of its splendid quality, as Schmidt & Hoffmann's.[48]

The decade of the 1880s was a period of transition for the Schmidt & Hoffmann brewery. Both of the senior members of the firm passed away during the early half of the decade, Robert Hoffmann in 1882 and Charles Schmidt in 1884. The latter – son of the elder C. W. Schmidt – had been a partner in the brewery since 1861, when he bought his father's share in the business. C. W. Schmidt passed away during that same decade, in 1887, at the age of eighty-two.[49]

Carl F. Schmidt (son of Charles Schmidt) and Louis Hoffmann (son of Robert Hoffmann) assumed control of their respective family's interest in the brewery after the deaths of their fathers.[50] In 1887, however, a significant portion of the brewery's stock was sold to Ernst W. Mueller, who subsequently joined the company's management as secretary and treasurer. As a young man, Mueller had worked as a maltster inside his father's malting business, Peter Mueller & Company, which eventually grew

Below: The Cleveland Brewing Company plant at Hough and Ansel. Right: Ernst W. Mueller acquired a large interest in the Schmidt & Hoffmann brewery in 1887. For the next sixty years, the Mueller family remained active in the local brewing industry.

Werner D. Mueller Collection

Staff of the Cleveland Brewing Company in 1887. The stars painted on the beer kegs were called "brewer's stars," an industry symbol of purity and quality.

to become one of the largest malting operations in Cleveland.[51] His entrance into the Schmidt & Hoffmann brewery began a long association with the local brewing industry by Mueller and his family.

Ernst Mueller's arrival in the business marked the beginning of a new era for the old brewery. The firm, which had operated under the Schmidt & Hoffmann name for thirty-five years, was changed to the Cleveland Brewing Company, and the business began a period of accelerated growth. Evidence left by Mueller himself testifies to the apparent prosperity of the brewery already during his first year of association with the company. In an 1887 letter urging his cousin, Rudolph Mueller, to join the brewery's staff, Ernst Mueller wrote:

44

If you will come here the position with us is open for you at once, or if you prefer I will get along until spring and have you go on then. I would prefer though if you intend to come that you should come on here as soon as possible. We look for an increase in business next season, our beer having been at No.1 all this year, and would like to have you go to work at once pushing ahead for new trade.[52]

Although the characterization as "No.1" was a little exaggerated, the brewery did, indeed, rank among the city's largest, producing about 10,000 barrels of beer in 1887. Within a decade the brewery was turning out more than 40,000 barrels annually.[53] The growth was particularly significant in light of the highly competitive nature of the brewing industry during much of the 1890s. Rudolph Mueller, incidentally, accepted his cousin's job offer, and spent many years involved in the brewery.

Throughout the Cleveland Brewing Company's period of growth and expansion, management of the business seems to have shifted largely away from the founders' heirs and more toward Mueller and his family. In 1892, the officers of the brewery still showed strong representation by the founders' descendants: Louis Hoffmann was president; Carl F. Schmidt, vice president; and Ernst Mueller, secretary and treasurer. But, by 1896, management had undergone a visible change: Hermann Mueller was president; Rudolph Mueller, vice president; Ernst Mueller, secretary; and Julius Mueller, treasurer.[54]

Late in 1897, discussions began among several of Cleveland's brewery owners concerning a possible consolidation of a number of area breweries into a single company. The discussions were prompted by the unfavorable competitive environment which had developed throughout the decade. By June of 1898, a merger of nine Cleveland breweries and two in Sandusky, Ohio had been completed, and was christened the Cleveland & Sandusky Brewing Company.[55] Ernst Mueller's Cleveland Brewing Company was among the breweries which joined the combine, and Mueller became a key figure in the new company. He eventually held the office of president. Under the new ownership, the old Cleveland Brewing Company was routinely expanded, and it ultimately represented a significant portion of the combine's total brewing capacity.

After nearly seventy years in continuous operation, the brewery ceased production of beer in September of 1919 in compliance with statewide prohibition. Although the facility continued in use by the combine producing non-alcoholic beverages during prohibition, the historic brewery never again produced beer.[56]

The early 1850s saw a handful of other attempts at the commercial manufacture of lager beer in Cleveland, most of which were only marginally successful. Bavarian immigrant John Bishop commenced the manufacture of lager in 1852 on Broadway near Pittsburgh Avenue.[57] Long-time Cleveland resident Frederick Weidenkopf set up a lager brewery on Canal Street around 1855. Weidenkopf was best known for his family's popular Weidenkopf's German Tavern on Seneca

(West 3rd) Street.[58] In the early 1850s, Irishman Mathias Mack brewed lager beer in "the Angle," an Irish neighborhood north of Detroit Avenue. Beer garden owner John Dangeleisen was an early lager beer brewer, doing business on Forest (East 37th) Street. Jacob Mueller established a lager beer brewery on Vega Avenue in 1858.[59] It ultimately grew to become the city's largest brewery under the ownership of Isaac Leisy.

The year 1857 witnessed the founding of two Cleveland lager beer breweries which, perhaps more than any others in the city, exemplify the force with which the Germans commandeered the American brewing industry during the mid-nineteenth century. It was during 1857 that German immigrants Carl Ernst Gehring and Leonard Schlather both took leave of their employment as brewers at John M. Hughes' ale brewery in the Flats to launch brewing ventures of their own.

The C. E. Gehring Brewing Co.

Carl Ernst Gehring has been called "the father of the Cleveland brewing industry." And, indeed, the title is justified. Although Gehring's brewery was not the biggest in Cleveland, nor the first, nor even the most widely-known, Gehring himself was the epitome of the nineteenth century immigrant brewer. He came to the new land with little. Through old fashioned hard work and simple determination, he made a success of himself in true German style. And Gehring, perhaps more than any other Cleveland brewer, was an advocate for his trade, always being at the center of efforts to better the brewing industry.

Gehring came to America in 1848 from his birthplace of Goeppingen, Württemburg, Germany where he had apprenticed in a brewery since the age of fourteen. After a short stay in Lancaster, Pennsylvania, he came to Cleveland seeking work in a brewery. Having been among the first European-trained brewers in the city, Gehring found employment easily. His first job was at the Eagle Brewery on Michigan Street. However, he was soon working instead at Truman Downer's Spring Street Brewery where, after the business was sold to John M. Hughes in 1850, Gehring remained for several years as brewmaster.[60]

By 1857, John M. Hughes had decided that his ale brewery was in need of expansion. Thus, construction of an entirely new brewery was begun just a few blocks from the old works. It was quite possibly this interruption in operations that prompted Gehring to set out in business for himself. Responsibility to his old employer, however, was not neglected. Upon the completion of Hughes' new ale brewery, it was noted that, "Mr. Hughes acknowledges himself indebted to his brewer, Mr. Chas. E. Gehring, for many valuable improvements suggested by him – and also that ale of his brewing cannot be excelled by any in the Western country."[61]

Carl Ernst Gehring

With a capital of $600, Gehring set up his brewery in 1857 in a small frame building near his home at Pearl (West 25th) Street and Brainard Avenue (later renamed Gehring Avenue). As the demand for lager beer was still a little dubious, ale and porter were produced as well as lager. During his first year, Gehring brewed 1,800 barrels and was his only employee, "combining in his person everything possible: brewmaster, salesman, deliveryman, and collector." It was said that, in order to make ends meet, Gehring's wife took on sewing jobs until the brewery began to show a profit.[62]

An 1878 survey of Cleveland's manufacturing firms gives some idea of the growth and level of production achieved by Gehring's brewery in two short decades. As reported by the survey, operations had been consolidated two years earlier into a magnificent new brewery which fronted Brainard Avenue, and stretched adjacent to Freeman Street through to Pearl Street. Included in the new plant was a 155-barrel brew kettle (the largest in the city at the time), thirty-six fermenting tanks, a malthouse, two ice houses, and six lagering cellars "with their labyrinths of vats on vats, holding thousands upon thousands of barrels of beer." The malthouse was capable of malting 12,000 bushels of barley annually. This extraordinary amount, however, was said to be only one-fifth of the brewery's yearly consumption. The remainder was obtained from independent malteries. It was also reported that Gehring owned seven ice-harvesting facilities throughout the city, all of which were needed to serve the brewery. Twenty-five men were employed at the works, and six teams were used for local delivery to saloons and beer gardens. One traveling agent was kept on the road to secure out-of-town wholesalers. As a result, Gehring beer was shipped not only throughout Ohio, but also to western New York, western Pennsylvania, Virginia, and West Virginia. The brewery sold 15,783 barrels of beer during 1878.[63] It is safe to assume that, by this time, Mrs. Gehring was no longer sewing for extra income.

In order to be close at all times to the operation of the business, Gehring and his family resided on the brewery's premises. In fact, the back wall of the Gehring home was connected to the brewery, and steam which was generated for brewery use also heated the family residence.[64] Indeed, the Gehring brewery was a family-operated business through and through. Carl Ernst Gehring, Jr. was the first of Gehring's four sons to enter the brewery, serving as assistant brewmaster. He worked under the supervision of long-time brewmaster William Dertinger, who was married to Gehring's

A Gehring bottle label and an early advertisement for Gehring's Beer.

oldest daughter. Another son-in-law, Gustav A. Weitz, also held a position in the brewery. Son Frederick W. Gehring, or "F. W." as he was called, was bookkeeper at the brewery for many years. His brother, John A. Gehring, started as the brewery's collector and ultimately succeeded the elder Gehring as president. Albert Gehring, the youngest of the Gehring sons and a graduate of Harvard University, was also a director of the brewery.[65]

The Gehring operation, like many other German-owned breweries, experienced its most prosperous years during the 1880s. The German-American population was ever-increasing, dozens of heavily-frequented beer gardens thrived in most major cities, and the production of beer often struggled to keep pace with demand. With business soaring, Gehring spent $150,000 in 1885 to construct an entirely new, larger brewhouse. Ale and porter were no longer produced at the plant as they had been in earlier days; the demand for lager beer now forced its exclusive manufacture. By 1888, Gehring was producing about 68,000 barrels of lager beer annually, more than four times the brewery's output of a decade earlier.[66] In a family diary, one of Gehring's grandsons recorded his childhood memories of the brewery's heyday, and of the elder Gehring himself:

I often saw my grandfather walking across the paved courtyard where the brewery wagons were lined up at night on his way from the office building to the Brew House. He always wore dark gray suits and stiff bosomed white shirts. He was rather austere...His house fronted Pearl Street with the brewery buildings to south and east just adjoining. A large lawn and garden gave light and cheer from the north on which all the living rooms fronted. A tunnel-like passageway led from the back yard thru the cold storage section of the brewery to the courtyard — a short cut to the office...The Gehring Brewery was not the largest Cleveland brewery but it was the best earner on barrels put out. It earned steadily $120,000 each year, net. Gehring's Beer was generally regarded as the best Cleveland beer and one of the best in Ohio.[67]

On March 5, 1893, Carl Ernst Gehring died at age sixty-three, his death caused by a long-endured liver condition. Perhaps more than any other Cleveland brewer of his day, Gehring had been a champion of the preservation and advancement of the brewing industry. For several years, he served as the president of the Local Association of Brewers of Cleveland, and presided over the proceedings of the Thirteenth Annual Brewers' Congress when that event was held in Cleveland in 1873. As a leading member of the Agitation Committee of the U.S. Brewer's Association, Gehring played an active role in developing the brewing industry's position regarding the ever-present temperance movement. And, in true allegiance to his chosen profession, Gehring campaigned for American adoption of the strict German brewing laws which prohibited the use of anything but pure ingredients in brewing.[68]

Gehring had also been active in the community. He was elected to City Council in 1873 and held the office of Cleveland Police Commissioner from 1875 to 1876. Among the local organizations with which Gehring was connected over the years was the Jones Home for Friendless Children, the Altenheim home for the elderly, and the German Hospital, which later became Fairview General Hospital. He also served as president of the Forest City Bank on Cleveland's west side for a number of years.[69]

At the time of his death, Gehring's estate was valued at $1 million, the bulk of which was bequeathed to his wife and children. The brewery had been incorporated in 1892 as the C. E. Gehring Brewing Company. Shares were held by each of Gehring's immediate family members.[70] By the late 1890s, disagreements had arisen within the family concerning management of the brewery. After several "bitter family meetings," it was decided that the Gehring brewery would be sold to the Cleveland & Sandusky Brewing Company, a consolidation of breweries in those two cities which was just beginning to fully take shape early in 1898. F. W. Gehring became closely involved with the development of the consolidation and, once the combine was officially complete, F. W. was appointed the first president of the new company.[71]

F. W. Gehring

Shareholders in the Gehring brewery received a healthy $1,250,000 cash for the brewery, in addition to stock in the combine.[72] The Gehring brewery was the largest local brewery to join the Cleveland & Sandusky Brewing Company at its inception. Indeed, it is likely that the combine would not have fully materialized without the participation of the Gehring brewery, given the competitive formidability of those breweries which chose to take no part in the consolidation. In 1901, the Gehring brewery produced 90,000 barrels of beer and employed ninety-five men, nearly one-third of the combine's total work force.[73] The plant remained one of the Cleveland & Sandusky Brewing Company's key facilities until brewing was halted there in 1918.

Although the entire brewery complex was destroyed by fire in 1927, Gehring Avenue survives today as a humble monument to one of Cleveland's most respected and successful brewers.[74]

The L. Schlather Brewing Co.

Leonard Schlather's brewery – which also eventually became part of the Cleveland & Sandusky Brewing Company – enjoyed success much like that of Carl Ernst Gehring's over the years. Schlather started his brewery during the same year as Gehring (1857) and only a few blocks away, on York (West 28th) Street. But this was not the extent of Gehring and Schlather's association. The two had been schoolmates back in the old country, both hailing from Württemburg, Germany. And it was side-by-side with Gehring at the old Hughes ale brewery in the Flats that Schlather was first employed in Cleveland. The two were said to have sustained "a warm personal friendship" throughout their years in Cleveland.[75]

The alleged circumstances under which Leonard Schlather emigrated to America comprise one of those stories which, though possibly quite accurate, possess the unique flavor of family lore. In 1853, Frederick and Christian Schlather, two of Leonard's older brothers, had decided to make the long journey to America. As the story goes, just at the time of their departure, the boys' mother became excessively grief-stricken over losing her two eldest sons to the voyage. Christian, who was described as "not very strong," became distraught at the sight of his mother's dismay, refusing to make the trip. As sailing arrangements had already been made, it was quickly decided that the boys' younger brother, Leonard, would take Christian's place. Without any preparation, save for the packed belongings of his brother, nineteen-year-old Leonard Schlather set sail for America.*[76]

Schlather first located in Altoona, Pennsylvania where relatives on his mother's side of the family were involved in brewing. He was offered work at the brewery, and it was here that Schlather gained his first exposure to the brewing industry, "acquiring a thorough knowledge of the business, theoretical and practical, mechanical and commercial."[78] Quite possibly at the encouragement of Gehring, Schlather came to Cleveland in 1856 and became a brewer at the Hughes ale brewery.

Schlather commenced to brew his own beer in 1857 in much the same, small way that most early brewers began. His first accommodation was a two-story frame building on York Street near Bridge Avenue, in which Schlather assembled a modest brewery. Indicating its level of sophistication is the fact that the brew kettle had a meager capacity of just four barrels. By 1861, however, improving business warranted the purchase of a parcel of land on the northeast corner of York Street and Carroll Avenue, just half a block south of the original location. Expansion of the brewery was soon under way. It was said that Schlather himself cut and hauled much of the necessary timber from Rocky River, Ohio, where – somewhat coincidentally – he would later own a lavish summer home situated on a large estate.[79]

In 1878, Schlather undertook a major reconstruction of his brewery, the original frame buildings being replaced with stylish new brick and concrete structures. The brewery was designed by local architect Andrew Mitermiler, who designed a multitude of Cleveland's brewing plants over the years. Clearly impressed by the "elegant new

Above: Leonard Schlather.

Below: A cardboard advertising sign, circa 1895. Large quantities of Schlather's Export were undoubtedly shipped to – among other points – Pittsburgh, where Schlather had established his own distribution facility as early as 1878.

---

*Incidentally, Christian Schlather did eventually make the trip to America, where he worked as shipping clerk in Leonard Schlather's brewery for a time.[77]

50

The King Can Do No Wrong

The typical nineteenth century brewery was a particularly conspicuous establishment. Various obstructions, such as old beer wagons, empty kegs, or retired brewing vats often littered the premises. Spent grains, soaked with half-fermented beer, were routinely discarded indiscriminately, left to rot in the sun. And, perhaps worst of all, the unmistakable odor of a thriving brewery tended to hang relentlessly over its neighborhood. Naturally, if a brewery happened to be situated in a somewhat congested portion of the city, friction between the brewer and his neighbors was inevitable. An angry west side resident, complaining about Schlather's brewery, wrote to the editor of the *Cleveland Leader* in 1874:

> *Mr. Leonard Schlather is the happy and royal owner of a brewery on the corner of York and Carroll streets, which he manages in the most princely style. Indeed, Mr. Schlather is a model of an American citizen, illustrating at once the sovereignty of Europe and the progressive genius of the glorious United States. He is an industrious man. Others may think it a small thing to quit work on Saturday evening and never do another stroke till Monday. Not so with him. No day in the week finds him idle. The cooper's hammer, the engine's whistle, the rattle and bang of the beer wagons are ever heard at Mr. Schlather's brewery. "Progressive," we said, so he is. At first he was content to occupy his building and premises just as other old-fashioned people do. Then he saw a nice brick sidewalk which was doing no one any good to speak of, and he appropriated that with his perfumed barrels and wagons and filled the gutter outside the curb with a living stream from his tanks and hogsheads. It is true no one could pass without stepping out into that filth, but who could object to that on reflecting that Mr. Schlather was making such good use of the pavement. And the police (bless their honest soles) were not slow to see the propriety and fitness of this arrangement. If a lot of praying women should block up the sidewalk for five or ten minutes it would be totally different. You see praying is one thing and making beer is altogether another. "Go on thereare," said the functionary with the brass buttons, and on went Mr. Leonard Schlather. But Mr. Schlather observed that York and Carroll streets were never more than half used, and so he extended his domain over portions of the street, occupying it with coal, old tanks and barrels, and to wash his beer wagons. Now it is perfectly plain that if the neighbors should all occupy the sidewalk this way Mr. Leonard Schlather might be put to some trouble and inconvenience; so the police took special pains to enforce the sidewalk ordinance on those neighbors. But the worst of it all is that some of those ungracious neighbors undertook to say that they had as good right to the sidewalk as Mr. Leonard Schlather, and that his royal brewery was a nuisance and an everlasting annoyance every day of the week, and especially on Sunday. But the police could not be fooled with any such nonsense, and, tapping Mr. Leonard Schlather on the shoulder, told him to be of good cheer and go on. Let us see now what is the secret of Mr. Schlather's success. It is in the principal of royalty by which his noble like has been governed. "The King can do no wrong" is the motto of Mr. Leonard Schlather.*[83]

Incidentally, the reference to "a lot of praying women" blocking up the sidewalk was probably not quite as facetious as it might sound. A common practice of local temperance associations was to assemble an outfit of bible-toting members for the purpose of embarking on a tour of selected breweries, distilleries, or saloons, where enthusiastic prayer would then ensue. As admittance to the called-upon establishments was invariably denied, the ritual usually took place on the sidewalk out front.

The Schlather brewery, circa 1910. Designed by local brewery architect Andrew R. Mitermiler, the plant stood at the corner of York (West 28th) Street and Carroll Avenue.

Above: Two concrete date-plaques were rescued from the exterior of the Schlather brewery before its demolition during prohibition. They are preserved in a house formerly owned by the Schlather family in Zoar, Ohio.

brewery," editors of *Western Brewer* magazine featured the completed project in one of their editions. The editors declared that, "the world cannot but be pleased to see such evidences of the material progress of our ancient art, and such a noble monument to Gambrinus as Mr. Schlather has created."[80] A congressman and friend of Schlather once wrote of the complex, "I always pass by the brewery, which occupies a square bound by York, Carroll and Bridge sts., the whole being a magnificent specimen of architecture and massive as a castle of old, with a feeling of awe."[81]

In 1879, the new brewery employed about fifty men and produced over 27,000 barrels of beer, the largest output of any Cleveland brewery during that year. Routine enlargement continued throughout the following years and the brewery grew to be a dominant presence in the neighborhood. Expansion had made it necessary for Schlather to acquire additional parcels of land along Bridge and Carroll Avenues, upon which were erected various support buildings, such as keg washing facilities, storage of delivery wagons, and stables for the delivery horses. Interestingly, Carroll street was one of the first in Cleveland to be brick paved. Undoubtedly, this was no coincidence. A muddy thoroughfare and the tremendous weight of a fully loaded beer wagon often spelled disaster.[82]

Schlather resided at or near his brewery for much of its existence. In 1881, after expansion of the brewery had overtaken the small frame dwelling in which Schlather and his family lived, a finely-appointed Italianate-style house was built on the northwest corner of York and Carroll, just opposite the brewhouse. The home stood for nearly a century, greatly outlasting most of the brewery buildings. It fell victim to a fire in the 1970s.[84]

However, Schlather's summer home in the Cleveland suburb of Rocky River, Ohio gained particular notoriety. Beginning with the purchase of a modest three acres of land in 1872, Schlather built a beautiful estate which eventually grew to claim a total of 97 acres overlooking the scenic Rocky River Valley.[85] Schlather and his second wife, Sophia, were avid travelers and as the years passed, the Rocky River estate evolved into somewhat of a monument to their

Leonard and Sophia Schlather pose in the yard of their Rocky River estate. After the death of his first wife (Catherine Buckes), Leonard Schlather married Anna Catherine Sophia Schwarz of Wheeling, West Virginia in 1897. One biographer wrote, "Notwithstanding their disparity in age, Mr. and Mrs. Schlather were in hearty sympathy in their life aims." Leonard and Sophia traveled abroad together frequently, collecting art, books and antique furniture from all over the world. After Leonard's death in 1918, Sophia spent the remainder of her years living at the Rocky River estate. She was active in a number of charitable endeavors. Among the many recipients of her benefactions was the Altenheim Home for the Elderly, Cleveland Day Nursery, Three Arts Club, Cleveland Orchestra, and Lakewood Historical Society. Prior to Sophia's death in 1955, she had donated $100,000 to the Rocky River Public Library for construction of the "Leonard Schlather Wing." When she died, many of the antique furnishings, books, and art objects which adorned Sophia's Rocky River home were bequeathed to the library for permanent display in the new wing. Included was a large oil portrait of Leonard Schlather, which still hangs at the library today.[88]

frequent trips abroad. The grounds featured an exotic Japanese rock garden, complete with arched Moongate bridges. The residence itself was decorated throughout with antique furniture from France, a number of genuine oriental rugs, and a collection of valuable paintings by European artists.[86] (Although most of the art was presumably acquired during trips abroad, it was rumored that one particular painting in the collection was the prize of a bidding war between Schlather and John D. Rockefeller at an art auction.) Despite it being customary for large estates to be christened with a name which conveyed the beauty and serenity of the place, Schlather's estate bore no special title. When questioned on the subject, Leonard Schlather modestly commented, "No, I haven't any other name for my country place than Schlather's

Farm. They hadn't got the farm-naming habit when I bought the place, almost forty years ago, and it's been just a plain farm ever since."[87] Throughout much of the late nineteenth century, Schlather and his wife spent their summers enjoying the seclusion of their Rocky River estate.

In the meantime, Schlather's brewery had enjoyed continuous growth. The company was incorporated in 1884 as the L. Schlather Brewing Company, with a capitalization of $500,000. The annual output amounted to about 50,000 barrels of lager beer, the primary varieties of which were Pilsener and Kulmbacher styles.[89] By the mid-1890s, production averaged between 70,000 and 80,000 barrels per year, and advertisements for Schlather's beer indicated at least five different varieties: Standard Lager, Select Export, Pilsener, Kulmbacher, and Munich, all manufactured under the supervision of long-time brewmaster John Schneider.[90]

Leonard Schlather's summer home in Rocky River, Ohio.

Primogeniture – the right of inheritance of the eldest son – was a widely-observed tradition in brewing during the 1890s and early 1900s. Many of the old-time immigrant brewers had grown old and decided to bequeath the product of their life's work on to their offspring; their *male* offspring. If the old-time brewer, however, happened not be blessed with a male child, he found himself facing a bit of a dilemma as he approached his later years. Leonard Schlather, the proud father of five lovely daughters, was one of those unfortunate early brewers who was left with no one to pass the reins when the time came for his retirement. Schlather's son-in-law, Mars E. Wagar, spent several years as the brewery's secretary and treasurer, and it appeared as though he might ultimately inherit management of the brewery. He was from a prominent family of local pioneers who settled in the western suburbs of Cleveland. A writer for the *Cleveland Press* once wrote that, "In M. E. Wagar, L. Schlather found an individual who, while not a great genius or the profoundest thinker, was extremely popular, a frank man, steadfast as an anchor, a student of men."[91] Having become involved in other affairs, Wagar severed his connections with

A brass and porcelain serving tray, circa 1895.

the brewery in 1898, a move which was reportedly the cause of "much comment."

Desirous of retirement, and with no alternative in sight, the aging Schlather sold his brewery to the Cleveland & Sandusky Brewing Company in 1902 for a rumored $1.5 million. Schlather had been brewing about 90,000 barrels annually, and it was reported that the plant boasted a capacity of 150,000 barrels. Thus, the Cleveland & Sandusky company stood to enjoy a significant boost in total production with the acquisition of the Schlather brewery. However,

officials for the combine noted that Schlather's control of more than sixty saloon properties in Cleveland and elsewhere – which the combine would inherit as part of the deal – was also a major factor in the purchase.[92] Among the most valuable of the outlets was the Casino Cafe, which Schlather himself established in 1889. Located on Superior Avenue just off Public Square, the Casino was an exclusive restaurant and saloon catering to Cleveland's social elite. Among the attractions were a large palm garden, a finely appointed billiard room, and live musical entertainment. The saloon's lavish interior featured a number of enormous murals depicting the consumption of beer in ancient times, and carrying German rhymes such as "Hopfen und Malz Gott erhalts" (Hops and Malt May God Preserve). The focal point of the saloon's interior was a dramatic circular oak staircase, featuring an abundance of intricately hand-carved ornamentation.[93]

Although Schlather's desire to withdraw from active business life was the reason given for his retirement, he achieved that goal only partially. Upon the acquisition of his brewery by the Cleveland & Sandusky Brewing Company, he was elected to that company's board of directors, a post which he held well into his later years. However, Schlather's many pursuits over the years went far beyond the brewing industry. He had been a director of the Immigrant Protection Society, a co-founder of the old Sheriff Street Market House, an active member of the Cleveland Chamber of Commerce, and life member of the Western Reserve Historical Society. His involvement in local banking, too, was extensive well into "retirement." He served as vice president of the People's Savings Bank, and as a director of the Union National Bank of Cleveland and the Society for Savings. After a long and active life, Schlather died in 1918 at his home across from the brewery.[94] Just one year later, the brewery produced its last barrel of beer, the victim of statewide prohibition.

Inside Leonard Schlather's Casino Cafe. In its later years, the establishment was known as Weber's Restaurant.

Chapter Three

Menace And Maturity

No era in Cleveland's history witnessed a greater level of growth and development of the city than did the period during the Civil War. The tremendous demand for war materials, coupled with the cutting-off of goods from the south, caused a torrential increase in manufacturing activity within the city. Iron ore shipped from the upper Great Lakes regions began building Cleveland's iron and steel industry. The discovery of oil in western Pennsylvania meant that Cleveland was rapidly becoming a major petroleum refining center. Spurred by these and other important developments, countless new industries sprung up inside the city. As industry burgeoned, the population swelled. Between 1860 and 1865, the number of inhabitants in Cleveland increased a full fifty percent, more than any other northern city. One essayist commented,

The progress of the city was never more marked than in 1863, particularly in the increase of population, the improvement of business, the building of new offices, factories, and houses, the extent and activity of trade, and the large business done by the railroads.[1]

Anthony Zappitelli Collection

Indeed, by the time the Civil War came to an end, Cleveland had irreversibly transformed itself from a commercial village into a primary center of industry.

Naturally, Cleveland's brewing trade, like virtually all local consumer goods industries, shared in the prosperity of the city's blossoming industrial character. Although a surprising two-thirds of Cleveland's eligible work force (and, thus, much of its beer-consuming population)

ultimately went away to fight for the northern cause, the loss was largely offset by the simultaneous influx of newcomers into Cleveland and the extensive manufacturing activity. The city entered the war with approximately a dozen breweries in operation. Already in 1863, about twenty were brewing beer in the city. And the growth continued well beyond the war's end. In 1865, beer production of Cleveland's breweries totaled 50,000 barrels. A decade later, local brewers were turning out more than 133,000 barrels a year.[2]

Nevertheless, the Civil War years presented numerous obstacles for Cleveland's brewers. A federal tax on beer, which was something entirely new to the brewing industry, was instituted to help finance the war effort. A tax of $1 per barrel of beer went into effect on September 1, 1862. Perhaps more offensive than the tax itself was the government's classification of beer within the same product category as hard liquors, characterized as "unnecessary luxuries which were prejudicial to the public good."[3] Many brewers vehemently objected to the classification, fearing that it would add fuel to an already growing temperance movement in America. In the end, their complaints resulted in little governmental action, and the federal tax became a way of life for the brewing industry.

Cleveland brewers were quick to react to the beer tax. In October of 1862, local brewery owners announced that the price of ale and beer would be increased by $1 per barrel to absorb the new tax.[4] Signed by fourteen of the city's brewers, the notice also cited the rising costs of raw materials and labor as an additional cause of the price increase. Although it was strictly intended to be a war-time measure, the beer tax was not repealed at the conclusion of the war as expected. Rather, a federal tax on beer has remained intact to this day.

The institution of a federal beer tax had an unexpected outgrowth which, over the long term, proved to be invaluable to the brewing industry. In order to work with the government to establish mutually acceptable methods and procedures for collection of the tax, brewers were compelled for the first time to organize themselves into a united group. In November of 1862, the United States Brewers Association was formed in New York City, thereby

> *federating all brewers and kindred trades into one great national combination for the purpose of protecting their common interests and insuring a uniform, faithful and conscientious obedience to the new law throughout the land.*[5]

This joining of forces gave brewers a strong voice in government and yielded great benefits to the industry in the ensuing years.

At the local level, as well, the banding together of brewers where previously there had been none, provided the industry with means of combating potential menaces to brewing.

58

Although the city's brewers had maintained an informal association for years, the "Cleveland Brauer Verein" (Cleveland Brewers Association) was officially incorporated in 1874.[6] The owners of the city's three largest breweries – Isaac Leisy, Leonard Schlather and Carl Ernst Gehring – were the association's trustees. Also in 1874, the "Liquor Dealers' and Brewers' Association" was established. The stated purpose of that organization was to help the retailers escape the Sunday drinking restrictions promoted by temperance activists.[7] Indeed, the temperance movement – more than any other potential hindrance to the brewing industry – forged a strong alliance among brewers everywhere.

A Temperate America

Over-indulgence in drink has been blamed, at different times in history, for everything from crime and poverty to the very moral decay of civilization. And there has always been a segment of the population that believed that the simple removal of alcohol from public temptation was the only means of salvation. This belief powered the tremendously widespread temperance movement of the nineteenth and early twentieth centuries. And while the word "temperance" implied that mere moderation in drink was the goal, the great majority of the movement's proponents intended something entirely more serious. Complete abstinence from drink was felt to be the only "cure" for drunkenness. And outright *abolition*, of course, was the only means to true abstinence. Thus, from a fairly early point, the total eradication of alcoholic drink from society was at the heart of the temperance movement in America.

Organizations formed for the expressed purpose of promoting anti-alcohol sentiment have existed in America since the nation's very beginnings. Usually grown from religious circles, these activist groups were strictly local in nature and rarely boasted membership of more than a few hundred.[8] They relied on "moral suasion" as their primary tool, preaching personal responsibility and decrying the perils of alcohol use. Briefly in the 1840s, a faction known as the "Washingtonian" movement gained wide notoriety. Its

Ohio Historical Society

By the 1890s, virtually every small town in Ohio had a local temperance headquarters.

NO. 3.

Ohio is often called the birthplace of prohibition due to the large amount of temperance activity which took place in the state throughout the nineteenth century. Temperance publications such as this edition from 1835 were common in Ohio.

popularity was in the fact that its membership was comprised entirely of reformed drunkards, thus adding a unique potency to their admonitions against drink. In 1845, there were no less than three branch societies of the Washingtonians in Cleveland.[9] (It is wondered whether members of those societies would have been dismayed to learn that old George Washington himself was known to have been a home-brewer and a lover of good beer!) But, aside from a few extraneous outgrowths, the temperance movement in the early nineteenth century was primarily in the hands of the religious. Successes were measured not in sweeping reform, but in the salvation of the individual.

It was only after passage of what came to be known as the "Maine Law" in 1851 that the temperance crusade began to affect real change in America's drinking habits. The first of its kind in the country, the law prohibited the manufacture and sale of all alcoholic beverages throughout the entire state of Maine.[10] Bolstered by that victory, temperance activists everywhere gained new confidence in their ability to rescue society from the evils of drink. And, perhaps more importantly, many were awakened to the fact that legislation was a vastly more effective weapon than the old-fashioned "personal pledge" system common in early temperance societies. In 1852, for example, a group of Cleveland temperance activists put forth a third party candidate for Governor who vowed to fight for statewide prohibition in Ohio.[11] Although his bid was unsuccessful, it was apparent that the temperance movement – both locally and nationally – had moved largely out of the religious arena and into the legislative one.

Beer, per se, was not the main target of the temperance crusade in its early days. Rather, whiskey and other distilled spirits were seen by the majority as the primary menace. And, indeed,

A crowd gathers to watch a group of prohibitionists accost the owner of Mader's saloon. While most saloonkeepers undoubtedly dreaded the imminent appearance of the "visitation band" at their establishments, others found it to be good for business. One German saloonkeeper was brutally quoted in the *Plain Dealer* as saying, "By h—ll, dem vimmens pass me by; I lose all de sale of many glasses after dey go out of de saloon."

brewers did everything possible to promote that notion. In 1863, the *Cleveland Leader* proposed (as did many brewers) that beer might even be a *solution* to the problem: "Whiskey is a fatal and filthy compound which steals away the brains of its votaries. The extensive manufacture of beer is suggested to supply the demand for drink, it being less intoxicating and injurious."[12] Even so, the most ardent of the temperance advocates disparaged any and all alcoholic beverages. It was noted in 1846 that Cleveland's temperance associations (which at that time numbered five, boasting some 4,000 members) were among the first in the nation to vow abstinence from not just distilled spirits, but from wine and "all that could intoxicate."[13]

And anyway, beginning in the 1850s, the focus of most temperance activists was entirely on the saloon, with little distinction being acknowledged between the various grades of intoxicants served therein. In 1853, City Council passed an ordinance prohibiting the Sunday operation of saloons in Cleveland, the first in a long list of marginally successful temperance-oriented actions.

The law was promptly ignored by the great majority of the city's 150 liquor establishments. Enforcement was half-hearted at best. A full year after adoption of the ordinance, the *Leader* commented,

Inclement weather was not enough to keep these devoted prohibitionists from blocking the entrance of D. Corcoran's saloon.

Since the city authorities have ceased making any further efforts to enforce the Sunday liquor ordinance, rowdyism and

drunkenness on the Sabbath day have fearfully increased.

On Saturday night, when most men have their week's earnings to themselves, the trouble begins. By Sunday night the devotees of appetite are pretty well cleaned out in purse, and injured in health and morals. Police seem to disregard the noise, and drinking in this city.

An inefficient police is worse than nothing because they are a heavy expense on the tax payers and stand in the way of better men...There is a screw loose somewhere that needs tightening, and we call the serious attention of our...citizens to it.[14]

The same fed-up writer made the tongue-in-cheek suggestion that enforcement of the Sunday law ought to be carried out for one single day, then dropped, so that "years hence, we may point back to the memorable day on which no liquor was sold in Cleveland."

The onset of the Civil War stagnated the temperance movement in America as attentions were diverted to more patriotic concerns. But, with the end of the war came a powerful resurgence in the cause. In 1874, "the women's crusade" was born, the defining component of which was the founding of the Women's Christian Temperance League in Cleveland on March 13th.[15] The primary tool of the organization was the much-feared "visitation band" – a virtual mob of bible-carrying women who visited area saloons, distilleries and breweries, bullying owners to cease business immediately. Indeed, the fired-up and threatening demeanor of the band often yielded a pledge from the owner to abandon the liquor business forever. (Whether the pledge was actually carried out, of course, was another matter.) After only three months, the League proudly reported that they had visited three distilleries, eight breweries, thirty-five hotels, forty wholesale liquor dealers, and eleven-hundred saloons. Under the changed name of the Women's Christian Temperance Union, the group went on to become one of the most important organizations in the ultimate enactment of National Prohibition in 1920.

In Ohio, the temperance movement of the nineteenth century culminated in 1883 when activists succeeded in placing a statewide prohibition amendment on the Ohio ballot. Campaigners worked tirelessly to promote the amendment, particularly in rural areas where support for prohibition was likely to be highest. Meanwhile, the local "wet" faction warned, somewhat clumsily, against the problems that would result from passage of the amendment:

If prohibition wins the farmers will be unable to sell surplus grains, and pork and beef will come down to such an extent that farmers will not be able to clothe their children in silks and satins, and to give them pianos. Schoolhouses will disappear, because there will be no money to pay teachers...We have raised $75,000 to spend principally in Cincinnati and Cleveland, and we are going to teach prohibitionists to let our business alone.[16]

In the end, the prohibition amendment failed, but the margin was alarmingly narrow; out of a total of 721,000 votes cast, more than 323,000 favored prohibition.

Of course, Cleveland's brewers recognized the threat of the temperance movement long before the campaign of 1883. When the United States Brewers Association held its thirteenth annual convention in Cleveland in 1873, the temperance menace was plainly the lead issue of the gathering. In his welcoming address, local brewer Carl Ernst Gehring remarked that

You have gathered, gentlemen, from near and far in the interests of that large trade you represent, and you will at this Convention devise ways and means to protect its interests, and to foster your trade so that it may ever be progressive. You are here...above all, to remind us of a necessary and important duty open to all of us, resisting to the utmost those citizens throughout all the States who consider our business a crime and a sin against society. To argue this matter and convince them of their error is one of our chief labors.[17]

In addition to serving as president of the Cleveland Brewers Association, Gehring was a member of the USBA's "Agitation Committee," which was assigned the task of overseeing all issues relating to the anti-alcohol efforts. For much of the nineteenth century, the USBA's singular defense against prohibition was the fact that the brewing industry, through taxation, contributed a surprising percentage of the U.S. government's total revenues – as much as twenty percent in 1873, for example.[18] "If brewing were to cease," queried the brewers, "how would this revenue be replaced?" Until institution of the personal income tax in 1913, even the shrewdest of temperance rationalists had no viable response.

Labor In The Brewery

The temperance movement was not the only perceived threat to the well-being of the brewing industry during the nineteenth century. At the 1886 convention of the United States Brewers Association, issues of brewery labor were at the forefront. The disastrous outcome of a number of recent labor conflicts around the country (for example, the notorious steelworkers' massacre in Homestead, Pennsylvania) was fresh in the minds of employers and workers alike. And the USBA was eager to address what it simply called "the labor question." Brewery workers in a number of cities had organized themselves and approached owners with demands for improved working conditions, and a handful of unpleasant strikes had ensued. The length of the work day – which, in many breweries, could be up to fourteen to eighteen hours – usually topped the list of workers' complaints. Salary issues were often not in question, as brewery workers were typically paid as well as, or sometimes better than, those in other industries. Rather, the eight-hour-day was plainly the goal of most brewery labor organizations. In early struggles with owners, many workers considered it a victory if they were able to negotiate a ten- to twelve-hour work day.

In Cleveland, the city's breweries together employed about 300 men in 1878. By the turn of the century, the number had grown to well over 500. But, in comparison to just about any brewing city in America, Cleveland boasted an unusually calm and subdued brewery labor movement. The *Wächter und Anzeiger*, a Cleveland German-language newspaper, wrote of the local brewing industry:

Relations between employers and employees have always been the best possible. Those who work in the brewing industry are paid, on average, better than those in other branches of industry. In all breweries, the highest union scale prevails. In slow times, the number of employees is not reduced and the number of work hours remains the same.[19]

Despite the reportedly good conditions, the first evidence of organization among the city's brewery labor came in 1872 when local brewery workers formed the "Bierbrauer Unterstutzungsverein" (Beer Brewers Aid Society).[20] Similar societies had served as the base for actual labor unions in Cincinnati and New York, two of the earliest and strongest brewery union cities in the country. However, the Beer Brewers Aid Society in Cleveland was more concerned with celebrating the brewer's trade than protesting whatever harsh working conditions may have existed in the city's breweries. In 1873, the society hosted a gala affair attended by brewery workers from all over the state. The gathering paraded through the streets of Cleveland – stopping at more than one beer garden along the way – with a German marching band at its head and waving colorful flags which depicted the various occupations within the brewery. The march terminated at Haltnorth's Garden, where the society was presented with a large silk banner featuring a likeness of King

Brewer's Union No 17

Gambrinus, the patron saint of beer. An enthusiastic speech was later made by society president Anton Kopp regarding the menace of the temperance "fanatics."[21] Labor issues were plainly not among the society's immediate concerns. Relations between the owners and their employees were, by all accounts, free of conflict.

However, the tremendous expansion of the brewing industry which occurred throughout the 1880s and 1890s began to impose a natural separation between worker and owner. The typical brewing plant was no longer a three- or four-man operation as in the old days. As the industry grew, it became common for a brewery to employ a multitude of workers, each with a very specific skill or function. As a result, full-blown unionization among labor was imminent. In Cleveland, the Beer Brewers Aid Society had evolved into an organized union – known as the Gambrinus Assembly of the Knights of Labor – by June of 1886. The following year, the union joined the National Union of the Brewery

The local brewer's union was a very fraternal bunch. Picnics and outings, such as the one pictured here, were common.

Workmen of the United States as Cleveland Local #17.[22] Reports from the national union, however, indicated only good relations in Cleveland. A study was conducted by the national union in 1888 concerning the local labor situations across the country. The results showed that, in nearly every city, the brewery worker's battle for better working conditions was being lost and that, "only on the Pacific Coast, in Cleveland, and in Syracuse was the condition of the union a good one."[23]

Naturally, minor disputes did arise between owner and worker from time to time. When the local union's first labor contract expired in 1888, Cleveland brewery owners, in a show of solidarity, refused temporarily to renew the contract. A strike was threatened by the union, but it was later called off in anticipation of the owners' eventual cooperation. A similar conflict occurred in 1890 and again in 1893.[24] In 1895, the local coopers' union attempted to organize a boycott against one of the city's largest breweries for using non-union kegs. The campaign, however, lost some of its momentum when it was rumored that the circular which announced the boycott had been printed at a non-union "rat shop."

In the end, all such disputes between owners and workers were resolved without major incident, usually in favor of the workers. Indeed, the Cleveland Local #17 once admitted, "It has to be mentioned that in many cases the Brewery Owners agreed that their workers were right, and step by step were pushed back from their offensive to a defensive condition."[25]

Even so, there certainly must have been forces other than simple compassion that formed the owners' relatively submissive stance over the years. Probably one of the more significant factors was the local brewing industry's near total dependence on its home market throughout the latter part of the nineteenth century. Although Cleveland brewers exported a large amount of beer outside the city during the 1860s and 1870s, shipping began to slow significantly after about 1880. The decrease was caused primarily by the advent of artificial refrigeration, which negated the advantage that Cleveland brewers enjoyed of unlimited supplies of ice harvested from Lake Erie. With much of their export business having disappeared, local brewers became far more dependent on their home trade. Thus, they were highly susceptible to the threat of a beer boycott – the fundamental weapon of brewery labor. Realizing that a boycott would be the likely result of any serious breakdown in labor relations, and with no other substantial markets to help compensate for such a disaster, brewery owners in Cleveland were quick to avoid major conflict.

Another influence may have been that, in comparison with some of the larger brewing cities, many of Cleveland's breweries were relatively small, and the owners and their families often resided right at or near the brewery. Consequently, the owners seem to have been, by most accounts, quite involved in the day-to-day operations of the brewery and, thereby, knew many of their employees personally. This situation must have helped, if

The symbol of Local #17 conveyed brotherhood and cooperation.

65

only a little, to create a mutual resistance to conflict. From this standpoint, the local union's claim that the owners "agreed that their workers were right" seems to hold some degree of validity.

Regarding labor relations, perhaps most noteworthy among Cleveland's brewery owners was Isaac Leisy. His west side brewery employed more men than any other during much of the late nineteenth century. One observer said of Isaac Leisy that "No head of a firm could be more popular with his employees, he frequently putting himself to much inconvenience for their special benefit."[26] And it was said that, at the Leisy brewery, "all worthy employees are to have every consideration consistent, in the way of improving their home life."[27] In 1886, the Leisy brewery employed as many as eighty men, a substantial portion of the city's total number of brewery hands.[28] Indeed, it is not unreasonable to surmise that Isaac Leisy's personal endorsement of the working man's cause may have played an important role in Cleveland's undeniably mild brewery labor movement. After all, any potential uprisings among brewery labor would certainly have been crippled if a significant portion of its members – satisfied with the conditions of their employment – refused to participate, thereby forcing an environment of negotiation rather than confrontation.

Isaac Leisy & Company

There are few names as closely identified with Cleveland's brewing history as is the name Leisy. Throughout the late 1800s, and well into the next century, there was nary a Clevelander whose thirst was not quenched at one time or another by an ice cold Leisy beer. For three generations, the Leisy family's gigantic brewery at Vega Avenue and Fulton Road turned out barrel after barrel of what many considered to be the city's finest beer. The Leisys themselves, too, enjoyed great popularity among Clevelanders. Their involvement in the community, their concern for the welfare of employees, their obvious wealth and success, and – perhaps most important to many – their unwavering commitment to producing a superior brew all contributed to the tremendous local respect for the Leisys and their products.

The story of Leisy beer in Cleveland began in June of 1873, when the city hosted the Thirteenth Annual Brewers Congress, held at the West Side Rink. Brewers from around the country converged on the city to discuss brewing-related issues and fraternize with industry compatriots. Among those in attendance at the Congress was brewer Isaac Leisy, part owner of the Leisy & Brothers Union Brewery of Keokuk, Iowa. Leisy, like the other attendees, could not have helped but be impressed

Cleveland State University

Isaac Leisy and his brothers came to Cleveland in 1873 and founded a beer-making dynasty which lasted for three generations.

by the fertile market that Cleveland offered its brewing enterprises. The city's industrial development had burgeoned nonstop since the Civil War, the level of European immigration into Cleveland was reaching new highs, and more than twenty-five breweries throughout the city enjoyed a booming trade. It must have been just these conditions that lead Isaac Leisy to pull up stakes in Iowa and seek the purchase of a brewery in Cleveland. Within four short weeks of his visit, Isaac Leisy and two of his brothers, August and Henry, had purchased the brewery of local entrepreneur Frederick Haltnorth, thus marking the beginning of a long-lived Cleveland brewing dynasty.

The brewery – in what was then Brooklyn Township – was originally established in 1858 by brewer Jacob Mueller, who sold the works to Frederick Haltnorth in 1864.[29] Haltnorth was involved in a number of different enterprises in Cleveland for many years, most notably Haltnorth's Gardens at Willson (East 55th) Street and Woodland Avenue. The large beer garden was among the city's most popular. It is likely that Haltnorth's involvement in the brewing business was motivated primarily by the need to supply his garden with ample quantities of beer. That notwithstanding, the brewery was turning out a large amount of beer – as much as 12,000 barrels annually – at the time of its sale to the Leisy brothers.

Isaac, August and Henry Leisy came to America in 1855 with their mother, father, brothers and sisters – a party comprised of fourteen Leisys in all. Coming from their ancestral home in Friedelsheim, Bavaria, the Leisys settled on a large farm in rural Iowa, where many fellow members of the Mennonite faith had also started life in the new land. Several of the Leisys were brewers by trade, and young Isaac – after finding work on the family farm to be distasteful – sought to become

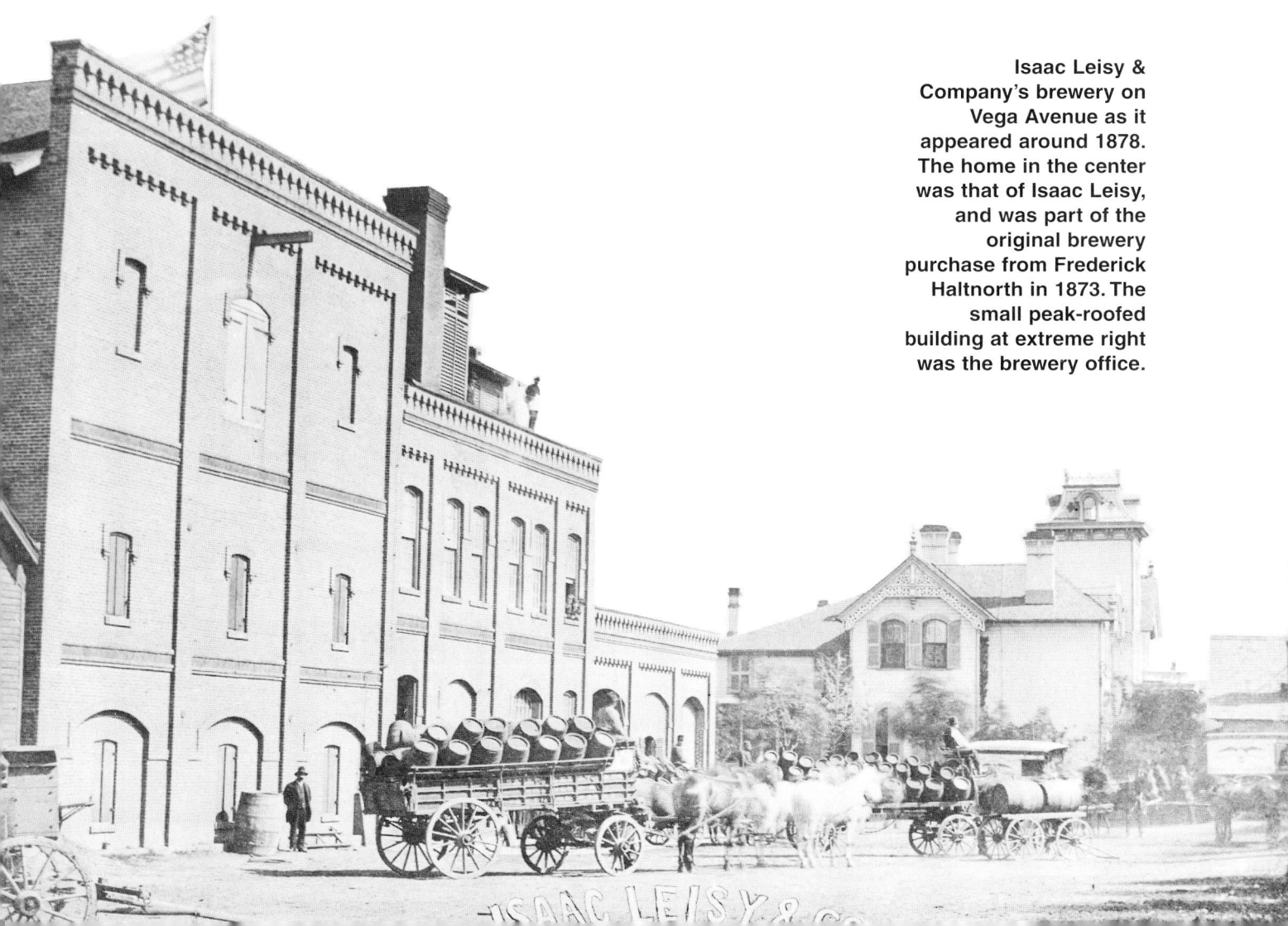

Isaac Leisy & Company's brewery on Vega Avenue as it appeared around 1878. The home in the center was that of Isaac Leisy, and was part of the original brewery purchase from Frederick Haltnorth in 1873. The small peak-roofed building at extreme right was the brewery office.

a brewer as well. His first employment in the beer-making trade was at a brewery in Warsaw, Illinois. However, Isaac was soon working instead at the brewery of William J. Lemp in St. Louis, where he remained for several years. While on a trip to Friedelsheim to visit his old home, Isaac married a cousin, Christine Leisy, and chose to remain in Germany for a time. Carrying on his career as a brewer, Isaac worked briefly at a brewery in Dürkheim.[30]

Upon his return to America in 1862, Isaac was persuaded by his father to come to Keokuk, Iowa and join two of his brothers – John and Rudolph – in a brewery venture there. Along with Jacob Baehr (who would later own a brewery in Cleveland), the Leisy brothers took over a Keokuk brewery and commenced business in 1862 as the Leisy & Brothers Union Brewery. Business at the Keokuk brewery was good, but Isaac soon yearned for something of grander proportions. As one biographer put it, Isaac was "ambitious to engage in business in some city of importance where he could have a wider field for the exercise of his talents."[31] It was undoubtedly this desire for new opportunities that led Isaac to Cleveland.

While Isaac Leisy had been busy with his brewery in Keokuk, his brothers Henry and August were engaged in pursuits in other parts of the country. August – one of the few Leisys who did not become a brewer at an early age – operated a furniture business in Missouri. Henry, however, followed in the family tradition and worked as a brewer in St. Louis and Milwaukee.

During the 1880s, the Leisy brewery produced three varieties of beer. "Budweiser" was not a trademarked brand name as it is today. Rather, it referred to the style of beer brewed in the European city of Budweis.

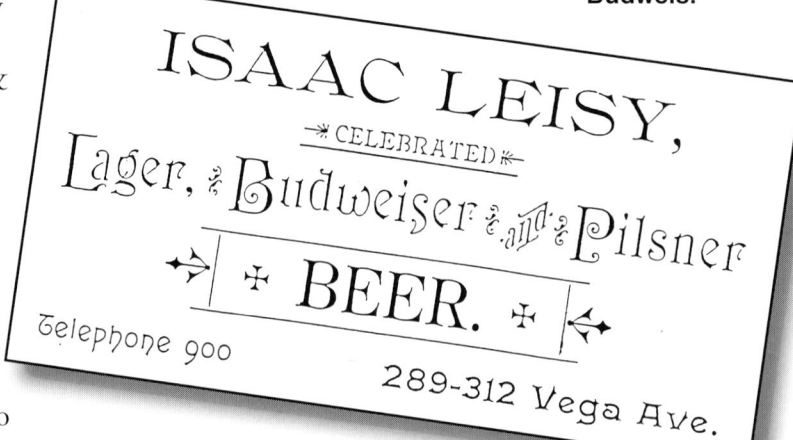

ISAAC LEISY,
CELEBRATED
Lager, Budweiser and Pilsner
BEER.
Telephone 900
289-312 Vega Ave.

A Leisy teamster making his daily rounds.

Anthony Zappitelli Collection

68

On July 2, 1873, Isaac, August and Henry Leisy bought Frederick Haltnorth's brewery in Cleveland for $120,000.[32] Interestingly, a portion of the capital was supplied by John, Jacob and Henry Laysy, who operated a local distillery under the name of J. Laysy & Company. Distant relations of the Leisy family, the Laysys were a branch of the original Swiss lineage which did not emigrate to Bavaria as Isaac's ancestors had done. It is surmised that the Laysys may have played more than just a financial role in the Leisy brothers' decision to come to Cleveland. Whatever the case, the Laysys sold their interest in the brewery to Isaac not long after business commenced.

There are a variety of stories concerning exactly how it happened that the Leisys came to purchase Haltnorth's brewery. One source states that Isaac Leisy toured the brewery while in Cleveland for the brewers' convention. Having found it to be "so every way satisfactory to him," Leisy allegedly approached Haltnorth on-the-spot and beseeched him to sell the brewery. However, more reliable sources show that Haltnorth, in fact, actively sought the sale of his brewery, even engaging the services of an agent to help secure a buyer.[33] The agent brought Leisy and Haltnorth together shortly after the conclusion of the brewers' convention. It was said that the final purchase price was negotiated over a late night card game between Leisy and Haltnorth. By the following morning, Haltnorth had come to regret the price, but honored the agreement nevertheless. "My word is my word," said Haltnorth.[34]

Isaac Leisy & Company was the name given the new firm as Isaac held the largest share among the brothers. Included in the purchase of the brewery was a large and stylish residence which had been the home of Frederick Haltnorth and which sat just near the brewery buildings. As head of the concern, Isaac enjoyed the benefit of residing in this home, while August and Henry lived in smaller houses further down Vega Avenue.

The Leisys approached the business of making and selling beer in Cleveland with unusual vigor. After all, Cleveland offered Isaac and his brothers opportunities which simply were not present in rural Iowa. For example, the complex network of rail lines which sprouted from the city in all directions allowed for efficient distribution of beer to locations outside the Cleveland area. And, indeed, distant markets were aggressively pursued by the Leisys right from the start. The brothers established their own distribution depot in Pittsburgh early on. By 1878, the Pittsburgh facility was doing enough business to warrant the relocation of Henry Leisy to that city for the purpose of overseeing the extensive trade there. During the same year, it was noted that Leisy beer was being handled by wholesalers as far away as San Francisco, although surely this must have been an isolated and short-lived arrangement. The costs of transportation would certainly have been prohibitive.[35] Nevertheless, it is clear that the Leisy brewery prospered from the very beginning.

Bottled beer was a rarity during the mid-1800s. It was not until after the turn of the century that brewers of lager beer began to bottle their product on a large scale.

In keeping with their ambitious charge to develop business, the Leisys sought to cultivate a local market for *bottled* beer to supplement the traditional kegged sales. Bottling was something which was almost entirely ignored by the great majority of the day's lager beer brewers. In fact, what little lager beer bottling did take place in the early days was conducted almost exclusively by independent bottlers. Many such bottlers found great profits in buying kegged beer direct from brewers, bottling it with or without the brewer's permission, and selling it themselves, often under their own names. Predictably, an arrangement of this sort was unacceptable to the Leisys. The early bottling of lager beer was a tricky process which often proved detrimental to the quality of the beer. And far be it from the brothers to allow some outside bottler the occasion to recklessly tamper with the good Leisy name. Accordingly, the Leisys built their own bottling works in the spring of 1878 across Vega Avenue from the brewery.[36] Although it represented a modest percentage of total output, bottled beer continued to be a priority at the Leisy brewery throughout the remainder of the pre-prohibition years.

Despite the early success of the Leisy brewery, both Henry and August Leisy gave up their interest in the business to Isaac in 1882 and left Cleveland to take up farming in Wisner, Nebraska. Their reasons for doing so are not entirely clear, although a family member later postulated that August and Henry – having grown up in rural regions of Germany – were simply not suited for urban life. In addition, it was suggested that the two brothers may have found it difficult to reconcile their strict Mennonite background with the reaping of large profits from the manufacture of alcoholic beverages.[37] Whatever the case, the business continued to flourish under Isaac's sole direction.

This life-size statue of King Gambrinus, "the patron saint of beer," adorned the Leisy brewery.

Creating A Landmark

In 1883, Isaac Leisy commissioned Cleveland brewery architect Andrew Mitermiler to design a grand new Leisy stockhouse (an ice house where beer was aged) adjacent to the original brewery buildings. This new structure not only marked the beginning of a wholesale metamorphosis of the Leisy plant, but also largely determined the architectural character that the entire complex would reflect for the next seventy-five years. Visually, the Leisy brewery was one of the most extravagant of the city's brewing plants. It included a number of unique architectural features. A life-size statue of King Gambrinus – "the patron saint of beer" – adorned the roofline until a 1909 windstorm earned it a new perch in the brewery yard. A series of unusual circular emblems spanned much of the brewery's main facade, symbolizing the many rows of aging casks within. And atop the 1883 stockhouse was a large mock beer keg impaled through its fattest part by the brewery's weather vane.

70

The brewery, however, was only one element of the charming eight-acre Leisy premises. It is interesting to imagine what the first-time visitor saw as he traveled down Vega Avenue from Pearl Street to the brewery. First was Isaac's majestic brownstone mansion with its white marble-pillared porticos and copper-plated towers. Built in 1892, the home was alleged (although falsely) to have a pipeline running directly from the brewery to the living room such that Isaac's guests might be treated to the very freshest beer possible.[38] Just past the mansion was a spectacular park-like setting that included a pond, numerous flower gardens, walking paths, several gazebos, and two large greenhouses. During warm summer days, the many exotic plants which were grown inside the greenhouses were moved outdoors to enhance the other greenery. (The fact that Isaac served on the Cleveland Board of Park Commissioners was an indication of his affection for nature.)

Left: Isaac Leisy's mansion on Vega Avenue, built in 1892.

Below: A green-house which sat in the yard next to the Leisy brewery.

The Leisy brewery, with Otto Leisy's residence in the foreground.

Just beyond the lawn and gardens sat the residence of Isaac's son, Otto Leisy. The large Victorian-style house was part of the original brewery purchase from Frederick Haltnorth in 1873. A number of architectural revisions were made over the years so that its appearance would complement that of the adjacent brewery buildings. Finally, having arrived at the brewery gate, visitors were confronted with the mammoth brewery itself and all of its architectural splendor. Certainly, the Leisys took great pains to make visiting the brewery grounds a pleasurable experience.

In its heyday, the Leisy brewery was a bustle of activity. With its many different departments and functions, the plant was highly self-sufficient. There was a blacksmith shop which manufactured brewery tools, horse shoes, barrel rings and countless other items. A fully-equipped woodworking shop was also on brewery grounds for the manufacture and repair of delivery wagons. The woodworking department also built saloon fixtures for the many Leisy-owned saloons throughout the city. When the brewery closed during prohibition, the Leisy family chose to keep the woodworking shop open, doing business as the Fulton Manufacturing Company. There was, of course, a cooperage to supply the necessary hundreds of beer kegs and brewery casks. A complete harness shop was maintained, as were stables which housed nearly 250 delivery horses.[39] The bottling department was kept busy at all times as well, eliminating the complications of employing outside bottling firms. Additionally, the Leisy brewery was one of the few local breweries that malted its own grain rather than buying from independent malteries. This process alone required its own five story building and two eighty-foot-high silos each with a storage capacity of 50,000 bushels of barley.[40]

Inside the brewery was "Der Sternwirt," where visitors and workers could enjoy an ice-cold mug of Leisy's Beer.

Clearly, the Leisy brewery dominated its primarily residential neighborhood. There was perhaps no other Cleveland brewery more intimately linked to its neighbors and its community. In an early newspaper article, many of the area's oldest residents recalled how the brewery was virtually the lifeblood of the neighborhood during the days before prohibition. A local storekeeper told how the chief topic of conversation in his store from morning until night was beer – *Leisy* beer. A barber, whose shop was just a few doors down from the brewery, complained about the sharp decline in business after the plant closed during prohibition. He used to give haircuts to everyone from the brewery, including the Leisys. A local saloonkeeper, who used to drive a Leisy beer wagon in his younger days, proudly announced that he had never drawn a glass of beer that was not Leisy's.[41] Other residents undoubtedly recalled the days when the Leisys paid for brick pavement of area streets, or funded the development of Lincoln Park, or supplied neighbors with electricity from the brewery's power plant when storms caused blackouts.[42] Indeed, the Leisys took pride in playing a role in the well-being and betterment of their adopted neighborhood and city.

Isaac Leisy was described as "a man of great energy and fully alive to the modern methods of doing business."[43] One observer went so far as to say of Isaac, "No brewer has ever displayed greater energy."[44] Many credited Isaac's economic success to his unusual charisma. In his later years, however, Isaac began to suffer failing health. Most of his winters were spent in the South, away from the harsh northern climate. He was a regular visitor of health resorts in both America and Europe. On July 11, 1892, after a two-week illness, Isaac passed away at age fifty-four at his home on Vega Avenue. The cause of death was cited as "apoplexy of the heart."[45] Son Otto I. Leisy was vacationing in Europe at the time and was cabled immediately to return home. After all, it would be Otto who would assume control of the family business.

The Second Generation

Otto I. Leisy was but nine years old when his father moved the family from Iowa to Cleveland. He grew and matured along with the brewery. Upon Isaac's death, it was time for Otto to assume his father's position as head of the firm. And although the Leisy brewery had grown into the city's largest and most prosperous brewing enterprise by the time of Isaac's death, Otto faced an industry very much different from that of his father's day. Industry-wide over-expansion during the 1880s, coupled with the economic panic of 1893, sparked intense competition among brewers throughout the last decade of the century. When nine Cleveland breweries joined two in Sandusky to form the Cleveland & Sandusky Brewing Company in 1898, Otto flatly refused to be involved in the consolidation. In a letter to the *Plain Dealer*, Otto defiantly wrote,

> *My firm has existed in Cleveland for over a quarter of a century; has prospered by honorable methods of trade, thereby obtaining, possessing and enjoying the confidence of the same. By its former methods my company proposes to preserve and maintain its trade, and in a fair way compete with its opponent, the huge beer trust.*[46]

Indeed, throughout the remainder of Otto's reign, the Leisy brewery fought vigorously with the Cleveland & Sandusky Brewing Company for business. And despite the cut-throat competition, the Leisy brewery clearly flourished under Otto's management. In 1898, just over 100,000 barrels of Leisy beer were sold, while nearly 300,000 were sold in 1913.[47]

Like most brewers of the day, the Leisys owned a large number of saloon properties

A tin serving tray advertising the I. Leisy Brewing Company, circa 1900.

The First Leisy Jingle?

In 1911, the Leisy brewery published a song extolling the virtues of Leisy's Special Brew. The tune was called "A Toast," and sheet music was given to Leisy customers. Radio, of course, was still many years away. The hope in distributing sheet music was that families would gather around the piano and, in essance, perform their own Leisy beer commercial. Below are some of the lyrics.

On the banks of old Lake Erie,
    there's a windy, smoky town;
Even so, the town is wealthy
    and the men of great renown;
Manufacturing and building,
    handsome homes and women too;
And the people are all happy
    cause of Leisy's Special Brew.

What is as good as Leisy's Beer?
    Leisy's Beer? Leisy's Beer?
Its better than wine, so fill up your stein.
    Let's have some Leisy's near.
Its good for the fat and its good for the thin.
    Its good when you're feeling blue.
We'll pass up the Beef and the Iron and Wine
    for Leisy's Special Brew.

If the parched and sandy desert
    were up on the market placed
Mighty few would buy for farmland
    any of that fruitless waste
But if someone would irrigate
    the land with Leisy's Brew
There would be a lot more farmers
    where there now are very few.

Way back there in the summer
    of the fifteenth century
The Spandiard Ponce DeLeon
    sailed forth some sights to see
He was looking for a fountain
    to restore his worn out youth
But he found a spring of Leisy's beer
    and he's living yet for sooth.

Young George Speedum once last summer
    out upon an auto ride;
Motor stopped out in the roadway,
    couldn't start it though he tried;
Carburator and magneto
    sparked until he turned the crank;
But he found he had no gasoline
    when he opened up the tank.

He filled it up with Leisy's Beer,
    Leisy's Beer, Leisy's Beer;
You never have seen a faster machine
    speed her up with gasoline;
Its good for the motor and steering wheel
    its good for the driver, too;
Feed your car, nothing's quite on par,
    with Leisy's Special Brew.

Down in Boston lived a maiden
    named Miss Priscilla Brown;
She had once been quite a beauty,
    and a favorite in the town;
But her face had lost its color
    from her cheeks the rose fled;
Though she used six or eight cosmetics
    before she went to bed.

She ought to try some Leisy's Beer.
    Leisy's Beer, Leisy's Beer;
Its better than Milkweed or Pompeian cream,
    so keep some Leisy's near.
Its good for the pink and its good for the pale,
    There's no end to what Leisy's will do;
We'll pass up the Beef and the Iron and Wine
    for Leisy's Special Brew.

throughout Cleveland and elsewhere. With the constant fight for business, brewers sought to protect their sales by achieving *exclusive* placement of their beer in saloons. This goal was often most easily accomplished through outright ownership of the saloons. By the time prohibition was enacted, more than 200 "outlets," as they were called, had been owned and operated by the Leisy brewery. In 1914, the Pontiac Improvement Company was incorporated by the Leisys to act as a holding company for the saloons. The new company was likely the result of recent legislative attempts to ban brewers from owning their own drinking establishments.[48]

Otto I. Leisy

The first decade of the twentieth century was perhaps the most prosperous period for the Leisy brewery. Great wealth was amassed by Otto Leisy and his family during this time. Otto's financial involvements, however, went far beyond brewing. He was a large stockholder in both the Ashtabula Worsted Mills and the National Woolen Mills of Cleveland. He had also been heavily interested in the old Forest City Railway Company before its absorption by the Cleveland Railway Company. Otto was active in the banking business as well, serving as director of the Lincoln Savings & Banking Company and as vice president of the Pearl Street Savings & Trust Company.[49] But, of course, beer was Otto's primary business, and he was well acquainted with many of the country's prominent brewers. Otto traveled to Europe regularly. On one such voyage, Otto booked passage on the now historic *Lusitania* which, just a few years later, would be at the center of America's involvement in World War I.[50]

Most of Otto's later years were spent at his eighty-acre summer estate at the top of Fairhill Road, east of what is today Martin Luther King Boulevard. The property was known as "Hochwald" – *high forest*. Originally, the retreat was meant only for weekend summer get-aways, while the family's full-time residence continued to be on the brewery grounds. However, by 1905, the advent of automobiles and the growing industrial unpleasantries of the city lead Otto to begin construction of a permanent residence at Hochwald. A stately thirty-six-room mansion, described as "1905 contemporary," was erected on a spot which featured a panoramic view of the entire city of Cleveland.[51] In its day, the lavish home was the scene of many parties and much-noted

After the turn of the century, most brewers made home deliveries of bottled beer.

social events, testifying to the lofty social status attained by the Leisys.

After more than twenty years at the head of Cleveland's largest brewery, Otto I. Leisy died at age fifty-one on March 1, 1914. Local newspapers, one of which called Otto "Cleveland's benefactor," detailed the numerous civic affairs in which the millionaire brewer played a major role. During Mayor Tom L. Johnson's notorious fight to reduce city trolley fares to 3¢, Otto was said to have come forth with a $200,000 donation toward the cause. Mayor Newton D. Baker, who walked to the Leisys' Fairhill Road mansion during a blinding snowstorm to deliver his condolences, said of Otto,

> *His belief in Cleveland was intense. He thought it the finest city in the world in its possibilities and was willing to give his money and time for its advancement...Mr. Leisy's death is a distinct loss to the city of Cleveland.*[52]

On the very day of his death, Otto was scheduled to deliver a $50,000 bank note to the city for development of the first public playground on the west side. The Leisy family saw to it that Otto's final act of philanthropy did not go unfulfilled.

The presidency of the Leisy brewery was left vacant for several years after Otto's death. Otto's sister, Amanda Corlett, joined the brewery as vice president in 1914. In the same year, cousin Hugo A. Leisy (son of August Leisy, one of the three original founders) left a career in banking in Nebraska to come to Cleveland and fill the position of secretary and treasurer of the brewery.[53]

Just as Isaac Leisy had died on the cusp of a new era in brewing, so too did Otto pass away on the verge of a rapidly changing industry. After 1914, beer consumption in America started a long downward slide ending in National Prohibition. Much to the credit of the new Leisy management, the Leisy brewery bore the difficulties remarkably well. It was correctly predicted that household consumption of beer would represent a profitable opportunity for brewers. Thus, the Leisys invested heavily in an enormous new bottling plant on the northwest corner of Vega Avenue and Fulton Road, finished in 1915. Only two years later, yet another new bottling facility was begun adjacent to the main brewhouse. By the end of 1917, more than thirty percent of Leisy's output was packaged in bottles, compared to only five percent in 1910.[54]

By 1917, more than thirty percent of Leisy's Beer was packaged in bottles, compared with just five percent in 1910.

It is likely that the Leisys' heavy emphasis on bottling was largely driven by their hopes for success of a new brand called Leisy's Bevera – a non-alcoholic malt beverage launched in response to the growing prohibition agitation. The new brand seems to represent the Leisys' acceptance that prohibition was imminent. The vigorous promotion of Bevera indicated that the company fully intended to remain active in the beverage business regardless of prohibition. Advertisements for the new brand boasted, "It is as good for children as for grown ups. It is the universal drink of the day."[55] Bevera was sold everywhere: soda fountains, drug stores, grocers, confectioners, hotels, restaurants and amusement parks – everywhere, that is, except saloons.

Production at the Leisy brewery peaked in 1918, when 565,493 barrels of Leisy beer were consumed during the year.[56] It does not appear, however, that sales of Bevera contributed significantly to the brewery's banner year. When production of real beer ceased for prohibition, the company's sales quickly dwindled to near zero. Non-alcoholic malt beverages like Bevera simply did not have a widespread market. And although the Leisys also manufactured a full line of flavored soft drinks, the business was unable to remain profitable for long. In 1923, the closing of the Leisy brewery was marked by the pouring of six thousand barrels of Bevera into the sewer.[57] A half-century of Leisy beer in Cleveland had come to an end. For the next ten years, the venerable old brewery would remain idle.

The Baehr Brewery

When Isaac, August and Henry Leisy first came to Cleveland in 1873, they were likely to have previous knowledge of the city's promising beer market. Among the partners in the old brewery back in Keokuk, Iowa was fellow German Jacob Baehr, who had left Iowa in 1866 to establish a brewery in Cleveland. Henry Leisy, in fact, ultimately married one of Baehr's daughters.[58] There is little doubt that word of Baehr's success in Cleveland had reached the Leisys prior to Isaac's initial visit for the Brewers' Congress. And, indeed, although Jacob Baehr passed away just weeks before Isaac's trip to Cleveland, the Baehr name was well-known in Cleveland's brewing circles for many years.

Jacob Baehr's brewery was not a typical establishment of its day. Although brewery work was no easy affair under any circumstance, Baehr must have run an *exceptionally* tight ship. No employee at the brewery was permitted to engage in "lewd talk" while on duty, and Baehr employed no man who was not a proven, regular church-goer. Perhaps even more revealing was Baehr's strict policy that no beer carrying the Baehr name would be sold to anyone who was known to use alcohol in any but a moderate manner.[59] In a time when beer was primarily a working-class indulgence (and, indeed, a time when the working class was not known for its moderation), Baehr's righteous business philosophies were not standard practice. The old brewer's strict Mennonite upbringing may have outweighed his entrepreneurial drive.

Jacob Baehr, a native of Heidelberg, came to America in 1850 and found his first employment as a cooper in New York City. At the behest of a brother living in Cleveland, who called the city "a second Heidelberg," Baehr came to the shores of Lake Erie and established a cooperage on Carroll Avenue.[60] In 1857, Baehr was encouraged by friend John Leisy to move to Iowa and join in the Leisy & Brothers Union Brewery there. Although business was good in Iowa, Baehr returned to Cleveland in 1866, apparently preferring the urban life. Baehr employed his long experience as a brewer, establishing a small lager beer brewery on Pearl (West 25th) Street near Church Avenue in 1866. While Baehr tended to the duties of the brewery, his wife ran the family's small saloon in the front portion of the building. The entire Baehr family, which numbered no less than ten, lived on the upper floor of the brewery.

In the early days, it was a common occurrence in the operation of a German-owned brewery that, after the passing of its proprietor, the widow assumed management of the business. Indeed, the death of Jacob Baehr in 1873 did not spell ruin for his brewery. Under the name of

Mrs. Jacob Baehr's Brewery, the widow Magdalena Baehr took over supervision of the business and, for the next twenty-five years, remained at its head. A biographer paid tribute to the ambitious widow:

With eight children, the youngest not even a year-and-a-half old, and suddenly without a husband, Mrs. Baehr admirably united the role of loving mother with that of shrewd business woman. Busy from early morning till late, looking after all details of the brewery, and never leaving an eye from raising her children, Mrs. Baehr achieved some surprising results. From the 3,000 barrels of beer that were made in 1873, she took the yearly sales of the brewery to 25,000 barrels, personally making sure that every drop of beer reached its destination in the city.[61]

Mrs. Baehr produced a selection of six different brews: Vienna, Kulmbacher, Pilsener, Franciscaner, Lager, and Extra Export. Despite its name, the Extra Export brand was probably not shipped out of town; Mrs. Baehr confined her business exclusively to the city of Cleveland, believing strongly in the "home industry principle."[62] Beer which was termed "export" connoted a premium variety and was offered by many brewers who engaged in little or no shipping.

The 1890s seem to have been a particularly progressive decade for Mrs. Baehr's brewery. The *Western Brewer* reported in 1892 that several improvements were being made at the brewery, among them a new brewhouse, new stockhouse,

Magdalena Baehr, Cleveland's "widow brewer."

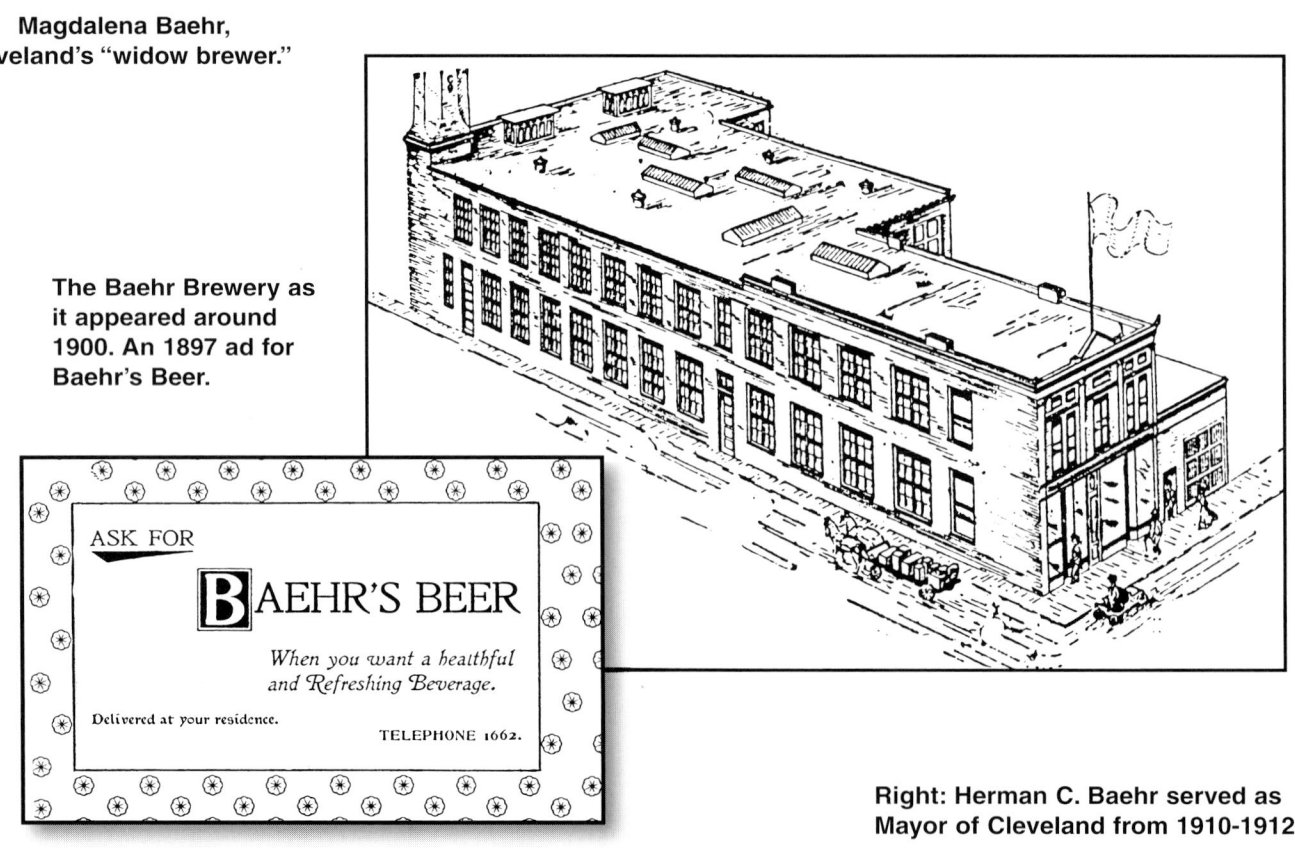

The Baehr Brewery as it appeared around 1900. An 1897 ad for Baehr's Beer.

ASK FOR

BAEHR'S BEER

When you want a healthful and Refreshing Beverage.

Delivered at your residence.

TELEPHONE 1662.

Right: Herman C. Baehr served as Mayor of Cleveland from 1910-1912.

78

improved racking (kegging) facilities, enlarged grain storage, and a new wash house.[63] In 1894, Mrs. Baehr, who generally did not involve the brewery in a great deal of promotional activity, advertised her bottled beer in *Cleveland Town Topics,* a magazine published exclusively for the city's social elite. Indeed, Mrs. Baehr's saloon adjacent to the brewery had become a fashionable spot. By virtue of her perseverance and independence, Mrs. Baehr won the admiration and friendship of many prominent Clevelanders, including Senator Marcus Hanna and local politician James Barnett.[64] It was, in fact, this exposure to political circles that sparked one of Mrs. Baehr's sons, Herman C. Baehr, to pursue a political career that culminated in his serving as Mayor of Cleveland from 1910 to 1912.*

In 1898, the aging Mrs. Baehr decided to sell the family brewery to the recently organized Cleveland & Sandusky Brewing Company. Sons Emil and Herman C. Baehr were kept on at the brewery as brewmaster and manager, respectively. Herman was placed on the board of directors of the Cleveland & Sandusky company. Mrs. Baehr spent her final years living on Cleveland's west side and engaging in philanthropic activities. In 1901, the Cleveland & Sandusky Brewing Company closed the Baehr plant and transferred its production to the Phoenix brewery at Columbus & Willey Streets, thereafter known as the Baehr-Phoenix branch of the combine.

---

*Baehr succeeded Mayor Tom L. Johnson, regarded as one of the great urban reformers of his time. Johnson's defeat by Baehr – the result of a hotly contested election – made national headlines. Interestingly, Johnson was the political arch rival of Marcus Hanna, a close family friend of the Baehrs.

Chapter Four

The Beer Barons

Like every other American industry, the brewing of beer was greatly impacted by the post-Civil War industrial boom. Beginning in the late 1870s and carrying well into the following two decades, brewers across the country invested heavily in new and expanded facilities. Seemingly overnight, wood frame structures and hand-powered brewery tools gave way to immense architectural wonders and widespread mechanization. Shipping of beer to new and distant markets became common, spurred by increased production and expanded channels of transportation. Between 1880 and 1893, annual U.S. beer production climbed from about thirteen million barrels to well over thirty-four million barrels.[1] Without question, the industry had leaped headstrong into a new era of beer-making: the age of the Beer Barons.

While a strong economy and an ever-growing immigrant population increased the *demand* for beer, the *supply* was made

University of Wisconsin

possible by the technological developments in brewing created during the 1870s and 1880s. And, of the many innovations, the most important was unquestionably artificial refrigeration. A brewing industry analyst wrote in 1903,

> *The application of refrigeration to the brewing industry was the means of implanting in it the germ of indefinite expansion...In the development of nearly every operation in the brewery – in the cooling of the wort, in fermentation, in storage of beer and hops, in racking, in bottling, and even in the operation of malting – artificial refrigeration has played an important part. Indeed it may be said that the wonderful progress made in the art of brewing during the last twenty-five years is mainly attributable to the introduction of artificial refrigeration in the brewery.*[2]

In the old days, the necessity of cold temperatures, particularly in the brewing of lager beer, presented a constant challenge to the brewer. The harvesting of natural ice – a bothersome and sometimes expensive affair – was the brewer's sole option, and brewing was conducted only as the supplies of ice allowed. Undoubtedly many frustrated brewers nursed their beer through the various stages of production only to find that the ice needed for proper aging of the beer could not be had, thus dooming the brew to imminent spoilage. By the 1870s, however, a number of viable machines for the manufacture of "artificial ice" began to appear. They were followed closely by systems for the outright refrigeration of entire spaces within the brewery. Suddenly, the brewer's most arduous task – the digging of underground cellars, the cutting and hauling of ice, the fight against melting, etc. – was completely eliminated. The technology was embraced by brewers everywhere. The entire lagering process was, for the first time, brought above ground, and brewing could be carried on year round. In short, artificial refrigeration took brewing out of the dark ages and placed it squarely into the modern era.

The extensive use of steam power in the brewery was another important development during the late 1800s. Although the employment of steam power in industrial settings was anything but new, it was only during the last two decades of the nineteenth century that its use in brewing gave rise to extensive mechanization in the typical brewery. In countless applications, the use of steam now replaced manually-powered equipment. The far-reaching effects of steam power in brewing are perhaps best demonstrated by one sarcastic observer's comments after witnessing a steam engine in operation in a brewery:

The engine is sixteen horsepower. It can, at the same time, grind the malt, sift it, throw it into the mash tub, let in boiling water that it has made to boil, stir up the malt and water, draw it off, pump it up stairs and throw it into the kettle, heat the kettle of liquid until it boils, throw it out into the coolers, cool it, force and carry it off into vats, ferment it, chafe it, and draw it off beer. With a little practice the engine could be taught to drink the beer.[3]

While cleanliness and visual appeal were paramount in the design of a brewery's exterior, the interior spaces were rarely afforded the same degree of aesthetic consideration. The early brewery was often a dark and dingy place.

Certainly the most visible outgrowth of this wave of technology and mechanization in brewing was a dramatic change in brewery architecture. At the most basic level, the addition of above-ground stockhouses (made possible by artificial refrigeration), as well as the construction of boiler houses to generate steam power, began to change the fundamental layout of breweries. Steam power, incidentally, also added the obligatory smoke stack which stood guard over the brewery grounds and puffed thick, black smoke into the sky. However, functionality was not the only factor that impacted late nineteenth century brewery architecture. With their newfound affluence, brewers were also concerned with the style and aesthetic appeal of their places of business. Brewers in most regions were experiencing some of their most profitable years ever, and optimism within the industry was at a high point. Breweries were designed to be virtual monuments to the success and prosperity of the brewing company and its owner. Towering steeples, an abundance of stylish concrete trim to contrast the red brickwork, and even decorative statues were characteristic of the typical brewery.

In earlier days, the design and layout of a brewery was a relatively simple matter, almost always being undertaken by the builder. But, with the advent of countless new technologies and mechanical apparatus in the brewery, coupled with the increased focus on cosmetic appeal, architects who specialized exclusively in the design of breweries became a necessity. In Cleveland, virtually every brewing plant in the city was completely or substantially rebuilt during the 1880s and early 1890s. Nearly all of them were designed and supervised by a single local architect, Bohemian immigrant Andrew R. Mitermiler. Somewhat of a confidant to the local brewing industry, Mitermiler became the local authority in brewery design. He is credited with planning more than a dozen of Cleveland's breweries, to wit: the Leisy, Schlather, Gehring, Oppmann, Stoppel, Muth, Mall, Baehr, Cleveland, Diebolt, Schneider, Pilsener and Standard breweries.[4] It is surmised, as well, that Mitermiler designed a multitude of breweries outside Cleveland.

Andrew R. Mitermiler

Distant Markets

Now commanding immense brewing facilities with all of the latest innovations and efficiencies, many brewers found themselves with excess brewing capacity. In order to operate at peak efficiency, wider beer sales were required. This often meant expanding into new geographical markets further from home. While the early part of the nineteenth century witnessed little long-distance shipping of beer, the 1880s and 1890s saw countless brewers sending their beer anywhere the railroads could carry it. However, shipping beer over any distance sometimes proved to be a burdensome endeavor. Bottled beer, for example, simply did not travel well. Thus, beer was shipped in kegs, then bottled in the locale where it was to be sold. Bottled beer was crucial to the success of any brand encroaching on new territory because it avoided direct competition for saloonkeepers' limited number of beer taps. But bottling in every city where a brewer wished to establish his brand was no easy task. Brewers had two choices: either employ the services of a local independent bottler, thus relinquishing quality control to an outside party; or bear the large expense of establishing a bottling facility in each new market. Indeed, both scenarios were played out by brewers, each having its own advantages and drawbacks.

The high costs of transporting beer to its destination was another menace to brewers who shipped. In order to prevent spoilage of the beer, shipments needed to be packed in ice sufficient to last the duration of the trip. In fact, it often happened that the space consumed by ice was greater than that of the beer. As much as ten thousand pounds of ice were required to protect a railroad car full of beer, depending on the distance and climate of the destination.[5] Freight charges, of course, were impacted significantly, thus making out-of-town brews always more expensive to the consumer than local brands.

John Schneider, brewmaster at the Schlather brewery, was one of Cleveland's veteran nineteenth century beer-makers. As the typical brewery became increasingly mechanized during the 1800s, the role of the brewmaster grew in importance. (George Schneider Collection)

Moreover, in all but a few regions, the seasonal scarcity and price fluctuation of the ice itself could be an added obstacle to the shipping of beer. Until the advent of artificially-refrigerated rail cars (spearheaded, likely enough, by St. Louis brewer Anheuser-Busch), shippers often lived or died by the prevailing market conditions for ice. Cleveland brewers, though, were almost entirely immune to the difficulties associated with the need for ice. Lake Erie ice was harvested in enormous quantities, such that local brewers rarely faced shortages and never paid prices as high as those in most inland regions. In 1880, for example, while the cost of ice in Cincinnati averaged $5.80 per ton, the average price along Lake Erie was $2.46 per ton. The price in Cleveland could dip as low as $1 per ton in some seasons, whereas other areas could see the price driven as high as $40 per ton during a critical shortage.[6] Breweries in Cleveland, therefore, enjoyed a tremendous advantage during the mid-nineteenth century. Brewing could be carried on year round, and the inexpensive cost of ice created an important shipping trade. Each of the city's larger brewers – Leisy, Schlather, Gehring, and others – employed "traveling agents" to stimulate new business throughout the Midwest. Pittsburgh, because of its enormous beer trade, was a large recipient of Cleveland-brewed beer. At least a few Cleveland brewers maintained their own distribution depots in Pittsburgh. Indeed, during the post-Civil War years, as much as twenty percent of Cleveland's beer production was sent to markets outside the city.[7]

The arrival of artificial refrigeration at the end of the 1870s was a mixed blessing for Cleveland's brewing industry. While local brewers certainly enjoyed the ease and efficiencies of automated cooling in their plants, the new technology eliminated the brewing industry's dependence on natural ice. Along with it went Cleveland's advantage as a major ice-harvesting center. Shipping among the city's brewers dropped off sharply. Thus, while artificial refrigeration stimulated the shipping of beer for brewers in other regions, it actually curtailed shipping for Cleveland's beer-makers. And although a rapidly swelling population at home (particularly within the German segment) greatly helped to offset dwindling outside sales, Cleveland brewers certainly must have felt the loss just the same.

The National Brewers

As the shipping trade for Cleveland breweries had all but disappeared by the 1890s, the influx of "national" brewing companies into the city was just beginning. Increasing production efficiencies and expanding railroads gave rise to nationally-minded companies. Heavily-capitalized brewers like Pabst, Schlitz, Anheuser-Busch, and others were on a quest for coast-to-coast distribution of their products. Easy rail access and the large immigrant population made Cleveland an attractive market for the national brands, nearly all of which had a presence in Cleveland during the years before prohibition.

The Pabst Brewing Company of Milwaukee was perhaps the most aggressive shipping brewer of the nineteenth century. Pabst first established a bottling depot in Cleveland around 1896.[8] Interestingly, the facility was just next door to Patrick Gavagan's ale brewery on Briggs (East 22nd) Street, in a building formerly used as Gavagan's malthouse. In fact, it seems probable that there may have been some shared use of the bottling works between Gavagan and Pabst. Whatever the case, the Pabst facilities were later moved to larger quarters on St. Clair Avenue. Like many out-of-town shippers, the Pabst brewery owned a number of its own saloons and beer halls in Cleveland, among them "The Pabst" just off Public Square and "Pabst Hall" on Champlain Street.[9]

Anheuser-Busch engaged local bottler Frank E. Diemer for a number of years to package and distribute its Budweiser Beer and other brands in Cleveland. By 1910, Anheuser-Busch was instead being handled by the William Edwards Company, a local wholesale grocer.[10] However, at least one local drinking establishment – the Hofbrau Haus on Prospect Avenue – consumed so much Budweiser Beer that it bypassed the local agent and received its shipments directly from St. Louis.

The Milwaukee-based Jos. Schlitz Brewing Company was bottling its beer in Cleveland as early as 1883. Its first bottling works, at 20 Merwin Street, was managed by John Schlitz, nephew of the brewery's namesake.[11] (It was rumored that John had been exiled from Milwaukee by his family after exhibiting behavior unbefitting the reputable Schlitz name.) By the turn of the century, Schlitz beer was being bottled on East 55th Street near Chester Avenue under the supervision of J. W. Marshall. John Schlitz, incidentally, remained in Cleveland for a number of years and operated a saloon near Public Square, where he advertised "Fine Merchants' Lunch served free every day."[12]

The B. Stroh Brewing Company sold an enormous amount of beer in Cleveland. In 1892, the Detroit brewer established a warehouse and bottling shop in Cleveland at the corner of Bond (East 6th) Street and Theresa Court. The works was capable of filling 1,200 bottles of Stroh's beer daily.[13] Within just a few years, additional warehousing was acquired on Case (East 40th) Street south of Superior Avenue. This particular facility, however, was not blessed with good fortune. In a single year, the building was severely damaged on *three* separate occasions by run-away train locomotives violently colliding with the track-side structure.[14] Luck notwithstanding, Stroh's beer enjoyed a sustained popularity in Cleveland for many years.

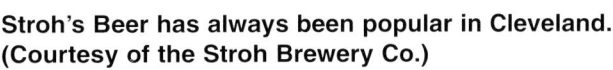

Stroh's Beer has always been popular in Cleveland. (Courtesy of the Stroh Brewery Co.)

The out-of-town brewers, while certainly cutting into the sales of local brands to some degree, were kept comparatively at bay in Cleveland prior to prohibition. Brewers in some other Ohio cities did not fare as well. In Youngstown, for example, the price wars between the local and foreign brewers came to a head when the price per barrel of beer sank from the regular $7 to a crippling $4 in 1896, finally forcing a truce among the combatants.[15] Due most probably to the Cleveland brewers' near total reliance on their home market, the local beer trade was diligently protected by the city's incumbents. One observer, though perhaps overstating the situation slightly, noted in 1902 that Cleveland's beer-makers "knew how to establish their position so well that brewers outside Cleveland never got any footing here."[16]

Carling & Co.

Among Cleveland's brewers, there is only one name which can rightfully be associated with the pursuit of a national market. That name is Carling. Indeed, during the decades which followed the repeal of National Prohibition in 1933, the Carling Brewing Company (initially known as the Brewing Corporation of America) grew dramatically until it ultimately ranked within the top five brewing companies in the nation.

However, the history of the Carling name in Cleveland dates from well before the heyday of the mid-twentieth century. In 1880, Sir John Carling, head of Carling & Company of London, Ontario, decided to expand his beer-making empire into the U.S. John S. Macbeth and Hugh Spencer – manager and brewmaster, respectively – were sent from Canada to secure arrangements for a new brewery in Cleveland.[17] What the messengers found was the old Rogers & Hughes Forest City Brewery at the corner of Seneca (West 3rd) Street and Canal. The brewery was purchased and production of the first American-made Carling brew commenced. Dubbing the works the London Brewery, Macbeth and Spencer began building up a trade for Carling's line of ale, porter and brown stout.

Right from the start, shipping of Carling products to distant cities was a priority. The Chicago-based firm of Barrett & Barrett – manufacturers of all kinds of ciders and vinegars – was hired as the American agent for the Carling brews. With distribution facilities in Baltimore, Chicago, Peoria, St. Paul, and Kansas City, Barrett & Barrett was well-qualified to carry the Carling brands to a wide market.[18]

After the deaths of two senior partners of Carling & Company in Ontario, Sir John Carling sought to divest the company of its U.S. properties. John S. Macbeth, manager of the brewery in Cleveland, was confident that the reputation he had established for the Carling products in America would endure. And so, in 1884, Macbeth raised the necessary capital to purchase the brewery and the rights to continue production of Carling's ale, porter and stout.[19] The following year, the brewery was moved into a former malthouse and distillery on West River Street (now Riverbed Road) where "a perennial spring of the purest water (an indispensable essential to good ale and porter) gushes forth from the earth."[20]

By 1891, Macbeth had sold his interest in the concern to the distribution agents Barrett & Barrett, and the business was reorganized as the Barrett Brewing Company. A mammoth new six-story brewhouse was erected next to the older buildings, boosting brewing capacity to an impressive 150,000 barrels annually.[21] Brothers Charles R. and William H. Barrett were the firm's officers, and the latter moved from Chicago to Cleveland to oversee operation of the brewery. Under the Barretts' management, the Carling brands remained in production, and widespread shipping continued as before. Indicating the company's ongoing pursuit of markets well beyond Cleveland was the fact that the Barrett Brewing Company was the only Cleveland brewer to exhibit at the Columbian Exposition of the Chicago World's Fair of 1893.[22]

In 1898, the American rights to the Carling brands became the domain of the Cleveland & Sandusky Brewing Company when the Barrett brothers sold out to the new combine. The Barrett brewery was kept in operation by its new owners, although the name was changed to the Bohemian Brewing Company branch of the combine. Carling's ale, porter and stout were brewed at the plant until its closing in 1911, but shipping into distant regions ended with the departure of the Barretts. It was not until after prohibition that the Carling name would resume its climb toward national prominence.

Life As A Beer Baron

The unprecedented advancements of the brewing industry throughout the 1880s and 1890s – the technology, the splendid architecture, the widening geographic markets, and, of course, the *wealth* – all conspired to elevate the typical brewer from craftsman to mogul, from artisan to tycoon. These immigrants who, only a few decades earlier, landed on unfamiliar shores weary and uncertain of their future, captured the American dream to an extent they could never have imagined. Their wealth carried them onto the boards of the most influential financial institutions and, for some, lead to prestigious careers in local politics.

Throughout their coming-of-age in America, the Beer Barons did not forget their German roots. On the contrary, with seemingly unlimited financial resources, brewers were dedicated to the preservation of German heritage in their adopted country. Particularly in the areas of music, drama, literature, and art, brewers were almost always at the center of activity. For example, virtually every German brewer in the city was a member of the Cleveland Gesangverein (singing society), arguably the most German of all local organizations. In fact, brewers C. W. Schmidt and Robert Hoffmann, owners of the Schmidt & Hoffmann brewery, were among the handful of local Germans who founded the Cleveland Gesangverein in 1853. Leonard Schlather, as well, was a founding member. He often acted as "marshal" of the group's social events. Cleveland periodically hosted the annual Saengerfest (singing festival), an event which gathered members from singing societies across the country to share musical performances and compositions. Brewers rallied behind the event. Albert Gehring, son of pioneer brewer Carl Ersnt Gehring and a director in his father's brewery, was himself a successful composer. One of his works, *In Mai,* was performed by Metropolitan Opera baritone Lawrence Tibbett at the 36th annual Saengerfest held in Cleveland in 1927.[23] Albert Gehring also authored a number of books on art, music, literature, poetry and philosophy.

Brewers also enjoyed paying tribute to the lives of venerable figures in German society. C. W. Schmidt was "president of the day" when more than 6,000 Germans took part in a celebration of the hundredth anniversary of the birth of Alexander Von Humboldt, a revered

Few nineteenth century brewers were more "baronial" than Isaac Leisy.

German philosopher. The day-long celebration, which took place in 1869, was called "one of the grandest in the history of the city."[24] When a collection was taken up in Cleveland for the erection of a monument in Wade Park to commemorate the beloved German composers Schiller and Goethe, nearly all of the city's brewers were on the list of contributors. The amount of the contribution made by brewer Leonard Schlather was matched only by the chairman of the monument committee. Schlather was also a major backer behind the building of a monument to Richard Wagner at Edgewater Park.

Patronage of the arts was then (as it is now) an open invitation into "high society." And brewers, or at least the most successful of them, were often high-ranking members of the elite social hierarchy. However, these were men who in many instances were recently "self-made" and relatively new to the ways of wealth. Their appetite for extravagance, grandeur and abundance was evident in their lavish residences, their dress and their lifestyles. As one brewing historian pointed out, the German brewers occasionally tended to overindulge, sometimes developing "habits of ostentation unfamiliar to puritan American society."[25] This, coupled with the undying allegiance to their German heritage, set the brewers apart somewhat from other industrialists. They were, therefore, a very close-knit group. Brewers who competed with each other for business by day often fraternized by night. Cleveland brewers Joseph Diebolt and George Gund, for example, sometimes traveled together, taking their families on extended vacations through Europe.[26] (Diebolt and Gund, incidentally, lived in mansions just across the street from one another in Cleveland Heights.) And many of Cleveland's wealthy brewers spent summer get-a-ways together in the German community of Zoar, Ohio, about sixty miles south of Cleveland. The beauty and serenity of the region, as well as the old world way of life preserved by the Zoarites, reminded many German immigrants of their youth in the old country. Some brewers, Leonard Schlather among them, even owned property in Zoar.

The Leisy's "Hochwald" estate exemplified the opulent lifestyles of the nineteenth century Beer Barons.

The brewers' children, as well, were often expected by their parents to join the virtually closed society of brewers. Inter-marriage among brewing families was extensive. Albert Gehring was married to Irma Mueller, daughter of Cleveland brewer and maltster Hermann Mueller.[27] Henry Leisy of Isaac Leisy & Company was married to Lissette Baehr, the daughter of Cleveland brewer Jacob Baehr.[28] And John J. Beltz, son of local brewery owner Joseph Beltz, was married to the daughter of Gottfried Kuebler, a Cleveland brewmaster. Nevertheless, when it was proposed that Ernst Mueller of the Mueller malting and brewing family marry a daughter of brewer Leonard Schlather, Mueller graciously declined. Much to the chagrin of Schlather, not one of his five daughters married into a brewing family. After all, Schlather himself was married to the daughter of a respected West Virginia brewer.[29]

The Beer Barons of the late nineteenth century numbered many in Cleveland. By the late 1870s, a handful of the city's brewers had already begun to adopt new technologies and invest in immense and stylish new plants. Certainly most deserving of early Beer Baron status were brewers Isaac Leisy, Leonard Schlather and Carl Ernst Gehring. In 1884, the combined output of those three brewers accounted for an amazing sixty-six percent of the

The entry way to Isaac Leisy's Vega Avenue mansion. Local prohibitionists used this photo to demonstrate the great wealth amassed by the city's brewers.

city's beer production among a total of eighteen brewing firms.[30] However, as beer sales rose steadily throughout that decade, other local brewers – anticipating continued increases – began boosting capacity as well. The Chamber of Commerce reported that, in 1884 alone, between a quarter and a half million dollars had been invested in the expansion and improvement of the city's breweries, increasing total brewing capacity by as much as twenty-five percent over the previous year.[31] And, indeed, brewers' expectations did not go unfulfilled. Local beer consumption continued to climb well into the beginning of the 1890s, fostering more expansion and generating substantial profits for brewers. Many Cleveland brewers who had endured typically humble beginnings were soon commanding thriving brewing enterprises. They had clearly joined the ranks of the Beer Barons.

Andrew W. Oppmann

Andrew W. Oppmann epitomized the image of the late nineteenth century Beer Baron. His ascent into the fraternity of millionaire beer-makers was as swift and dramatic as that of any brewer in Cleveland. The small frame structure in which Oppmann brewed his first batch of beer grew into a palatial brewery, one of the most architecturally extravagant in Cleveland. In his personal character, too, Oppmann fit the Beer Baron mold: Hard-working, industrious, successful and *German.* As was common among the early Beer Barons, Oppmann's first fortune spurred others. He invested heavily in local real estate, a legacy inherited and managed by Oppmann descendants still today.

Having worked in a number of breweries throughout his youthful travels, Oppmann's skills as a brewer were finely honed by the time he arrived in Cleveland in 1871. He had been lured here by west side brewery owner Frederick Haltnorth, who met Oppmann while traveling out-of-town and urged him to come to Cleveland and become Haltnorth's brewmaster.[32] Oppmann accepted the offer. But, in 1872, after just a few months in Haltnorth's employ, the ambitious Oppmann left his position and acquired the brewery of Adam Schumann at the corner of Columbus and Willey Streets.

The growth of the Oppmann brewery between 1880 (above) and circa 1895 (right) gives some idea of the progress of brewing during that period.

The Adventures of Youth

In a brief autobiography, Andrew W. Oppmann recounted a rather adventurous youth before settling in Cleveland in 1871. He came to America in 1863 at the age of nineteen from his native Bavaria, where he had apprenticed in a number of breweries. After sampling life in a variety of American cities, Oppmann found work in a St. Louis brewery. But the young immigrant soon became restless. Along with several friends, Oppmann departed for Kansas, where he and his cohorts intended to establish a small town. Once past Fort Leavenworth, however, the caravan was attacked by "bushwhackers" and all of the group's belongings were looted. Discouraged and broke, Oppmann joined the Cavalry of the U.S. Army in Fort Leavenworth and embarked on a wagon train journey to deliver ammunition and supplies to western forts. On the very first day of the excursion, Oppmann's troop came upon the same bandits who had robbed him; "bloody revenge" was exacted.

At the end of the five-month journey, Oppmann arrived back in Fort Leavenworth with a fondness for the adventure of traveling the deep wilderness of the untamed west. In February of 1866, Oppmann and a group of war comrades set out on horse-back for California, spending much of the journey hunting buffalo for food and fighting off bandits (or "prairie guerrillas" as Oppmann called them). After eight months, the expedition arrived on the west coast well-worn but intact. In San Francisco, a brewer and friend of Oppmann introduced him to the captain of a steamship which traveled between the west coast and Hong Kong. Oppmann recalled the acquaintance: "After we emptied a few bottles of genuine Los Angeles, we sealed our friendship."

The twenty-two year old Oppmann was offered the position of second steward on the steamship *Colorado*. He promptly set sail for the Orient.

But life at sea was monotonous for the young immigrant, whose stated goal was "to see the world." Once back in California, Oppmann left his stewardship on the *Colorado* and set out for Panama via coastal steamship. Stopping in Mazatlan, Acapulco and San Jose along the way, Oppmann arrived in Panama and, after a few days, walked the forty-mile distance to Aspinwall, Colon. Here, Oppmann concluded, "I had enough adventures and wanted now to apply my time to my profession." From Aspinwall, Oppmann sailed through the Caribbean Islands and up the east coast to New York, where he found work in a brewery. The job was unsatisfactory to him, and so he decided to travel to Chicago in search of a brewmaster's position. At the Mueller Brothers Brewery in Chicago, Oppmann found a job in which he intended to remain for good.

On October 11, 1871, the Great Chicago Fire changed the young brewer's plans dramatically. Wrote Oppmann, "The fire robbed me of everything except my courage and self-esteem." Free passage out of the city was granted to anyone who wished to leave, and so Oppmann left the devastated city for parts unknown. He eventually settled in Cincinnati, where he secured work in the employ of a brewers' supply firm. It was during a sales trip for this company that Oppmann met Cleveland brewery owner Frederick Haltnorth, who offered him a job as brewmaster at the Haltnorth brewery. Having passed through Cleveland during his early travels, Oppmann was aware of the city's growing importance as an industrial center. Thus, he eagerly accepted Haltnorth's offer. And the rest, as they say, is history.[37]

The small west side brewery had experienced little success in the five or so years since its establishment. The founder, Adam Schumann, lost control of the works in 1871 as a result of unpaid debts.[33] Oppmann, nevertheless, was not discouraged by the business' less-than-glorious past. Although the situation had not significantly improved by 1874 (the brewery ranked as the city's eighteenth largest among a total of twenty-six), Oppmann's patience and determination eventually brought prosperity. In 1884, sales of Oppmann's beer were more than five times that of a decade earlier, and the brewery was the fifth largest in Cleveland.[34] And success was not fleeting. Business remained strong for the next several years, and the venture continued to grow at a rapid pace.

Born in Bavaria in 1844, Andrew W. Oppmann was an active supporter of German culture in America. He was a co-founder and president of Cleveland's "Bayerischer Unterstuetzungsverein," the Bavarian Benevolent Society. Under Oppmann's guidance, the organization ultimately joined with others around the country to form the Bavarian National Association of North America.[35] And Oppmann, it appears, was not slow to take action when outside forces threatened preservation of the German way of life. He was named as one of the instigators of the somewhat notorious "West Side Riot" of 1874.[36] The ugly episode was the result of a clash between local temperance marchers and a group of equally fervent *non*-supporters of the cause.

Andrew W. Oppmann possessed that certain German quality that made him a near-obsessive problem solver. Finding many of the old "tried and true" methods of brewing to be lacking, Oppmann often sought a better way. As a result, the inventive brewer was the holder of several patents for equipment involved in the brewing process, including a mechanized system for exchanging full beer kegs for empty ones from one floor of the brewery to another. Of particular note, however, was Oppmann's "Patent Mash Machine," which he actively marketed to other brewers. After observing the Oppmann machine in operation at a Pittsburgh brewery, editors for the *Western Brewer* declared themselves "greatly pleased with its work."[38]

Like many German brewers of his day, Andrew Oppmann had little or no interest in bottling his beer. The bulk of any brewer's trade during the nineteenth century was in the saloons, where draught beer was a must. Many brewers simply saw no great need for bottled beer. However, a handful of Oppmann's senior employees apparently believed otherwise. In March of 1889, the Anhaeusser Co-Operative Bottling Company was set up by Herman Anhaeusser, Gottlieb Kuebler and Henry Boehmke. The trio worked at Oppmann's brewery as collector, brewmaster and vice-president, respectively. The organization was formed expressly "for the purpose of buying, bottling and selling the beer manufactured by The Oppmann Brewing Company."[39]

Bottling facilities for the Anhaeusser company were just across Columbus Street from the Oppmann brewhouse in a building formerly occupied by the brewery's offices.[40] A great deal of the Oppmann-brewed beer which was bottled at the Anhaeusser works was sold under the label "The Anhaeusser Malt Tonic." (It was not at all uncommon for bottlers to buy kegged beer and re-sell it under their own name.) The product was clearly not aimed at the same saloon-going consumers who drank beer. Despite the fact that the malt tonic undoubtedly contained *at least* as much alcohol as the rest of the brew made at Oppmann's brewery, it was sold primarily to households as a health aid. One observer recalled that the nuns of a nearby convent were among the most loyal customers of The Anhaeusser Malt Tonic.

Andrew W. Oppmann with his son and grandson. Unlike the great majority of his fellow Beer Barons, Oppmann did not pass along a beer-making legacy to his offspring. Rather, after making his fortune, Oppmann sold his brewery and entered the business of real estate.

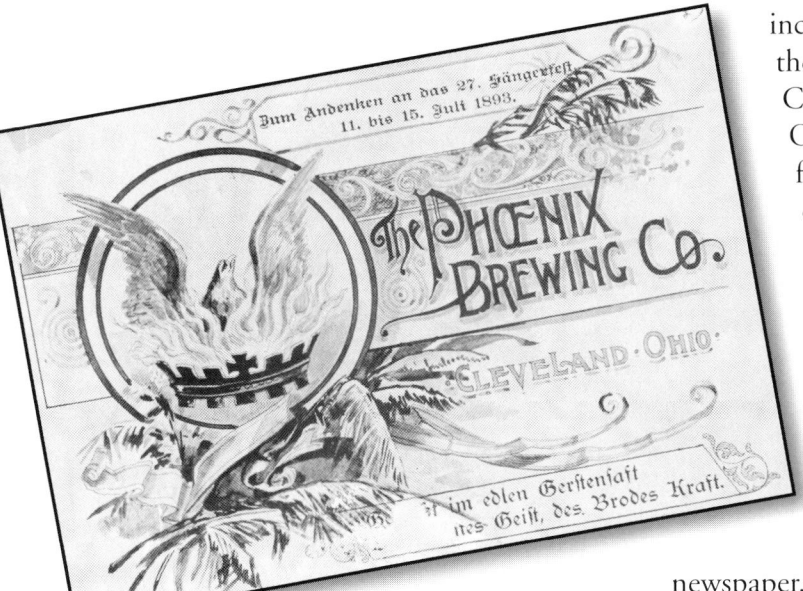

The Oppmann Brewing Company became the Phoenix Brewing Company in 1891.

The brewery was incorporated in 1887 as the Oppmann Brewing Company. Andrew Oppmann held about forty percent of the company's outstanding stock, representing the largest single share. Among the other stockholders in the company was Philip Gaensslen, once called "one of the most influential German citizens of Cleveland." He was a successful business owner and an officer of *Der Wächter am Erie*, the local German-language newspaper. Many of Oppmann's employees also owned stock in the company.[41]

On the Fourth of July, 1889, Oppmann's brewery was severely crippled by a fire requiring nearly a dozen fire steamers to extinguish. Although the cause of the fire was not certain, several witnesses believed that nearby fireworks must have been the culprit. The following morning, the *Plain Dealer* remarked,

The crew of the Oppmann brewery, circa 1890.

> *Yesterday's pyrotechnic displays ended with a great finale which drew many people from all over town. The old brewery of the Oppmann Brewing Company, on the corner of Columbus and Willey streets, is now a mass of ruins....The flames spread in short order in every part of the building and at one time it appeared as though the entire neighborhood was doomed.*[42]

The loss was estimated between $30,000 and $35,000. There was worry that the brewery would not be put back into operation in time to help fill the heavy summertime demand for beer. Andrew Oppmann quelled that concern by declaring that brewing would resume immediately "by the old system of hand work."[43]

In place of the burned portion of the brewery, Oppmann erected a colossal new brewhouse following the fire. The structure reflected all of the grandeur of the day's architectural style in breweries: high peaks and towers, fancy and decorative rooflines, and even a statue of King Gambrinus adorning the facade. Yet, by 1891, Andrew W. Oppmann had elected to retire from the business of brewing to pursue other endeavors. Selling his interest in the brewery to the remaining stockholders, Oppmann spent many of the following years involved in the development of a section of real estate at West Boulevard and Madison Avenue. The large residential complex ultimately came to be known as Oppmann Terrace.

With Oppmann's withdrawal from the brewery, the name of the business was changed in 1891 to the Phoenix Brewing Company.[44] The name – borrowed from the mythological phoenix which rose from its own ashes to live again – was intended to symbolize the re-establishment of the company after the devastating fire at the brewery two years earlier. Indeed, the remainder of the decade seems to have brought good fortune to the Phoenix brewery. By 1897, no less than 50,000 barrels of beer were being sold annually.[45]

In 1898, the Phoenix Brewing Company was sold to the newly-formed Cleveland & Sandusky Brewing Company. The Phoenix plant was the second-largest producer among the nine Cleveland breweries which joined the consolidation. In 1902, the beer production of the Cleveland & Sandusky's Baehr brewery was transferred to the Phoenix plant, which was known from that point forward as the Baehr-Phoenix brewery. In spite of the facility being one of the combine's newest and presumably best-equipped plants, the Baehr-Phoenix brewery was shut down in 1908 amidst attempts to better consolidate the combine's beer production.[46] The brewery never reopened.

Andrew W. Oppmann, incidentally, passed away in the summer of 1910 at age sixty-six. He died one of the wealthiest real estate owners in Cleveland. Despite the fact that Oppmann remained disassociated with the brewing business locally for the last twenty years of his life, he had been an officer of the Kansas City Brewing Company since its inception in 1906.[47] In his final years, the inventive and entrepreneurial spirit which characterized Oppmann for much of his life lead him to work tirelessly toward the realization of a somewhat unique dream. Having visited the Grand Canyon, Oppmann was compelled by the notion that descent into the gorge by mule-back could be replaced by a modern electric railway tunneling from the head of the canyon down to the Colorado River. Although Oppmann repeatedly went before Congress with his proposal, the plan never came to fruition.[48]

George Muth & Son

With little exception, early biographies of America's nineteenth century Beer Barons described in grandiose detail the assumed cunning and keen business sense which brought success to the brewer. These qualities were often characterized as almost prophetic visions of the future prosperity of the brewing industry. In reality, many of these captains of industry came into the field of brewing quite as a result of haphazard circumstance. The story of German immigrant George Muth and his son George V. Muth, whose brewery sat on Cleveland's west side for nearly half a century, details just such a case.

Around 1867, Gottfried Reindl established a small lager brewery on Buckley Street near Burton (West 41st) Street.[49] The brewery site had all of the usual requirements for making lager beer: a hillside into which cellars could be dug, access to a constant supply of pure water, and proximity to a large pond for the harvesting of ice. It became apparent early on, though, that Reindl would be neither successful in his business nor entirely forthright in his dealings. In 1867, the crafty brewer issued a mortgage on his brewery and its equipment to one Johann Schmidtbauer in order to secure a $1,500 debt. Just two days later, Reindl issued a second mortgage on the very same property to a Mr. Severin Elk as collateral for a cash loan of $1,800. Schmidtbauer, the first

George V. Muth and his
brewery on Buckley Street.

mortgage holder, sold his note in January of 1868 to Nicholas Alten who, in turn, sold it to George Muth.[50] Reindl promptly defaulted on both mortgages and, naturally, conflict ensued.

By the Fall of 1868, the issue of who held legal right to possession of the brewery had yet to be sorted out. Severin Elk, the second mortgage holder, took it upon himself to conduct a public auction of the brewery property in order to recoup his interest. Muth, who was likewise determined not to lose his investment in the note, appeared on the day of the auction to inform the crowd that the property in question was encumbered by *his* mortgage, issued two days prior to Elk's. As a result of that announcement, Muth's bid of $800 was the only one placed, and Elk was compelled to accept the bid and relinquish his claim on the property.[51]

Bolstered by his new acquisition, Muth's complete lack of experience in brewing apparently did not dissuade him from pursuing cultivation of the business. Taking on his brother Matthias Muth as partner, the eager entrepreneur set out to make a success of his new-found enterprise. However, the firm of Muth & Brother was put to an abrupt and unfortunate end in 1871 when Matthias hung himself to death in the brewery's attic. The resulting inquest found that, given the victim's financial stability and favorable position in the community, "temporary insanity" was the only possible explanation.[52]

Once recovered from the loss of his brother, Muth carried on with the brewery, bringing son George V. into the business. Together, father and son spent the next ten years transforming the business into one of the city's most prosperous late nineteenth century brewing concerns. By the time the elder George Muth passed away in 1881, the younger George V. had attained experience enough to take over sole direction of the business. In 1885, to accommodate sales which had more than doubled from a decade earlier, Muth replaced the original brewery with an imposing new brick structure – "an adornment for the neighborhood."[53]

In 1895, George V. Muth was struck with a case of blood poisoning which caused the amputation of his right foot. Choosing not to recruit others to run the brewery on his behalf, Muth decided to find a buyer for the business and retire on the proceeds of the sale. Brewers Carl A. Strangmann and John M. Leicht came to Cleveland from Alexandria, Virginia in 1896 and purchased Muth's brewery for $100,000.[54] The two partners had been involved with breweries in several eastern cities, most recently the Robert Portner Brewing Company of Alexandria. Their new venture in Cleveland was incorporated in July of 1896 as the Star Brewing Company, named for the traditional "brewer's star" which had always appeared on kegs of Muth's beer. The plant was aggressively expanded so that, by 1898, production had reached about 13,000 barrels annually.[55]

It was during that same year that many of the city's breweries were being acquired by the newly-formed Cleveland & Sandusky Brewing Company. And, indeed, the Star Brewing Company was among the first to join the combine. Strangmann left Cleveland to engage in the brewing business elsewhere, while John M. Leicht remained in Cleveland and became vice president of the Cleveland & Sandusky company. The Star brewery was operated by the combine until 1913, when its doors were closed and the property sold.

George V. Muth, incidentally, continued to reside in his home across the street from the brewery until 1899 when ongoing health problems took his life.[56]

Joseph Stoppel

Joseph Stoppel was well known among Cleveland's tavernkeepers well before he brewed his first barrel of beer in 1859. Since his arrival in Cleveland in 1848, the German immigrant was engaged as a "distiller, rectifier, and manufacturer of vinegar and cordials." His business had achieved a reputation for producing quality wares, and Stoppel sought to capitalize on that good standing by expanding his line of products. Recognizing that the ever-increasing number of Germans in the city was spurring demand for lager beer, Stoppel elected to enter the beer business. Accordingly, construction was started on a new brewery on Canal Street at the foot of Ohio Street. In 1859, Stoppel began business as the J. Stoppel & Company's Belle View Brewery.[57]

Throughout the next decade, the growth of Stoppel's brewery paralleled that of Cleveland's thriving brewing industry. In 1869, the business was incorporated by Stoppel and several cohorts as Stoppel's Actien* Brewery.[58] Despite his financial successes, Joseph Stoppel never fully embraced life in America, and commitment to his enterprises in Cleveland appears to have been somewhat less than total. In 1872, Stoppel returned to Europe, selling the brewery to the firm of J. Kraus & Company for $50,000. However, the new owners were not successful and their mortgage with Stoppel soon fell into default. Had it not been for this unfortunate turn of events, Joseph Stoppel may never again have stepped foot on American soil. As it was, he returned from Europe in 1877 and promptly sued all who had been involved in the operation of the brewery (including his own mother-in-law, who had since become a partner in J. Kraus & Company). The legal action forced the brewery into public auction in 1878, and Stoppel regained control of the business when his was the high bid.[59]

The Stoppel brewery on Commercial Street.

With the brewery back under his control and on sound footing, Joseph Stoppel returned to Europe in 1883 – this time to live out his remaining years. Sons Alphonso and Omar Stoppel took over the brewery, doing business as Stoppel's Sons & Company.[60] Like most local brewers, the Stoppel brothers enjoyed rising beer sales throughout much of the 1880s. In 1887, the brewery was reorganized as the Stoppel Co-Operative Brewing Company. Cash raised

---

*"Actien" is the old spelling of the German word "Aktien," meant to indicate that the brewery was jointly owned by a group of stockholders.

from the sale of stock in the new company – which amounted to $200,000 – was used to erect an entirely new brewing facility on Commercial Street near Canal, where beer production commenced in 1888.[61]

Advertisements for the brewery promoted Stoppel's "Extra Vacuum Lager," indicating that the Stoppels employed the newly-developed vacuum fermentation technology. Conducting fermentation within a vacuum was said to eliminate the potential for bacterial infection in the beer. Many brewers were ultimately attracted to the technology because it substantially sped up the entire fermentation process. Supporters of the new technology, in debunking early skeptics, noted in 1891,

> *Already nearly one-tenth of the lager beer made in the country is made in Vacuum breweries, and not in one of them has there been any failure attributable to the system, while the product of many is well known to be in the front rank of fine beers.*[62]

In 1891, after the death of Alphonso Stoppel, the controlling interest in the Stoppel brewery was sold to a group of investors headed by local entrepreneur Joseph Erlanger. Also involved in the buyout was attorney Emil Joseph, son of Cleveland clothing magnate Moritz Joseph (founder of Joseph & Feiss).[63] Although the Stoppel family remained partial owners, the name was changed to the Columbia Brewing Company in 1891. Over the next several years, the brewery was under the control of various local businessmen. In 1898, the brewery was sold to the Cleveland & Sandusky Brewing Company. For the next two decades, the Columbia plant was one of Cleveland & Sandusky's workhorse breweries, turning out about 35,000 barrels of beer annually.[64] After passage of a statewide prohibition amendment in 1918, the brewery closed and never reopened.

Chapter Five

The Business of Brewing

While total U.S. beer production increased nearly thirty percent between 1890 and 1900, the last decade of the century was, for many brewers, not a favorable one. German immigration into America, which had been at its highest levels during the previous decade, slowed significantly after 1890.[1] The unforeseen economic depression early in the decade also had a significant impact on the situation, causing beer sales across the country to plummet by more than a million barrels between 1893 and 1894.[2] The exorbitant investment in plant expansions of the 1880s – the result of a grossly over-anticipated beer market – did not help matters. In short, industry-wide brewing capacity had expanded at a much faster rate than had actual beer consumption. Unable to afford the huge capital outlays committed to in more optimistic times, countless brewers found themselves struggling to maintain control of their businesses. The fight for customers intensified dramatically. And with the influx of nationally-shipping brewers into most major cities, the

U.S. brewing industry entered an age of unprecedented competition.

The most immediate manifestation of the increasing competition was a rash of price wars throughout the brewing industry. The price per barrel of beer to saloons – typically between $7 and $9 in most regions during the 1890s – could drop as low as $3.50 in the throes of battle.[3] In some cases, brewers sold beer at a price well below cost just to retain valuable customers, all the while hoping that the war would subside before insurmountable losses were incurred. In 1896, at the annual meeting of the Ohio Brewers' Association, it was proposed that the price of beer be fixed at $8 per barrel throughout the state. Cleveland brewers, however, refused to agree to the pact. Although the going rate per barrel was, indeed, already $8 in Cleveland, the local brewers pointed out that they were sometimes compelled to offer better prices to certain customers.[4] This, of course, was exactly the type of strategy that spurred price wars.

The brewers' invasive control over the saloon trade was another outgrowth of the worsening competitive environment. In order to edge out competitors, brewers made all manner of deals with saloonkeepers in exchange for the promise to sell only that particular brewer's products. Replacing old bar fixtures with new and fancier furnishings, making interest-free loans, paying for the saloonkeeper's annual liquor license, and as always, granting a "best" price on beer were just a few of the incentives offered to saloonkeepers. Of course, the saloonkeeper typically worked-off most of these expenditures through his beer purchases, but the lure was effective nonetheless.

The out-and-out ownership of saloons, too, was heavily engaged in by brewers. As owner of the property, a brewer could dictate that only his beer be sold on the premises. The saloonkeeper who leased his space from a brewery still bore the risk of entrepreneurship just the same as any other saloonkeeper. And, naturally, the brewers were less concerned about the profit margins of the saloonkeeper than they were about the volume of beer he was selling. Indeed, for the saloonkeeper, the situation was often bleak from the outset; frequently, a brewer's sole motive in setting up a new saloon was to compete directly with a nearby saloon controlled by a rival brewer. Thus, the competitive battle between brewers was often fought, reluctantly to be sure, between the saloonkeepers.

Price competition, saloon control and saloon ownership were all common means of survival for breweries during the 1890s. But each was tremendously expensive, and brewers often did not have the financial resources to compete. In fact, a great many became virtually cash broke as a result of the huge sums of money spent on capital improvements during the expansion frenzy of the previous decade. A number of long time immigrant brewers – most of whom had spent the better part of their lives building up their enterprises – were left with little choice but to sell out. Investors with ample capital for the high cost of competition began acquiring breweries, forming stock companies, and throwing their hats into the ring. Though many of the old-time brewers were able to retire in economic comfort, their proud status as Beer Barons had passed as quickly as it had come.

Meanwhile, the stream of new capital which flowed into the brewing industry as a result of the numerous buyouts and takeovers only intensified the competitive situation.

A Taxing Ordeal

Adding to the woes of brewers was the increase of the federal tax on beer in 1898 to help finance the Spanish-American War. The tax per barrel was doubled from $1 to $2, bringing loud cries from the brewing industry, but to little avail. The United States Brewers Association consoled its members by pointing out that the tax was clearly intended to be borne not by brewers or saloonkeepers, but by the consumer for the simple reason that "in fact neither the maker nor the seller could possibly bear it."[5] Brewers whole-heartedly embraced that interpretation of the circumstances, passing along the $1 increase to saloonkeepers, who then were expected to pass it on to consumers.

In Cleveland, the issue of the new tax sparked a heated row between brewers and saloonkeepers which, according to a local newspaper, "promised to eclipse the Spanish-American affair."[6] In June, 1898, the Cleveland Brewers Association circulated a notice to the retail establishments of the city informing them that the additional $1 per barrel tax would be shifted entirely to saloonkeepers. Not surprisingly, the notice was met with more than a little hostility from retailers. They promptly threatened to boycott local beer-makers and obtain all of their beer from out-of-town breweries. But the local brewers were not moved by the threats, knowing full well that virtually all brewers – out-of-town or local – would impose the same increase.[7] Brewers suggested that saloons ought to reduce the size of the 5¢ mug of beer from the standard sixteen ounces to fourteen ounces. This, the brewers urged, would yield more than an additional $1 per barrel, thus fully absorbing the tax and adding a slight profit increase as well. Saloonkeepers, firm in their conviction that brewers were simply gouging saloons, wanted nothing to do with the idea of reducing the size of the 5¢ beer. They pointed out that the government gave a seven-and-a-half percent allowance on the new tax, making the actual increase only 92-1/2¢ per barrel. Why then, asked the retailers, were the brewers demanding a full $1 increase from saloons? When all was said and done, the brewers held fast to their position, and saloonkeepers had no option but to give up the fight. The 5¢ beer, it was decided, would indeed be slightly reduced in size to compensate for the tax. In addition, growlers* would get nothing but "the exact measure" – no over-fills.[8]

Cleveland saloonkeepers were not alone in their plight. During the implementation of the new tax, the brewing industry unanimously clung to the assertion that it should not have to bear any of the increase. But, in the end, the tax had a devastating impact on brewers and saloonkeepers alike. Beer sales in the U.S. dropped by nearly one million barrels from 1898 to 1899, leading the *Western Brewer* trade journal to regret the industry's early stance on the tax issue: "The supposition that [brewers] could shift the burden of the added tax upon the dealer and the dealer in turn shift it upon the customer proved to be erroneous. In practice it would not work."[9]

Nevertheless, economic conditions improved significantly after the end of the Spanish-American War. Beer consumption rose sharply and the federal malt liquor tax returned to $1 per barrel in 1902.[10]

Amidst all of the strife suffered by brewers throughout the 1890s, there was one course of action which offered significant relief from the uphill battle for survival: consolidation with other brewers. Conglomerations, or "trusts" as they were called by many, were all the rage during the last two decades of the nineteenth century. The industrial revolution had boosted production efficiencies beyond

---

*A growler was a small tin pail used to fetch draught beer from saloons.

imagination. And with expanding transportation, communication, and financial markets, geographic boundaries were blurring for all industry. Strong competition was soon a fundamental part of business. In virtually every line of manufacture, the joining of forces with others in the same industry was an attractive refuge from the uncertainties of a changing marketplace. Brewing was no exception. Breweries throughout the country banded together in hopes of mounting a resistance to the perilous competitive environment.

However, the first impetus for brewery consolidations grew not from the threatening competitive climate, but from a torrent of foreign investors. In the late 1880s, British "syndicates" – driven abroad by economic depression at home – infiltrated the American brewing industry, buying up breweries at a surprising pace. The acquisitions were rarely made on an single-brewery basis. Rather, the English strategy usually consisted of gaining control of all or nearly all of a city's brewing plants, then forming a stock company to operate the plants as a single entity. Already in 1890, British-controlled brewery conglomerates were operating in Baltimore, Chicago, Detroit, St. Louis and some half-dozen other cities.[11] In order to gain control of a majority of the breweries in a given region, the investors typically offered brewery owners hugely inflated prices for their establishments. Such was certainly the case when English financiers came calling on Cleveland's breweries in 1889. Isaac Leisy, for example, was offered $1.5 million for his plant, despite the fact that his entire estate was valued at no more than $1 million upon his death three years later.[12] Likewise, Andrew W. Oppmann was tendered an offer of $250,000 for his brewery. But when the main building of his plant was completely leveled by fire only a few weeks later, the loss was recorded at just $35,000. The Schlather, Gehring and Stoppel breweries were also reportedly approached by the British investors.[13]

Although none of Cleveland's brewers ever sold out to English capitalists, the notion of consolidating all or some of the city's breweries into one company was toyed with throughout the 1890s. In 1892, it was said that a refusal to participate on the part of Isaac Leisy had killed a plan to join all the local breweries. Again in 1895, the plan was resurrected. Isaac Leisy had since passed away, and it was hoped that son Otto Leisy might be more amenable to the idea.[14] The Leisy brewery, as Cleveland's single largest producer of beer, would have been a desirable component of any conglomeration among the city's breweries.

The Cleveland & Sandusky Brewing Co.

It was not until late in 1897 that efforts to consolidate the local breweries moved passed discussion and began to fully materialize. The Cleveland Brewers Association (many of whose members favored a combine) appointed a committee of three to negotiate with Philadelphia financial broker John P. Persch, who became the central figure in arranging financing for the proposed consolidation. After several months of speculation and unconfirmed reports, the Cleveland & Sandusky Brewing Company was incorporated on February 8, 1898, and it officially took control of nine breweries in Cleveland and two in Sandusky, Ohio on June 7th of the same year.[15] The local breweries which joined the combine at its inception were the Baehr, Barrett, Bohemian, Cleveland, Columbia, Gehring, Phoenix, Star and Union breweries. The Sandusky contingent was made up of the Kuebeler and Stang breweries, which had merged in 1895 to form the Kuebeler-Stang Brewing & Malting Company.

The combine was capitalized at $6,000,000. Each of the brewers who sold their plants to the new company received a combination of cash and stock for their breweries.[16] John P. Persch was

said to have represented an "eastern syndicate" of investors who were the financial backers of the effort to consolidate Cleveland's breweries. In reality, however, it appears that no eastern parties were associated with the consolidation beyond Persch and a few of his associates. Although, indeed, it is almost certain that purchases of the combine's stock were ultimately made by eastern investors (the Guarantee Trust Company of New York was the company's financial agent), much of the initial cash needed to acquire the various breweries was raised by mortgaging the breweries themselves.

Persch, who reportedly made $250,000 for his involvement in setting up the Cleveland & Sandusky Brewing Company, was a bona fide specialist in brewery mergers. He had previously been at the center of attempts to join breweries in several cities throughout Ohio and Pennsylvania. At

Conquering The West

The Cleveland & Sandusky Brewing Company was originally intended to be called the Cleveland Brewing & Malting Company.[17] Indeed, in its early stages, the venture merely sought to take in the major breweries of Cleveland. It was only after the recruitment of the two breweries in Sandusky that the name was changed and the combine took on much larger proportions. The Kuebeler-Stang Brewing & Malting Company was producer of the venerable Crystal Rock Beer, ostensibly brewed using water from the Crystal Rock spring just outside Sandusky. For years, the brand was well known to visitors of Cedar Point, where the Crystal Rock Castle served thousands of frosty mugs of beer to the Sandusky amusement park's thirsty guests every summer. More importantly, Crystal Rock Beer dominated the entire beer market between Cleveland and Toledo. Not only would the Cleveland & Sandusky Brewing Company inherit Crystal Rock's good sales, but it would also gain valuable inroads for the combine's other brands in new territories.

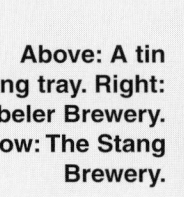

Above: A tin advertising tray. Right: The Kuebeler Brewery. Below: The Stang Brewery.

The critical importance of the region west of Cleveland was evident when the combine decided in 1904 to erect an entirely new brewery in Lorain, Ohio.[18] Located about half-way between Sandusky and Cleveland, Lorain boasted a good beer market, due mainly to its unusually large amount of heavy industry and, thus, the large labor force. The combine had maintained a distribution depot in Lorain for many years, and it was on the site of this depot that the brewery was constructed. However, undoubtedly much to the anger of the local prohibitionists, a nearby church had to be removed to make way for the brewery.[19] The Lorain plant was the only new brewery ever built by the combine; all of the others had been inherited from previous brewers. The Lorain brewery remained active until 1918.

Crystal Rock was a hit with the ladies. An 1899 advertisement made a bold claim: "Crystal Rock Beer regulates woman's ills. A glass or two used faithfully each day insures prompt and painless periods."

the very time he was finalizing the Cleveland and Sandusky arrangement, Persch, along with the Guarantee Trust Company, was involved in litigation surrounding the unsuccessful attempt to consolidate Toledo's breweries.[20]

Once the formation of the Cleveland & Sandusky Brewing Company was completed, Persch and his cohorts had little to do with the new concern. At the initial time of incorporation, the company's officers were comprised of a group of attorneys from the Cleveland law firm of Squire, Sanders & Dempsey, counsel for the brewers.[21] As operations began, it was the brewers themselves who took over management: F. W. Gehring of the C. E. Gehring Brewing Company was president; Jacob Kuebeler of the Kuebeler-Stang Brewing & Malting Company was 1st vice president; Ernst Mueller of the Cleveland Brewing Company was 2nd vice president; and William H. Chapman was secretary and treasurer. Among the directors were Herman C. Baehr of the Baehr brewery, Henry Boehmke of the Phoenix brewery, Emil Joseph of the Columbia brewery, John M. Leicht of the Star brewery, Simon Fishel of the Bohemian brewery, and Frank Stang of the Kuebeler-Stang breweries. The offices of the Cleveland & Sandusky Brewing Company were opened on the eleventh floor of the American Trust Building on Public Square.

The Cleveland & Sandusky Brewing Company was formed, as stated by its management, "for the purpose of overcoming the evils of a ruinous competition."[22] But the purported desire for peace and harmony among Cleveland's brewers was not to be fulfilled. Already in February of 1899, accusations were flying concerning alleged unfair trade practices by the combine. When Otto Leisy charged that the Cleveland & Sandusky company had instigated a price war, secretary Chapman adamantly denied the accusation:

> We shall not engage in any beer war with Mr. Leisy or anyone else. It would demoralize business, and while we could undoubtedly hold out longer than any rival we have in the field, still we would not care to engage in anything of that kind.[23]

At the same time, Chapman admitted that all the makings of a full blown price war were present:

> *It is a fact that in particular instances Leisy is selling beer for less than the standard price of $7 a barrel, and we have been obliged in some instances to do the same thing...There are often cases where some man's trade is very much desired. In such cases a better rate can be made to him.*[24]

Otto Leisy, of course, denied that he or anyone other than the combine was responsible for the price cutting. This type of squabbling was characteristic of the near constant friction between the combine and the independents throughout the years before prohibition.

 The independent brewers of Cleveland were not the only faction launching charges against the combine. After a brief investigation by the Ohio Attorney General's office, the Cleveland & Sandusky Brewing Company was declared to be in violation of Ohio antitrust laws in the spring of 1899, and was ordered by Attorney General Frank S. Monnett to cease business immediately. The combine, of course, fought Monnett's findings and the $1,950 fine imposed on them for ignoring the order to discontinue business.

 Testimony was taken from several of Cleveland's independent brewers in an effort to prove that the combine was operating as a trust. Local brewer Anthony J. Diebolt told of rumors that the combine lured saloonkeepers away from competitors by offering cash bonuses of up to $300 to carry the combine's beer. The "common talk," according to brewer George F. Gund, was that the Cleveland & Sandusky company routinely sought to lease or buy saloon properties where a competitor's beer was being sold. The saloonkeeper was then given an option to either switch to the combine's beer or be evicted. More pertinent to the issue at hand was Gund's testimony that the combine's activities were undertaken not in the name of the individual constituent breweries, but in the name of the Cleveland & Sandusky Brewing Company as a single entity.[25] Nevertheless, Monnett's attack on the alleged trust soon lost its zeal, and in the end, the combine was allowed to continue in operation.

 For several years, rumors abounded to the effect that the Cleveland & Sandusky Brewing Company's ultimate objective was to build a massive conglomerate which would encompass breweries in regions well beyond Northeast Ohio.

Ernst W. Mueller

Late in 1898, F. W. Gehring stepped down as president of the Cleveland & Sandusky Brewing Company, and vice president Ernst W. Mueller took his place. During a time when many brewers were struggling for their very survival, Mueller was credited with building the Cleveland & Sandusky company into a thriving enterprise. Indeed, far more than any other individual, Ernst W. Mueller shaped the combine's early years.

Born in Alsenz, Bavaria in 1851, Mueller came to America with his parents while still a child. He grew up working in his father's malting business in Cleveland before taking control of the old Schmidt & Hoffmann Brewery in 1887. By the time his brewery became part of the Cleveland & Sandusky Brewing Company in 1897, it was among the largest in the city.

Mueller, who died in 1931 at age seventy-nine, spent nearly his entire life involved in the brewing and malting business in Cleveland. Son Omar E. Mueller inherited his father's legacy, operating the Cleveland Home Brewing Company until his own death in 1946.

Workers pose in front of the Schlather brewery.

Below: The Cleveland & Sandusky Brewing Company acquired Starlight Beer when it purchased the Schlather brewery in 1902.

In fact, just days after formation of the Cleveland & Sandusky company, newspapers reported that brewers from all over Ohio were soon to be absorbed by the combine. Within a few months, the myth grew to almost ridiculous proportions. It was believed that Cleveland's breweries planned to join with those of Columbus, Cincinnati, Dayton and Toledo to form a virtual statewide beer monopoly.[26] Of course, nothing on that scale was ever developed.

Again in 1902, similar rumors circulated. This time, the hearsay caused the Cleveland & Sandusky company's stock to jump dramatically in both price and trading activity. It was said that the combine had secured options to purchase the Leisy, Gund and Diebolt breweries, and that a giant merger with brewery conglomerates in Pittsburgh and Buffalo was imminent. One local stock broker, proclaiming the rumors to be absolutely true, justified his position by saying, "There is nothing else that could possibly give the securities such a boom as they have enjoyed during the last few weeks."[27]

Outlandish speculation aside, it is true that the Cleveland & Sandusky Brewing Company sought to – and, indeed, did – absorb local competitors from time to time. The combine's acquisition of the L. Schlather Brewing Company in 1902 was the first such case. The purchase, which involved a reported $1.5 million, shifted the balance between the combine and the local independent brewers significantly.[28] The Schlather brewery added about 90,000 barrels to the combine's annual beer sales and gave it control of some sixty saloon properties. After the Schlather takeover, combine-brewed beer accounted for fully seventy-five percent of all beer sold in Cleveland and sixty percent of that sold in Northeast Ohio. Incidentally, Leonard Schlather joined the Cleveland & Sandusky company's board of directors after the takeover, a fact which was considered an important aspect of the deal. His long experience in the local brewing industry was considered a highly valuable asset.

Late in 1906, discussions between the combine and Stephen S. Creadon began concerning a possible buyout of Creadon's Standard Brewing Company. Although the brewery had been established just a few years earlier, it was particularly well-equipped to compete in the saloon trade as the majority of its stock was held by saloonkeepers. Creadon had made a reputation for himself as a "hands-on" competitor in the beer business, and the combine felt that he would be a valuable addition to the board of directors. One director said,

We thought Creadon was a good man, representing the Catholic element, Irish element, and he was the kind of man we thought that could go out and mix with the people, be more in daily direct touch with the trade.[29]

The buyout was all but consummated when, at the last minute, objections were raised by Herman C. Baehr and Ernst Mueller of the combine over the $650,000 purchase price, which they felt was highly inflated. In the end, the takeover was called off.[30]

Scandal Among The Brewers

In March of 1907, the Fishel Brewing Company of Cleveland was absorbed by the Cleveland & Sandusky Brewing Company. The transaction set off a heated debate not only between the combine and the independents, but between opposing factions within the combine itself. Highly publicized by local newspapers, the controversy boiled for nearly a year, and the competitive environment for Cleveland's brewers was never more turbulent.

Simon Fishel's first involvement in the beer business came in 1889 when he purchased the Bohemian Brewing Company on Pearl (West 25th) Street. The brewery became one of the constituent plants of the Cleveland & Sandusky Brewing Company in 1898, and Fishel was made general manager of the combine. By 1904, internal disputes had developed within the company's management, ultimately resulting in Fishel's resignation.

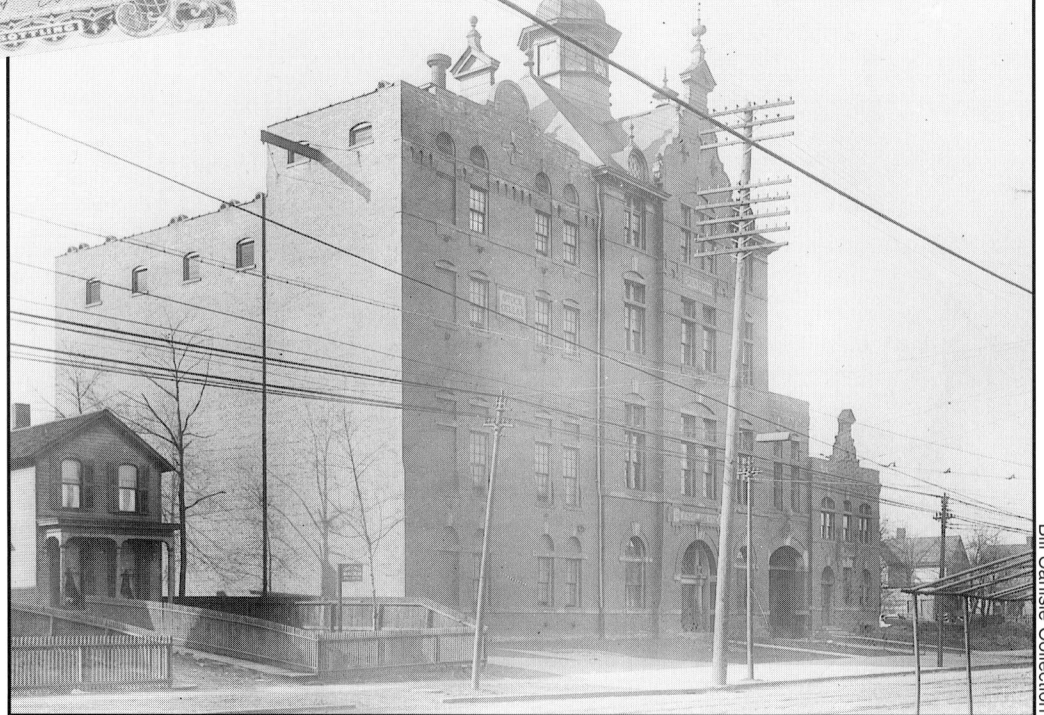

The bottle label of Fishel Brewing Company's $500 Bond Beer mimicked a real cash bond certificate.

The Fishel brewery on East 55th Street. The Cleveland & Sandusky Brewing Company would continue to operate this plant until 1962.

Bill Carlisle Collection

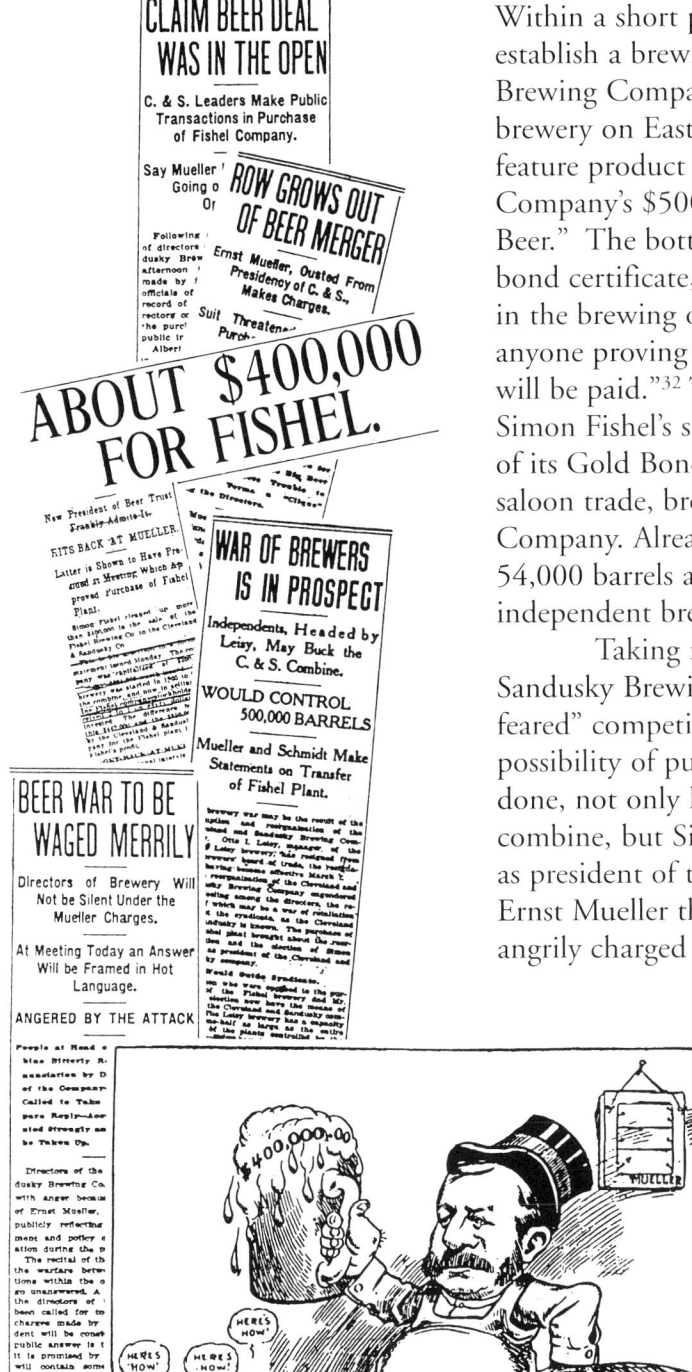

Within a short period, arrangements were under way by Fishel to establish a brewing venture of his own. Early in 1905, the Fishel Brewing Company made its first batch of beer in a brand new brewery on East 55th Street near Grand Avenue.[31] The company's feature product was a bottled beer called "Fishel Brewing Company's $500 Bond Beer," later altered to "Gold Bond $500 Beer." The bottle label, which was designed to mimic a cash bond certificate, vowed that no "injurious substitutes" were used in the brewing of the beer. It was further promised that "To anyone proving this statement false Five Hundred dollars ($500) will be paid."[32] The integrity of the promise was assured by Simon Fishel's signature and the company seal. The novel theme of its Gold Bond beer, together with aggressive solicitation of the saloon trade, brought quick success to the Fishel Brewing Company. Already in 1906, the company was selling a surprising 54,000 barrels annually, ranking it as the city's third largest independent brewer.[33]

Taking notice of Fishel's quick rise, the Cleveland & Sandusky Brewing Company – which called Fishel its "most feared" competitor – decided early in 1907 to investigate the possibility of purchasing Fishel's brewery.[34] When all was said and done, not only had the Fishel operation become part of the combine, but Simon Fishel himself had supplanted Ernst Mueller as president of the Cleveland & Sandusky company. A furious Ernst Mueller threatened legal action to block the purchase. He angrily charged that some of the details of the takeover – mainly the fact that he would be deposed as president – were not revealed to the board of directors when a vote was taken on the buyout. Only after the purchase was approved did it become known that Simon Fishel had been offered the presidency of the combine. Mueller told one newspaper reporter that a "clique" within the combine had been making efforts to oust him from the organization ever since he opposed the company's purchase of the Standard Brewing Company several months earlier.[35]

Meanwhile, Simon Fishel and the

Local newspapers followed the Fishel controversy with great interest.

111

stockholders in the Fishel Brewing Company stood to profit greatly from the takeover by Cleveland & Sandusky. The purchase price totaled $850,000 in cash and stock in the combine, about $440,000 of which went to Fishel stockholders.[36] The remaining $410,000 went to Fishel himself, a fact which was heavily objected to by Mueller and his supporters. Others, however, saw nothing wrong with Fishel's exorbitant profit. They believed that Fishel's ability to build his concern into a successful enterprise in such a short period of time deserved whatever reward resulted from it. Stockholders in the Fishel company, who unanimously approved the buyout, had few qualms about Fishel's personal profit. On the contrary, after receiving a nearly two-for-one profit, the stockholders threw a party at the brewery in Fishel's honor and presented him with a gold watch in appreciation of his shrewd negotiation on their behalf.[37]

But Ernst Mueller and his sympathizers stood strong in their assertion that the Fishel takeover was arranged by inappropriate means. The combine answered those charges by releasing the minutes of a meeting in which the Fishel purchase was unanimously approved by the combine's board of directors, Mueller included. Officials off-handedly admitted that, indeed, Mueller "probably was not informed" prior to the buyout that he would be replaced as president of the combine. But the officials maintained that the approval of the directors was binding regardless of that small oversight.[38]

Adding fuel to the fire was an announcement by Otto Leisy that, as a direct result of the Fishel takeover, he refused to continue as a member of the Cleveland Brewers' Board of Trade. The group was formed in 1903 as a result of the ongoing price wars and saloon manipulation by brewers.[39] A tacit agreement had been in force by the Board of Trade for some time and had been successful in stabilizing beer prices and controlling competitive tactics as concerned saloons. Thus, fighting between the combine and the independents had cooled somewhat. However, Simon Fishel, it was said, repeatedly refused to involve his brewery in any price fixing, believing that free competition should prevail. In fact, it was implied that the rapid success of Fishel's brewery was largely the result of his renegade competitive practices. Fishel reportedly bragged openly about cutting deeply into his competitors' trade. In response to learning that Fishel was to become president of the combine, Otto Leisy allegedly exclaimed, "This means war!"[40]

Indeed, as Leisy certainly believed, the combine's recruitment of Simon Fishel as president was a virtual declaration of the company's intent to adopt some of the less-than-friendly competitive tactics for which Fishel was famous. A supporter of Mueller wrote,

> *Mr. Mueller is criticized as not having displayed an aggressive enough policy as president. He has always acted on the policy of having good goods, good prices and good customers, rather than one of aggressive competition which only provokes retaliation and business war.*[41]

Amidst all of the accusations and recriminations, Mueller vowed that he would soon be re-established in the beer business to compete with the combine. Indeed, after declining an offer to become general manager of the Leisy brewery, Mueller gained control of the old Beltz Brewing Company just weeks after the Fishel takeover. The brewery, at East 61st Street and Outhwaite Avenue, was reorganized as the Cleveland Home Brewing Company, and Mueller was back in business. He was quoted as saying, "I hope my prestige and experience will secure for me much of the business of my old friends."[42] Indeed, a great many saloonkeepers who had been customers of the Cleveland & Sandusky company promptly transferred their patronage to Mueller's new venture, showing that their allegiance was to him, irrespective of his company affiliation. This kind of loyalty was particularly strong within German circles, where Mueller was well-known and respected as a supporter of various German organizations and activities.

Just when it seemed that the Fishel controversy had begun to pass, two Cleveland & Sandusky stockholders – prominent architect Frank E. Cuddell and former brewer Carl F. Schmidt – distributed a circular to combine stockholders demanding an official accounting of the Fishel deal. The circular made a number of bold accusations, the most severe of which was that certain directors of the combine had secretly shared in Fishel's $410,000 profit from the buyout. In response to the charges, the combine held a series of hearings at which Ernst Mueller, Simon Fishel, and various others testified as to the circumstances of the Fishel takeover. Although no proof of misconduct was uncovered, the fact that the enormous purchase price had pushed the combine into virtual bankruptcy was revealed.[43]

In the end, no legal action was ever taken in connection with the Fishel buyout, and the conflict eventually faded. Ironically, it was common knowledge that Fishel's departure from the Cleveland & Sandusky company in 1904 had been due to an earlier personal dispute between Mueller and himself. After Mueller was unseated as the combine's president, one local reporter summed up the situation by writing, "Fishel lost no time getting in harness again."[44]

Fishel's Reign

Simon Fishel's first two years at the head of the Cleveland & Sandusky Brewing Company were inauspicious. Although the addition of the Fishel plant boosted sales, the heavy debt incurred to finance the purchase took a toll on the company's profitability. In 1908, the combine recorded a net loss of more than $285,000. During that year, there were reports that Fishel had tired of his post and intended to resign and take a "much needed rest."[45] Vice-president John M. Leicht, according to the reports, had been named as Fishel's replacement. But the rumors did not bear out. Fishel, in fact, remained president of the combine until his death in 1917 at age seventy.[46] Sons Theodore Fishel, and later Oscar J. Fishel, succeeded him as president of the combine.

By 1910, the Cleveland & Sandusky Brewing Company had fully recovered from its financial woes and showed respectable profits throughout the remainder of Simon Fishel's reign. Production was streamlined with the closing of the Baehr-Phoenix plant in 1908, the Bohemian plant in 1911, and the Star plant in 1913. The company's beer sales remained steady at about 500,000 barrels per year.

Fishel's valuable Gold Bond brand (which was now produced under the Cleveland & Sandusky Brewing Company name) joined Crystal Rock as one of the combine's leading products. Although these two brands were clearly the company's mainstays, additional brands were also marketed. In 1905, a beer called Kellersaft was introduced by the combine. Interestingly, the title came from a contest in which the company invited the public to submit potential names for its new product. A great deal of fun was had over the fact

A post card advertising Kellersaft Beer, circa 1905.

that the winning name, which translates as "cellar juice," was submitted by an area clergyman. One observer commented, "Its dollars to doughnuts the worthy pastor is no stranger to the 'juice of the cellar.'"[47] The lucky reverend won a $100 cash prize for his entry.

Another brand, Clicco-Brew, was introduced in 1914 but was short-lived. Writers for the *Western Brewer* predicted the brand's brief life. Discussing the need for quality and morality in beer advertisements, the trade journal cited Clicco-Brew newspaper ads as "an example of poor judgment." In particular, the authors objected to the depiction of overly festive social scenes and the "conviviality" of the advertisements. The writers insisted, "It is from pictures and suggestions of this sort that the prohibitionist forms his impressions and chooses his text."[48]

The Cleveland & Sandusky Brewing Company made Carling Ale and Porter at its Bohemian branch until prohibition.

Among the combine's other brands prior to prohibition were Fishel's Kulmbacher, Frieden, Carling Ale and Porter, Schlather Pilsener, and Starlight. The rights to the Carling name were inherited from the constituent Barrett Brewing Company, which was licensed by Carling & Company of London, Ontario to produce the brands in America. The Starlight and Schlather Pilsener brands were both acquired with the combine's purchase of the L. Schlather Brewing Company in 1902.

By 1918, the Cleveland & Sandusky Brewing Company, like all brewers, was beginning to suffer from the looming prohibition threat, wartime restrictions, and rising taxes. The combine shut down its Columbia, Gehring, Kuebeler, and Lorain breweries in 1918 after passage of Ohio's statewide prohibition amendment, which was to take effect one year later.[49] By September of 1919, only the Fishel, Schlather, and Stang branches remained active, each producing "near beer" (nonalcoholic beer) and/or soft drinks. While the combine was destined to fare better than some during the dry years, its heyday was gone forever.

During formation of the Cleveland & Sandusky Brewing Company in 1898, three additional breweries in Cleveland were slated as willing participants in the combine, each of which ultimately dropped out of the deal before consummation. The withdrawing concerns were the Diebolt Brewing Company, the Pilsener Brewing Company, and the Jacob Mall Brewing Company.[50] Certainly the shape of Cleveland's brewing industry during the early 1900s would have been radically different had any of these companies joined the combine. All three shared a common characteristic: they had survived the turbulence of the 1890s remarkably well, and their best years were destined to come just after the turn of the century. By 1907, the Diebolt, Pilsener, and Jacob Mall (by then changed to the Gund Brewing Company) plants ranked as Cleveland's second, third, and fourth largest independent breweries, respectively.[51] Thus, their choice to be competitors, rather than constituents, of the combine was of great significance.

The Diebolt Brewing Co.

The Diebolt Brewing Company was one of Cleveland's great pre-prohibition beer-makers. In 1902, a writer for the Plain Dealer commented on the Diebolt brewery: "This is one of the most prosperous breweries in the city and its constantly increasing business is attributable entirely to its liberal business methods and the superiority of its products."[52] Indeed, with its venerable Diebolt's White Seal Beer leading the way, the company grew to enormous proportions. By 1912, the mammoth brewery consisted of six large buildings covering four acres of land at Pittsburgh Avenue and East 27th Street. Many Clevelanders still recall the brewery's fortress-like horse stables, which far outlasted all of the other buildings. The defining feature of the stables was a large horse's head which protruded from the building's facade above the main doorway. When the unique structure was demolished in 1979, Clevelanders mourned the last remnant of one of the city's great brewing enterprises.[53]

Anthony J. Diebolt first came to Cleveland in 1887 from his birthplace of Buffalo, New York, where he had learned the brewing trade while in the employ of brewer Gerhard Lang. Once in Cleveland, the twenty-one year old Diebolt found work at the Bohemian Brewing Company on Pearl (West 25th) Street, then owned by Wenzl Medlin. Interestingly, Medlin had also spent time working for Gerhard Lang's brewery in Buffalo. It seems likely, therefore, that Diebolt and Medlin first became acquainted in New York. And, indeed, it is entirely possible that Diebolt's decision to travel to Cleveland may have been prompted by his friendship with Medlin.[54]

The mammoth Diebolt brewery on Pittsburgh Avenue.

Nevertheless, Diebolt only remained in his cohort's employ for little more than a year. In 1888, he left his job at the Bohemian brewery and purchased Louis Lezius' share in the old Lezius & Uehlein brewery on Pittsburgh Avenue at Jackson (East 27th) Street. The new firm of Diebolt & Uehlein, however, was short lived. August Uehlein left in 1889 to pursue other endeavors. He was replaced in the business by Edward A. Ruble, an acquaintance of Diebolt's from Buffalo.[55] Once again, though, Diebolt soon found himself without a partner when Ruble passed away in 1891. Optimistic about the brewery's future, Diebolt purchased Ruble's interest from his estate and organized the Diebolt Brewing Company.[56]

Over the next twenty years, beer production at the Diebolt brewery expanded at an astonishing rate. When Anthony Diebolt first bought an interest in the brewery in 1888, the business was selling about 4,000 barrels of beer annually. A decade later, sales had grown five-fold to more than 20,000 barrels. And by 1907, the brewery was capable of turning out a healthy 80,000 barrels per year.[57] The flagship Diebolt's White Seal brand, promoted as "The Triumph of Brewing," undoubtedly accounted for the lion's share of Diebolt sales. However, other brands were produced as well, among them Diebolt's Standard Lager, Diebolt's Bohemian Export and Diebolt's Malt Tonic.[58]

In addition to its beer business, the Diebolt Brewing Company operated the Cleveland Hygeia Ice Company at the brewery address on Pittsburgh Avenue. Begun around 1908, the subsidiary manufactured large quantities of "artificial" ice for wholesale purposes. By the mid-1910s, fully one-third of the brewery grounds was used for ice storage. Long chutes carried the ice blocks from the plant down to the rail tracks in the valley behind the brewery site. Continuing well into prohibition, the ice business undoubtedly became one of the company's primary sources of income after the production of beer was stopped.[59]

Like many brewers, the Diebolt company concentrated on bottled beer during the years just prior to prohibition. As the saloon trade deteriorated (due largely to the efforts of the Anti-Saloon League and other prohibitionist groups), brewers began to target the household as the primary consumer of beer. Thus, sizable investments to enlarge and improve bottling facilities were common throughout the industry. The Diebolt brewery opened an entirely new bottling plant in 1915, the modern features of which were highlighted in both the *Western Brewer* and *Brewer's Journal* trade magazines. Interestingly, the latter publication described the new bottling facility as "architecturally plain and devoid of all useless ornamentation."[60] It seems that efficiency, not style, was now the primary consideration of most brewers, many of whom had undoubtedly begun to feel the decline of their industry.

Brewing Diebolt beer was a family affair. Anthony Diebolt served as the company's president. Two of his brothers, Joseph A. and Mathias L. Diebolt, came from Buffalo in 1893 and filled the positions of vice-president and secretary-treasurer, respectively. A fourth brother, Frank Diebolt, worked in the family business as a brewer for a time. Brother-in-law Joseph A. Irr was the brewery's collector throughout the 1890s. And his son, Anthony J. Irr, held a brewer's position after his graduation from the Wahl-Henius Institute, a respected Chicago brewing school.[61] Although the

Diebolt's father had no official job in the company, it was said that the brewery's prosperity was "largely owing to the advice of Andrew Diebolt, the father of these young men, who is a common-sense man, of the same stamp as Christian Morlein, of Cincinnati."[62]

Like the family business, the family itself was particularly close-knit. Along with a sister, the Diebolt brothers, none of whom ever married, lived much of their adult lives together in their Cleveland Heights residence. Coincidentally or otherwise, the home of George F. Gund, owner of the old Jacob Mall Brewing Company, sat just across the street.

The Jacob Mall Brewing Co.

Jacob Mall

The Jacob Mall Brewing Company enjoyed a long history in Cleveland. It began in 1859 when brewer Jacob Mall and saloonkeeper Paul Kindsvater took over the brewery of Martin Stumpf on Hamilton Avenue. By 1871, Mall was alone in the business. The works – known as the Lion Brewery – had since been moved to Davenport Avenue along the shore of Lake Erie. Jacob Mall was among the earliest German brewers in the city. He came to Cleveland from his birthplace of Baden, Germany in 1853 and worked as brewmaster at the old Schmidt & Hoffmann brewery. When he died in 1891 after nearly forty years of brewing beer in Cleveland, Mall was the oldest active brewer in the city. A local publication wrote, "Jacob Mall was a gentleman of the old school who in their direct, simple, German manner move unerringly to their goal."[63] After Mall's death, his son-in-law, Gustav Kaercher, took control of the brewery. Under his direction, business grew significantly and the plant was expanded.

But the historic brewery enjoyed its greatest success after 1897, when George F. Gund came to Cleveland and purchased a controlling interest in the firm. Gund was no stranger to the business of brewing. His father headed the mighty John Gund Brewing Company of LaCrosse, Wisconsin, once the largest brewery in that state outside of Milwaukee. When he reached the age of twenty-one, Gund joined his father's brewery as secretary and treasurer. In 1891, he ventured out on his own, traveling to Seattle to buy H. J. Claussen's share in the Claussen-Sweeney Brewing Company. Two years later, the company joined two other breweries to form the Seattle Brewing & Malting Company, of which Gund was eventually elected president.[64] In 1897, the forty-two-year-old entrepreneur severed his connections with the Seattle combine and came to Cleveland.

A tin serving tray, circa 1899.

Gund's first order of business with his new brewery in Cleveland was to cultivate a *household trade* for his beer. As a characteristically German operation, the Jacob Mall brewery had paid little attention to household consumers, focusing exclusively on the saloon business. But Gund recognized that there was a strong future in home consumption of beer. Thus, bottling of

117

the new Gund's Crystal Bottled Beer began on February 1, 1898 in the company's newly erected bottling plant.[65] The long-time kegged product, Mall's Crystal Lager, remained in production as the draught counterpart to the new bottled beer. A second bottled beer, called Ye Old Lager, was introduced later, made especially for the "family trade."[66] It is interesting to note that, while serving as president of the Seattle Brewing & Malting Company, Gund distributed beer to such far away places as China, Japan, and Guatemala. Now in Cleveland, Gund did not pursue markets outside of the immediate area.

George F. Gund

To inaugurate the new century, the name of the brewery was changed on January 1, 1900 from the Jacob Mall Brewing Company to the Gund Brewing Company.[67] The brewery, by this time, had gained a distinct reputation as being the most modernly equipped brewing plant in Cleveland, keeping abreast of all the latest technological innovations. Among those modern conveniences were the brewery's own electricity plant and subsequent incandescent lighting throughout; smoke eliminators to reduce the amount of emissions from the boilers; automatic crib feeders in the horse stables; and, in the bottle shop, automatic filling machines which "reduced the work to play." The Gund brewery was also an early adopter of the revolutionary "Cork Crown" bottle cap, the ancestor of which is predominant even today.[68]

During the first week of 1912, a brand called Gund's Finest Beer was introduced. The growing importance of the household trade to the Gund brewery was evident in the features which accompanied the new brand. It was decided, for example, that the standard wooden bottle case used by all brewers for decades was inappropriate for households. "Filth, dirt and disease lurk in the pockets of the partitioned wood" was the claim.[69] Thus, bottles of Gund's Finest were packaged in modern disposable cardboard cases, each of which

The Jacob Mall brewery.

contained eight individual cartons holding three bottles. Every carton, furthermore, included a coupon for Gund's new "Profit-Sharing Plan," a system whereby consumers could exchange their coupons for merchandise in a brewery-issued premiums catalog. Items in the catalog ranged from small kitchen gadgets to major household appliances. This type of promotion was designed to attract housewives, encouraging them to order the family supplies of beer just as they did milk, eggs and other groceries. Incidentally, the introduction of the Gund's Finest brand marked the retirement of the old Crystal Bottled Beer.

George F. Gund was involved in a diverse collection of enterprises in addition to beer-making. He was president of the Gund Gold Mining Company and a director of the Rambler-Caribou Mining Company. (One of Gund's

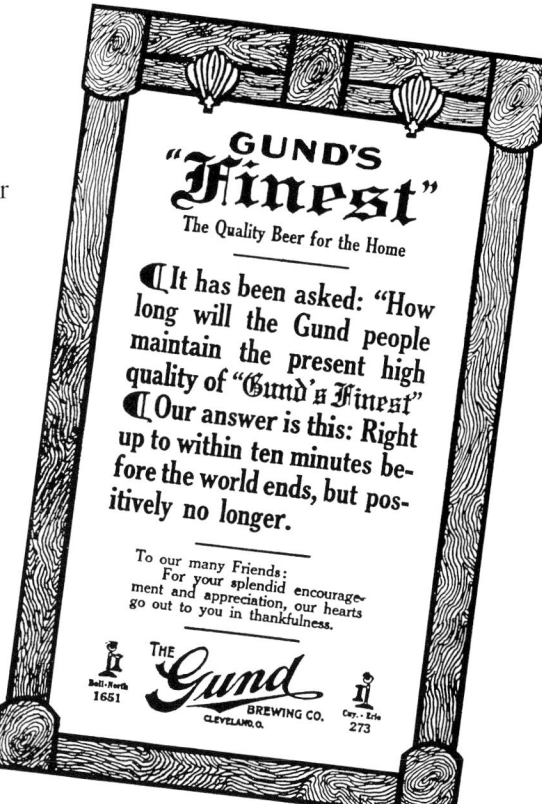

youthful pastimes had been panning for gold in Alaska.[70]) Banking, too, was another of Gund's pursuits. Back in Seattle, he had been associated with the Puget Sound National Bank and the National Bank of Commerce. In Cleveland, Gund was a director of the Broadway Savings & Trust Company and the Woodland Avenue Savings & Trust Company. He was also a director of the Cleveland Life Insurance Company, the Cleveland Realization Company and the Realty & Rental Company.[71]

A tin advertising sign, 1915.

But, of course, Gund had grown up in a brewing family, and it was beer which was the foundation of Gund's success. Not surprisingly, therefore, Gund was always active in affairs concerning the well-being of the brewing industry. For many years, he served on the Labor Committee of the United States Brewers Association. He was also president of the Ohio Brewers Association for a time. And when Cleveland's brewery owners re-established a local trade association in 1903 after a several year hiatus, Gund was elected president. He was also an active member of the local association of bottlers.[72]

After a long and successful career, George F. Gund passed away in March of 1916 at age sixty. His son, George F. Gund II, came to Cleveland from his home in Seattle to take over management of the family business. Since his graduation from Harvard Business School in 1909, George II had spent his young manhood exploring the wild west, a love he had shared with his father. He ranched in Nevada, studied animal husbandry in Iowa, rode broncos in Wyoming, and worked as a silent film stunt man in early Hollywood westerns.[73] Finally settling in his boyhood home of Seattle, George II took a position at the Seattle National

Bank. It was a job which foreshadowed George's later career in banking, a career which culminated in his heading the gargantuan Cleveland Trust Company.

Upon his arrival in Cleveland in 1916, George II took his father's place at the helm of the Gund brewery and began placing his personal stamp on the business. He introduced a new brand of beer called Gund's Clevelander, destined to become a local favorite. Bottle labels of Gund's Clevelander depicted a jubilant Moses Cleaveland overlooking the city which bears his name, and holding a mug of the beer which does the same. The slogan was "A Wonderful City – A Wonderful Beer."[74]

The Gund family closed the brewery in May of 1919 when statewide prohibition took effect in Ohio. Having since become involved in a variety of other affairs, the Gunds did not wish to venture into new beverage-related fields. The company's entire reserve of beer was transferred to the Pilsener Brewing Company which was authorized under a special arrangement to sell the last stocks of Gund Beer.[75]

The Pilsener Brewing Co.

The phrase "P.O.C." was a cornerstone in Cleveland's brewing industry for more than a half-century. Even today, many years after its disappearance from bar tops and beer stores, P.O.C. Beer still lingers in the memories of Clevelanders. Dubbed "Pride Of Cleveland" (not by the brewery, but by its patrons), the venerable brand was the city's top selling beer at various points in its history. Its maker, the Pilsener Brewing Company, occupied an enormous complex at the corner of West 65th Street and Clark Avenue, fondly known as "Pilsener Square." Although most of the brewery still survives, it stands quietly in decay and gives little sense of the high regard in which Clevelanders once held the beer brewed within its walls.

The history of the Pilsener Brewing Company began in 1892 when Bohemian immigrant Wenzl Medlin established a brewery on Gordon (West 65th) Street near Clark. Medlin had come to America in 1866 and, for the next twenty years, was employed in various breweries and malteries in Chicago, Milwaukee, Buffalo, and Jersey City. In 1886, he came to Cleveland and purchased the brewery at the corner of Pearl (West 25th) Street and Vega Avenue, which had been operated for a number of years by William Aenis & Company.[76] Here, Medlin established the "Wenzl Medlin Bohemian Brewery." Three years later, Medlin sold the brewery to his manager, Simon Fishel, but continued to work as brewmaster there until leaving to establish the Pilsener brewery.

Medlin's new enterprise began production in 1892. Known as the Medlin Pilsener Brewing Company, the brewery's primary brand was called Extra Pilsener Beer. Medlin, after all, was one of the very few brewers in the city who had learned his art in the world-famous brewing city of Pilsen, Bohemia. In addition to brewing the

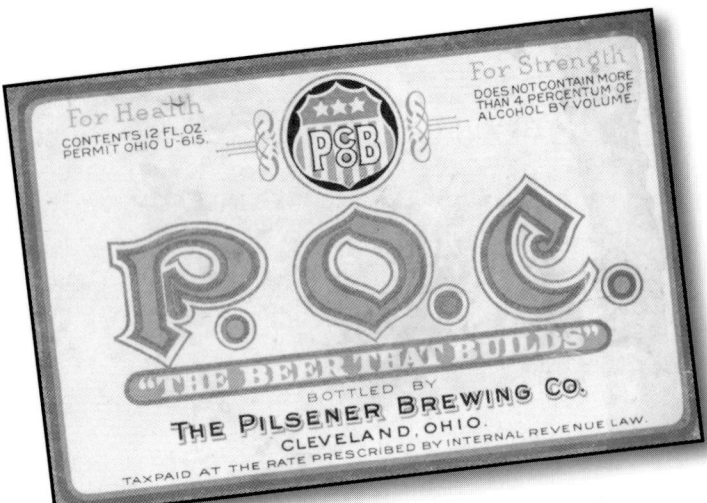

P.O.C. was a mainstay in Cleveland for half a century.

Wenzl Medlin founded the Pilsener Brewing Company in 1892.

beer, Medlin was also the brewery's manager and treasurer. Vaclav Humel, a local merchant, was president.[77]

The brewery, however, did not meet with immediate success. Unable to pay its creditors, the company passed into bankruptcy early in 1894. Under Vaclav Humel's direction, the firm's affairs were put back in order and all debts were settled by the end of that same year.[78] The company resumed business as The Pilsener Brewing Company; Medlin's name was dropped from the firm, thus indicating his diminished position in the brewery after the bankruptcy. Medlin, in fact, had planned to divorce himself entirely from the Pilsener brewery and establish a new brewing venture in Ashtabula, Ohio.[79] However, in the end, he remained in Cleveland and continued in his role as brewmaster. Just as with his earlier Bohemian Brewery, Medlin ultimately relinquished managerial duties to others while he concerned himself exclusively with matters of brewing.

Once back in business, the Pilsener brewery's troubles seemed to disappear. Beer sales grew rapidly throughout the remainder of the decade: 6,000 barrels in 1894; 16,000 barrels in 1895; 18,000 barrels in 1896; 22,500 barrels in 1897; and 26,000 barrels in 1898.[80] The steady growth spurred expansion of the brewery. An entirely new five-story brewhouse was completed in 1901. It was followed by a new boiler house, new stables, and new pitch house. A bottling plant was added in 1906, and the Extra Pilsener Beer made its first appearance in bottles sporting a stylish yellow label cut in the shape of a shield. The premium variety, Extra Pilsener Gold Top, featured decorative gold foil on the bottleneck, as well as a higher price: "The recollection of quality remains long after the price is forgotten."[81] The brewery also bottled a brand known as Zunt Heit.

In 1907, the Pilsener Brewing Company began using the monogram "P.O.C." as a slogan for its Extra Pilsener Beer, thus initiating what would become the company's keynote for most of its history. By mid-1914, P.O.C. had graduated from slogan to full-fledged brand name, taking its place at the head of the Pilsener line of beers.[82] The running theme of P.O.C. Beer was the mystery of what the letters meant. Baited with few clues, the consumer was left to his own imagination for the answer. A "P.O.C. Guessing Contest" was even promoted by the company at one point, the premise of which was to guess the meaning of the P.O.C. letters. Such gimmicks were designed only to bolster the public's curiosity and ended in no

The automobile stimulated home delivery of beer.

121

Pilsener Square

In June of 1915, the Pilsener Brewing Company unveiled the results of a $300,000 plant expansion. The focal point of the project was a new three-story building fronting Clark Avenue housing the new company offices, the new bottling department (capable of filling 5,000 bottles per hour), an assembly hall, a kitchen, and a rathskeller. Adjacent to this building was a new "fireproof" garage capable of holding the company's thirty delivery trucks and wagons. With the brewery's domain now extending over onto Clark Avenue, the intersection of West 65th Street and Clark became known as "Pilsener Square."

The Pilsener Brewing Company promoted its new plant using the slogan, "Where Cleanliness is Paramount." To herald its new additions, the brewery conducted a week-long open house, inviting the public to inspect its expanded premises. Groups of twenty-five were escorted through the various departments while receiving "a little talk about the ideals of the Pilsener Brewing Company."[83] The tours concluded in the rathskeller where guests were treated to refreshments and entertained by a live orchestra. The brewery claimed that it was host to an estimated 35,000 visitors during the open house, and that "no doubt many prohibitionists were converted."

With its 500-seat rathskeller, the new Pilsener addition often hosted employee functions and executive social gatherings. Reporting on the 1916 convention of the U.S. Brewers' Association held in Cleveland, the *Brewer's Journal* detailed the festivities of one such gathering at the Pilsener brewery. A dinner party was held at the brewery during the convention in honor of John M. Leicht, a former executive of the Cleveland & Sandusky Brewing Company. A hearty dinner was served in the rathskeller while entertainment was provided by cabaret dancers from Cleveland's Hippodrome Theater. After dinner, the men were all treated to the brewery's own "P.O.C. cigars."[84] The party then retired to the assembly hall, where moving pictures were shown featuring the Pilsener executives' recent automobile excursion through the city's parks, footage of the old Star brewery on Buckley Street (once owned by John M. Leicht), and a presentation of the film "Hoyt's – A Temperance Town." Although not reported, it is assumed that P.O.C. beer was consumed well into the night.

A post card featuring the 1901 brewhouse at Pilsener Square. This building remains today.

clear revelation of P.O.C.'s true meaning. Throughout the brand's long duration, the originally intended meaning of the P.O.C. initials was deliberately obscure.

At least one interpretation of P.O.C. – "Pride Of Cleveland" – gained enough favor over the years to become almost common knowledge. Indeed, writers for the *Western Brewer* had submitted this phrase as their official guess already in 1915. Although some P.O.C. advertising of the 1930s carried "Pride Of Cleveland" as a slogan, it was presumably used only in response to the popularity of the phrase. After all, the brewery plugged many expressions into the P.O.C. initials over the years, such as "Pleasure Of Course" or "Pilsener On Call." Ironically, as late as the 1950s, the Pilsener Brewing Company itself could only speculate as to the original meaning behind the P.O.C. letters. A television commercial which aired during that decade stated, "History records are not complete on this subject, but it is thought that they originally represented 'Pilsener Of Cleveland.'"[85] Certainly the creators of P.O.C. had little idea that the mystery would live to baffle even the company itself!

Workers at the Pilsener brewery.

Brewers have always been active sponsors of bowling teams and other sporting organizations.

Whatever the exact meaning of each of the letters, the evidence does suggest that P.O.C. was intended to highlight the fact that Pilsener's brands were made and marketed exclusively in Cleveland. The brewery's advertising throughout the 1910s invariably included messages such as "No need for Clevelanders to use a product of any other city when such excellent products of our own city are available."[86] Countering the actions of the invading national brewers, too, was a regular practice of the Pilsener brewery. For example, when the long-running "Schlitz in Brown Bottles" ad campaign made its appearance in Cleveland, Pilsener answered by offering P.O.C. in clear bottles each wrapped in dark paper. The brown bottle, as Schlitz ads explained, kept its beer from spoiling if exposed to light. Pilsener argued that the consumer ought to be able to see the beer's clarity and absence of foreign matter before drinking it. As expressed by one P.O.C. ad, "Clear bottles protect you. Dark wrappers protect the beer."[87] The individually wrapped bottles, however, undoubtedly became too cumbersome (both for the consumer and for the brewery) and the idea was discontinued.

The Pilsener Brewing Company was controlled largely by Bohemians for over thirty years. Throughout the 1890s, the company's management was comprised of various local Bohemian businessmen, presumably stockholders in the brewery. Many remained for only a short while, and turnover among the directors was frequent. But from 1904 until the onset of prohibition, the Pilsener Brewing Company was under the unchanged direction of president Vaclav Snajdr, vice-president Carl Anders, treasurer James C. Wolf, and secretary Frank Kratochvil. Vaclav Snajdr, probably the most notable Bohemian to be connected with the Pilsener brewery, was the founder and long-time editor of *Dennice Novoveku*, a local Bohemian-language newspaper. He was also credited with leading the promotion and fund raising to build the grand Bohemian National Hall on Broadway Avenue, still in use today.[88] Carl Anders, the vice-president, was a successful Cleveland building contractor. The Pilsener brewhouse was among the many local structures built by his firm. James C. Wolf and Frank Kratochvil had each been associated with the brewery as early as 1898. Both remained directors of the company until well after the repeal of prohibition in 1933.

Not surprisingly, Pilsener beer was brewed at the hands of primarily Bohemian brewmasters. Founder Wenzl Medlin, of course, was the first. Among his successors prior to prohibition were Joseph Liska, Jaro Pavlik, Vinzenz Spietschka, Zdenek Sobotka, and Frank Knopp. The last named, who started as Pilsener brewmaster in 1916, remained at the brewery throughout prohibition making near beer – or "spoiled beer" as Knopp called it.[89]

Incidentally, Wenzl Medlin held stock in the Pilsener Brewing Company until 1899 when he sold his interest and began a small weiss beer brewery at his home address on Pearl (West 25th) Street. Both his output and his success, however, were limited. By 1904 the brewery was no longer active. In 1912, Medlin died at age sixty-three. By the time of his death, the Pilsener Brewing Company had grown considerably, though Medlin never shared in that success. His portrait, nevertheless, hung at the brewery for several years – "a tribute to its founder."[90]

Chapter Six

The Saloon

The corner saloon has always been an essential ingredient in the makeup of the brewing industry. Virtually the sole outlet for beer throughout the nineteenth and early twentieth centuries, the saloon was the brewer's lifeblood. Beer, after all, was first and foremost an imbibery of the saloon, and only secondarily a household product. But even in the early days, the "take-home" trade was conducted through the saloons as well. Small tin pails called "growlers" were used to carry beer from saloons, and they represented a significant portion of the typical saloonkeeper's business. Later, the ease and convenience of bottled beer doomed the growler to extinction, but even bottled beer was dispensed primarily through saloons. It was not until after the repeal of prohibition in 1933 that new retail channels for beer began to develop. As America's mobility increased, particularly after World War II, so too did "off-premises" consumption of beer. For more than a century prior, however, brewers built their trade and amassed their fortunes through neighborhood drinking establishments.

The typical pre-prohibition saloon was a unique place. Much like the traditional corner grocery, saloons were usually family-run operations. While the saloonkeeper busied himself behind the bar pouring shots of whiskey and drawing mugs of beer, his wife tended to the obligatory free lunch counter. The free lunch was a time-honored saloon tradition. Every purchase of beer or whiskey earned the patron a visit to the free lunch spread. The type of food offered by any particular saloonkeeper depended entirely on his nationality. Of course, whatever the food, it was always a little heavy on the salt, thereby stimulating the urge for just one more mug of beer. One jaded saloon-goer complained about the nature of the free lunch in 1913:

125

The corner
saloon was
the brewer's
lifeblood
during the
late nineteenth
and early
twentieth
centuries.

*Most of the modern free lunch 'layouts' would kill a horse. They consist
of a dozen different kinds of food, and nothing that would really appeal
to the palate. One good joint of roast or corned beef is better than a
dozen dishes of pickled this, and pickled that, and pickled almost
anything that was never eaten in Germany.*[1]

Complaints aside, the nationality of a saloonkeeper affected not just the type of lunch he
served, but usually determined the character and style of the entire establishment. For instance, it
was said that Irish saloons contained only stand-up bars and no tables. In German places, tables
were a must. Likewise, the German saloon welcomed the entire family through its doors: women,
children and all. The Irish places, meanwhile, were strictly a man's domain.[2] Indeed, the many
differences in beliefs, customs and tastes among the various saloon-going ethnic groups were almost
always reflected in their neighborhood drinking spots.

That being the case, the local saloon often developed into an important social center for
immigrants, providing an oasis from the tribulations of working-class life. It was a place where

126

immigrants could fraternize with their own kind, talk in their native language, discuss topics of mutual concern, and generally escape – if only temporarily – the hardships of assimilating into a society not always accepting of foreign ways. Saloons served as meeting places for ethnic-based social organizations such as singing societies, gymnastic clubs, dance groups, literary clubs, and countless others. And so, for its patrons, the saloon was much more than a place to drink beer. It was where friends and neighbors came together to participate in their community.

For the saloonkeeper, his establishment was a business above all else. It was his livelihood. And making a go of it was not always a simple matter. Slim profits, high license fees, anti-saloon sentiment, and a variety of other threats menaced saloonkeepers constantly. And the brewers (without question the most important of the saloonist's suppliers) did little to improve the situation. Until the late nineteenth century, beer-makers by and large did not interfere with the retail end of the business. Throughout much of the 1800s, the roles of each party were pretty well fixed: the brewer *made* the beer, and the saloonkeeper *sold* the beer. But, by the last two decades of the century, the competitive environment within the brewing industry had changed dramatically. Industry-wide brewing capacity had reached surplus levels, and the fight for customers intensified. The overt control of saloons, among other tactics, became a powerful weapon in the brewers' arsenal. In controlling the retail trade, brewers sought *exclusive* sale of their particular product in saloons, thereby locking out competitive brands of beer. Often, the saloonkeeper had little choice but to succumb to the brewer's manipulation.

The very nature of the relationship between brewer and saloonkeeper became more complex. In the old days, a brewer employed a "collector," who often did little more than take and fill the saloonkeeper's beer order. In his stead, there was now a bona fide salesman, replete with pressure tactics and all. The brewery man often came into a prospective customer's saloon bearing gratuities such as complimentary glassware and serving trays (custom-lettered for the brewery, of course). Large wall hangings, providing an appealing decoration and an advertisement for the brewery at the same time, were popular giveaways. The smart brewery man commonly bought rounds of beer for the entire place.[3] Pretentious thought it may have been, it was an effective (and popular) tactic. A big smile and a flashy entrance

Most saloons were the domain of only one brewer. Edd's Place, for example, was clearly marked as a Schlather saloon.

were trademarks of any good brewery man.

Once all of the obligatory pleasantries had been tendered, it was usually simple price competition that sealed the deal. The saloonkeeper would be offered a price slightly lower than the going rate in exchange for his promise to sell only the beer of the sponsoring brewery. However, there was no easy recourse for the brewer in the event that the saloonkeeper decided (as many certainly did) to break the commitment and seek a better price from a rival brewery. This inevitably lead to bitter price wars, often so damaging that the brewers themselves were forced to call a truce. Breweries in many cities, including Cleveland, set up brewers' associations for the expressed purpose of establishing and enforcing strict guidelines regarding the pricing of beer, thus avoiding the sting of heated price battles.

One of the more effective methods of saloon control concerned the buying and selling of saloon fixtures by brewers.[4] The many necessities in setting up a saloon – the bar, the backbar, tables, chairs, beer-tapping apparatus, and a myriad of other utensils – represented a large investment for the prospective saloonkeeper. For those unable to secure financing, startup costs were often prohibitive. This, of course, is where the brewer came in, offering to supply the necessary fixtures on credit, often on an interest-free basis. The brewer required only that the saloonkeeper agree to sell the brewer's beer, and *only* his beer, throughout the duration of the debt repayment. Such arrangements could involve a number of years, thereby securing a long-term captive customer for the brewer.

For already-established saloons, this strategy was equally effective. In many cases, the various items used in the running of a saloon had simply been inherited from the previous owner. And in light of the sometimes rough environment of a heavily-frequented saloon, it is no surprise that its fixtures became worn and in need of replacement over time. What better way, after all, to entice a new clientele into your establishment than by sporting a fancy new mahogany bar and backbar? Or a new set of barroom tables and chairs? Or adding a billiard table? However, the typical saloonkeeper was far from moneyed. Profit margins being what they were, capital improvements were usually few and far between. Indebtedness to a brewer, therefore, was often the only option. Interestingly, some breweries (such as the Leisy brewery in Cleveland) even employed a staff of woodworkers to produce the various bar fixtures themselves in order to cut costs.[5]

Another impetus for brewery control of the saloon trade originated from an unlikely source: the temperance factions. One of the favored tactics of the anti-saloon groups was to campaign for disproportionately high license fees for saloons.[6] The rationale was that by making the license unusually expensive, the "grog shops" – that is, those establishments where lewd and drunken behavior ran wild – would not be able to afford the fee and would thus disappear. City and state governments subscribed to the idea in astonishing numbers, objecting neither to the

The Log Cabin Cafe was a popular spot on Cleveland's east side.

notion of eliminating the troublesome saloons nor to the prospect of boosting revenues from the respectable ones. The concept was, however, flawed from the beginning. Brewers would not sit idly by and watch their outlets be knocked off one by one. Instead, the brewers stepped in and paid the high license fees for those high-volume saloons that were important to their trade and their profits. Again, the only string attached was the exclusivity provision. The net result of the high license fee, then, was to strengthen the brewers' hold over the retail business.

But the ultimate control of a given saloon meant simply owning that saloon. And brewers were large holders of saloon properties. Even in cases of brewery ownership, though, the saloon was usually run by an independent entrepreneur. The prices of beer were fixed by agreement with the

"Drawn In Homely Language"

In supplying new saloons with all of the necessary implements and appliances to begin operation, the brewer's aim was to lock his competitors out of that particular establishment and maintain exclusive sale of his product there. Saloonkeepers, many of whom would otherwise have no means of getting started in business, readily agreed to work off the debt in beer purchases. And so, everyone was happy – happy, that is, in the beginning. However, once the saloonkeeper realized that a rival brewer would grant him a lower price on beer if he would break his commitment to the first brewer, pleasantries quickly subsided, and a melee typically ensued.

Such was the case in 1891 when brewers Diebolt & Ruble took legal action against saloonkeeper Henry Bringman for violating the conditions of an agreement made between the parties. Bringman was discovered selling both Schlather beer and Oppmann beer in his establishment despite a contract to sell only Diebolt & Ruble's beer. The agreement involved some $600 worth of saloon fixtures including a bar, backbar, cigar cabinet, ice box, glassware, playing cards, window shutters, and a host of other items. Bringman was to buy his beer from Diebolt & Ruble at the price of $8 per barrel, fifteen percent of which was to be applied to the $600 debt until fully paid. The agreement, however, was found to be poorly worded – "drawn in homely language" – leaving Bringman with a gaping loophole. As written, the agreement stated that the saloonkeeper was to buy "all" Diebolt & Ruble's beer, instead of "only" their beer. Consequently, Bringman argued that the agreement was completely unenforceable as he could not possibly buy "all" of the brewery's beer. The contract, he insisted, was thus null and void from the beginning.

This type of folly undoubtedly plagued brewers who engaged in the saloon game. A large brewery, after all, might enter into as many as a hundred such agreements every year. And the very nature of the saloon business virtually assured that there would be a goodly share of "bad apples" in every bushel.

brewery, and the saloonkeeper's monthly lease payment was partially worked-off through beer purchases. Naturally, selling competitive brands of beer on the premises was strictly disallowed. In Cleveland, all of the breweries owned at least a handful of their own saloons. The Leisy brewery was most probably the leader, owning more than 200 saloons by the time prohibition was enacted.[7] The Schlather brewery owned properties throughout Ohio, particularly in the southeast part of the state along the Ohio River. In 1902, the Cleveland & Sandusky Brewing Company claimed that no less than seventy-five percent of its beer production was secured against competition by sales through its own retail outlets.[8] Indeed, the final goal in creating "tied houses" was to establish a protected channel of sales for every barrel of beer produced.

The Saloon Under Attack

One historian estimated that, by the early part of the twentieth century, as many as eighty-five percent of the saloons in America were either owned or sufficiently controlled by breweries. The brewing industry as a whole was said to have invested about $70 million by 1909 in its quest to takeover the retail trade.[9] That the brewers achieved their goal was plainly apparent on every street corner. For the benefit of both customers and rival beer-makers, the brewers marked out their territory in gaudy fashion. Saloon fronts were cluttered with large advertising signs extolling the virtues of the particular brand of beer sold within. Writers for the *Western Brewer* found this trend toward saloon front advertising to be frivolous and wished that the brewers would

> *proceed to cut off the sign nuisance, so prevalent in most cities, which compels them to furnish kindling wood to their saloons in the shape of costly signs that sooner or later make their way into the fire-box, to make room for other signs more elaborately painted by a competitor. We could name a single brewery whose sign bills average from $300 to $500 a week.*[10]

The commandeering of the retail trade by the brewing industry caused a profound change in the nature of the saloon business in America. At best, the brewers made it increasingly difficult for entrepreneurs to make a respectable living. At worst, the takeover resulted in nothing less than the utter deterioration of the saloon nationwide. In most cases, the true level of detriment probably lay somewhere in between those assessments. But one thing is certain: the brewers' manipulation of the saloons did nothing to help curb the growing anti-saloon sentiment in America. When the prohibition forces focused all of their efforts squarely on the poor moral conditions of the typical saloon, the brewing industry's half-hearted pledge to improve the situation ended in little genuine

Powerful groups such as the Anti-Saloon League and the Women's Christian Temperance Union appealed to America's sense of morality in their campaign to abolish the saloon.

Carrie Nation (far left) visited Cleveland in 1906. She is shown here after one of her famous hatchet-in-hand saloon raids on the L&C Cafe on Public Square.

action. And so, while distilled spirits had largely been the target of temperance activists during the nineteenth century, it was instead the brewing industry – for its support and sponsorship of the "grog shop" – that became the main enemy of the prohibitionists.

For saloonkeepers, brewery dominance of the saloon trade was a no-win situation. The brewers' agenda was decidedly *not* that of the saloonists. While the saloonkeeper simply wanted to run a secure and profitable business, the brewer was out to fight to the death with his competitors. And his choice of weapon was the unwitting saloonkeeper. After all, if a few innocent bystanders happened to get swept away by the torrent, the brewers probably considered it a small price to pay for the survival of their mammoth brewery enterprises.

Certainly the most damaging aspect of brewery control over the retail trade was the resulting growth in the number of saloons. When a brewer was successful in obtaining the exclusive business of a particular outlet, the usual counter-measure from the rival brewers was to open a saloon of their own on the opposite corner, or just down the block, or even right next door. By 1898, the situation in Cleveland had become so competitive that the brewers came together and agreed to close down many of the unprofitable saloons, which were said to number in the hundreds.[11] One year later, it was clear that little had changed. Calling the duplicate saloon warfare a "perfectly legitimate" business strategy, William H. Chapman, secretary and treasurer of the

Cleveland & Sandusky Brewing Company, openly discussed his firm's tactics: "If [a competitor] buys a saloon where our beer has been sold, it has been our policy to lease a place two or three doors away and start our man in business again. We find we are able to hold our own in that way."[12]

Forced now to compete with a neighbor (or two, or three) for customers, the saloonkeeper's sales decreased expectedly. While the brewers may have been able to absorb the resulting losses, the saloonkeeper could not. Many were forced to exit the business, broke and beleaguered. Others resorted to less-than-honorable means in an effort to survive. Various enticements – gambling, prostitution, under-age liquor sales – were sponsored by unscrupulous saloonkeepers. And the brewers, while not openly endorsing any such activity, were certainly not willing to undermine the entrepreneurial spirit of an ambitious saloonkeeper.

In Cleveland, the "saloon problem" (characterized as such even by the saloonkeepers themselves) was a topic of great public concern. Between 1885 and 1899, the number of saloons operating in the city grew from 1,418 to 1,978. And well into the new century, the number was consistently above 2,000. In a single twelve-month period spanning 1903 and 1904, 119 new saloons were opened in Cuyahoga County, nearly all of them being inside Cleveland proper.[13] A constant battery of local and state legislation attempted to curb the saloon business throughout the late 1800s and early 1900s. Laws prohibiting the sale of alcohol on Sunday were common. For decades, one after another of Sunday closing ordinances was passed in Cleveland, most failing in enforcement and ending in repeal.

Most of the legislative efforts, however, sought far more than mere restriction of the saloon's hours of business.

Sunday Was a Large Day for Cleveland Saloonkeepers.

Sunday closing laws were a futile attempt to curb the "saloon problem."

132

A host of state and local laws was passed after the turn of the century with the objective of inflicting serious harm on the saloon trade. In 1904, the Brannock Law gave several residential districts in Cleveland the power to vote saloons out of their neighborhoods entirely. The liquor interests, though, were not flustered by this particular piece of legislation. They pointed out that fewer than 200 of the city's saloons were at risk under the provisions of the law.[14] Nevertheless, a number of the city's residential areas did, indeed, make good use of the law and ejected saloons from their communities.

The Dean Law was adopted in 1909. It required that saloonkeepers not be issued a license until swearing under oath that they had 1) never allowed gambling in their establishment, 2) never sold alcohol either to under-age or intoxicated persons, 3) never admitted "improper females" (i.e., prostitutes) into their saloon, and 3) never been convicted of any felony.[15] The hope, of course, was that all wrong-doers would voluntarily admit their crimes and thus be denied licenses.

In 1909, the Rose Law was passed, giving every county in Ohio the right to abolish the saloon trade by popular vote.[16] Although none of the major cities was in jeopardy of losing its saloons, a great number of rural counties voted public drinking spots out of existence. The law did not prohibit the manufacture of alcoholic beverages, but a large number of breweries located in the affected counties were forced to shut down nonetheless because the saloons had been their sole sales outlets. Brewers who shipped beer into those counties, too, were most certainly hurt by the Rose Law.

For Cleveland's brewers, perhaps the most harmful of the anti-saloon laws was the 1913 revision of the Ohio License Code, which imposed a statewide limit of one saloon license for every 500 inhabitants. In Cleveland (where the number of saloons had been the highest in the state), legal saloons were reduced from 2,116 before the law to 1,258 after adoption.[17] While the city's brewers were undoubtedly distraught by the legislation, local saloonists strongly supported it. The owner of a saloon on St. Clair Avenue summed up the "honest" saloonkeepers' point of view: "By limiting the number of saloons it would prevent the competition that at present exists among saloonkeepers, and would enable every man in the business to make a living without resorting to illegal methods...It would result in a better class of men engaging in the business."[18] When the law was first proposed, the *Plain Dealer* could not find a single saloonkeeper who was not in favor of the clause limiting saloons to one for every 500 in population. It is suspected, however, that the more than 800 saloonkeepers who were put out of business by the law might have objected if polled.

In hopes of avoiding just this kind of wholesale crippling of the saloon trade, brewers made attempts – lackadaisical though they may have been – to clean up the saloon situation. In 1907, the Ohio Brewers Association established a Vigilance Bureau whose stated function was to seek out those saloons which were "violating the moral sense of the community."[19] Reports were to be made with local authorities concerning such places, and the Brewers Association itself was supposedly authorized to begin legal proceedings against the troublesome saloon owners. When Cleveland law enforcement authorities launched an attack on the city's vice-ridden saloons in 1905, the local brewers made the following resolution:

> We, the brewers of the city of Cleveland, through the Brewers' Board of Trade, commend the city administration for the activity displayed in attempting to abate dives and grogshops with sitting-room attachments. We urge the administration to go even further than stationing policemen in front of such places, and urge the arrest of all boys and girls patronizing such places and the arrest of the proprietors if they do not strictly obey orders.[20]

Of course, this kind of talk from the brewers was free-flowing. Their actions, however, did not match their professed concern. After all, the brewers' own manipulation of the retail trade was largely the cause of the poor condition of the saloons. Occasionally, a reformed saloon was offered up as proof of the brewers' sincerity. One skeptic asserted that this merely showed that the brewers were "willing to throw overboard a child or two to satisfy the wolves of public opinion, hoping to make their escape with the greater part of the family uninjured."[21]

A Rebellion: The Standard Brewing Co.

By the turn of the century, the saloonkeeper's plight had become critical. Fed up with the hardships of brewery manipulation, saloonkeepers in many cities banded together, pooled their resources, and built breweries of their own to provide themselves with an alternative source of beer. In Cleveland, at least a few early attempts were made to establish saloonkeeper-operated breweries. In 1902, the Greater Cleveland Brewing Company was organized by a group of Cleveland saloonkeepers.[22] The company was headed by Alois Michel of Michel & McDonough's saloon, one of the day's most frequented downtown drinking establishments. It was reported that more than 100 of the city's saloonkeepers had committed to buying stock in the new company. That notwithstanding, the venture never fully materialized, and Cleveland saloonkeepers remained without an alternative source of beer. A similar attempt to establish a brewery among the local saloonkeepers – to be called the Cleveland Co-Operative Brewing Company – had also failed to take shape about a year earlier.[23]

The first Standard brewery on Sackett Avenue.

On Christmas Eve day of 1903, a small west side brewery doing business as the Kress Weiss Beer Company was reorganized as the Standard Brewing Company.[24] Cleveland's only saloonkeeper-owned brewery was under way. The primary figure behind the venture was long-time saloonkeeper Stephen S. Creadon, and the majority of the firm's stock was held by other area saloonkeepers. One observer aptly described the circumstances surrounding Standard's formation:

A unique creation of the time is Standard: it is the brewery of innkeepers. Whereas the local brewing industry began with the first brewers being innkeepers as well and then giving up their inns when their business was good enough, now it is turned around. The innkeepers have joined in sufficient numbers to build a brewery of their own.[25]

Stephen S. Creadon grew up in "the Angle," a close-knit Irish community on Cleveland's near west side, north of Detroit Avenue. As a young man, Creadon involved himself in a number of pursuits before setting up a saloon and grocery business at the corner of West 25th and Detroit.[26] Just across the street from Creadon's establishment sat the Forest City Savings Bank, where friend and fellow Irishman John T. Feighan worked as a bank teller. Together, the two spearheaded creation of the Standard Brewing Company.[27] It is clear that one of their primary goals was to supply beer to saloonkeepers who were suffering the manipulations of the city's competition-entrenched breweries. Perhaps selection of the name "Standard" was significant in that regard; Webster's Dictionary defines the word as "a model to be followed or imitated." That aside, the founders undoubtedly also recognized the potential advantage of establishing the city's only Irish-run brewery. The Irish population in Cleveland was second only to the German.

In keeping with the Irish spirit, the flagship product of the Standard brewery for more than half a century was a brand entitled Erin Brew, first introduced in 1904. Writers for the *Brewers Journal* commented,

> *There is no doubt that the selection of the brand name 'Erin Brew' was a happy one. It is short; easy to repeat and remember; and the rollicking quality associated with Irish tradition is strictly in harmony with the purpose of the product to stimulate good fellowship and promote good nature.*[28]

Stephen S. Creadon in caricature.

Despite the decidedly Irish character of the Standard Brewing Company's products, the company was careful not to alienate the large population of beer-consuming Germans. The Erin Brew logo was fashioned to incorporate both the English spelling and the German: "Ehren Brau."

The Standard brewery began business in the old plant of the Kress Weiss Beer Company on Sackett Avenue at West 32nd Street. Andrew Kress, the former owner, was one of the incorporaters of the new Standard company, and he remained active in the brewery after its reorganization, serving as general manager.[29] However, late in 1904, operations were moved to

Train Avenue near Clark, where a former flour mill was taken over by the company and converted into a brewery. Over the next several years, about $200,000 was spent to improve and enlarge the plant. A towering new brewhouse was completed in 1906. The following year, a four-story stockhouse was built. In 1908, an enormous bottling plant was erected across Train Avenue from the brewhouse. The new facility – capable of bottling 160 barrels of beer daily – was one of the most extensive bottling works in the city. Standard soon claimed to be "the largest independent bottlers of beer in Cleveland."[30] As the brewery complex grew, so too did beer sales. Between 1906 and 1910, annual beer production at the Standard brewery doubled from 35,000 to 70,000 barrels.[31]

In 1906, the Cleveland & Sandusky Brewing Company put forth an offer to purchase the Standard Brewing Company. The tendered price was about $650,000, a sum which was more than twice the amount of capital invested in the Standard company up to that point. Just as the deal was about to be finalized, certain directors of the Cleveland & Sandusky company sabotaged the purchase. Despite that fact, other sources reported that the buyout was deemed "unsatisfactory" by Standard stockholders.[32] It is likely that the stockholders – mainly saloonkeepers – wanted nothing to do with the Cleveland & Sandusky Brewing Company, seen by many as the primary instigator of the rampant saloon competition still prevalent throughout the city.

Be that as it may, the Standard Brewing Company's characterization as a "brewery of innkeepers" faded as the business grew. In order to finance its rapid expansion, the company issued a great deal of new stock over the years, thus diluting

A truck load of Standard bottled beer ready for delivery in 1911.

The Standard brewery on Train Avenue. Brewing began on this site in 1906 in a former flour mill.

the saloonkeepers' collective share in the brewery. By 1911, it was clear that the Standard brewery counted as much on the household consumer for business as it did on the saloon trade. Nutrition and wholesomeness were the central themes in the brewery's promotions, fashioned to appeal to housewives. Phrases like "choicest home beverage," "pure food tonic"

Loading dock at the Standard brewery.

and "liquid food" were coupled with the brewery's open invitation for public inspection of the modern, sanitary conditions under which Standard beer was made.[33] Post cards, which carried the following rhyme, were mailed to households throughout Cleveland:

Family soaps and Family teas
for the Family use are good ideas.
But the point you want to remember first
is Standard Beer for the family thirst.[34]

A brand called Full Weight Tonic was promoted along side Erin Brew, continuing Standard's theme of health and nutrition. The product, according to its bottle labels, "improves the appetite [and] gives tone to the nervous system."[35]

The Standard company, like many brewers, operated an ice business in conjunction with the brewery. The Lake City Ice Company was formed by the Standard directors in 1906. Its main ice-manufacturing facility was located at 2038 West 55th Street, south of Lorain Avenue. The company remained active well into prohibition, but operations had ceased by 1932.[36]

Throughout the Standard Brewing Company's pre-prohibition existence, the founders – Stephen S. Creadon and John T. Feighan – remained at the head of the business. Creadon was president while Feighan served as secretary and treasurer. Feighan, though, never relinquished his ties with the banking community. Ultimately, he worked his way into the position of vice president of the mighty Cleveland Trust Company, one of the largest banks in the Midwest.[37]

The long-time brewmaster at the Standard Brewery was Jaro H. Pavlik, the son and grandson of Bohemian brewers. It was most certainly that fact which accounted for one of Standard's early brands – Standard Old Bohemian Style Beer. In later years, Pavlik was employed at several other Cleveland breweries.[38] He retired in 1950 after working as a brewmaster for more than a half century.

The Standard Brewing Company was not the only newcomer to appear on Cleveland's brewing scene shortly after 1900. In spite of the fierce competition raging in the saloon trade, the brewing industry entered the new century with a promising outlook for the future. The federal tax on beer, which had doubled during the Spanish-American War, was brought back down to its former $1 per barrel in 1902. The population was growing rapidly. And financial markets were strong and healthy. Between 1900 and 1910, beer production in America skyrocketed from roughly forty million barrels annually to almost sixty million. Annual per capita consumption grew from sixteen to twenty gallons.[39] By all measures, beer-making was in its heyday.

Thus, a rash of new capital was attracted to the industry. New breweries began appearing in most regions. In Cleveland alone, five new brewing companies were formed during the first decade of the century: the Standard, Fishel, Cleveland Home, Forest City and Excelsior Brewing Companies. Most targeted the household consumer heavily. The saloon trade, after all, had been nearly exhausted by the older brewers. There simply was little room left for new competition in that segment of the beer business. In addition, the mounting anti-saloon legislation was effectively decreasing the number of outlets.

Indeed, even the long-time brewers began turning their attention toward the household consumer. It was infinitely less expensive than the saloon strategy, and it was far less competitive. Additionally, the very nature of the saloon had always limited the beer drinking population to men. The household trade brought women into the brewers' picture for the first time. The appearance of both the automobile and the telephone also helped stimulate brewers' interest in the household. Customers could now simply telephone the brewery and order a case of beer, which would be promptly whisked to the customer's door via automobile. Even suburban residents were now only a telephone call away from home delivery.

Bottled beer was a crucial aspect of the household business. By the turn of the century, a number of developments significantly improved the processing of bottled beer. For much of the 1800s, cumbersome tax laws had steered many brewers away from bottling a large percentage of their beer. The laws mandated that beer first be kegged, then removed to a building entirely separate from the brewery before it could be bottled. By 1900, these archaic laws were replaced by the "government pipeline" system.[40] The new procedure allowed brewers to pipe beer directly to their bottling equipment, providing that a tax assessor was present to gauge the amount of beer passing through the lines. This development, in turn, sparked advances in the quality and affordability of bottling equipment. Perfection of the Crown bottle cap, which eliminated the age-old problem of leakage, was also a boon to bottling. The Crown – still in wide use today – offered the first significant advance in bottle enclosures and was quickly adopted by all brewers. By 1909, no less than twenty percent of America's beer production was packaged in bottles.[41] The household consumer had become the new target for brewers everywhere.

The Cleveland Home Brewing Co.

In May of 1907, Ernst W. Mueller acquired a controlling interest in the Beltz Brewing Company at East 61st Street and Outhwaite Avenue and incorporated it as the Cleveland Home Brewing Company. Mueller had been ousted from the presidency of the Cleveland & Sandusky Brewing Company just weeks earlier, an event which set off an emotionally-heated row among the city's brewers. Early

in the dispute, Mueller and his supporters vowed to gain control of one of the independent breweries in order to do battle with the combine. Formation of the Cleveland Home Brewing Company was seen as the first step toward fulfilling that promise. But, once tempers cooled, Mueller found that he was clearly not interested in involving his new venture in the fierce and troublesome saloon warfare waged by the combine. As Mueller himself put it, "I and my associates are going into this business to make money – not war."[42] And anyway, there is evidence that suggests that Mueller's new company could not have afforded the heavy expense of head-to-head saloon battles. In a 1907 letter to a relative, Ernst Mueller described the circumstances of the new Cleveland Home company at its inception:

> *Though our subscriptions to the capital stock of our new undertaking are not what we*
> *should have liked, we have gone on with the preliminary organization, and have*
> *arranged to take possession of the Beltz plant as a going concern next Monday May 20th*
> *a.m. On account of an extremely tight money market and a general depression of all*
> *stock securities, we were handicapped considerably with our subscriptions, but have*
> *enough to swing the deal.*[43]

Ernst Mueller filled the office of president of the new company. Joseph Beltz, who had founded the brewery in 1876, was vice president. Carl F. Schroeder was secretary and treasurer. (Schroeder was among the handful of former executives at the Cleveland & Sandusky Brewing Company who resigned when Mueller was deposed as the combine's president.) Rudolph Mueller, cousin of Ernst Mueller, was the brewery's sales manager. The brewmaster was John J. Beltz, son of the founder.[44]

As declared in the very name of the company, the Cleveland Home brewery was aimed largely at the household consumer. Although saloons still represented the majority of most brewers' business, Mueller recognized that consumption of beer in the home represented a substantial opportunity for new sales. Among the brewery's feature products was a brand called simply The Home Beer. Others included Meister Brau, Yako (presumably the reverse of "okay"), and a low-alcohol product named Malt Liquid.[45] Bottling, of course, was of utmost importance. Initially, the bottling function was handled by independent bottler A. Weber, whose works sat just next door to the brewery. In 1914, bottling was taken over by the brewery: "The Cleveland Home Brewing Co. announces that in connection with its Brewery it has opened a Modern Bottling Plant, and is ready to supply for family use its Meister-Brau and Home Beer of extra quality."[46] Throughout the remainder of the pre-prohibition years, the Cleveland Home brewery (like all others) became increasingly dependent on household sales as saloons declined both in number and social stigma.

The Forest City Brewing Co.

The Forest City Brewing Company was organized in January of 1904 by a group of local Bohemians. Its chief promoters were Broadway-area merchants Michael Albl and Joseph F. Troyan, who filled the positions of president and secretary, respectively.[47] Interestingly, Troyan was a clothier by trade and Albl a grocer, suggesting little previous experience with the brewing industry for either.[48] However, enlisted as treasurer and general manager of the brewery was Vaclav Humel, an organizer and past executive of the Pilsener Brewing Company. Among the board of directors was County Commissioner John Vevera. Announcements of the company's formation made special mention of the fact that none but Bohemians were stockholders.

The brewery was located on Union Avenue at East 69th Street near "Slavic Village," a neighborhood known even today for its high concentration of Eastern Europeans. Construction of the plant began in the spring of 1904. Noted brewery architects Mueller & Mildner of Detroit designed the brewery, which was to be "modern and first-class in every respect." Of particular note was the fact that all of the brewery's vessels (fermenting tanks, aging casks, etc.) were of steel

The Forest City Brewing Company on Union Avenue.

construction. Wooden cooperage had traditionally served this purpose. The annual capacity of the works was to be 50,000 barrels, and the cost of its construction was estimated at approximately $225,000.[49]

Production of the company's feature brand – Select Pilsner Beer – commenced in 1904 under the supervision of brewmaster John Silhavy. (He was replaced in 1909 by Max Hansky, who came from West Virginia to fill the position.[50] Hansky remained brewmaster at Forest City until well after the repeal of prohibition.) Advertisements for the new brewery noted that bottled beer was their "specialty."

The Excelsior Brewing Co.

In July of 1905, the Excelsior Brewing Company began making beer in the former plant of the Standard Brewing Company at West 32nd Street and Sackett Avenue. The founder of the new firm was brewmaster Jacob F. Haller, who had come to Cleveland in 1903 after working in breweries in Kentucky, Toledo, Chicago and St. Louis. His first job here was that of brewmaster at the Diebolt brewery, a position with which he was soon unsatisfied. In 1904, he purchased the Goodfellows Hall on Pearl (West 25th) Street, which he continued to operate until founding the Excelsior Brewing Company.[51]

In its first year, the Excelsior brewery sold 10,000 barrels of beer, an impressive total for a relatively new and small brewery. A series of additions to the works was under way by 1907, due to the fact that "the progress which the business immediately enjoyed was far beyond the expectations of even the company itself."[52] New buildings were constructed, and the brewing capacity was boosted to 30,000 barrels annually.

Bill Carlisle Collection/Bob Bickford Collection

Jacob F. Haller and his Excelsior Brewing Company on Sackett Avenue.

Over the years, the Excelsior brewery enjoyed strong sales of its brands, Excelsior Success Beer and Golden Seal Beer. Enlargements to the brewery were frequent. As late as 1917 (when many brewers were beginning to feel the pains of the looming prohibition threat), the Excelsior brewery, optimistic about the future, was still investing in plant expansions.[53] Although the household consumer was clearly the primary target for Excelsior, the company did not entirely ignore the saloon trade. One advertisement read, "The Excelsior Brewing Company's Famous Lager – on draught or in bottles at all leading saloons." Like all others in Cleveland, the Excelsior brewery ceased beer production in 1919 when statewide prohibition took hold in Ohio.

Chapter Seven

Demise Of An Industry

On January 16, 1920, the Eighteenth Amendment to the U. S. Constitution went into effect, and America embarked on that "noble experiment" called National Prohibition. The Amendment, which had been ratified by the required thirty-sixth state exactly one year earlier, was surprisingly brief:

> *After one year from the ratification of this article the manufacture, sale, or transportation of intoxicating liquors within, the importation thereof into, or the exportation thereof from the United States and all territory subject to the jurisdiction thereof for beverage purposes is hereby prohibited.*
>
> *The Congress and the several States shall have concurrent power to enforce this article by appropriate legislation.*

> *This article shall be inoperative unless it shall have been ratified as an amendment to the Constitution by the Legislatures of the several States, as provided in the Constitution, within seven years from the date of the submission thereof to the States by the Congress.*[1]

The seven-year clause in the third section raises an interesting point. The Amendment's supporters wanted this period to be as lengthy as possible in the event that signing on the necessary thirty-six states proved difficult. The fact that it actually took little more than *one year* for ratification (Congress submitted the Amendment to the states in December of 1917) demonstrated that even the drys underestimated the support for prohibition.[2]

The Anti-Saloon League – formed in 1893 at Oberlin, Ohio – was far and away the single most important force in bringing about National Prohibition. Originally organized for the purpose of suppressing the saloon trade, the group's objective soon blossomed into something much bigger: complete riddance of the alcoholic beverage industry in America. Members of the Anti-Saloon League believed that the old-fashioned "moral suasion" employed by most temperance groups had proved wholly ineffective. They felt that an all-out war on liquor interests was the only means of making real progress. And the League was determined that the battle would be fought entirely in the political arena. In fact, the group's first president, Hiram Prince, was a five-time Republican Congressman from Iowa. The League conducted no saloon raids, no sidewalk prayers for the drunkard's salvation. Its efforts were aimed not at the drinker nor even at the saloonkeeper, but entirely at the politician. One historian characterized the Anti-Saloon League by writing, "It didn't care how much an officeholder drank, only how he voted on issues of temperance."[3]

For many of the Anti-Saloon League's best years, the organization's most visible figure was Reverend Wayne B. Wheeler, an Ohio clergyman who time and time again proved himself a master of political manipulation. His first notable victory came in 1905 when Wheeler launched the full force of the League against then Ohio Governor Myron Herrick in his bid for re-election.[4] Herrick had once vetoed a bill for local option (which would have given local governments in Ohio power to abolish saloons and/or alcoholic beverages), thus automatically declaring himself an enemy of the temperance cause. And, as such, Herrick was exactly the type of politician that the League was in business to eliminate.

Herrick was considered a virtual shoe-in for re-election as Governor. He was tremendously popular, a Republican in a primarily Republican state, and his opponent was an utter unknown. When election day arrived, however, Herrick was resoundingly defeated. Wayne B. Wheeler had successfully mobilized his troops, arranging 3,000 public meetings, distributing seventy-five million pages of literature, and conducting a widespread door-to-door campaign against Herrick.[5] Wheeler's victory sent a loud message to politicians everywhere. From that point forward, the power of the Anti-Saloon League was questioned by few, least of all politicians who wished to maintain their careers.

It was not long before the Anti-Saloon League's endeavors moved beyond the mere state and local levels and into the federal one. By 1913, a number of prohibition supporters had been seated in both houses of Congress, leading the drys to put their cause to its first real test. In December of that year, 5,000 members of the Anti-Saloon League, the Women's Christian Temperance Union and various other groups marched on Washington, presenting Congress with petitions calling for a Constitutional Amendment for National Prohibition.[6] The petitions made their way through the governmental labyrinth, surfacing in 1915 as a bill to be voted on by the House of

Wayne B. Wheeler was at the forefront of efforts to make National Prohibition a reality.

Representatives. The vote was 197 in favor, 190 against. Though not the required two-thirds majority, the outcome was a clear indication that National Prohibition was, for the first time, within reach. The Anti-Saloon League soon proclaimed itself "the strongest political organization in the world."[7]

The brewers, of course, did not remain entirely paralyzed as their industry began to disintegrate. Considerable efforts were put forth on various fronts to combat the momentum of the prohibitionists, but none were terribly effective. The brewers simply could not counter the omnipresent perception that anything they said or did was entirely self-serving. After all, drunkenness and the problems of the saloon had been rampant for years while the brewers had done little to abate the menace. The prohibitionists, meanwhile, were seen as moral purists, volunteering their time and energy for the betterment of society. Their motivation was above question. And throughout the duration of the prohibition fight, there was no equally-potent independent group to act on behalf of the "wet" viewpoint. There was no political machine to lobby government, publish literature, raise funds, campaign for political candidates – all of the

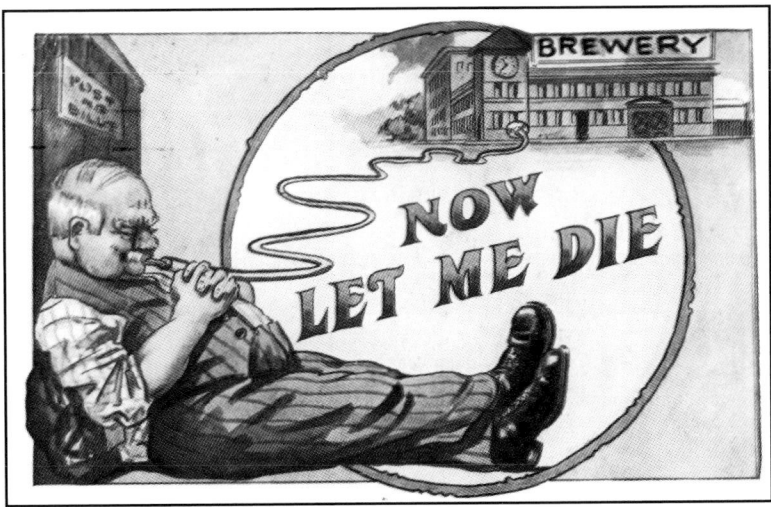

activities in which the drys were so proficient. In the end, the brewers were guilty of being short-sighted and disorganized, and of relying solely on their own devices to save themselves, a strategy that proved embarrassingly ineffective.

A partial explanation for the brewing industry's languid resistance to the dry forces was that many brewers simply did not believe that prohibition was a real possibility. Noisy temperance uprisings had come and gone throughout the nineteenth century, few of which succeeded in doing severe

A fairly typical example of prohibitionist propaganda.

damage to the brewing industry. Editors of the *Western Brewer,* as late as October of 1917, were blindly confident that the industry was in no danger:

> *The signs of the times are encouraging. They indicate that the tide has turned against prohibition. The Philadelphia Sunday Dispatch says the long-looked-for reaction has set in; fanaticism and social regeneration has run its course; there are signs on all sides of a return to national sanity.*[8]

John E. Stang, a director of the Cleveland & Sandusky Brewing Company, agreed with that assessment. Just three months before statewide prohibition was to take effect in Ohio, Stang told a newspaper reporter,

> *I don't believe that the sentiment of the majority is [in favor of prohibition] and if there isn't the sentiment there isn't going to be the fact. Were the prohibition question to be put to the voters of Ohio again what in your opinion would be the verdict? Wet without a doubt, and by a good big margin.*[9]

Stang's comments typified brewers' almost irrational assertion that prohibition would not succeed in destroying their industry.

Despite their lack of a cohesive battle plan, the brewers were not entirely helpless. Their enormous financial resources, their clout in government, their sheer numbers, and their strong trade association (The United States Brewers' Association) were not to be taken lightly. In wielding these weapons, though, the brewers were often seen as bullies trying to manipulate and buy their way out of a predicament which, many felt, was a result of their own doing. A group of Texas brewers, for example, was charged in 1915 with attempting to use funds to influence legislators in

145

favor of the brewery interests. Supporters of the brewers pointed out that they were merely exercising their Constitutional right to "petition the legislature and to combat hostile legislation."[10] In spite of the fact that the Anti-Saloon League was employing identical tactics with few reprisals, widespread publicity of the Texas affair (and others like it) brought a dark cloud over the brewing industry's defense efforts. It was painfully clear that the playing field was anything but level.

For years, the brewers' keynote argument against prohibition was the fact that the brewing industry paid an enormous amount of taxes. Beer taxes supplied as much as twenty percent of the U.S. government's total revenues in some years. There was, according to the brewers, simply no way that government could function without revenues from the brewing industry. Adoption of the Sixteenth Amendment in 1913, which instituted a federal tax on personal income, completely erased what had been the brewers' most compelling defense.[11] The government would no longer be dependent on the brewing industry, and the drys (who, of course, backed the Amendment whole-heartedly) heralded this as a pivotal development. They had objected to taxation of the liquor interests for decades, asserting that it legitimized an illegitimate industry.

As harmful as the Sixteenth Amendment was to brewers, the war in Europe, and its ultimate evolution into World War I, was more damaging still. Anti-German sentiment swept across the country, and brewers (the great majority of whom were of German descent, and devoutly so) were accused of being German sympathizers. Suspicions of a connection between the brewing industry and German propaganda resulted in highly-publicized Senate hearings on the subject.[12] In reality, the brewers were as patriotic as any other group, buying huge quantities of Liberty Bonds, sending their sons off to war, and generally doing what was expected of every American citizen. Nonetheless, negative publicity persisted. The prohibition activists did everything possible to amplify and exploit the brewing industry's deteriorating image. Certain dry factions in Ohio even made it their battle cry that "pro-beer is equivalent to pro-German."[13]

World War I also did much to nullify the aid which the brewing industry would certainly have otherwise received from the German-American Alliance, a group once called "the most formidable foe of the drys."[14] The brewers were large contributors to the Alliance, whose members numbered two million in 1914. The Alliance's strategy was to appeal to the American sense of liberty and freedom, stressing that prohibition took away the individual's right of choice. But as the German population became increasingly persecuted by suspicions of anti-American activities, their cries of freedom and liberty seemed almost sacrilege. In fact, by 1918, Congress had ordered the Alliance to disband – the result of investigations that determined the organization had conducted itself in an unpatriotic manner.[15]

The war-time shortage of food, too, had a tremendous impact. Brewers had always gone to great lengths to promote the fact that beer was made with natural grains, resulting in a wholesome, food-like product. As war-time shortages worsened, the prohibitionists charged that the liquor industries monopolized the nation's grain supply, thereby curtailing the production of *real* food essentials. The government agreed. Distillers were the first to be targeted. In 1917, the government's Food Control Law prohibited the use of any grain in the manufacture of distilled spirits for beverage purposes, effectively putting the distilling industry out of business. And the following year, grains were briefly cut off to brewers.[16] The prohibitionists were at the forefront of these initiatives. After all, shutting down the brewing and distilling industries for the purposes of the war effort was certainly a step in the right direction toward doing away with the trades altogether.

The war-time restrictions, coupled with the fact that a large number of states had enacted their own prohibition laws, rendered the National Prohibition Amendment somewhat academic in many regions. In Ohio, statewide prohibition was adopted in the November elections of 1918 and went into effect May 26, 1919, a full six months prior to National Prohibition.[17] It was Ohio's fourth attempt in five years to enact a statewide prohibition law. In the 1917 effort, it initially appeared as though the drys had won, but the final count of votes showed a slim wet majority of 1,798 with more than a million votes cast. One observer wrote,

> *The Anti-Saloon League, which conducted the campaign for the prohibition amendment, was not willing to concede the election when they seemingly had victory within their grasp. The Anti-Saloon League forces had spent many times the amount of money that the opposition had to spend. They had worked hard and defeat was a bitter pill for them to swallow, so bitter, in fact, that they almost at once raised the cry of "fraud," and threatened to contest the election if the wets won...The fact that this is the third defeat should convince them that the people of Ohio do not want prohibition, and should deter them from forcing another election upon the state for several years to come.*[18]

That interpretation, of course, proved false the following year, when Ohio's brewers were plunged into statewide prohibition.

"One-Half of One Percent"

When the Eighteenth Amendment was ratified in 1919, there were 1,217 licensed breweries in America. For the great majority of brewery owners, the future looked bleak. Most had not sufficiently prepared themselves for the possibility of prohibition. Indeed, many simply sold their plants and equipment at a fraction of their original investments and never looked back. Others, however, were determined to continue in business in new fields.

The most common alternative for brewers was the manufacture of low-alcohol cereal beverages, commonly called "near beer." The only required modification to the brewery was the addition of a de-alcoholizing machine, which reduced the alcohol level of the regular beer to the legal one-half of one percent by volume (pre-prohibition beer contained as much as seven or eight percent alcohol). Many brewers had already perceived a demand for low-alcohol brews long before prohibition. In 1917, one source counted 189 near beers on the market, acknowledging that its list was probably incomplete.[19] A number of factors stimulated early production of near beer. Increasing household consumption of beer caused more women to develop a taste for malt beverages. Many, however, disliked the high alcohol content of traditional beer. In addition, as the saloon trade began to crumble under the strain of public disfavor, low-alcohol products opened up new retail outlets for brewers, such as grocery stores, drug stores, soda fountains, and movie theaters. And there was a significant market for near beer in regions which were dry as a result of local option laws.

Near beer was also attractive to brewers before prohibition as it was not taxable as real beer.[20] The federal tax on beer had been raised from $1.00 per barrel to $1.50 in 1914, then doubled to $3.00 per barrel in 1917 as a war measure. It was doubled yet again to $6.00 per barrel in 1919.[21] Near beer, meanwhile, was classified as a soft drink and avoided taxation altogether until 1917, when a mere 1¢ per gallon tax was instituted.[22]

While near beer may have been a reliable supplement to regular beer during the pre-prohibition years, brewers found it terribly difficult to survive solely on the manufacture of low-alcohol products once prohibition was enacted. Near beer simply never gained the degree of popularity that brewers hoped for, due largely to the fact that bootlegged beer was readily available in most regions. Then, too, there was no question that the de-alcoholization process – which consisted of boiling off the access alcohol – compromised the flavor of the finished product. In 1920, brewers produced about 286 million gallons of near beer. By 1932, the number had dwindled to about 85 million gallons.[23]

Nevertheless, brewers by the hundreds turned to the production of near beer at prohibition. Many did so simply because they lacked the capital or the expertise to enter other lines of business. Near beer allowed them to use existing equipment and supplies, employ the knowledge and experience of the existing staff, and retain many of the same customers and channels of distribution. Simply stated, it was the path of least resistance, particularly for those brewers who had steadfastly denied that prohibition would become a reality and now found themselves unprepared for the new challenges.

A brewer's pre-prohibition success in the beer business was not necessarily an indication of his ability to do well in the near beer arena. For example, the Leisy brewery, for decades Cleveland's largest-producing brewery, did not fare well in the cereal beverage market. Since 1917, the Leisys had been producing a near beer called Bevera, promoted with the cheerful motto: "Laugh and grow fat. Drink and keep well."[24] But, like most near beer products, Bevera was unable to compete with the illegal flow of real beer, not to mention the saturation of countless other cereal beverages struggling to survive. In 1923, after failure of the brand had become obvious, about 6,000 barrels of not yet de-alcoholized Bevera were poured into the sewer as prohibition agents looked on.[25] Stripped of its equipment (which was sold to breweries in Canada, Mexico and Cuba), the Leisy brewery sat idle for the remainder of prohibition.

Likewise, the Diebolt Brewing Company's venture into the near beer trade was short-lived. Diebolt's Perlex was introduced in May of 1919 just as the sale of real beer became illegal under Ohio's prohibition amendment. But efforts to

Despised by brewmasters and beer drinkers, the de-alcoholizing machine removed the alcohol (and a significant amount of the flavor) from beer, thus creating "near beer." This particular unit served the Pilsener Brewing Company.

Prohibition agents witness the destruction of 6,000 barrels of beer at the Leisy brewery in 1923.

stimulate sales of the new brand seem to have been somewhat half-hearted. Little, if any, advertising was undertaken. After four years of fledgling sales, the Diebolts quit the beverage business altogether in 1923.[26]

However, for many, confidence in the future of near beer was surprisingly high. The Cleveland & Sandusky Brewing Company, under the changed name of the Cleveland-Sandusky Company, was initially so optimistic about its cereal beverage business that the company believed the saloon trade could be salvaged with near beer:

Social features that attracted thousands to the saloons will be maintained as far as possible. Mahogany bars will remain, with white-aproned men serving cereal beverages, and the larger places will have orchestras, professional entertainers, pool tables, lunch counters and reading rooms. The places will be available for religious services and other public meetings. Classes in naturalization will also be held.[27]

Of course, the notion that saloons without alcohol would draw customers proved false, particularly as speakeasies flourished virtually unchallenged throughout the city.

Nevertheless, the Cleveland-Sandusky Company, under the guidance of president Theodore Fishel and vice-president Oscar J. Fishel, carved out a respectable existence in the manufacture of cereal beverages during much of prohibition. In 1920, the firm's offices in the American Trust Building were moved to the newly-renamed Gold Bond Building adjacent to the old Schlather brewery on Carroll Avenue. The Schlather plant, as well as the Fishel brewery on East 55th Street and the Cleveland brewery on Ansel Avenue, were put to work making near beer and soft drinks. The Gold Bond brand, as in the old days, remained the company's feature product. In an effort to console beer drinkers mourning the loss of real beer, ads for

Two of the Cleveland-Sandusky Company's prohibition brands.

Kuebler's MALT TONIC

ALCOHOL 2% BY VOL.

A NUTRITIOUS MALT TONIC, REFRESHING AND INVIGORATING, MADE FROM CHOICE MALT AND IMPORTED BOHEMIAN HOPS.

THE CLEVELAND-SANDUSKY CO.

NON-TAXABLE

"Bola"

INVIGORATING BEVERAGE

A HEALTHFUL NUTRITIOUS

MIN. CONTENTS 12 FL OZ

SERVE COLD

The Cleveland and Sandusky Company

CONTAINS LESS THAN ½ OF 1% OF ALCOHOL BY VOLUME

Bob Kay Collection

149

the new Gold Bond urged, "Life is still worth living – and you can have Gold Bond...just as much a good old pal as ever – but now made to conform to existing regulations."[28] Other cereal beverages manufactured by the company over the years included Bola, Starlight Brew, Fifty-Fifty, and New York Special Brew.

The company's operations in Sandusky were kept active as well. Although the Kuebeler plant was closed, the Stang brewery – doing business as the Crystal Rock Products Company – began making near beer once statewide prohibition took effect in 1919. The new product was sold under the old familiar Crystal Rock name. John E. Stang was quoted as saying, "Yes, we've decided to call it 'Crystal Rock,' for the old beer has made a host of friends and I am going to keep the name alive as long as I am around."[29] After all, a well-known brand name was one of the few assets to which brewers could cling as their industry disintegrated before their eyes. Indeed, those brewers who had succeeded in developing good name recognition for their beers before prohibition were the most likely to redirect their efforts into the production of near beer during prohibition.

Such was certainly the case with the popular P.O.C. brand name, kept alive throughout the dry years by the Pilsener Brewing Company. In fact, few local brewers were as committed to the cereal beverage market as was Pilsener. And success was evident. After six years of prohibition, the Pilsener Brewing Company still maintained its own distribution depots in Ashtabula, Mentor and Lorain.[30] The P.O.C. cereal beverages were handled by independent dealers throughout Ohio. As late as 1930, the company was producing no less than *seven* different brands of near beer.

The old Excelsior brewery, reorganized as the Eilert Beverage Company upon prohibition, also had great confidence in the future of near beer. Brewery founder Jacob F. Haller sold the works to Henry F. Eilert in 1919, but Haller remained involved in the new company as its vice president. Eilert, a German immigrant, was familiar to Cleveland's brewing trade, having worked at several local breweries before prohibition. And Eilert was well-

Above: Pilsener brewmaster Frank Knopp draws a glass of not-yet-de-alcoholized beer from an aging vat in 1932.

Right: A 1932 billboard. Although Knopp's hand "never lost its skill," the brewmaster was less than happy with his prohibition-era brew. He called his de-alcoholized beer "spoiled beer."

seasoned in other beverage fields, too. For years, he operated a wholesale wine and liquor establishment on Lorain Avenue near the West Side Market.[31] Prohibition had put him, like the brewers, out of business. Now in his new venture, Eilert brewed a number of different near beers, among them Muenchner Double Brew, Eilert's Clev-Ale, and Golden Seal. The latter was named for Jacob Haller's pre-prohibition beer of the same name. The new Golden Seal was advertised as being "Nearest To The Old Famous."[32]

Eilert's cereal beverages were distinguished from the competition somewhat by the fact that Eilert did not employ any type of de-alcoholization process. Rather, his products were brewed using a method which produced virtually no alcohol in the beer, thus eliminating the need for flavor-damaging de-alcoholization. Henry F. Eilert flatly asserted, "We don't make near beer; it's real beer."[33] This point, of course, was vigorously promoted. Whether the consumer shared Eilert's enthusiasm over that distinction is an open question.

Another Cleveland brewery which put its faith in the near beer business upon prohibition was the Standard Brewing Company. The brands included Standard Special, Old Bohemia Brew, and the paradoxically-titled Full Weight.[34] However, by 1922, the company was taking a new direction. The name was changed to the Standard Food Products Company and efforts got under way to involve the firm in a variety of food-related businesses, among them dairy products, meat packing, frozen foods and soft drinks.[35] By 1930, the company's cereal beverages were low on its list of products.

Indeed, by the late 1920s, most brewers who were still pinning their survival strategy on the manufacture of near beer were living a precarious existence. Many, it seemed, merely sought to stay afloat as long as possible, keeping their plants operative in hopes that the repeal of prohibition might soon appear on the horizon. The Cleveland Home Brewing Company, for example, barely survived prohibition making a marginally-successful near beer called Yako, first introduced in 1917 and advertised as "Cleveland's Favorite Beverage."[36] Liquid malt and ice were also manufactured. Ernst W. Mueller nursed the company through the lean years until his death in 1931. Herman Schmidt, one of the company's initial investors, took over after Mueller's death. Schmidt was succeeded by Otto W. Beltz, and later by Ernst W. Mueller's son, Omar E. Mueller.

The Forest City Brewing Company, doing business as the Forest City New Process Company, eked out a living making its cleverly-titled X-L-N-T De-Alcoholized Beer. The company also owned the local franchise for Zem-Zem grape juice.[37] However, shrinking profits finally caused president Frank E. Albl, son of the brewery's founder, to halt operations in 1930.

Nearly all Cleveland brewers ultimately abandoned the production of near beer during prohibition. Of the city's nine breweries in operation in 1919, only one (the Pilsener brewery) was still making near beer in 1933.[38] That aside, near beer did play a crucial role in the sustenance of the brewing industry during the dry years. While sales were rarely what brewers

Bottling at the Standard Brewing Company.

hoped, many were able to negotiate passable profits. Thus, near beer helped to keep the brewing industry from complete collapse during the dry years. It kept breweries active, equipment intact, and brewmasters employed.

Entering New Fields

The manufacture of soft drinks was another common alternative for brewers at prohibition. The typical appliances in the brewery – the vats, the piping, the bottling equipment, etc. – accommodated the manufacture of all types of sodas and juices. For brewers who elected to produce near beer, the addition of soft drinks was a natural extension. The profit margins, however, were significantly lower for soft drinks than they had been for beer, rendering distant shipping too expensive. (Even today, most soft drink manufacturers ship their product in concentrate form, and bottle it locally.) Sales, therefore, were typically confined to local markets, limiting the potential for growth. Rather than introducing their own line of soft drinks, many former brewers engaged in franchise agreements with nationally-advertised brands. Brewers purchased the concentrate from the manufacturer, transformed it into the drinkable product, bottled it, and distributed it in their territory. But with countless brewers now turning to the soft drink industry for survival, the market was soon flooded with new products, and only the most aggressive survived.

A number of Cleveland brewers produced soft drinks during prohibition. Perhaps most active was the Cleveland-Sandusky Company, offering no less than six different lines of soft drinks over the years. The Leisy Brewing Company, although it put the lion's share of its efforts behind the Bevera cereal beverage, briefly tried its hand at the carbonated soft drink business. Production of Leisy's root beer, ginger ale, orangeade and loganberry ended when the company closed its doors in 1923.[39] The Eilert Beverage Company also marketed a wide variety of sodas, among them Eilert's Pep and EBCO Cola.[40] The Pilsener Brewing Company set up a subsidiary – the P.O.C. Products Company – to produce P.O.C. Ginger Ale and two franchise brands, Dr. Swett's Root Beer and Parfay Cola.[41] The Standard Brewing Company found success with its Creadon's Ginger Ale, named for brewery founder Stephen S. Creadon after his death in 1921.

Before closing in 1923, the Leisy brewery produced a full line of soft drinks, including Leisy's Old Fashion Root Beer.

The making and selling of ice was a popular activity for brewers during prohibition. Most had invested in ice-making facilities to serve the needs of their breweries during the wet years, and some had already been involved in the ice business for decades when prohibition came. The Diebolt Brewing Company, for instance, had been operating its Cleveland Hygiea Ice Company on the brewery grounds since 1908. And the business continued well into the dry years. With a number of major rail lines running just behind the plant, the ice company developed a substantial wholesale trade, selling large quantities to local ice distributors.

The sale of ice directly to households was also an important aspect of many brewers'

LEISY'S Old Fashion ROOT BEER
THE ISAAC LEISY COMPANY CLEVELAND, OHIO.

Bob Kay Collection

152

The Cleveland-Sandusky Company's exhibit at a soft drink trade show during prohibition.

survival during prohibition. It created a sort of symbiotic relationship between the brewer's various product lines. Households which were already receiving daily ice deliveries might as well obtain, for example, their weekly supply of soft drinks at the same time. This type of "bundling" added convenience for the customer while increasing sales for the brewer. With that logic in mind, many brewers branched out into other lines of business which involved routine deliveries to residences. In 1928, the Pilsener Brewing Company was reorganized as the Pilsener Ice, Fuel & Beverage Company.[42] Coal and other fuels for the home were marketed right alongside ice and beverages. The Standard Brewing Company marketed a variety of household food items in addition to its extensive ice business. The Cleveland Home Brewing Company, aside from its manufacture of near beer and ice, made liquid malt for households. Liquid malt, also known as malt syrup, was a necessity for home brewers (the Volstead Act, which specified exactly what was and was not legal under the Prohibition Amendment, did not forbid the making of beer in the home for private consumption).[43]

One field to which a significant number of brewers turned at prohibition was that of real estate. Their extensive purchase of saloons throughout the late 1800s and early 1900s transformed many brewers into bona fide experts in the valuation, purchase, management, leasing and sale of real estate. Most brewers still retained large holdings of former saloon properties which could be reconditioned for new uses. Indeed, of those brewers who managed to maintain their fortunes well into the dry years, most accomplished it

Before and after. The Diebolt brewery was demolished in 1928 to make way for the rail approach to the Union Terminal. The Diebolt brothers fought a five-year court battle to save the structure, but finally lost.

through the business of real estate.

The Diebolt brothers – Anthony, Mathias and Joseph – were among the many former brewers who engaged themselves in real estate activities. Somewhat ironically, the Diebolts' Pittsburgh Avenue brewery and ice plant (their single most valuable property) was taken away from them by millionaire real estate developers Oris P. and Mantis J. Van Sweringen. Builders of Cleveland's Union Terminal (Terminal Tower), the Van Sweringens sought to take control of the Diebolt property by eminent domain so the land could be cleared to make way for the rail approach to the Terminal. In the end, the Diebolt brothers lost their five-year court battle with the Van Sweringens, and the brewery was razed in 1928.[44]

With the brewery gone, the Diebolts turned their attention entirely to their real estate firm, located first in the Keith Building and later in the Hanna Building. Business was good during the early years. When Mathias Diebolt passed away in 1934, his estate was valued at $1.7 million, the bulk of which represented his one-third ownership of the real estate company.[45] However, the prolonged Depression of the 1930s and the onset of war during the following decade conspired to sabotage the Diebolts' success in real estate. Anthony Diebolt died in 1940, and Joseph Diebolt followed in 1946. The latter, who had inherited both of his brothers' estates, held assets valued at just $20,000 at his death.[46]

The Gunds in Cleveland

The Gund family, like the Diebolts, involved themselves in real estate during prohibition. But unlike the Diebolts, the Gund family was destined to build and maintain great wealth for many years to come – more so, in fact, than any other brewing family in Cleveland. Ironically, the Gunds were the only local brewers who elected not to try their luck in the soft drink and near beer business. Rather, as soon as statewide prohibition was adopted, the Gunds sold their inventory of beer to the Pilsener Brewing Company and turned their attention to real estate and other pursuits.

George F. Gund II and his mother, Mrs. Anna M. Gund, set up the Gund Realty Company in 1922 and ran it from the former brewery offices on Davenport Avenue. Gund was president and secretary, Mrs. Gund was vice president, and Louis F. Roether (who had been an officer of the brewery in years past) was secretary.[47] The company owned and managed a number properties in the downtown area and throughout Greater Cleveland. Many had been former saloon properties.

However, George F. Gund II had found another pursuit to which he would ultimately direct the bulk of his attention during prohibition. In 1919, he purchased the Kaffee Hag Corporation, a small producer of coffee, for $130,000.[48] What attracted Gund to the company was its exclusive process for removing caffeine from coffee without compromising the flavor, the first accomplishment of its kind. Initially, Gund marketed his new decaffeinated coffee under the name Night Cap, later changing it to Kaffee Hag (German for *Coffee Grove*) to better identify with the corporation name. Already in 1921, the company – doing business out of the old brewery – was capitalized at $1 million dollars and was operating branch facilities in Chicago and New York.[49]

George F. Gund II

The flourishing Kaffee Hag brand caught the attention of W. K. Kellogg, head of Battlecreek, Michigan's famous Kellogg Company. Kellogg's focus on health and nutrition had been the niche that built the company into one of the world's largest food manufacturers. For decades, Kellogg had experimented with a variety of products which would allow coffee-drinkers to avoid its harmful drug, caffeine. In 1927, Gund sold the Kaffee Hag Corporation and its valuable patents for the decaffeination process to the Kellogg Company for $10 million, paid mostly in Kellogg stock. Gund subsequently joined Kellogg management as vice president of sales. He left a few years later amidst reports of internal disagreements as to the future of the Kaffee Hag brand. Kellogg eventually sold the product to General Foods, which renamed it Sanka.[50]

George F. Gund II's enormous stock holdings in the Kellogg Company (which split five-for-one in 1936, earning Gund $850,000 in dividends) were the basis for the Gund family fortune. Gund used his earnings to invest in a wide array of businesses, among them the Cleveland Trust Company, Ohio's largest bank. In 1937, Gund was elected to the bank's board of directors and, in 1941, he was made president. For the next twenty-five years, Gund remained at the head of Cleveland Trust and was its single largest stockholder. Sitting on the boards of more than thirty corporations over the years, Gund was long regarded as the wealthiest man in Cleveland.

Despite his tremendous fortune, Gund's public persona was one of thrift and frugality. He drove what one observer called "a battered old Buick" and clung to a favorite overcoat well beyond its best days. Son George F. Gund III recalled,

> *And yet when we were at the Ritz-Carlton in Boston for Thanksgiving he'd make sure every light was on in every room. He said, 'I have stock in Con Edison and I want them working for us while we're having dinner.*[51]

What most did not know, including his own children, was that Gund was a philanthropist at heart. Even prior to establishing the George Gund Foundation in 1951, Gund gave generously, but anonymously, to scores of charities and institutions. Among his favorites were the Cleveland Museum of Art, the Salvation Army, Harvard University, Trinity Cathedral and the Cleveland Foundation. At the time of his death in 1966, George F. Gund II held assets valued at more than $600 million, the largest estate ever recorded in Cleveland.[52] He left much of his wealth to the George Gund Foundation, which continues today to support hundreds of social, educational and artistic endeavors in Greater Cleveland.

Several of Gund's children inherited their father's entrepreneurial spirit. Of the siblings, perhaps most in the public eye are George III and Gordon Gund, owners of the Cleveland Cavaliers NBA basketball team since 1983. The brothers have been involved in professional sports for decades, first buying the California Seals hockey team in 1976 and moving them to Cleveland. Renaming the team the Cleveland Barons, the brothers hoped to resurrect the glorious past of Cleveland's 1937-1973 hockey team of the same name. But poor game attendance and lukewarm fan interest caused the Gunds to merge the team with the Minnesota North Stars in 1978, and the Barons passed into oblivion once again. The Gunds later sold their interest in the North Stars to buy another hockey team, the San Jose Sharks, which they still own today.

The Gund children – George III, Gordon, Agnes, Graham, Geoffrey and Louise – share a family fortune which was estimated in 1996 at $2.1 billion by *Forbes Magazine*.[53]

Chapter Eight

Happy Days Are Here Again

Almost from the very moment the Eighteenth Amendment was ratified, efforts were under way to repeal National Prohibition. The Association Against the Prohibition Amendment (AAPA) was formed in Washington D.C. in 1919. Its members were comprised mainly of big industry, which believed that prohibition would have a harmful impact on American labor, one group which was particularly disinclined to give up its beer and whiskey. Undoubtedly more important to the AAPA's members was their prediction that the government's loss of revenue from liquor industries would result in higher taxes for big corporations. By 1926, the AAPA had enlisted companies like General Motors and Standard Oil to support their cause.[1]

But the loudest objections to prohibition stemmed from the rash of corruption and violent crime which commenced simultaneously with the law's adoption. It was clear at a very early date that the Prohibition Bureau was destined to fail

miserably in its efforts to enforce the Volstead Act – the set of laws which actually defined prohibition. Congress initially appropriated the grossly insufficient sum of $5 million dollars annually for operation of the Prohibition Bureau, indicating the miscalculated belief that prohibition would be met with widespread patriotic obedience. By 1932, the budget was increased to $16 million, but was still far short of what was needed.[2] Bootlegging, speakeasies, organized crime and political corruption proliferated in cities across America.

Cleveland, certainly as much as any city, suffered the unbridled flow of illegal beer and liquor throughout prohibition. In 1931, one group counted 2,545 speakeasies in Cleveland compared with just 1,028 saloons in the city in 1919.[3] The illicit drinking spots were supplied with liquor from organized crime syndicates. Names like Lonardo, Porello, Milano, and others were synonymous with bootlegging in Cleveland. Gangs such as the notorious Mayfield Road Mob

Left: A Cleveland cop poses with his "catch" – a makeshift brewery – in 1927. This particular scheme involved pasting Canadian beer labels on bottles of Cleveland-made beer in order to throw authorities off the trail.

Below: Confiscating a rail car full of Canadian beer at Cleveland's Terminal Warehouse in 1930.

fought viciously with other mobsters for monopoly of the city's immense liquor trade. Some 100 violent deaths were attributed to gang warfare in Cleveland during the dry years.[4] And the authorities were either helpless to gain control over the situation or, in many cases, were well-paid *not* to do so.

The means by which bootleggers disguised and moved their product were often quite clever. In 1922, two Cleveland barbers were convicted and sent to prison when it was discovered that their "Love Me Dearie" hair tonic was actually pure grain alcohol. The name of the front company, the Million Dollar Hair Tonic Company, took on a special significance when authorities determined that the barbers had circulated just about $1 million worth of booze before being caught.[5]

This flagrant lawlessness motivated a variety of factions to campaign aggressively for significant modification of the Volstead Act or outright repeal of the Eighteenth Amendment. Among the groups which pounded the pavement against the evils of prohibition were the Women's Organization for National Prohibition Reform, the Moderation League, the Crusaders, and others. (It was ironic that the driving energies behind many such repeal organizations were women; it, of course, had been mainly women who first gave life to the anti-alcohol movement in the mid-nineteenth century.) As the Anti-Saloon League had so adroitly demonstrated, political office was the only effective tool for real change as concerned prohibition. And so, those interested in bringing about an end to the Eighteenth Amendment focused their efforts squarely on political channels. The emergence in 1931 of presidential candidate Franklin D. Roosevelt and his strong pro-repeal platform was a Godsend for anti-prohibitionists everywhere.

However, even before the president-elect took office in 1933, the legislative foundation upon which prohibition rested was beginning to give way. The government's dire need to generate new revenue during the Depression, coupled with the nation's epidemic unemployment, was forcing legislators to see prohibition with new eyes by the latter part of 1932. Under the Volstead Act, it was left entirely up to Congress to define what constituted an intoxicating beverage. At the

158

time the Volstead Act was being drafted, it was determined that beverages containing more than one-half of one percent of alcohol by volume would be classified as intoxicating. But the Congressional power to alter that figure at will gave that body the ability to, in effect, nullify prohibition without an outright repeal of the Eighteenth Amendment. In March of 1933, Congress did just that. In the interest of jobs and revenue, the Cullen Bill was passed, making legal the manufacture and sale of beer containing 3.2 percent alcohol by weight on April 7, 1933.[6] The bill also imposed a federal tax of $5 per barrel of beer, plus a license fee of $1,000 annually per brewery. For all intents and purposes, the dry era was over. Later in the year, National Prohibition was quietly and uneventfully repealed by ratification of the Twenty-First Amendment to the U.S. Constitution.

April 6, 1933 was known across the country as New Beer's Eve, as 3.2 percent beer became legal at 12:01 a.m. on April 7th. In cities from coast to coast, anxious crowds gathered outside breweries, restaurants and taverns hoping to get a taste of legal beer for the first time in thirteen years. Within the first twenty-four hours beer was back, rejoicing Americans consumed an amazing total of 1.5 million barrels of beer.[7]

Clevelanders were denied the bells and whistles of New Beer's Eve by Mayor Ray T. Miller's decree that no beer be sold until daybreak on April 7th.[8] But the urge for mass revelry did not, by any means, go unfulfilled in Cleveland. In fact, local beer drinkers began their celebrating back on March 31st when the Ohio Senate passed the Ackerman Bill, a piece of legislation which paralleled the federal Cullen Bill. That evening, State Senator Joseph N. Ackerman (champion of the state's beer bill) arrived home via the Union Terminal train station. More than 3,000 turned out to greet the man-of-the-hour and take part in the fireworks, speeches, and parades which filled Public

On March 31, 1933, some 3,000 Clevelanders gathered on Public Square to welcome home State Senator Joseph N. Ackerman, champion of Ohio's beer bill.

Square and downtown streets well into the night. The exultant crowd lifted Ackerman onto its shoulders and carried him through the terminal, cheering wildly as they went.[9] Ironically, the first mass celebration of beer recorded in Cleveland history included no beer at all.

New Beer's Day, April 7th, was a different story entirely, as thousands quaffed 3.2 percent beer in crowded drinking spots throughout the city. None of the beer, however, was Cleveland-brewed. Local brewers announced that they would not have any beer ready for consumption for several weeks:

> TO THE PUBLIC...The undersigned brewers are the owners of plants which were established before the advent of prohibition. In the past we sold a quality product; we pledge ourselves to sell only a quality product in the future. Sufficient time has not elapsed between the passage of the Federal and Ohio laws to permit us to lawfully manufacture and age our product; WE ARE NOT WILLING TO PUT OUR BEER ON SALE ON APRIL 7th BECAUSE IT WOULD THEN BE AN INFERIOR PRODUCT DUE TO LACK OF AGING. At an early date Cleveland-made legalized beer will be available for sale, and an announcement will be made in the newspapers as to deliveries.

The Cleveland Home Brewing Company   Forest City Brewery, Inc.
The Cleveland & Sandusky Brewing Company   The Pilsener Brewing Co.
The Eilert Brewing Company   The Standard Brewing Co.[10]

Left: A truckload of beer – the first in Cleveland – arrives from the Renner brewery in Akron, April 7, 1933.

Above: L. E. Christopher, right, receives the first case of beer from Nathan Rosa, manager of the Miller-Becker Bottling Company.

Cleveland wholesalers scrambled to secure shipments of beer from outside sources. The George J. Renner Brewing Company in Akron – one of the first breweries in the state to turn out beer – shipped several thousand cases of its old famous Grossvater Lager to Cleveland. Beverage Distributors, Inc., a local beer distributor, had a shipment flown in by airplane from the Atlas Brewing Company in Chicago. Another distributor sent fifteen trucks to Pittsburgh to collect 15,000 cases of Tech Beer.[11] (Many such "beer convoys" traveling the country's highways were equipped with armed guards for protection against hijackers.) Still, in many restaurants and taverns, the demand far outweighed the supply:

An airplane full of Chicago-brewed beer arrives at Cleveland Airport, April 7, 1933.

At 5:25 p.m. at Otto Moser's, 50 faces dropped, and pleasant conversation changed to a chorus of groans. The stream of amber liquid from the spigot had dwindled to dripping foam. "That's all of it," said the bartender. "We can't get any more for a while." The 50 men looked very sorry indeed. "We've got a half-barrel of near beer left in the cellar," the bartender declared. "We'll have it connected up in a couple of minutes." Three men stayed. They had ordered sandwiches.[12]

Cleveland Breweries Awaken

Those brewers who had been engaged in making near beer when 3.2 percent beer became legal were in the best position to quickly supply the overwhelming demand. For most such brewers, turning out real beer was simply a matter of shutting off the de-alcoholizing unit at the end of the production process. As Cleveland's lone producer of near beer in 1933, the Pilsener Brewing Company was the first local brewery to get its product on the market. But, long-time brewmaster Frank Knopp (who called prohibition "wasted years" in the practice of his art) refused to hurry his inaugural brew. It was not until Thursday, May 4th – almost a full month after legalization – that the first P.O.C. Beer rolled out of the West 65th & Clark Avenue brewery. At the head of the Pilsener company were many of the same Bohemian families who had controlled the brewery in pre-prohibition days: Adolph F. Humel, son of one of the brewery's founders, was president; Fred J. Anders, whose father was a company officer in earlier days, was vice president,; and Frank Kratochvil was secretary, having filled that office since well before prohibition.[13]

Following several weeks behind the introduction of P.O.C. was the Cleveland Home Brewing Company's release of its Clevelander Beer on May 26th. The Clevelander brand was a product of the Gund Brewing Company before prohibition, but Cleveland Home president Otto W. Beltz felt the name's local pride attributes justified its resurrection by him. Meister Brau, a dark beer, was introduced the following week. Each of these brands, however, ultimately ranked behind what became the company's cornerstone product, Black Forest Beer. Named for the renowned

Not long after the return of 3.2 percent beer was announced, artist Ted Voyse took these photos inside the Pilsener Brewing Company.

Black Forest woodlands of the German Rhineland, Cleveland Home's new brand was reportedly brewed using a formula developed in Bavaria in the eleventh century.[14] In October of 1933, Black Forest Beer made its unique debut when it was taste-tested by the female cast of *Vanities* playing at the Palace Theatre. The unveiling was declared a resounding success: "These girls know their beers, and if Cleveland folks react as enthusiastically as the girls did, the brewery will have a difficult time keeping up with demand."[15]

The Standard Brewing Company had its Erin Brew Beer on sale by the end of May, despite the fact that production of near beer had been halted at the plant several years earlier. Like all other brewers, Standard struggled to keep pace with the initial demand for beer. The company hired fifty new employees during the first week of legalization and added 100 more over the following month.[16]

The Eilert Brewing Company at West 32nd and Sackett was among the most anxious to get its brew on the market once Congress ruled 3.2 percent beer legal. As early as December of 1932, owner Henry F. Eilert (who came out of retirement to re-open his brewery) was already soliciting orders for beer in anticipation of an early lift to the restrictions. As one of only two Cleveland brewers holding a brewing permit for near beer, Eilert intended to have some 30,000 cases of real beer ready for release the minute the law allowed.[17] However, the plan was thwarted by a handful of obstacles, among them delays in governmental permission to issue new stock, as well as a law suit brought by investors in the former Eilert Beverage Company. Nevertheless, the new Eilert's Supreme Lager made its way onto the market by June 10, 1933 and the company was soon reporting healthy sales.[18]

The Cleveland & Sandusky Brewing Company's plant on East 55th Street was put back into operation in 1934.

The Cleveland & Sandusky Brewing Company experienced difficulty readying itself for legalization of beer. Completely depleted of cash from several years of shrinking profits, the company sought unsuccessfully to borrow funds to refurbish one of its brewing plants. Finally, president Hascal C. Lang made an appeal to the company's stockholders and bondholders, informing them that bankruptcy was imminent unless the necessary capital for re-entry into the beer business could be raised.[19] The investors acceded, and production of beer got under way. The Stang plant in Sandusky was the first of the company's breweries to be put back on line. On July 13, 1933, it was proudly announced that Gold Bond Beer shipped from Sandusky was ready for sale in Cleveland.[20] Within a year, Crystal Rock Beer and a new brand, Old Timer's Ale, were on the market as well. The company's Fishel brewery on East 55th Street (the last new brewery to be built in

Cleveland before prohibition) resumed operations in 1934. Under the slightly modified name of the Cleveland-Sandusky Brewing Corporation, the company would operate its East 55th Street brewery for many years to come.

A New Environment

By the end of summer of 1933, seven of Cleveland's old breweries had been put back into operation and were pumping out beer as fast as their brewmasters would allow. For local beer drinkers, the days of old were back. But, for brewers, times had changed dramatically. Very little, except maybe the beer itself, resembled the pre-prohibition days. Perhaps the most pronounced difference was the seemingly unending degree of governmental regulation of brewing immediately after repeal. The widespread crime associated with illegal trafficking of alcohol during the Volstead years gave rise to the notion that the beer and liquor trades, though now legalized, required heavy monitoring and control by the government. Then, too, there still remained a large segment of the population which did not favor the repeal of prohibition; tighter governmental control helped to quell the opposition. The fact that prohibition was repealed largely to create new government revenue also promoted a strict regulatory environment. Virtually every aspect of the brewing business became scrutinized and regulated. Sizes of containers, information on beer labels, types and locations of advertising, beer delivery procedures, and countless other issues were all controlled by governmental regulation.[22]

Heavy taxation was another new factor for brewers. For the better part of half a century before prohibition, brewers paid a federal tax of just $1 per barrel. It was only during times of war that the tax was temporarily increased. But the $5-per-barrel tax which Congress imposed upon legalization of 3.2 percent beer was fully intended to be a permanent fixture. State taxes were something new as well. Between 1933 and 1939, the average state tax on beer was $1.17 per barrel.[23] Despite the hardships of heavy taxes, the brewers typically raised few objections. After all, a well-taxed return to beer was better than no return at all.

As the initial fervor over repeal began to subside, brewers came to the realization that the Depression was having a severe impact on sales. Nationwide beer consumption in 1934 (the first full year after repeal) was about thirty-seven million barrels, compared to an average of sixty-two million barrels annually between 1910 and 1917.[24] To stimulate sales, resurrection of the pre-Volstead mainstay – the 5¢ draught beer – was the goal of both brewers and retailers. Wholesale beer prices, however, were greatly affected

For brewers, the post-repeal "honeymoon" did not last. Crowded taverns and booming beer sales soon gave way to slim profits and mounting costs of operation.

The Brewery That Never Was

With the repeal of National Prohibition in 1933 came a flurry of entrepreneurial interest in the brewing industry. After all, a little capital and a lot of ambition was all it took to start a brewery and to cash in on what many expected to be a gold mine industry. A great number of such ventures never found their way off the drawing board. The Old Tavern Brewing Company of Cleveland, while getting a little farther than some, nonetheless ranks among those would-be beer-making enterprises which never quite made it to fruition.

Charles J. Koepke, a former director of the Cleveland Home Brewing Company, was the mastermind behind the Old Tavern Brewing Company. By June of 1934, Koepke

had found a site for his brewery, signed a ten-year lease for the property, hired a brewmaster, and determined that his product would be called "Old Tavern Ale."[21] The brewery was to be housed in the old Brown-Graves Company building at 1804 East 55th Street. A reported $100,000 was to be spent equipping the plant, and brewmaster John Ereshe was to oversee the project. No beer – only ale – was to be brewed. In anticipation of Old Tavern Ale's imminent release, an advertisement was placed in the 1934 Cleveland Directory (above).

However, for reasons which were curiously well-concealed, Old Tavern Ale never made its grand introduction, and no brewery was ever outfitted at 1804 East 55th Street. In the end, the venture amounted to nothing more than an unfulfilled vision and a couple of prematurely-placed advertisements.

by the federal and state taxes. Although several taverns and restaurants offered 5¢ beer during the first few days after legalization, retailers quickly learned that profits could not be sustained at that price. As a result, most were forced to charge 10¢ for draught and 15¢ for bottled beer. By 1937, confidence in the return of 5¢ beer was waning: "Everyone hopes that one of these days it will be possible to purchase a real 5¢ glass of beer – but that day is a long way off."[25]

In Cleveland, the price issue came to a head in September of 1933, when the city's brewers engaged in a brief but heated price war. The Cleveland Brewers Association had been formed earlier in the year to help establish local beer prices. Communications among the members broke down when the Pilsener Brewing Company suddenly cut its price from $16 per barrel to $14. Other brewers retaliated by cutting prices to $12 per barrel. Some made the mistake of announcing in advance that their price would be dropped the following day, only to find that rival brewers had gotten to their customers the night before with the same price. Within a few weeks, all of the city's brewers were locked at $12 per barrel, a price which was reportedly about $2 below cost. Finally, a truce was called and the normal prices were re-instated. But the damage was severe. One brewer estimated his losses at $2,000 per day during the price war.[26]

Weighing heavily on the price issue was the government's elimination of brewery control over retail channels after prohibition. In earlier days, brewers were somewhat shielded from price competition by outright ownership of saloons. The saloonkeeper was a "captive" customer in that situation, thus alleviating the brewer's need to undercut the competition. But with saloons and taverns now entirely outside of their control, brewers were thrown into hand-to-hand combat for the retailers' business.

Another new problem facing the brewers was that of labor unions. Although unions certainly existed in the breweries before prohibition, a new issue had quietly developed during the dry years. While the brewers' union laid essentially dormant during prohibition, the Brotherhood of Teamsters had gained enormous strength due largely to industry's growing dependence on the transportation of goods by automobile. Thus, when breweries across the

Strikers outside of the Cleveland-Sandusky Brewing Corp.'s East 55th Street brewery, 1935.

country began to re-open, the question of which union had jurisdiction over brewery deliverymen and drivers quickly escalated into a heated conflict. The International Union of United Brewery Workers, based in Cincinnati, was one of the few *vertical* industrial unions still operating in America. As such, it faced a large degree of opposition from trade-specific unions, which believed that a separate union should exist for each different trade within a given factory. The American Federation of Labor, as well as the Cleveland Federation of Labor, shared this view. Both organizations ruled in favor of the teamsters in their disagreement with the brewers' union.

Cleveland ultimately became the focal point of the nationwide jurisdictional dispute between the teamsters and the brewery workers. After two years of violent clashes and frequent truck blockades at the city's breweries, 250 members of the Cleveland Local #17 of the brewery workers union went on strike on April 19, 1935. The local union had consistently refused to accept the ruling that drivers should be under teamster control. The strike was called when the last of Cleveland's brewery drivers transferred their membership to the teamsters. Throughout the debate, brewery owners asserted their neutrality. As secretary of the Cleveland Brewers Association, John W. Marshall (former mayor of Cleveland) commented that, "The employers are the innocent third parties to this dispute and are caught in the middle, where they can do nothing about it."[27] Nevertheless, the local brewer's union accused owners of collusion with the teamsters, and they refused to end the strike until all beer drivers were back under their domain. They also accused the city's breweries of employing armed guards to intimidate strikers.

Feeling the need to prepare for the upcoming summertime surge in beer sales, the brewery owners replaced many of the strikers with non-union workers in order to continue brewing operations. This brought harsh reaction from the International Union of United Brewery Workers, which promptly organized boycotts against Cleveland-brewed beer in outside cities such as Pittsburgh, Akron, Toledo and Cincinnati. The teamsters, in support of the local brewers, retaliated by boycotting all out-of-town beer in Cleveland.[28]

Finally, after seven months, the ruinous boycotts and violent picket-line episodes came to an end. An agreement was reached among the warring factions whereby the dispute would be suspended until the two unions could formally agree on a settlement. Cleveland's brewery workers returned to their posts in November of 1935. Local owners, meanwhile, assessed the damage. It was said that the city's breweries lost about $400,000 per month during much of the conflict.[29] The Cleveland-Sandusky company was perhaps the hardest hit. In Sandusky, where the clashes had been most violent, the company's Stang plant was closed for good after strikers had successfully prevented it from operating with replacement workers. Equipment from the brewery was eventually moved to Cleveland.

The Newcomers

The Great Depression, coupled with all of the new difficulties of running a brewery in the post-repeal era, caused a high mortality rate among breweries after 1935. During the decade following that year, the number of breweries operating in America dropped from 766 to 468.[30] A large part of the decline was due to an over-anticipated demand for beer. Fueled by the prospect of great profits, there was a virtual mad rush to re-open old breweries or build entirely new ones immediately after 3.2 percent beer was legalized. But many years would pass before beer consumption would again reach pre-prohibition levels in America. The Depression eroded disposable income among the working class, and beer sales simply did not climb at a fast enough rate to support all of the country's newly-refurbished breweries.

Those who had been active in the brewing industry before prohibition were on the strongest ground after repeal. Many had made great names for their beer in earlier days, a substantial asset in the new environment. Their experience and knowledge of the fundamentals – the brewing process, sales promotion, beer distribution, etc. – allowed them to focus exclusively on the myriad of new challenges and complexities within the beer business.

Conversely, the countless "newcomers" to brewing were at the greatest risk of failure. They came to the industry with no name-recognition, no history to promote, no long-term relationships with retailers, and no experience in the many peculiarities of beer-making. As it became evident that supply was outgrowing demand, the newcomers were often forced out of the market. Although the majority of post-repeal breweries in Cleveland were operated by veteran brewers, a handful of newcomers entered the local brewing industry. And, indeed, it was these brewers who struggled more than the others, and who ultimately did not survive the harsh conditions.

Jack H. Harris

The Forest City Brewery, Inc.

Early in 1933, the old Forest City brewery on Union Avenue was acquired by "a syndicate of prominent Cleveland business men" headed by former Cuyahoga County Commissioner Jack H. Harris.[31] Taking over breweries in several Ohio cities, Harris and partner Carl F. Lang made large investments in the brewing business as soon as legalization of beer seemed likely. The partners bought the New Philadelphia brewery in New Philadelphia, Ohio and began making beer there in 1933. They also gained control of the defunct Windisch-Muhlhauser brewery in Cincinnati. It was originally intended to be renamed the Forest City Brewery of Cincinnati, but was instead incorporated as the Lion Brewery, Inc. in 1933.[32] The old Heubner brewery in Toledo was another of the partners' early targets, but that venture never came to fruition.[33]

Harris and Lang incorporated their Cleveland operation as the Forest City Brewery, Inc. in March of 1933 with plans to put their first brew on the market by the end of May.[34] Sales were strong right from the start. According to a later promotional brochure, the brewery lead the city in beer sales in 1934, accounting for about twenty-five percent of the beer sold in Cleveland during that year.[35] An important aspect of Forest City's early success was the fact that it occupied one of the newest brewing plants in Cleveland. Built in 1904, all of its equipment was intact at the time of repeal, and presumably little rehabilitation was necessary to begin brewing. In contrast, beer production at some of the city's other breweries was hampered by the necessity of large-scale plant overhauls.

The company's main product throughout its existence was a brand called Waldorf Beer, brewed under the supervision of Max Hansky, Forest City brewmaster since 1909. The brewery produced a wide variety brews under the Waldorf banner. There was Waldorf Lager, Waldorf Pilsner, Waldorf Special Dark, Waldorf High Proof, Waldorf Half & Half, Waldorf Red Band, Waldorf Samson Brau Lager, and Waldorf Samson Ale. The last two varieties, whose labels sported a rendering of the biblical Samson, were so named for their alcoholic strength. There were also two seasonal brands, Waldorf Golden Bock (spring) and Waldorf Harvest Brew (autumn).

After 1935, the entire Waldorf line was promoted with the slogan, "Champagne of Beers." Milwaukee's far more famous Miller High Life Beer had coined the phrase, "Champagne of *Bottled* Beers," in 1906 and used it for decades afterward. It is difficult to imagine that the Miller Brewing

Company did not object to Waldorf's use of the slightly-modified slogan, but no evidence exists to suggest that a conflict arose. On occasion, the Forest City brewery even taunted the issue in ads which bragged, "There is only _one_ 'Champagne of Beers' – Waldorf."[36] Whatever the case, Miller eventually dropped the word "Bottled" from its slogan, thus matching exactly the Waldorf slogan. This did not occur, however, until many years after the Forest City brewery had passed out of existence.

In addition to Waldorf, the company produced a brand called Old Bohemian Style Pilsner Beer, brewed both in Cleveland and at Harris and Lang's New Philadelphia brewery. For a brief period, the Forest City brewery also made DeWitt Beer and Ale exclusively for the DeWitt hotel chain.

Despite its promising start, the Forest City brewery encountered difficulties once all of the city's other breweries had geared up production. Local competition did severe damage to sales of Waldorf, and the company slid into bankruptcy in 1939. Jack H. Harris had sold his interest in the brewery during the previous year, and had turned over the presidency to partner Carl F. Lang.[37] In 1940, a group of investors lead by former State Representative Joseph G. Ehrlich bought the Forest City brewery and its assets for $135,200 and continued the manufacture of Waldorf beer and ale. Among the investors were individuals associated with the Beverage Bureau of Louisville, Kentucky and the George J. Meyer Malt &

Waldorf was the Forest City brewery's primary brand line after prohibition.

Below: The Forest City brewery on Union Avenue.

Bill Carlisle Collection

Grain Corporation of Buffalo. Joseph G. Ehrlich served as the brewery's president and secretary.[38]

Business was not much better for the new owners than it had been for the old ones. In 1944, Ehrlich, who had acquired all of the company's outstanding stock by that time, sold the brewery to the local Brewing Corporation of America for a reported $477,000.[39] The plant was used until 1946 by Brewing Corporation, makers of Carling's Red Cap Ale and Carling's Black Label Beer, to handle overflow from its main brewery on Quincy Avenue.

The Sunrise Brewing Co.

Another newcomer to the local brewing scene, the Sunrise Brewing Company, ended its brief life exactly as Forest City did, selling out to the Brewing Corporation of America during the same *week* as Forest City. Formed in 1933, the Sunrise company did business in the old Gund brewery on Davenport Avenue. The Gund family had long ago developed interests far removed from brewing and, beyond leasing the plant to the new company, the Gunds were not involved in the venture. The Erie Sales Company, a manufacturer of liquid malt, had occupied a portion of the old brewery during prohibition. Two of that firm's directors – Abraham Miller and Joseph Hecht – organized the Sunrise Brewing Company.[40] Veteran Cleveland brewmaster Jaro Pavlik, who worked at the Pilsener and Standard breweries before prohibition, was hired to supervise production of the new Sunrise Beer. Pavlik also acted as vice president.

After installation of entirely new brewing equipment, the Sunrise brewery began operations in July of 1933 with an annual capacity of about 75,000 barrels. The new Sunrise Beer arrived on the market August 24th and was offered in both light and dark varieties.[41] Initially, only kegged beer was available. However, bottling began early in 1934, and advertisements for Sunrise Beer in bottles proclaimed, "Socially, it is above reproach – no embarrassment from (pardon us) burping."[42] A money-back guarantee backed up that rather unusual claim. Aside from Sunrise Beer, the company's brands included Old German Lager Beer and Golden Dawn Lager Beer.

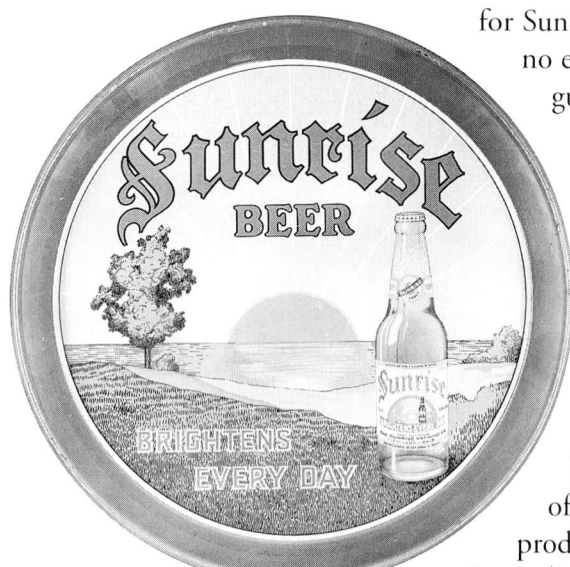

A tin advertising tray, circa 1935.

Late in 1934, the Sunrise Brewing Company became embroiled in a highly publicized controversy which, in little more than a few months, resulted in the brewery's loss of its operating license, seizure of the brewery by the U.S. Alcohol Tax Unit, and a court-ordered sale of the company and its assets. Among the charges launched in a Federal action against the company was that Sunrise employees were routinely instructed to illegally recycle tax stamps from already-sold kegs of beer for reuse on subsequent kegs. It was also charged that beer production records were falsified to reflect smaller-than-actual output levels.[43] In addition to ordering the sale of the company to pay the $12,000 in imposed fines, the court also instructed the firm's officers to retire completely from the business of brewing.

With little delay, the company was sold to brothers and local businessmen David and Harry Frankel, who became president and vice president, respectively. Unofficial reports noted a sale price of about $125,000.[44] Retaining the Sunrise Brewing Company name, the brewery resumed operations on March 29, 1935 after having been idle since January 1st. Jaro Pavlik was kept on as brewmaster and the

The Sunrise Brewing Company occupied the former Gund brewery on Davenport Avenue.

production of Sunrise Beer continued as before.

In celebration of Pavlik's thirty-fifth year as a brewmaster in 1938, the company added two new brands, Cheerio Ale and Tip Top Beer. The latter brand was said to have been brewed according to "dusty recipes" long ago perfected by Pavlik's father and grandfather, both of whom had been brewmasters in Kuttenberg, Bohemia.[45] Already by 1939, Tip Top Beer had overtaken the old Sunrise brand as the brewery's lead product, and the company name was thus changed to the Tip Top Brewing Company.

For several years, there were rumors that the Tip Top Brewing Company was connected with organized crime. The rumors remained just that – rumors – until 1940, when a major portion of the company's stock was transferred to Alfred Polizzi, a well-known Cleveland mafia boss.[46] Polizzi, or "Big Al" as he was commonly known, was no stranger to the beer business. He, along with several cohorts, established the Lubeck Brewing Company in Toledo in 1933.* Among those in charge of the Lubeck operation was Edward C. Stanton, former Cuyahoga County Prosecutor turned mafia lawyer.[47] In true allegiance to mafia syndication, some of the packaging of Lubeck Beer was handled by Chicago's Manhattan Brewing Company, also known as "Al Capone's

*The company was named after the city of Lübeck in northern Germany. Perhaps of some symbolic significance was the fact that Lübeck was the thirteenth century birthplace of the notorious Hanseatic League, a mafia-like syndicate of commercial organizations.

brewery."[48] In Cleveland, Polizzi and his associates set up the Lubeck Distributing Company to handle local distribution of Lubeck Beer, promoted with the ominously happy slogan, "The Beer That Makes Friends."[49] It was only after the Toledo brewery closed in 1939 that Polizzi took control of the Tip Top Brewing Company, which subsequently added Lubeck Beer to its brand line.

While World War II restrictions on grain were a source of consternation for most brewers, Polizzi managed to turn it into an asset for his organization. The state's exclusive control over sales of hard liquor in Ohio was relaxed during the war-time shortages, allowing private wholesalers to import liquor from other states to help alleviate the growing scarcity. Seeing an opportunity, Polizzi had more than 1,500 cases of liquor shipped to Cleveland from Chicago. Much of the liquor was then offered to Tip Top retailers, thus helping to create illegal "tied houses" for the brewery. In turn, the unlimited supply of liquor at Polizzi taverns attracted more customers, ultimately resulting in more beer sales. Among the other illicit bonuses enjoyed by Polizzi's tied-house retailers was a lawyer on retainer to defend owners against liquor violations, and a special fund used to guarantee repayment of retailers' bank loans.[50]

In 1944, Polizzi sold the Tip Top Brewing Company to the Brewing Corporation of America for $400,000.[51] The brewery was immediately shut down, and its war-time grain rations were transferred to Brewing Corporation's Quincy Avenue plant for use in the manufacture of its Carling brands. The Tip Top Distributing Company (successor to Polizzi's Lubeck Distributing Company) remained in business well into the 1960s, distributing Pabst Blue Ribbon Beer and other brands. For most of those years, the company did business out of a portion of the former Tip Top brewery. Later, it moved its operations to Scovill Avenue.[52]

"Big Al" Polizzi, incidentally, moved to Florida after selling the Tip Top brewery. Despite his purported desire to shed his criminal ways, Polizzi's dark past followed him south. When he attempted to join an exclusive Florida country club, for example, he was refused membership on the basis of his criminal record. Nevertheless, his business enterprises in Florida were apparently legitimate ones. He involved himself mainly in real estate and was ultimately credited with building much of the city of Coral Gables.[53]

Alfred "Big Al" Polizzi, testifying before a Senate committee on organized crime.

A Grand Re-Opening

Just a few days after 3.2 percent beer was again legal in Ohio, the *Plain Dealer* published a brief tribute to the men who had built and ruled Cleveland's brewing industry in the days before prohibition. Reading somewhat like a eulogy, the article concluded:

> And now beer is back, but not the men that made it. And though Milwaukee may still have its Uihleins, St. Louis its Buschs, New York its Ruppert, there are no more barrels or bottles with Cleveland's grand old names upon them. They are gone, all of them, from the realm of brewing.[54]

It was true that many of Cleveland's venerable brewing names – Schlather, Gehring, Diebolt, Gund, etc. – were never again to be synonymous with beer. But the *Plain Dealer's* assertion that "all of them" were gone was a bit premature. One local brewing family was destined to resume its proud brewing legacy in Cleveland. Not long after the fervor over repeal had subsided, it was announced by Herbert F. Leisy (son of Otto I. Leisy and grandson of brewery founder Isaac Leisy) that his family's historic Vega Avenue brewery would be put back into operation. After several months of preparation, the first shipment in fourteen years of "good ol' Leisy's Beer" rolled out of the brewery yard on May 14, 1934 – more than a year after legalization of beer.

Most of the city's other breweries had resumed business amidst a sort of panicked rush to fill a gaping demand for beer. Little attention was paid to re-establishing brand reputations or reminding consumers of the rich traditions of brewing. Rather, simply churning out beer, as fast and as much as possible, was the singular goal. In contrast, the Leisy brewery re-opened with the style and finesse characteristic of its pre-prohibition heritage. The fanfare began a full eight weeks before the first Leisy brew made its appearance. New York City ad agency Fuller & Smith & Ross was hired to design a series of somewhat *nouveau* newspaper ads designed to set Leisy's Beer apart from its competition and rekindle the once auspicious Leisy reputation. The ads, which carried no logo or product signature (a bold

approach for the time), whimsically reminisced about the days when the Leisy brewery was the nucleus of its neighborhood and a revered Cleveland institution. The refreshing "soft sell" attitude of the ads caused one observer to comment, "Here is a really intelligent departure from the dogmatic announcements of too many breweries who took refuge in trite phrases and uninteresting illustrations."[55]

In conjunction with the advertising campaign, "old timers" from around the west side were invited to special gatherings at the brewery to taste-test the new Leisy's and compare it with their recollections of the pre-prohibition counterpart.[56] Likewise, there were parties at the brewery for "children under 35" who had never tasted Leisy beer, but whose opinions were nevertheless much sought by Carl Faller, head brewmaster at the Leisy brewery since 1900. Under Faller's watchful eye, three Leisy brands were in the works: Leisy's Premium, Leisy's Special Brew, and Leisy's Extra Pale. Each had been brewed before prohibition, or "the Interlude" as Leisy management called it.[57]

On the big day, May 14th, the brewery grounds were crowded with prominent citizens invited to take part in the celebration of Leisy's return. A number of news reporters were on hand,

Above: Preparing the aging vats at the Leisy brewery.

Left: Brewmaster Carl Faller (left) and Herbert Leisy sample some Leisy Beer.

and radio personalities even broadcasted live accounts of the complimentary brewery tour. The feature of greatest interest on the tour was the brewery's ancient beer cellar, a series of long arched-ceiling tunnels fifty feet below ground where beer was aged before the advent of artificial refrigeration. Dubbed the "Gay Nineties Rathskeller," the atmospheric cellar was reconditioned for use as a hospitality center for visitors of the brewery.

The high point of the celebration occurred when the ceremonial first shipment of Leisy beer left the brewery destined for the mayor's office. Mayor Harry Davis would become the first Cleveland citizen to have a case of Leisy's. As the truck passed through the brewery gate, it broke a white ribbon draped between the gate posts and tripped a switch that illuminated two twenty-foot high Leisy neon advertising signs, one along the West Shoreway and the other at the corner of East 107th and Carnegie Avenue.[58] The crowd later retreated to the Gay Nineties Rathskeller, where

Earl L. Johnson, who served as Leisy's vice president of sales, was a key part of the brewery's re-opening after prohibition. It was a great loss to the brewery when Johnson was killed in an airplane crash in 1947.

quantities of Leisy beer were consumed well into the night. The "Leisy's Saturday Night Singing Society" entertained the gathering with a number of old favorites while local radio station WTAM broadcast the performance live.[59]

The following day, the hoopla over Leisy's return continued. Airplanes equipped with loud-speakers circled the city blaring the news "Leisy's Is Back," the same phrase which was featured in radio commercials and double-page ads in local newspapers. The new fleet of thirty-six Leisy beer trucks scurried around the city, their horns sounding the first few notes of "How Dry I Am." There was also a six-horse beer wagon – newly painted with the blue and cream Leisy colors – making deliveries downtown.[60] Back at the Leisy plant, neighbors gathered around as the brewery's three-pitch steam whistle blew at noon for the first time since 1917. The whistle was well-known to the neighborhood's oldest residents, one of whom expressed his joy over its return:

Leisy produced three different brands of beer upon its re-opening: Supreme Lager, Special Brew, and Extra Pale.

That whistle – it's good music to me. I heard it many many times when I was a boy. When it blew in the morning I knew it was time to get up. When it blew at noon it was time to go home from school for lunch. When it blew in the evening it was time for dinner. I lived by it, set my watch by it. Life these last years has not been the same without it.[61]

For the first several weeks after Leisy's return to the market, there was not enough of the product to go around. It was even discovered that unscrupulous tavernkeepers, unable to procure a sufficient supply of Leisy's, were selling other brands under the Leisy name. The problem became so rampant that Herbert Leisy finally placed ads in the local newspapers warning beer drinkers of the impostor brews.[62] But relief from the Leisy shortage came two months after the brewery's opening when the production capacity was doubled from 120,000 to 240,000 barrels annually. Within a short time, the Leisy brewery was proclaiming itself the sales leader in Cleveland. The company's advertising slogan was thus cleverly modified from "Leisy's Is Back" to "Leisy's Is Back – In Front."[63]

From Automobiles To Ale

The Leisy Brewing Company was not the only Cleveland brewery to make a splashy entrance into the market after repeal. The Brewing Corporation of America, doing business in the former plant of the Peerless Motor Car Company on Quincy Avenue, also attracted a great deal of attention upon its grand opening. Some 20,000 visitors took part in the brewery's open house festivities on June 15, 1934 as the first batch of American-brewed Carling's Red Cap Ale made its debut.[64] Host of the gala affair was Peerless president James A. Bohannon, whose determination to rescue the Peerless stockholders from a declining automobile industry gave rise to the Brewing Corporation of America. Also prominent among the group was E. P. Taylor, owner of Brewing Corporation of Canada, which granted Bohannon the American rights to the Carling brands. Among the honored guests was Col. J. Innes Carling, whose grandfather founded the Carling empire in Canada in 1840.

James A. Bohannon

"From Automobiles To Ale" was the popular headline of newspaper and trade journal articles detailing the unusual story of how a suffering automobile manufacturer sought refuge in the production of malt beverages. Peerless auto sales, like those of countless other car-makers, declined sharply after the stock market crash of 1929. Producers of luxury cars like Peerless were hardest hit. The American consumer simply no longer had the means (or the taste) for extravagance. Auto production was halted at the Peerless plant in 1931, and president James A. Bohannon began a search for alternative lines of business in which to engage the company. The prospect of the Eighteenth Amendment's repeal was much in the news, and Peerless decided to pursue the possibility of entering the beer business. Bohannon later explained how Peerless became associated with Carling:

> Having lived in Detroit, right across the river from Canada, I always had a proper respect for Carling's. In fact, during prohibition, long before I ever got into the brewing business, people paid up to a dollar a bottle for it. On a quality basis, I associated it with Cadillac, Steinway and Tiffany.
>
> So when at Peerless we had the chance to acquire the American rights, formulas and technical assistance of Canadian Breweries, Ltd.*, brewers of Carling's Ale, we were quick to take advantage of it.
>
> We had a big, modern plant and lots of ambition, and they had the name. It was a natural commercial wedlock.[65]

James A. Bohannon was, in every sense of the phrase, a man of big proportions: big of physical stature, big of character, and big of ambition. It was, therefore, not in his nature to approach the business of brewing in merely the same way which others had done. Indeed, Brewing

---

*Brewing Corporation of Canada was reorganized as Canadian Breweries Limited in 1937.[66]

Corporation of America was the virtual antithesis of Cleveland's other breweries. The company's emphasis on *ale*, for one thing, set it apart from most brewers. Although the rights to produce Black Label Beer were acquired in addition to that of Carling's Ale, it was the ale, not the beer, to which Brewing Corporation of America was wholly devoted. The strategy was to cultivate, on a large scale, a sort of elite "following" for ale in America – something attempted by few brewers and accomplished by fewer still. It was a strategy to which the brewery would cling for many years, but one which would later be abandoned to assure the survival of the company.

Brewing Corporation of America also differed from other local brewers in the sense that it did not consider itself a "local brewer" in any sense. Having cut his teeth on the automobile industry (which was anything but a locally-oriented industry), James A. Bohannon was not inclined to limit the potential of his new venture to a small geographic region. From the very beginning, Bohannon set his sights on a market which encompassed regions well beyond Greater Cleveland. And the pursuit of that market, more than any other single facet of the company, became the life-force of the Carling products in America over the next forty-plus years.

Chapter Nine

An End To Depression

The Great Depression, coupled with the brewing industry's inability to achieve a return to the much-sought 5¢ beer, was the fundamental cause of disappointing beer sales during the first several years after the repeal of prohibition. But as the nation's economic woes began to dissipate by the early 1940s, the brewing industry's outlook for the future brightened significantly. Despite the multitude of constraints brought on by World War II, signs that beer-making in America was returning to its pre-prohibition glory were nevertheless visible. Between 1939 and 1945, national per capita consumption of beer rose from 12.3 to 18.7 gallons.[1] By the end of the war, sales of beer in America had climbed well beyond the industry's former peak year of 1914, and an industry-wide optimism prevailed.

Thus, despite initially poor sales, America's love affair with beer was alive and well after prohibition. The typical consumer, however, was very different now than he had been prior to the Volstead years. Attitudes had changed. Habits had changed. Indeed, *life* had changed. Consumers were far more mobile than they had been in earlier days, and the corner drinking spot was no longer the social center of its neighborhood. Electric refrigerators were now a common household amenity, bringing beer into the home on a wide scale. In turn, women, who by and large did not drink beer in the old days, were now heavy consumers of it. Beer was no longer strictly a product of the saloon. Rather, in the post-repeal era, brewers would have to adapt to the undeniable fact that "off-premises" beer consumption would be a dominant facet of their industry.

Cleveland State University

For brewers, the most immediate impact of consumers' changed drinking habits was a marked shift in demand for packaged beer versus draught. Beer in bottles had started to

Packaged beer was a crucial aspect of any brewer's business after prohibition. Left: Canning P.O.C. Beer at the Pilsener brewery. Below: Bottling Erin Brew Beer at the Standard brewery.

become popular just before prohibition. Even in the best years, however, bottled beer rarely constituted more than twenty percent of total beer sales. But, after repeal, the percentage grew rapidly. Already in 1936, nearly *forty* percent of beer brewed during that year was packaged in bottles and cans. And the percentage continued to escalate. Even the most liberal predictions for the future of packaged beer fell far short of what consumers ultimately demanded. By 1940, more than half of America's beer was consumed from packages; by 1950, the figure had grown to well over seventy percent.[2]

Although most brewers clearly recognized the trend toward off-premises beer consumption, many still clung to their age-old inclination to make kegged beer the priority. Thus, brewers introduced all kinds of keg-like contraptions for the off-premises beer drinker. For example, the Leisy brewery enjoyed mild success with its "Leisy Growler," a small oak vessel resembling an inverted bucket in size and shape. It held one-eighth of a barrel of beer and required the use of a *bicycle pump* to provide the air pressure necessary for tapping. The Forest City brewery sold its Waldorf Beer in a similar package known as "The Tankard."[3] Of course, consumers found such containers to be awkward and inconvenient, preferring the ease of bottles and cans.

Tavernkeepers, as well, found great convenience in packaged beer. It was far less troublesome than draught beer, which required the constant maintenance of a complicated and often temperamental tapping apparatus. Packages also allowed a tavernkeeper to offer a wider variety of brands without adding expensive tapping equipment. In many cases, too, the slightly higher price of packaged beer improved profit margins for the tavernkeeper.

The introduction of beer in cans in 1935 increased consumers' interest in packaged beer immensely. Cans were much lighter and took up less space in the refrigerator than bottles. They required no deposit, and consumers liked the idea of drinking from a fresh receptacle never before used by anyone else (bottles were still largely encumbered by the return/deposit system). Also, cans were far less fragile than bottles. For brewers, cans offered significant economic benefits. One Cleveland brewer noted that one case of his canned beer weighed

180

fifty-five percent less than a case of bottled beer, and consumed about sixty-five percent less space, all of which had a tremendous impact on the brewer's shipping costs.[4] In addition, cans protected beer from flavor-damaging light and required a shorter pasteurization period.

Most brewers who canned a portion of their beer opted for the compactness of the flat-top style of beer can. However, some could not afford the cost of adding canning equipment, and thus preferred the "Cap-Sealed" cone-top beer cans, which could be filled and sealed using bottling equipment. The Crown Cork & Seal Company, makers of bottle caps, saw the flat-top design as a threat to its livelihood. As a sort of pre-emptive strike, the company became one of the early manufacturers and promoters of cone-top beer cans. They emphasized that cone-tops did not require the consumer to use a special opener, as did flat-top cans. Nevertheless, the cone-top beer can eventually lost favor with both the public and the brewing industry. By the mid-1950s, cone-top cans had disappeared from use.[5]

Prompted by the popularity of the beer can, bottle manufacturers launched the first throw-away beer bottles in the mid-1930s. A variety of "low profile" bottle configurations were designed to compete with the economical shape of the beer can. The amount of glass used per bottle was curtailed as much as possible to reduce weight. Cans, after all, had the potential to do serious damage to the bottle industry, particularly after war-time shortages of metal had ended.

In Cleveland, several brewers subscribed to the idea that throw-away packages were the wave of the future. The Forest City brewery was an early champion of disposable beer containers. The company's Waldorf Beer was the first Cleveland brand to be sold in cans. As such, Forest City took great pains to convince yet-skeptical retailers of the benefits of cans: "Once the consumer realizes the remarkable convenience of canned beer – which single test convinces – then your sales run steadily on. As a force for new business – and more profit in business – canned beer is unique."[6] Waldorf Beer was also marketed in throw-away "Steinie" bottles.

The Waldorf "Steinie."

In 1935, the Leisy brewery unveiled the new "Leisy Schooner," a throw-away bottle whose near can-like shape was promoted as "trim and close-rigged." Leisy was the first brewer to employ this particular bottle design (known as the "Stubby"). The company had great confidence in its future. From land, air and sea, news of the Leisy

To herald the introduction of the Leisy "Schooner" bottle, sailers paraded through downtown barking the news.

Schooner's arrival was spread. Men dressed as sailors roamed downtown streets heralding the new product. A boat traveling the Lake Erie shore from Sandusky to Erie, Pennsylvania broadcasted the news. A blimp even circled the city with the new product message. Billboards featured a pipe-smoking sea captain professing, "I sez it's gonna make history."[7]

Cleveland State University

Bottling at the Leisy brewery.

There was perhaps no one more optimistic about the future of the throw-away beer bottle than James A. Bohannon, president of Brewing Corporation of America. In 1945, in an unprecedented move, Bohannon completely eliminated his draught beer business and concentrated *exclusively* on the throw-away bottle.[8] The long-neck "bar bottles" were even discontinued as Bohannon, in his quest to capture a national market, aimed all of the brewery's resources at the off-premises consumer.

Bohannon's strategy – decades ahead of its time – proved costly for Brewing Corporation of America. Tavern sales, of course, were seriously impacted by the elimination of the returnable bottle. Those tavernkeepers who chose to continue carrying the Carling brands reluctantly did so with the new throw-away bottle. This, in turn, created conflict with city waste collection authorities, who objected to the tremendous amount of refuse generated by taverns using the throw-aways.[9]

But, worst of all, acceptance of the throw-away bottle among household consumers was not nearly as extensive as initially anticipated. America's war-time mentality, which placed a premium on conservation, still dictated consumers' purchase habits. The throw-away bottle, therefore, was seen by some as wasteful. After all, the return/deposit scenario was a time-honored institution, and consumer attitudes would not be changed overnight. In the end, committing exclusively to the throw-away bottle proved a serious mistake for Brewing Corporation of America, and returnable bottles were soon reinstated at the brewery.

Although throw-away containers would ultimately dominate the brewing industry, it was a slow evolution. Those brewers who approached the trend cautiously and allowed consumers to dictate their own rate of acceptance found the greatest success with non-returnable containers.

Spreading The Word

As off-premises consumption of beer escalated after prohibition, so too did advertising by brewers. In pre-Volstead days, brewery advertising had typically been limited to saloon signage, the occasional newspaper ad, and give-aways such as serving trays or glassware lettered with the brewery name. To some degree, the need for brewers to advertise before prohibition was precluded by the "tied house" system. The customer simply did not have the luxury of choice since most saloons carried the product of only one brewery. But with the tremendous growth of packaged beer in the 1930s and 40s, there was an increasing number of situations in which side by side competition occurred. Consumers could now choose their brand. And, of course, every brewer was eager to make certain that his brand was chosen more often than the competitor's. Advertising, therefore, became a priority among brewers.

The growth of the mass media, too, spurred an increase in beer advertising. There were simply far more advertising vehicles available after prohibition than before. Electrically-illuminated billboards, increasing numbers of (and more specialized) magazines, radio broadcasting, and television broadcasting all offered new opportunities for beer-makers. Radio, in particular, was attractive to advertisers, and brewers used it in great numbers. At the time prohibition was repealed, there were some 600 radio stations operating nationwide, and more than nineteen million households owned a radio set. Even so, the medium was barely out of its infancy. In the years to come, radio would evolve into a great "godlike presence," as one historian called it.[10]

In Cleveland, virtually every local brewer was involved to some degree in radio advertising. The Standard Brewing Company broadcasted a daily radio program on WGAR called "Column of the Air" beginning in 1935 and continuing until well after the war. The news-oriented program was hosted by local commentator Sydney Andorn, who brought "a mood of gayety and humor" to the news stories.[11]

The Sunrise Brewing Company hosted "You Be The Judge," a weekly program on WHK featuring a mock court trial in which the listening audience actually determined the verdict. Retailers distributed entry cards on which listeners indicated their vote of "guilty" or "not guilty." The cards were then returned to the brewery and the verdict was revealed on the following week's program. Participation was encouraged by a weekly prize of $25 in cash awarded to one lucky listener.[12]

Musical programs were a popular

"Beer Is For Pigs!"

Hollywood actor Jim Backus was once asked to describe his most embarrassing moment. He responded with the following story:

Some years ago, I was working for a Cleveland radio station doing a man-on-the-street interview show. My sponsor was a local beer company, Pride of Cleveland Beer.

One night I managed to do a broadcast from the stage of a nightclub that was the "in" place in town.

I interviewed their star performer and several show girls. To give an international flavor to the show, I decided to interview the club's wine steward.

He said he'd worked in such prestigious places as the Adlon Hotel in Berlin, Maxim's in Paris and Shepheard's Hotel in Cairo. With his imperious manner and Viennese accent, the show was going along beautifully.

Then I asked the steward what his duties were. He pompously explained, "I advise people on the correct wines to go with each course. For example, they want claret with their sole when I will only allow them to have a fine chablis."

Suddenly, I realized I was sponsored by the Pride of Cleveland Beer company and this man was talking only about wines.

So I said, "And undoubtedly you recommend to many diners that they drink Pride of Cleveland Beer with their meal." He glared at me. After a long pause, the wine steward thundered, "Beer is for pigs! Beer under any condition is slop!

"It not only dulls the taste buds, but it causes gas! Perhaps if you're outdoors picnicking, a swallow of Heineken's is permissible. But that garbage you mention, never! Phooey!"

And that was my most embarrassing moment. As he walked away, all I could do was weakly say, "We now return you to the station for an interlude of organ music."

My show was canceled the following day.

format for brewery sponsorship. During the 1930s, the Pilsener Brewing Company hosted a musical program on WGAR consisting entirely of "happy rollicking songs by The Pilseneers."[13] The Cleveland-Sandusky brewery sponsored a show known as "Morgan's Musical Inn" on WGAR and a program called "The Gold Bond Polka Party" on WJMO.[14] The Standard Brewing Company made a bold move in 1952 when it decided to sponsor Cleveland's now-legendary "Moon Dog Show," an early rock & roll radio program. The daily show was hosted by pioneer disc jockey Alan Freed, who is credited with coining the phrase *rock & roll* on his show.[15] The Standard brewery, it seems, was interested in cultivating a younger market for its Erin Brew Beer.

However, the most popular program format for brewers was sports. The Leisy brewery was the long-time sponsor of the daily "Leisy Sports Review," hosted by venerable sportscaster Tom Manning. The program's guests over the years included such famous sports figures as Tris Speaker, Johnny Kilbane, Joe Lewis, Jack Dempsey, and Jesse Owens. The program signed off with the familiar first few notes of "How Dry I Am," the same jingle blared by Leisy delivery trucks.[16]

In 1948, the Standard Brewing Company signed-up as the sponsor of radio broadcasts of Cleveland Indians baseball games. The move soon proved a master stroke as the Indians climbed their way to the World Series, and ultimately won the 1948 Championship. A record number of listeners tuned in as play-by-play announcers Jimmy Dudley and Jack Graney professed the virtues of Erin Brew Beer between innings of the games. Sales of radio sets in 1948 were higher in Cleveland than in any other city in the country.[17] And,
by 1949, sales of Erin Brew were higher than that of any other beer in Cleveland. Naturally, the Standard brewery clung to its affiliation with the Cleveland Indians for several years afterwards. In 1951, Indians right-fielder Bob Kennedy was hired by Standard as a bona fide Erin Brew salesman. Beer distributors and beverage store owners were treated to regular sales calls by the star player, autographs and all.[18]

The Pilsener Brewing Company was a long-time sponsor of radio broadcasts of Cleveland Barons hockey games. Pilsener management was a strong believer in the power of radio advertising. President Frank B. Sullivan once said, "Radio programs of high quality and diversified scope add prestige to a trade name to an extent that makes that name almost a household word."[19] During the late 1940s, the Barons (who had won four Calder Cup Championships since the team's founding in 1937) were among those "programs of high quality" for Pilsener.[20] Hoping to duplicate the Standard brewery's success with the Indians in 1948, the Pilsener Brewing Company bolstered its sponsorship of the Barons for the 1949-50 hockey season. The brewery became the *sole* radio sponsor of game broadcasts, and created the "P.O.C. Hockey Network." In addition to local radio station WJW,

Jimmy Dudley (left) and Jack Graney called the 1948 World Series games for Erin Brew Beer. The Standard Brewing Company's sponsorship of the Cleveland Indians had a tremendous impact on beer sales.

stations in Ashtabula, Canton, Sandusky, Elyria and Youngstown were included on the new P.O.C. network.[21] The brewery also sponsored a number of televised Barons games. Not surprisingly, Pilsener enjoyed the right of exclusive beer sales at the Cleveland Arena, where it dispensed P.O.C. Beer from the "Pilsener Cellars," a Viennese-style pub in the north lobby of the Arena.[22]

Artwork for a P.O.C. billboard. Brewers used virtually every advertising media available after prohibition.

The War

The Japanese attack on Pearl Harbor on December 7, 1941 plunged America into a new era. Brewing, like all other industries, was greatly impacted. However, the conflict in Europe had affected American brewers long before Congress' declaration of war. In July of 1940, the "Defense Tax" was instituted, raising the federal tax on beer from $5 to $6 per barrel.[23] The tax increase severely crippled the nation's smaller brewers. Those who had not developed extensive sales volume found it difficult to absorb any portion of the tax. Sales for these smaller brewers dwindled, and many were forced out of business.

In Cleveland, Henry F. Eilert's brewery was the first casualty of the war tax. The brewery's name had been changed in 1940 from the Eilert Brewing Company to the King's Brewery, Inc. to better identify with the company's feature products, King Kole Beer and King's Ale. Interestingly, King Kole Beer was the brainchild of a group of Chicago businessmen who sought to establish the brand as a national product.[24] The beer was to be advertised on a national basis and brewed by independent licensee-breweries in various regions. Each participating brewer was to pay a fee to the Chicago firm for rights to brew and sell King Kole in their particular territory. By 1934, as many as eight breweries (Eilert among them) had signed up for the plan. But, in the end, the scheme failed to fully take shape, and the Eilert brewery became the only company to actually market King Kole. Nevertheless, the brand enjoyed respectable sales locally. Henry F. Eilert later added King's Ale as the sister product. Both brands were promoted with the obvious slogan, "Fit For A King."

Increased tax burdens finally pushed the King's Brewery into default. Unable to pay its creditors, the brewery was declared bankrupt in 1941 and the company's assets were liquidated. Henry F. Eilert spent the remainder of his years in retirement. He died in 1952 at age eighty-one.[25]

War-time increases in the federal beer tax were not capped at $6 per barrel. Rather, the tax was boosted to $7 per barrel in 1942 and raised again to $8 per barrel in 1944. Despite burgeoning war-time beer sales, the increased tax took a financial toll on the nation's smaller brewers. Though many undoubtedly anticipated a reduction of the tax at war's end, those hopes were never fulfilled. The $8 tax remained intact until 1951, when it was increased yet again in the interest of the Korean War.[26]

Left: Due to war-time shortages of tires, the Standard Brewing Company dusted off one of its pre-prohibition delivery wagons and put it into service during World War II.

Below: A truckload of Crystal Rock Beer leaves Cleveland for Camp Van Dorn in Mississippi. During the war, Cleveland brewers supplied large quantities of beer to the armed forces.

Of course, throughout World War II, the high federal beer tax was just one item on a long list of hardships for the brewing industry. Shortages of just about everything imaginable – labor, brewing materials, bottles, kegs, etc. – were a constant source of aggravation for brewers. Under "War Food Order 66," both malt and hops became rationed materials in February of 1943. A series of subsequent amendments to the order progressively reduced the quantities available to brewers. The amount of grain rationed to any particular brewer was based entirely on his pre-war usage. At its worst, Order 66 denied brewers about one-third of their pre-war brewing materials. Reduced output was the result. Many brewmasters, however, were assigned the troubling task of re-formulating their brew in order to require less grain per batch.[27] Many brewers simply eliminated entire brands from their product line. The Cleveland-Sandusky Brewing Corporation, for example, discontinued its Gold Bond Beer. The Brewing Corporation of America halted production of Black Label Beer. (Both brands were resurrected after the grain restrictions were lifted.)

The war-time shortage of tin was of particular menace to brewers as most were unable to secure enough bottle caps to fill orders for bottled beer. Many brewers compensated by promoting beer in quart-sized bottles, thereby reducing the necessary number of caps. The Pilsener Brewing Company instituted bottle cap drives, urging the public to save their caps and bring them to the brewery for recycling. But consumers were reluctant to make special trips to the brewery for something as seemingly insignificant as bottle caps. So, Pilsener placed a number of large collection bins throughout the city. The bins (which, oddly enough, were made of tin) doubled as advertising signs, prominently featuring the P.O.C. logo.[28]

By and large, brewers were strong supporters of the war effort. Many still remembered the key role which World War I had played in bringing about National Prohibition. Naturally, prohibitionists were eager to repeat the scenario, while brewers were determined to avoid it. Thus, brewers were often at the forefront of all kinds of patriotic activities. The Brewing Corporation of America was awarded the "Minute Man Flag" in 1942 when nearly 100 percent of its employees had purchased war bonds, accounting for more than ten percent of the brewery's total payroll.[29] The Leisy Brewing Company did its part by donating all of its outdoor billboards to the Red Cross to promote its War Fund Drive. Of course, a conspicuous bottle of Leisy's accompanied the Red Cross message.[30]

Brewers also supplied enormous quantities of beer to the government for shipment to troops overseas. Early in the war, many brewers were asked to reserve fifteen percent of their beer production for military use. Cleveland brewers reportedly sent about one million bottles of beer *per week* to the armed forces during the war.[31] The beer was packaged in squat throw-away bottles and in cans painted with an olive drab, non-reflective coating which prevented the reflection of sunlight once discarded.

A Post-War Boom

With the end of World War II came one of the most prosperous periods in American brewing history. Federal restrictions on grain were lifted in 1947, and the brewing industry experienced a sales boom during that year which would remain unsurpassed for more than a *decade* afterward. As availability of brewing equipment and construction materials increased, breweries across the nation began bolstering production to meet the soaring demand for beer. In 1939, expenditures on brewery enlargement totaled only about $20 million; however, in 1947, brewers spent an impressive $110 million, a figure matched by only a handful of other U.S. industries.[32]

The Brewing Corporation of America launched the first and most vigorous post-war expansion program among Cleveland's brewers. Between 1945 and 1948, the company spent an astounding $7.2 million on capital improvements at its Quincy Avenue plant.[33] Certainly James A. Bohannon's decision to convert the brewery to exclusive use of throw-away bottles in 1945 accounted for a large portion of the expenditures. But a mass increase in brewing capacity was the main objective, as Bohannon pressed ever-forward toward his ultimate goal of national distribution for Carling's Red Cap Ale.

The Pilsener Brewing Company, as well, aggressively expanded its plant after World War II. Under the direction of president Frank B. Sullivan, about $5 million was spent between 1948 and 1951 to improve and enlarge the brewery at West 65th and Clark.[34] The Pilsener company had been purchased in 1935 by the large Cleveland-based City Ice & Fuel Company, suppliers of artificial ice and coal for home heating. In 1935, the company had gross revenues of more than $25 million, and operated in twenty-three states and Canada. City Ice & Fuel's involvement in brewing was the result of efforts to diversify its fields of business amidst shrinking demand for both ice and coal in the home. Professing to its stockholders that "there are great possibilities for future expansion in this business," City Ice & Fuel acquired breweries in New Orleans, Miami and Granite City, Illinois in addition to the Pilsener brewery in Cleveland.[35] Over the next thirty years, City Ice & Fuel (renamed City Products Corporation in 1949) was an active player in the U. S. brewing industry.

The Pilsener brewery enjoyed good sales of its P.O.C. beer throughout the 1940s, ending the decade with production of about 360,000 barrels in 1949. After the death of long-time Pilsener brewmaster Frank Knopp in 1947, Carl Fromm came from the Ohio Brewery, Inc. in Columbus to join Pilsener as head brewmaster.[36] Fromm oversaw much of the brewery's post-war modernization efforts, and he remained Pilsener's brewmaster throughout its most prosperous years yet to come.

The Standard Brewing Company, like Pilsener, finished the 1940s in good condition, although production was sluggish for the first year or two after World War II. Brewing was hindered by the continued shortages of raw materials. In 1946, the company was still only able to produce about half as much beer as in pre-war days. For brewmaster Gotthold Kuebler, the concern was not so much the *quantity* of the materials as it was the *quality*. For the duration of the war, the brewery was forced to use hops grown in Oregon instead of

Above: The Pilsener brewery, like most, enjoyed tremendous prosperity just after World War II.

Left: Looking west down Train Avenue. On right and in distance is the Standard Brewing Company's $4.5 million post-war plant expansion.

Cleveland State University

188

Kuebler's much-preferred Czechoslovakian hops. One observer noted, "It all worried Kuebler, who whittled constantly to keep his nerves calm."[37]

However, by 1948, after government rationing of malt and hops ended, expansion at the Standard brewery got under way. Initially, the company intended to spend about $3 million for enlargement. However, by the time the project was completed in 1950, costs had escalated to $4.5 million.[38] The new facility – which officially opened on April 20, 1950 – attracted a great deal of attention. Of particular note was the new, "ultramodern" bottling and canning facility, the entire operation of which could be orchestrated from a single master control panel. Standard officials were especially proud of the canning line, which was capable of filling and sealing a revolutionary 210 cans per minute. In all, the new additions to the Standard brewery boosted annual production capacity from 400,000 to 550,000 barrels.[39] Before the war, Standard had limited its market to a fifty-mile radius of Cleveland. With completion of the expansion program, the brewery moved well beyond that boundary, shipping Erin Brew Beer into parts of Ohio, Michigan, Pennsylvania and New York.[40]

Above: The Standard brewery's new canning line was capable of filling 210 cans per minute.

Below: Gleaming new aging tanks at the Standard brewery.

Beer At A Premium

As the economy burgeoned during the post-war years, a number of regional brewers put significant efforts behind establishing "premium" brands of beer. Premium beers were distinguished from non-premium beers mainly by the use of ultra-high quality ingredients and, therefore, were sold for a higher price. A large number of beer-makers had already launched premium brands by 1940, but war-time shortages caused many brewers to abandon them, if only temporarily. It was not until the mid-1940s that brewers began to revisit the idea of establishing a premium beer category. It was felt that, as consumers' buying power increased, a certain segment of the population would prefer a better-quality, more expensive product. This was born out by the relative popularity of premium-priced national brands like Budweiser, Schlitz and Pabst. Indeed, to a large degree, it was the

189

infiltration of brands like these that caused regional brewers to offer similarly-priced products.

In 1939, the Leisy brewery introduced Leisy's Dortmunder Beer, brewed according to the style of beer made for centuries in the great brewing city of Dortmund, Germany. Ads for the new premium brew asserted, "Dortmunder is not an imitation of its European namesake – it is an *absolute match*."[41] The Dortmunder brand, distinguished by the gold foil wrapped around its bottle neck, was the crowning achievement of long-time Leisy brewmaster Carl Faller, who passed away just a few months after the new product's release.[42] (At the time of his death, Faller was America's oldest active brewmaster at age eighty-three.) After the war, promotional activities for Dortmunder were strengthened, and the brand remained Leisy's premium brew for many years.

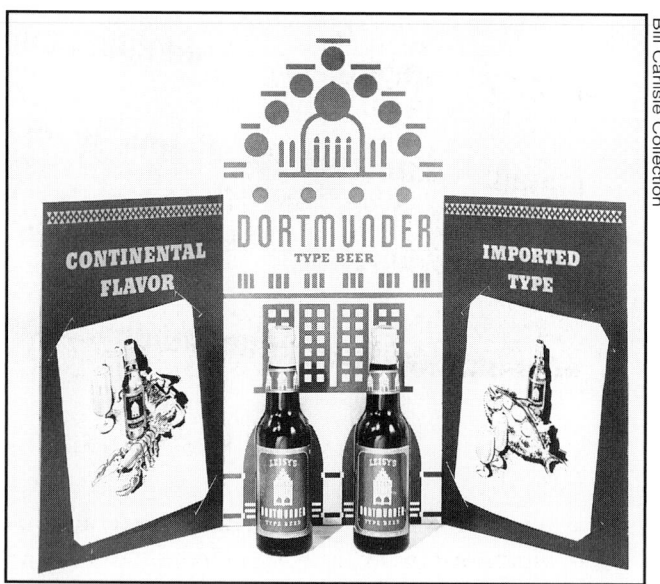

Bill Carlisle Collection

Dortmunder Beer was the Leisy Brewing Company's long-time premium brand.

The Cleveland-Sandusky Brewing Corporation's entry in the premium category was a brand called Brewmaster's Special, named in honor of brewmaster Frank P. van de Westelaken. Having joined Cleveland-Sandusky in 1937, van de Westelaken was elected president of the brewery in 1940.[43] He succeeded Oscar J. Fishel, who resigned after Cleveland-Sandusky stockholders voted against a proposal to sell the company to Brewing Corporation of America for $93,000. Van de Westelaken, of Dutch descent, was a sort of patriarch in the close-knit community of American brewmasters. He had served as president of the Master Brewers' Association of America for several years and taught courses on brewing at the University of Chicago. He also authored a monthly column in *Modern Brewer* magazine. Prior to prohibition, the veteran brewmaster worked in breweries in Newark, Milwaukee, New York, Baltimore, Buffalo and Chicago.[44]

Van de Westelaken successfully guided Cleveland-Sandusky through the war years and, by 1944, the company's East 55th Street brewery was operating at near capacity.[45] During that same year, the company launched its 100th anniversary celebration (the Stang brewery in Sandusky, one of the original eleven breweries which formed the Cleveland-Sandusky company, had origins dating back to 1844). The year-long celebration concluded with a well-

Frank P. van de Westelaken

190

attended luncheon at Hotel Statler, at which the company was presented with an award from the Cleveland Brewers Association. Long-time employees of the company were also honored at the luncheon. For several years after the anniversary, Crystal Rock Beer – which originated at the Stang brewery – was proudly promoted as "Ohio's Oldest Beer."[46]

The Cleveland-Sandusky brewery anticipated a bright future for premium beers after the war. In 1947, the company announced that nearly its entire advertising budget for the year would be allocated to Brewmaster's Special.[47] Only a small portion would be spent on its non-premium brands, Crystal Rock Beer and Old Timer's Ale. That notwithstanding, the company's strategy had shifted by 1949. Gold Bond Beer, discontinued during the war, was re-introduced, replacing Brewmaster's Special as the company's premium brew. Initially, the Gold Bond bottle label encountered legal difficulties due to its similarity to a cash bond certificate, but governmental authorities ultimately granted permission for its use.[48] For the remainder of Cleveland-Sandusky's years, Gold Bond was the company's mainstay product.

Early in 1940, the Pilsener Brewing Company released its premium brew, Toby Ale – "the taste thrill of the year."[49] The name was borrowed from a figure in Anglo folklore, Toby Fillpot, who allegedly drank 2,000 gallons of beer without eating.[50] The Pilsener brewery, however, did not put strong efforts behind marketing Toby Ale, and the brand remained only a minor contributor to the company's beer sales. By the late 1940s, Toby Ale had been discontinued.

The Cleveland Home Brewing Company entered the premium beer market when it launched Sonny's Premium Beer in 1939. The brand was the namesake of Alessandro "Sonny" DeMaioribus, vice president, secretary and general manager of the brewery. The Sonny's brand was used for many years but never achieved particularly good sales. And, anyway, by the end of the 1940s, the Cleveland Home brewery was beginning to suffer far greater problems.

Above: A billboard outside the Cleveland-Sandusky brewery on East 55th Street.

Below: Brewmaster Special was named for Frank P. van de Westelaken.

The First Post-War Casualty

It is unusual how many Clevelanders still recall the Cleveland Home Brewing Company's spectacular Black Forest Beer advertising sign which sat on the hillside along Cleveland's West Shoreway for many years. The brilliant neon lights blinked on in phases: first was the silhouette of the forest, then the castle in the distance, then the leaping deer, and finally, one by one, the letters B-L-A-C-K-F-O-R-E-S-T. Cleveland Home president Omar E. Mueller, commenting on the gigantic sign, once wrote,

> *The most important consideration was to blazon our brand upon the public consciousness. In our case, it was of elementary importance that the beer consuming public be acquainted with the fact that there was such a beer on the market as Black Forest. For this purpose, we eventually decided that billboards of an outstanding size and artistic design would be the most effective media to bring our brand to the attention of the public. Advertising that does not evoke public interest is not patently of any value.*[51]

Not long after 3.2 percent beer was legalized in 1933, Omar E. Mueller succeeded Otto W. Beltz as president of the Cleveland Home brewery and proceeded to rebuild the company which his father, Ernst W. Mueller, had organized back in 1907. Throughout the 1930s, Mueller was particularly successful in placing Black Forest Beer in many of Cleveland's best social clubs, and the brand ultimately developed a sort of niche following among the local elite. As such, Omar E. Mueller took a personal interest in assuring that Black Forest maintained a high standard of quality. Son Werner D. Mueller recalled that his father drank exactly one bottle of the beer every evening with dinner in order to keep constant check over its flavor and consistency.

The Cleveland Home Brewing Company.

Throughout the war years and afterward, Omar E. Mueller delegated much of the Cleveland Home brewery's day-to-day responsibilities to long-time employee Sonny DeMaioribus. Sonny had first been employed at the East 61st and Outhwaite brewery while still a young lad, working as an office boy during his summer vacations from school.[52] After graduation from high school in 1916, he secured a full-time job at the brewery. However, Sonny's real notoriety was in local politics. He was elected to City Council in 1927 and spent two terms as council president. Sonny later became active in Cuyahoga County Republican affairs, eventually serving as party chairman for a number of years. Despite his long and busy political career, Sonny never left his position at the Cleveland Home brewery. On the contrary, as the years passed, Sonny assumed ever-greater control over the brewery's management.

Omar E. Mueller studies an oil portrait of his father, Ernst W. Mueller, who organized the Cleveland Home Brewing Company back in 1907.

For much of the post-war era, the Cleveland Home Brewing Company was plagued by dwindling beer sales. After production peaked in 1945 at 111,000 barrels, the company began a rapid downward spiral marked by the death of Omar E. Mueller in 1946.[53] The following year, the brewery suffered another loss when brewmaster George Lezius passed away at the age of eighty-two. Just days before his death, the venerable brewmaster was featured in an article for the *Ohio Tavern News*. The article told of Lezius' fifty-plus years as a beer-maker in Cleveland, dating back to the days when "the brewmaster was the czar of the brewery, a hard and sometimes testy taskmaker whose command was unquestioned even by the owner."[54] Lezius himself recalled his early days as a brewmaster: "Everything was by hand. There was no machinery. But it went like machinery when I yelled the orders."

Purchasing the Mueller family's stock in the company, Sonny DeMaioribus seized control of the Cleveland Home brewery following Omar E. Mueller's death. Sonny appointed his brother, Dr. Anthony D. DeMaioribus, a dentist, as the company's new brewmaster. (When asked why he was compelled to abandon dentistry for brewing, the brother explained, "In an Italian family you don't ask why, you do what the oldest member of the family tells you to do."[55]) The quality of Black Forest Beer was said to have declined noticeably after Lezius' passing, and sales dropped in similar fashion. Although the brewery was capable of producing 175,000 barrels annually, output amounted to just 35,000 barrels in 1951. In January of 1952, production was halted at the Cleveland Home brewery, never again to resume.[56]

Much of the brewery equipment was auctioned off early in 1952, as was the Black Forest trade name, which brought a paltry $500 from an anonymous bidder.[57] A group of urban

Sonny DeMaioribus was vilified in the local newspapers when he blocked attempts to build a public housing project on the site of his defunct brewery.

renewalists made efforts to acquire the brewery property for development of a low-income housing project. The plans were quashed largely by Sonny DeMaioribus' determination to get a good price for the land. He was quoted as saying, "If those housing people really want the property, why don't they offer us something for it?"[58] Ironically, a government-subsidized housing project occupies the site today.

The passing of the Cleveland Home Brewing Company was a bad omen for the city's remaining brewers. By the time the last keg of Black Forest Beer was tapped, local brewers had come to the brutal realization that the post-war salad days were over, and that tough times lay ahead. Competition among the large national brewers had spiraled up to full force by the early 1950s, and small brewers everywhere readied themselves for what would become a long and arduous fight for survival.

Chapter Ten

The Fatal Fifties

The character of beer-making in America in the years following World War II lends credence to the old adage that history repeats itself. In the post-Civil War era, brewers throughout the nation enjoyed a healthy rise in beer consumption which served as the impetus for a widespread surge in plant expansions and technological improvements. By the 1890s, optimism had turned to despair as industry-wide brewing capacity far outgrew the demand for beer. Competition intensified and countless brewers were forced either to consolidate with their peers or to cease business entirely. Likewise, the period after World War II was characterized by an initial sales boom followed by unrestrained expansion and modernization of brewing plants. Competition sharpened and the brewery mortality rate soared. By the end of the 1950s, the small American brewer had become an endangered species. Between 1947 and 1958, the number of operating breweries dropped from 465 to 252. And by 1965, the number was below 200.[1]

The fierce competitive situation within the brewing industry after World War II was the result of several factors. Certainly the rampant expansion of brewing plants throughout the industry was key. However, levels of beer consumption during the 1950s continually fell short of industry projections, leaving many brewers unable to use (and, thus, unable to afford) their newly bolstered brewing capacities. Annual per capita consumption of beer actually sank by eighteen percent between 1947 and 1958.[2] Brewers had incorrectly assumed that the strong post-war economy would automatically mean a reinstatement of beer as the national beverage. But beer was still largely associated with the corner tavern and was considered primarily a working-class beverage. The industry had failed to establish its product as a household staple in the minds of modern consumers. Brewers could hardly be blamed for the failure, given the pre-occupations of post-prohibition reconstruction, followed by the host of World War II restrictions on their industry. Nevertheless, when Americans made their great exodus to the suburbs during the whole of the 1950s, beer, by and large, did *not* go with them.

Recognizing the problem, the United States Brewers Foundation (USBF) instituted a series of advertising campaigns during the 1950s designed to alter public perceptions of beer, and thus stimulate sales. Mottoes such as "Beer Belongs" and "Beer – The Universal Beverage" were used to position beer as being suitable for all occasions and for all social classes. One particular set of magazine ads featured artist renderings of malt beverages being enjoyed in suburban and upper class social settings. Created especially for the USBF, the series of illustrations was entitled *Home Life in America*. Typical ad copy included lines like "Perhaps no beverages are more 'at home' on more occasions than good American beer and ale."[3]

Although the USBF ad campaigns did succeed in helping to build the desired consumer perceptions of beer, the effort did little to abate another of the fundamental problems facing the industry: the growing dominance of the nationally-shipping brewers. Virtually the defining element of the competitive environment throughout the 1950s was the fact that, while overall beer consumption remained relatively stagnant, production of the national brewers was climbing at a steady rate. In 1950, sales of the ten largest brewers in the nation accounted for about thirty-seven percent of total U.S. beer production. A decade later, the figure had grown to fifty-two percent. Sales of Anheuser-Busch alone rose from 4,928,000 to 8,477,000 barrels annually during the same period.[4] Such gains, of course, came entirely at the expense of the nation's small brewers.

In earlier days, there had always been at least one advantage that local brewers held over the shipping brewers: The high cost of transporting beer from the home brewery to distant markets made national brands more expensive to the consumer than local brands. But, after World War II, the costs of operating a brewery (particularly a small-producing brewery) rose drastically. The price edge once enjoyed by local brewers quickly began to erode. Virtually every aspect of beer production encountered inflating costs during the 1950s. For example, in 1956, Cleveland brewers reported that, in the preceding five year period alone, the cost of brewing materials increased between ten and thirty-two percent; costs of packaging supplies climbed between fifteen and twenty-five percent; delivery and transportation costs grew as much as twenty-nine percent; labor expenses increased nearly thirty percent; and real estate taxes were up more than twelve percent.[5] For small brewers with limited sales volume, such increases were nothing short of deadly.

In contrast, the national brewers were less impacted by the escalating costs of operation in two respects. First, the national brewers' enormous scale of production brought significant economies in the purchase of brewing materials and other supplies. Second, large profits allowed for frequent streamlining and modernization of brewing equipment, thus continually trimming production costs. The typical local brewer possessed neither of these advantages, and was thus engaged in a constant battle to maintain respectable profit margins. Most local brewers struggled to hang on to their price differential over the nationals as long as possible. By the mid-1950s, however, the price gap was closing fast in many regions as local brewers reluctantly raised beer prices to offset their mounting costs.

Brewers in Ohio suffered an additional obstacle to success. While the federal taxes on beer were uniform throughout the nation, state taxes varied greatly. The tax in Ohio, 36¢ per case of beer, was well above the average of 12¢ per case among the principal beer-producing states.[6] Many neighboring states had significantly lower tax rates. In Michigan, for example, the tax was 9¢. In New York, it was 7-1/2¢. The high tax in Ohio was doubly harmful. Not only did it cut into local brewers' profits, but out-of-state brewers who sold beer in Ohio were forced to seek added sales volume here to compensate for the high tax. This, of course, only worsened the competitive situation. Most Cleveland brewers sought to develop sales in low-tax states like New York and Michigan, thereby immunizing a portion of their output from the Ohio tax. But competitive pressures in those states were no less severe than anywhere else, and gaining a strong foothold in out-of-state regions was never easy.

Like most Cleveland brewers, the Standard Brewing Company tried to cultivate out-of-state markets to avoid Ohio's excessive beer tax.

Another challenge for small brewers was the increasing importance of competing with the national brewers in the advertising arena. By the early 1960s, American brewers were spending a remarkable $95 million annually on advertising, compared with just $6 million in 1938.[7] The national brewers had adopted mass media advertising as their tool of

choice in breaking new territory. Local brewers were often forced to step up their own advertising efforts in defense of their market. But advertising was expensive, and the typical small brewer simply could not match the enormous ad budgets of the shipping brewers. In 1959, for example, expenditures for spot television advertising among the twenty-two largest brewers in America averaged 39¢ per barrel of beer produced. The nation's remaining brewers, meanwhile, spent an average of less than 4¢ per barrel on spot television.[8]

Nevertheless, in Cleveland, the local brewers managed to maintain a continual presence on television. The Leisy Brewing Company aired the "Leisy Premiere Theatre" on Saturday evenings on WXEL. Hosted by actor Basil Rathbone of Sherlock Holmes fame, the program featured a first-run movie each week, interrupted periodically by Rathbone professing the wonders of Leisy beer.[9] The Cleveland-Sandusky Brewing Corporation sponsored a weekly half-hour drama called "State

Trooper," starring Rod Cameron.[10] And the Standard Brewing Company broadcasted a show on WEWS called "Ranch Ten-O-Two," featuring famous country singer Frank "Pee Wee" King and his band.[11] The program was named for Erin Brew's slogan of the early 1950s: "Formula Ten-O-Two."

Local brewers devoted the bulk of their television advertising dollars to sports programs. The Leisy brewery was

Basil Rathbone on the set of The Leisy Premiere Theatre.

197

Herbert F. Leisy (seated) looking over a promotional agreement with the Cleveland Indians in the 1950s.

When the Cleveland Indians won the 1954 American League Pennant, the Leisy Brewing Company toyed with the idea of introducing a brand called Leisy's World Series Beer. Although the brand never came to fruition, artist conceptions of the label survive.

the first to take advantage of televised sports. While fans of the 1948 World Champion Cleveland Indians eagerly anticipated the start of the 1949 season, it was uncertain whether the team's regular season home games would be broadcast on local television for the first time. Still a new and unproven medium at that time, television was approached by advertisers with apprehension. And none seemed willing to accept the high sponsorship price tag of the World Champion Indians. Just when it appeared that the season would begin without televised games, the Leisy Brewing Company stepped forward and paid $75,000 to sponsor telecasts of alternating home games throughout the season.[12] After all, television sets were rapidly becoming standard fare in taverns (where ball games were king), which created a unique opportunity for brewers to target beer drinkers right at the bar stool.

Legendary Indians pitcher Tris Speaker and local sports commentator Bob Neal were engaged by the Leisy brewery to call the games. Excitement over the Indians telecasts mounted quickly. At one point, it was even rumored that the Leisy brewery was planning a promotion whereby customers could lease a DuMont television set from the brewery and work toward ownership of the set by purchasing quantities of Leisy beer. However, the brewery denied the rumors, and no such promotion ever materialized.[13]

The Cleveland-Sandusky Brewing Corporation was sponsor of Cleveland Browns football game telecasts in 1955. The brewery had been unprofitable for three consecutive years, and president Homer Marshman hoped that promoting Gold Bond Beer and Old Timer's Ale with the Cleveland Browns would help turn the tide. Marshman, a local attorney who replaced Frank P. van de Westelaken as president of Cleveland-Sandusky in 1949, was a co-founder and president of the original Cleveland Rams football team. After 1954, he was a part owner and secretary of the Cleveland Browns. Marshman was also financially involved in horse racing locally, and the Cleveland-Sandusky brewery often sponsored telecasts of horse racing events.[14]

The Pilsener Brewing Company was best known for its radio and television coverage of Cleveland Barons hockey games. The brewery promoted its P.O.C. Beer on a variety of other sports programs as well. In 1950, Pilsener began airing a television show called "All Outdoors," featuring professional outdoorsmen demonstrating techniques in hunting, fishing, golf, tennis, archery, and other sports.[15] Another of Pilsener's television programs was the "P.O.C. Saturday Night Sports Club." Although the show consisted mainly of live boxing matches, viewers were occasionally treated to impromptu guest appearances by comedian Bob Hope.[16] (Hope had been friends with Pilsener president George S. Carter when both shared boyhood aspirations of becoming professional boxers.) The Pilsener brewery was also involved in professional tennis, establishing the "P.O.C. Trophy" for the International Pro Tennis Championship. The award made news in 1951 when that year's champion, Frank Kovacs, jumped in his car with the P.O.C. Trophy and sped away after the award ceremony. The usual policy was that the trophy remained in the hands of tennis authorities for display purposes. When asked to return the P.O.C. Trophy, Kovacs responded defiantly, "I won it on the court and I'm not giving it up until some one beats me."[17]

Television was a significant factor in the brewing industry during the 1950s. For those brewers

For me, here and in Hollywood

it's always

P.O.C. PILSENER BEER

says

Bob Hope

STARRING IN THE NEW PARAMOUNT PICTURES INC. FEATURE PRODUCTION "THAT CERTAIN FEELING" with Eva Marie Saint and Pearl Bailey

There is Nothing Finer Than P.O.C. Pilsener Beer... Regardless of Brand Name or Price

Comedian and native Clevelander Bob Hope was a childhood friend of Pilsener brewery president George S. Carter. As such, Hope appeared in a number of ads for P.O.C. Beer.

who could afford to exploit it, television was a new and efficient tool to reach a mass audience. But, far more than that, television was the impetus for an entirely new era in product advertising. In the past, the typical brewers' promotional efforts were largely disarrayed and rarely coordinated. But television gave rise to the modern advertising *campaign* – a highly-orchestrated, well-executed series of promotional efforts all conveying the same message and serving the same objective.

"That Genuine 51 Flavor"

In 1951, the Pilsener Brewing Company launched the "Genuine 51 Flavor" advertising campaign for P.O.C. Beer. Designed by local ad agency Meldrum & Fewsmith, the campaign was the first of its kind among Cleveland's brewers in that it demonstrated the tremendous power of the modern, multi-media promotional campaign. Genuine 51 Flavor was more than just a collection of ads. It was the grand unveiling of an entirely new P.O.C. Beer with a new taste and a contemporary new label. The new product represented a distinct break with the past and a bold move toward the future. Indeed, it reflected the very optimism which characterized America's booming post-war economy. Within a short time after the campaign's appearance, P.O.C. Beer climbed from the third sales position in Cleveland to first place, a distinction it would continue to enjoy for several years.

"Pilsener Pete" was the official ambassador of the new P.O.C. 51 Flavor.

The Genuine 51 Flavor campaign revolved around the claim that P.O.C. was re-formulated in 1951 based on the original recipe used by Pilsener's founders back in 1892.[18] Although that notion made for good advertising copy, it was probably not entirely true. America's tastes in beer had changed radically since the nineteenth century. Particularly after World War II, consumers were demanding lighter and milder beers. And the new P.O.C. Beer, described as "more light-bodied and milder," was formulated to answer that demand. The re-engineering of the P.O.C. brand to be less full-bodied marked the beginning of a rash of such product shifts among Cleveland's beers.

Another key element of the Genuine 51 Flavor campaign was P.O.C.'s contemporary label design. The fact that the new P.O.C. label bore an obvious resemblance to that of Schlitz Beer was undoubtedly not a coincidence. After all, Schlitz was the nation's best-selling beer in 1951, and it was national brewers like Schlitz against which the new P.O.C. Beer was designed to compete.

Genuine 51 Flavor was inaugurated under the direction of George S. Carter, who had joined the Pilsener Brewing Company as president on January 1, 1951. Carter came to Pilsener from the Leisy brewery, where he had spent four years as general sales manager and assistant to president Herbert F. Leisy. City Products Corporation, owner of the Pilsener brewery, hired Carter to help Pilsener revitalize its sales and endure the rapidly intensifying competitive environment. Sales of the brewery had peaked in 1949 at about 360,000 barrels, and then declined by ten percent in 1950.[19] Carter's immediate task was to reverse that trend. And that he did. By 1954, Pilsener had recorded a 200 percent increase in sales over 1951. Commenting on the unparalleled sales growth, Carter said,

The increase definitely shows that the Pilsener Brewing Company has succeeded in reversing the trend wherein the large national breweries have been overwhelming the smaller beer producers saleswise, and proves that so-called 'local' breweries cannot only continue to exist, but actually progress and grow.[20]

George S. Carter

Indeed, the Pilsener Brewing Company would prove to be the only one of Cleveland's brewers to mount a solid defense against the national brewers during much of the 1950s.

Impressed by the explosive success of the Genuine 51 Flavor campaign, Cleveland brewers responded with product changes and promotional efforts strikingly similar to P.O.C.'s. For example, the Standard Brewing Company's Erin Brew Beer (which had been unseated by P.O.C. as the city's largest seller) was reintroduced with a new recipe dubbed "Formula Ten-O-Two." A re-designed Erin Brew label had made its debut several months earlier. The modern, almost space-age characteristics of Erin Brew's new look were in sharp contrast to the old label, which had undergone few changes since the brand's inception in 1904. The gigantic ad campaign which heralded the new Erin Brew Formula Ten-O-Two was kicked off in May of 1953 with a gathering at Hotel Carter for Standard's distributors.[21] For the next three months, Clevelanders were barraged with radio, television, newspaper and billboard messages celebrating the arrival of Formula Ten-O-Two. Indeed, Standard had followed Pilsener into the era of the multi-media ad campaign.

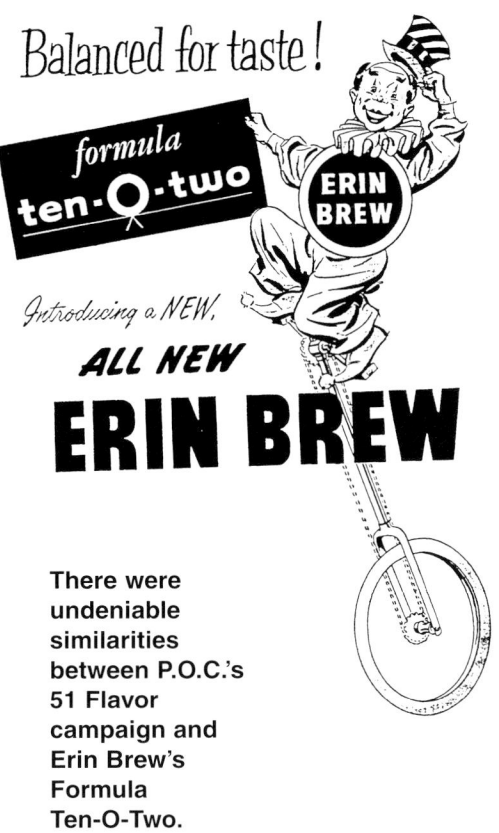

There were undeniable similarities between P.O.C.'s 51 Flavor campaign and Erin Brew's Formula Ten-O-Two.

The Cleveland-Sandusky Brewing Corporation responded to P.O.C.'s Genuine 51 Flavor by initiating its new Gold Bond "1953 Prize Beer."[22] Promotions centered around the fact that Gold Bond had won the "Star of Excellence" at a recent beer competition in Paris. In keeping with consumers' demand for lighter beers, the Cleveland-Sandusky brewery advertised its new Gold Bond as "99% sugar free." According to ads, "A whole case of Gold Bond contains less sugar than the average cup of coffee."[23] This particular claim, although surely true, was abandoned not long after government authorities issued a statement that such claims were misleading. According to the statement, all beers in their finished form have "little more than a negligible trace of sugar."[24]

Interestingly, while the Pilsener, Standard and Cleveland-Sandusky breweries sought to project an image of modernism for their products during the early 1950s, the Leisy Brewing Company took the opposite tack. Drawing upon its long heritage, the Leisy brewery built its 1952 promotions upon a celebration of its 90th anniversary (Isaac Leisy and his brothers had first brewed beer in 1862 in Keokuk, Iowa). Particularly from a news publicity standpoint, the campaign was highly effective. Local newspapers were attracted to the colorful story of Isaac Leisy and his brothers coming to Cleveland in 1873 to establish a brewing dynasty. "Since then," wrote one reporter, "enough Leisy beer to fill a good-sized lake has rolled out of the West Side landmark."[25] The 90th anniversary celebration marked the production of Leisy's 300 millionth gallon of beer.

Although the Leisy promotions were focused on the past, the brewery was cognizant of the fact that consumer preference was shifting away from full-bodied beer. In fact, Leisy was among the first in the industry to perceive a demand for lighter beer. As early as 1940, the brewery had introduced a brand called Leisy's Light. And with the trend becoming fully realized by the 1950s, Leisy's Light, sporting a new label design, became the company's principal brand. A 1952 television commercial related the rationale for Leisy's Light:

> *Most of us can remember when automobiles and even locomotives were built for bulk and weight rather than pleasure and usefulness. The popular idea then was that, in order to be good, a product had to be massive and heavy. Progress changed that false notion. Beer, too, has progressed. Today, people who like good beer are turning toward a lighter beer – particularly, Leisy's Light....Try it yourself and join the chorus that's singing, 'Go Lighter, Go Leisy's, Go Leisy's Light!*[26]

The "chorus" was loud for Leisy's in 1952. The 90th Anniversary promotion was a decided success, and sales were strong. However, the year 1952 was the last profitable one for the Leisy Brewing Company. By the following year, the brewery had started down a path of steady decline.

The End For Leisy's

When Herbert F. Leisy was born in 1900 in the mansion next door to the old Vega Avenue brewery, it was preordained that he would one day take his place at the head of the family beer business. After all, before Otto I. Leisy died in 1914, he had *mandated* that no majority of the company's stock could ever be sold to anyone outside the Leisy family.[27] It never was. Herbert F. Leisy possessed that same commitment to the family business when he re-opened the Leisy brewery after repeal. Particularly after the disappearance of all World War II restrictions on brewing, Leisy must have had high expectations for the success of the business. And, in fact, the brewery experienced its best post-prohibition year in 1949 when sales topped 330,000 barrels.[28] In just a few years, however, the Leisy brewery's outlook for the future had darkened under the pressures of competition. Herbert F. Leisy would spend much of the 1950s struggling to regain a sound footing for his brewery.

In an effort to replace some of its lost sales volume, the Leisy brewery launched Leisy's Mello-Gold Beer early in 1955. Brewery officials recognized that competing against the national brewers for the *traditional* beer drinker's patronage was becoming an increasingly difficult proposition. Thus, the new Mello-Gold was designed not to sway existing beer drinkers from their usual brand, but to cultivate an altogether new segment of beer consumers. Herbert F. Leisy explained, "Mello-Gold is aimed at a new, virtually untapped beer market....We feel it will appeal especially to women and the younger generation of potential beer customers, because of the bitter-free taste."[29] Mello-Gold was not available in draught, but was packaged in a unique slope-shouldered bottle with a stylish gold foil label. An aggressive promotional campaign was undertaken, the most notable feature of which was a series of radio jingles written and performed by musician Ray Charles. On television, the "Mello-Gold Girl" demonstrated the Leisy "spoon test" and urged viewers to try the experiment at home. The test consisted of comparing a spoonful of foam from Mello-Gold with that of any other beer to evaluate the bitterness of each.

Commenting on Mello-Gold, Herbert F. Leisy gave some hint of the degree to which Leisy management had pinned their hopes on the new brand:

Change is inevitable and desirable. Every thriving, successful organization changes and grows continually, impelled by inner strength and development, and driven by outside forces in the fields of its operation. We consider Mello-Gold another such step in our growth in Cleveland.[30]

The Leisy "Rathskeller" (old aging cellar deep beneath the brewery) was a sort of hospitality center for visitors to the plant.

However, in the end, Mello-Gold fell far short of expectations. Probably the largest obstacle to the brand's success was its unusually high price – higher, in fact, than any of Leisy's other products. The "vacuum aging" process necessary to remove all bitterness from the beer was very expensive, and significantly extended the length of the aging period. In addition, because the patent for this particular process was owned by other parties, the Leisy brewery paid royalties for its use. Thus, the brand's high price was all but unavoidable. But the idea that Mello-Gold's intended consumers – "women and the younger generation" – would be willing to pay a premium price for beer proved to be a gross miscalculation. By the end of 1958, Mello-Gold was no longer in production.[31]

Continuing its search for new "niche" markets, the Leisy brewery introduced Black Dallas Malt Liquor in 1956.[32] Many brewers had experimented with malt liquors in the 1950s in hopes of

Western Reserve Historical Society

Bock beer season was a special time at the Leisy brewery. Each spring, Leisy's "Billy Bock Contest" was held in the brewery yard. The rules? "Easy! Just show up with a goat." Goats were judged on a variety of characteristics and cash prizes were awarded. The largest goat won the grand prize of $200. Any goat that said "Baa" won a case of Leisy's Beer.

In 1949, Herbert F. Leisy hired a local artist to sculpt two goat statues and two polar bear statues to guard the brewery entrance. Today, the statues reside at the Cleveland Metroparks Zoo.

establishing an ultra-premium beer category in America. Malt liquor was typically priced higher than even the premium-priced national brands, and usually contained significantly more alcohol than regular beer. Although Black Dallas Malt Liquor was produced at the Leisy brewery for the remainder of the company's existence, the brand never accounted for a significant portion of Leisy's sales.

In 1958, Herbert F. Leisy embarked on a spirited effort to revitalize the family brewery. Although the company had suffered five consecutive profitless years, Leisy was determined not to let his brewery fade quietly into oblivion as so many others around the country had done. The root problem facing many small brewers during the 1950s was a lack of sales volume. Competition being what it was, most small brewers simply could not sell enough beer to cover the ever-increasing costs of operating a brewery. The Leisy Brewing Company was no different in this regard; added sales volume was the key to survival. With that in mind, early in 1958, Herbert F. Leisy negotiated the purchase of the George F. Stein Brewery of Buffalo, New York.[33] The Buffalo plant was shut down and production of the Stein brands transferred to the Leisy brewery. The brands were then shipped back to New York and sold in the markets where they enjoyed a long-standing popularity. This particular strategy among brewers was growing in practice by the late 1950s. It allowed for the addition of large increments of sales volume without incurring significant increases in production costs.

In another tactical maneuver, Herbert F. Leisy lured

George S. Carter away from the Pilsener Brewing Company to join the Leisy brewery as president in 1958. Leisy (who then became chairman of the board and chief executive officer of the brewery) heralded Carter as "the most capable man in the field."[34] And a local newspaper called Carter's move to Leisy "one of the most important developments in the brewery industry here in recent years."[35] Carter had worked for the Leisy brewery as general manager and assistant to the president before taking over the presidency of the Pilsener Brewing Company in 1951. While at Pilsener, Carter was credited with propelling P.O.C. Beer into the leading sales position in Cleveland and transforming the company into a formidable competitor of both local and national brewers. Upon his return to the Leisy brewery, Carter was quoted as saying:

> *This is a challenge for which I have been waiting a long time. The position of local and national breweries across the country is becoming more and more competitive each year. The situation today demands an excellent product, aggressive advertising, merchandising, and consistent hard selling to acquire and maintain a position of leadership. I consider the Leisy brewery and its fine name most eminently suited to prosper in this highly competitive industry.*[36]

Carter's first move at Leisy was to duplicate the strategy which he had employed to catapult Pilsener's sales several years earlier. Clearly reminiscent of P.O.C.'s esteemed Genuine 51 Flavor campaign, a new product called Leisy Pilsner Beer made a splashy entrance onto the market late in 1958. Full-page newspaper ads told how brewmasters Otto Kalsen and Carl Fromm (the latter formerly of the Pilsener brewery) painstakingly developed the new Leisy Pilsner Beer, replicating the brew of the famous Castle Brewery near Munich, Bavaria. When the product was finished, Herbert F. Leisy and George S. Carter flew to Bavaria to place the new Leisy Pilsner under the scrutiny of the brewmasters at the Castle brewery. Not surprisingly, the brew was judged "perfect in every respect" by the Bavarian brewers.[37] Beer drinkers in Cleveland, however, apparently did not concur, as Leisy Pilsner achieved only moderate sales.

The launch of Leisy Pilsner Beer in 1958 was the "last hurrah" for the Leisy Brewing Company. Less than one year later, the final batch of Leisy beer was produced at the old landmark brewery. Announcement of the plant's closing was made in October of 1959. Curiously, Herbert F. Leisy gave reports that the closing was merely a temporary measure, and that brewing would resume after certain plant improvements were completed.[38] That scenario, of course, never materialized.

As if to add insult to injury, a law suit was filed by the "Verband Dortmunder Bierbauer" (Association of Dortmund Brewers) against the Leisy brewery just prior to its closing. The Association insisted that the Leisy's Dortmunder brand infringed upon the products of Dortmund's breweries. Thus, the Association demanded that Leisy pay damages for its twenty-year use of the Dortmunder name. The suit was eventually dismissed for "lack of prosecution."[39]

Meanwhile, dismantling of the Leisy brewery had commenced by 1961. Much of the equipment, including the brewery's large copper kettles, was sold to a brewery in Athens, Greece. From the windows of their new home, the old Leisy kettles had a clear view of the Parthenon, a fact which Herbert F. Leisy jokingly hoped would bring some small degree of immortality to the Leisy brewery.[40]

Although the Leisy brewery would never again brew beer, the Leisy brands did remain available to Cleveland beer drinkers until 1964. When brewing ceased, Herbert F. Leisy made arrangements with the Canadian Ace Brewing Company in Chicago to take over production of the Leisy brands and ship them to Cleveland. Sales were handled through independent distributors, and the Leisy Brewing Company received royalties from the Chicago brewer for every barrel of Leisy beer sold.[41]

The closing of the once invulnerable Leisy Brewing Company foreshadowed the destiny of Cleveland's remaining brewers. The

Above: When the Leisy brewery closed in 1959, its gargantuan copper kettles were sent to a brewery in Athens, Greece.

Left: The main buildings of the Leisy brewery were demolished in 1974.

1950s had been difficult. Locally, all but the Carling Brewing Company ended the decade battered and weak. By 1964, the last of the great Cleveland beers were but a memory.

Prognosis Negative at Cleveland-Sandusky

As early as 1947, many brewers were already predicting a dim future for the brewing industry. Frank P. van de Westelaken, president and brewmaster of the Cleveland-Sandusky Brewing Corporation on East 55th Street, was among those who saw trouble on the horizon. After reporting on his company's favorable 1946 performance, van de Westelaken delivered a stern warning to stockholders:

> *While we find ourselves in a most favorable position at the moment, we should not be too optimistic as to the future....In particular, the higher cost of materials, and much more pronounced competition, will combine to make it increasingly difficult to maintain a respectable profit margin between the selling price of our product and the cost to produce it.*[42]

Those assertions proved painfully accurate in time. It was perhaps that very fact which lead van de Westelaken to leave Cleveland in 1949 and take a non-managerial position as brewmaster in a Nashville, Tennessee brewery.[43] Homer Marshman, a local attorney and Cleveland-Sandusky's chairman of the board, replaced van de Westelaken as president of the brewery. Sales of the company's Gold Bond Beer and Old Timer's Ale declined steadily as competition intensified and consumer loyalty to local brands waned. By 1952, the brewery was operating at a deficit, a condition which would continue for the next five years.

Like many brewers, the Cleveland-Sandusky Brewing Corporation struggled to identify new markets which might offer some relief from the overwhelming fight for the "core" beer drinker's patronage. On January 1, 1955, Cleveland-Sandusky resurrected one of its prohibition-era products, New York Special Brew, and launched an effort to build demand for the non-alcoholic malt beverage. The brand's primary target was the thirty-five percent of Ohio which was under some type of dry legislation. Retailers in such regions who carried New York Special Brew were given advertising placards which quipped, "We sell near beer here because no beer is sold near here."[45] Bolstered by initially good sales of the brand, an official at the Cleveland-Sandusky brewery said, in complete seriousness, "We may start an educational campaign to sell it to children, in a different container, of course."[46] Indeed, new markets were clearly in dire demand.

In August of 1956, a controlling interest in the Cleveland-Sandusky Brewing Corporation was purchased by Marvin Bilsky, who had come to the brewery one year earlier as vice-president and general manager. Three months after his arrival, he was elected as the company's president, replacing Homer Marshman. (At age thirty-

Gold Bond Beer was Cleveland-Sandusky's flagship brand for more than a half-century.

four, Bilsky was said to have been the youngest president of any American brewery.) Cleveland-Sandusky had been consistently unprofitable for several years and, in some sense, Bilsky represented the company's last hope for survival. Described as "a dynamic go-getter with raven hair and an Ernie Kovacs mustache," Marvin Bilsky possessed just the kind of enthusiasm which many stockholders felt had been lacking in the company's management.[47]

Marvin Bilsky came to the Cleveland-Sandusky brewery with a strong background in mass merchandising. For several years, he had been general manager of his family's wholesale bakery, the Bilsky Baking Company. Thus, he was not only well-versed in the ways of consumer goods marketing, but was a well-known figure among Cleveland's retail food industry. His long-time relationships with local grocery store owners and supermarket chains followed Bilsky to Cleveland-Sandusky and proved to be an invaluable asset to the company's beer sales. Crystal Rock Beer, after seven years in hibernation, was revived by Bilsky in 1956 for exclusive distribution through supermarkets.[48] The brand was not advertised, and was intended to serve as the low-price counterpart to the more expensive Gold Bond Beer and Old Timer's Ale.

Jaro H. Pavlik

When brewmaster Frank P. van de Westelaken left the Cleveland-Sandusky Brewing Corporation in 1949, his duties in the brewhouse passed into very capable hands. Taking van de Westelaken's place was veteran Cleveland beer-maker Jaro H. Pavlik, who was nearing his *sixtieth* year as a brewmaster. Pavlik was born into a brewing family in Kuttenburg, Bohemia, where he first apprenticed in a brewery at age fourteen. After traveling Europe and working in a number of different breweries, the twenty-year-old Pavlik rode steerage to America in 1897, settling in Cleveland. His first job was at the Pilsener Brewing Company, where he earned $10.50 per week working twelve hours per day, seven days per week. Lacking proper certification as a brewmaster in America, Pavlik left Cleveland to attend the prestigious Wahl-Henius Institute brewing school in Chicago.

With his Master Brewer's certificate in hand, Pavlik returned to the Pilsener Brewing Company in 1901 and was made head brewmaster. Although a job opportunity with a Mankato, Minnesota brewery briefly lured Pavlik away from his adopted city, his fondness for Cleveland soon brought him "home." From 1904 until 1929, Pavlik served as brewmaster at the Standard Brewing Company in Cleveland, making Erin Brew Beer and Standard Old Bohemian Style Beer. He later helped form the Sunrise Brewing Company, later renamed the Tip Top Brewing Company in honor of Pavlik's popular Tip Top Bohemian Beer. After brief employment with both the Brewing Corporation of America and the Cleveland Home Brewing Company, Pavlik retired in 1947. However, after more than a half-century of making beer, the seventy-year-old brewmaster found it difficult to stay away from his art for long. In 1949, he came out of retirement to fill the vacancy left by Frank P. van de Westelaken at the Cleveland-Sandusky brewery.

Once described as "a rosy-faced, white-haired gentleman with a fondness for dancing polkas to brass band music and smoking long porcelain pipes," Pavlik was among the most experienced brewers in the country in his later years. He had the unusual practice of rarely taste-testing his brews-in-progress. "If the smell and sparkle please me," he once said, "the flavor will take care of itself. After half a century of judging brews, one never makes a misjudgment." By 1950, Jaro H. Pavlik had brewed his last beer, again retiring from his life-long calling. Pavlik died in 1955 at the age of seventy-eight.[44]

Marvin Bilsky (right) with John Giunta, president of Stop-N-Shop Supermarkets. Bilsky's good relationships with mass merchandisers were a boon for the Cleveland-Sandusky brewery.

The "Gold Bond Walking Six-Pack" was one example of the inexpensive promotional activities Bilsky employed to rebuild the Cleveland-Sandusky brewery's sales.

Although Bilsky brought good retailer relationships to the Cleveland-Sandusky brewery, consumer loyalty to the company's brands continued to wane. And with little cash available for large-scale promotions, rebuilding demand for the company's beer represented a formidable challenge. As one optimistic observer noted, "The problem was to do it with one-tenth the ideal budget, and that's where the fun came in."[49] Indeed, limited funds did not dissuade Cleveland-Sandusky management from making an aggressive bid to recapture lost consumer patronage. Costly mass media advertising was largely foregone in favor of a less expensive, more "hands-on" approach. For example, when Gold Bond Beer was promoted in 1956 as being brewed using Laurentian Mountain Spring Water from Canada, a novel promotional gimmick was devised. Six female models, wearing three-foot high facsimiles of Gold Bond beer cans, visited taverns, beverage stores and supermarkets throughout Cleveland. The models (collectively known as the "Gold Bond Walking Six-Pack") were transported to their various destinations by a conspicuous horse-drawn wagon with two Canadian Mounties at the reins. Models were also permanently stationed at major supermarkets to act as *live displays* for the new Gold Bond Beer, "with that lively Canadian flavor."

Marvin Bilsky's charge to put the Cleveland-Sandusky Brewing Corporation back on solid ground met with initial success. Sales for the first four months of 1957 were sixty percent higher than those of the same period in 1956. Production at the brewery climbed from 103,000 barrels in 1957 to 111,000 barrels in 1958. During the latter year, the brewery declared its first stock dividend in years.[50] Indeed, it was the first sign that the brewery had finally shaken off the problems of its past.

Bilsky could now concern himself with building for the future. His hopes centered not just on re-establishing a local market, but on transforming Cleveland-Sandusky into a major regional brewer. Expansion and modernization of the brewery was made a top priority. In 1959, all of the machinery and equipment of the Star-Peerless Brewing Company in Belleville, Illinois was purchased and shipped to the Cleveland-Sandusky brewery for use in expansion of the East 55th Street plant.[51] And plans were under way to expand the brewery's sales territory from three states (Ohio, Michigan and Pennsylvania) to six.

In 1960, in an attempt to establish new revenue streams, the Cleveland-Sandusky brewery branched out into the distribution of wine. The company became the exclusive wholesale agent for Italian Swiss Colony Wine in a three-county region surrounding Cleveland. The idea was a practical one, as the sale of wine was conducted through many of the same outlets as the sale of beer, thus creating many natural economies. To Marvin Bilsky, wine represented a largely untapped market in Ohio. He pointed out that annual per capita consumption of wine in California was three gallons, while it was barely *one* gallon in Ohio. According to Bilsky, "Wine is not being pushed the way it should be. We are going out for floor-stacking and mass display merchandising in stores and supermarkets."[52]

Bottling Old Timer's Ale at the Cleveland-Sandusky brewery.

Despite the Cleveland-Sandusky company's stalwart determination to prevail over worsening conditions for small brewers, the company finally succumbed in September of 1962. Marvin Bilsky announced that beer production would cease immediately, and that the Detroit-based International Breweries, Inc. had arranged to take over production of Crystal Rock Beer, Old Timer's Ale and GB Beer (formerly Gold Bond Beer).[53] The Cleveland-Sandusky company retained the distribution rights to the brands in Northeast Ohio well into the 1960s, but none of them was ever again brewed in Cleveland.

Pilsener: "Goin', Goin', Gone"

Such read the 1963 newspaper headline which told of the auction at the old Pilsener brewery at West 65th Street and Clark Avenue.[54] One by one, bidders staked their claim on the various pieces of dormant brewing equipment. Production at the plant had stopped earlier that year when Pilsener's parent company, City Products Corporation, sold the brewery and its P.O.C. brand to the Duquesne Brewing Company of Pittsburgh. Despite local speculation that the new owners would keep the Pilsener plant in operation, it is not likely that the Pittsburgh brewer ever intended to do so. Rather, Duquesne's interest in the Pilsener Brewing Company most certainly laid entirely in the acquisition of the P.O.C. label. The brand still enjoyed a healthy market in Cleveland. With Pittsburgh only a short trucking distance away, economics dictated that the Pilsener brewery be closed and production of P.O.C. be transferred to Duquesne's home plant. Not unlike the demise of a number of other Cleveland brands, the once proud P.O.C. name became an ancillary product of a foreign brewer.

In contrast, just a decade earlier, the Pilsener Brewing Company's outlook for the future could hardly have been more promising. After George S. Carter joined Pilsener management as president in 1951, the company enjoyed sustained growth. P.O.C. Beer surpassed both Leisy's Light and Erin Brew to become Cleveland's largest selling brand by 1953. Sales in out-of-town markets,

Most of the Pilsener brewery complex – known as "Pilsener Square" – still stands today.

as well, climbed at a steady pace. Despite frequent plant expansion, the company found it difficult to supply the swelling demand. In fact, in order to help alleviate a sudden shortage of brewing capacity, Pilsener acquired the Franklin Brewing Company of Columbus, Ohio late in 1952.[55] As the Cleveland brewery struggled to fill orders at home, output from the Columbus plant was used mainly to supply beer to southern Ohio and out-of-state markets.

While many of Cleveland's other brewers had begun to feel the pains of worsening competition, it appeared that the Pilsener company might be among the fortunate few to survive as a strong regional brewer. By the mid-1950s, Pilsener's distribution area included Ohio, West Virginia, Pennsylvania, New York and some of the New England states.[56] The company heralded its fifth consecutive year of sales growth in 1955 as beer production reached 412,000 barrels for the year. The Columbus brewery had been closed after completion of an aggressive expansion program at the Cleveland plant. Nevertheless, in 1956, the Pilsener Brewing Company again found itself in need of more brewing capacity.

George S. Carter announced that $5 million had been earmarked for the purchase of additional brewing plants in Cleveland, or another major city, or both. The goal was to achieve an annual production capacity of one million barrels for P.O.C. Beer.[57] Management, it seemed, was well aware of the harsh reality facing most mid-sized brewers: stagnation bred failure. In the words of one local brewer, "In this industry there can be no standing still – a company either advances or loses ground."[58]

The year 1956 was a pivotal one for the Pilsener Brewing Company. In spite of the brewery's ambitious drive for regional dominance, sales that year were disappointing. Plans for acquisition of supplementary breweries were suspended, and the company's upward momentum was stymied.

Above: The Pilsener brewery promoted cooking with beer in 1951.

Left: The annual release of P.O.C. Bock Beer was cause for celebration at the Pilsener brewery.

211

Introduced in 1959, the decidedly sultry "Golden Girl" was P.O.C.'s answer to "Mabel," the popular (and far more wholesome) patroness of Carling Black Label Beer.

Inspecting the fermentors at the Pilsener brewery. While the nation's large brewers could afford the most modern, efficient brewing equipment available, most small brewers could not.

Although the brewery remained profitable over the next several years, the explosive growth which had characterized the company throughout the first half of the 1950s was never to be repeated. The resignation of George S. Carter in 1958 was a sign of things to come.[59] Five years later, the Pilsener brewery produced its final batch of P.O.C. Beer.

Without question, the intensifying competition among and between the national brewers during the late 1950s was a key factor in the Pilsener Brewing Company's decline. However, Pilsener's ownership by City Products Corporation also played a major role in the destiny of the brewery. By the late 1950s, priorities within the highly diversified City Products Corporation had begun to shift. The Pilsener brewery (as well as the parent company's breweries in Miami and New Orleans) diminished in importance as the parent company entered new, more profitable fields of business. In particular, City Products had spent a number of years – and millions of dollars – achieving a prominent position in the mass merchandising industry. By 1962, the company owned and operated hundreds of retail department stores across the country, and supplied wholesale merchandise to 2,400 Ben Franklin variety stores.[60]

The first sign of City Products' fading interest in brewing came in 1958 when the company's Miami brewery was sold to Anheuser-Busch.[61] Just a few years later, management announced its decision to divest itself entirely of all businesses deemed "not in keeping with its emphasis on merchandising."[62] Thus, both the Pilsener brewery and the brewery in New Orleans were put up for sale in 1962, and City Products abruptly exited the beer business. It remains an intriguing question whether the destiny of the Pilsener Brewing Company would have been radically different had City Products adhered to its early commitment to beer-making.

212

After buying Pilsener in 1963, the Duquesne Brewing Company produced P.O.C. Beer at its Pittsburgh plant for several years, shipping much of it to Cleveland. Somewhat ironically, P.O.C. was once again brewed locally when Duquesne closed its doors in 1972 and sold its entire line of products to C. Schmidt & Sons. The Philadelphia-based Schmidt had just recently taken over the former Carling brewery on Quincy Avenue. During its many years of production at the Schmidt plant, P.O.C. enjoyed good local sales. In fact, even after Schmidt left the city in 1984, as many as 10,000 cases of P.O.C. Beer were sent to Cleveland every month from the company's Philadelphia brewery. When the 125-year-old C. Schmidt & Sons finally fell victim to competitive pressures in 1986, it sought a buyer for the lingering P.O.C. label. No takers emerged.[63]

Death Knell at Standard

In August of 1953, John T. Feighan, co-founder of the Standard Brewing Company, passed away in his seventy-seventh year.[64] For just about a half-century, Feighan had been a director of the Standard brewery, taking over as president in 1933. It was under his shrewd guidance that the brewery rebuilt itself after repeal, and finally boasted Cleveland's largest selling brand of beer, Erin Brew, by 1951.

But, far more than a brewer, Feighan was a noted figure in the local banking industry. He started as an office boy at the Detroit Avenue Savings & Trust Company at West 25th Street and Detroit. Feighan recalled that his early responsibilities included everything from "scrubbing the floors to lugging the huge ledgers around."[65] He eventually climbed his way up to the position of vice president of the bank, by then renamed the Forest City Savings & Trust Company. Feighan was put in charge of the bank after its purchase by the Cleveland Trust Company in 1920. Thus, in his nearly sixty years as a banker, Feighan worked less than a half-mile from his birthplace in the Irish neighborhood known as "the Angle." He made many friends over the years, and it was said that Feighan knew 20,000 west-siders by name. Despite his long tenure in the brewing industry, Feighan was a banker at heart. He once commented, "If I had the opportunity to choose my career again, I would again choose banking."[66]

John T. Feighan

After John T. Feighan's death in 1953, George E. Creadon and John T. Feighan Jr., sons of the founders, took over management of the Standard brewery as president and treasurer, respectively. But their task would not be a simple one. The Standard Brewing Company had already begun to encounter many of the same problems threatening virtually every small brewer. Despite rising costs of operation and the growing formidability of the national brewers, Standard's management remained optimistic, rarely giving any indication that business was suffering. Nevertheless, the first hint of trouble at Standard came as early as 1956 when rumors circulated that the company was negotiating its sale to another local brewer.[67] Although George E. Creadon denied the rumors and asserted that "no such idea has ever been entertained," it was apparent that the company's outlook for the future was not entirely promising.

John T. Feighan Jr. became president of the brewery after the death of George E. Creadon in 1960.[68] Feighan, a graduate of Georgetown University and a Cleveland attorney, was determined that the Standard Brewing Company would, in his words, be "successful in withstanding the in-roads of the so-called national brands."[69] He fought valiantly to retain market share and counter the insidious competitive strategies of the invading national brewers. However, despite Fieghan's best efforts, conditions at Standard deteriorated. The once-sturdy Erin Brew brand suffered a debilitating plunge in sales, and was thus replaced in all but a few markets with a new product, Standard Premium Beer. But even with the introduction of the new brand, the brewery's situation did not improve. Between 1960 and 1961, about 200 Standard employees were laid off as the company's sales continued to plummet.[70]

In an effort to combat frequent price cutting among the national brands in Cleveland, the Standard brewery launched two new products, Red Velvet Ale and Red Label Beer, in 1960 and 1961, respectively. The brands featured innovative built-in price incentives. Red Velvet Ale, for example, was sold at the same price as a case of twenty-four twelve-ounce bottles, but was packaged instead in half-quart bottles, thus giving the consumer an extra quantity of beer in each case. Likewise, Red Label Beer was sold at regular prices, but cases of the new brand included twenty-eight bottles instead of the traditional twenty-four. The brands were cleverly promoted to retailers

By 1961, the veteran Erin Brew had been replaced by Standard Premium Beer.

with the slogan, "Offer the MOST in either Case!"[71] Upon announcing the new brands, Benton P. Bohannon*, chairman of the board at Standard, described the plight of his company: "The small and medium-sized brewer has the biggest fight on his hands. The big brewers are getting bigger and the small ones are getting squeezed out."[72]

Bohannon's comments could hardly have been more prophetic. Just weeks later, in May of 1961, it was announced that the Standard Brewing Company had made arrangements to sell its brewery to the F. & M. Schaefer Brewing Company of Brooklyn, New York. Schaefer was among those brewers making a bid for national distribution – "a big brewer getting bigger," as Bohannon might have characterized it. The sale price was reported to have been about $2 million, and the transaction allowed for Schaefer to continue production of the Standard labels.[73] But, of course, Schaefer Beer would constitute the bulk of the brewery's output, as the company aggressively pursued cultivation of new markets throughout the Midwest.

The Cleveland-based Carling Brewing Company was in the very throes of its battle for the top position among America's beer-makers when Schaefer took over the Standard brewery in 1961. As such, Carling management did not react favorably to Schaefer's move into Cleveland, and a venomous law suit between the two brewers promptly ensued. The Carling Brewing Company charged that Schaefer's Red Velvet Ale and Red Label Beer (which had been inherited from the Standard Brewing Company) were so-named in a "flagrant" attempt to confuse customers and infringe on the brand identities of Carling's Red Cap Ale and Black Label Beer. A spokesman for the Schaefer brewery insinuated an ulterior motive on Carling's part: "Strange that Red Label beer and Red Velvet ale have been on the

---

*Benton P. Bohannon (who was married to the step-daughter of George E. Creadon) was the son of James A. Bohannon, founder of Brewing Corporation of America, predecessor of the Carling Brewing Company.

market without complaint from Carling for some time, and that a suit should be instituted after our purchase of the Standard Brewing Company."[74] Rather than incur the expense of a lengthy court fight to save the brands, Schaefer reluctantly agreed to discontinue Red Velvet Ale and Red Label Beer in exchange for dismissal of the law suit.[75]

Competitive posturing aside, the F. & M. Schaefer Brewing Company was a welcome newcomer to Cleveland, and the firm enjoyed good prosperity here. The Schaefer name had not been entirely unfamiliar to Clevelanders. Early in 1961, Schaefer brewery president Rudolph J. Schaefer II had purchased a majority ownership of the Cleveland Browns football team along with co-investor Art Modell.[76] Schaefer held his interest in the Browns for many years, but ultimately sold out to partner Modell.

The F. & M. Schaefer Brewing Company heralded its arrival in Cleveland by parking a fleet of beer trucks on Public Square, each truck sporting the message: "America's Oldest Lager Is Cleveland's Newest Beer."[77] Rudolph J. Schaefer III was appointed by his father to oversee brewing operations in Cleveland. A new subsidiary, Schaefer Brewing Company of Ohio, Inc., was set up to brew and distribute Schaefer Beer throughout Ohio and neighboring states. Expansion of the Cleveland brewery was frequent; between 1961 and 1964, Schaefer spent approximately $1.5 million on enlargement and improvement of the Train Avenue facility. In 1964, Schaefer recorded its best sales year in history, producing 4,446,634 barrels of beer and ranking as the nation's sixth largest brewing company.[78]

In 1961, the Standard Brewing Co. was sold to the F. & M. Schaefer Brewing Co. of Brooklyn, New York. Schaefer left Cleveland three years later.

However, 1964 was also the last year that Schaefer Beer would be brewed in Cleveland. Reporting the company's intention to cease brewing at the Cleveland plant, a Schaefer official said,

Despite the fact that the acceptance of our product in the Cleveland area has established a satisfactory base for future sales growth, available capacity in our other plants, increased by the acquisition of the Hamm Brewery in Baltimore to satisfy eastern demand, makes continued production in Cleveland uneconomical.[79]

In addition to plants in Baltimore and Cleveland, Schaefer operated its main plant in Brooklyn and another facility in Albany. The F. & M. Schaefer Brewing Company continued its climb toward national status until decline set in during the mid-1970s.

The old Train Avenue plant was not quite yet destined to go the way of so many other defunct and decaying breweries around the country. Instead, Philadelphia-based brewers C. Schmidt & Sons, Inc., in its own quest for a national presence, moved into the Cleveland brewery and began producing its Schmidt's Of Philadelphia brand for distribution in the Midwestern states. With sales of just over two million barrels in 1964, C. Schmidt & Sons was the nation's fourteenth largest brewer.[80] Operations continued in the brewery until 1972 when, in need of more brewing capacity, Schmidt moved across town to the recently-closed Carling brewery on Quincy Avenue. For the next thirteen years, C. Schmidt & Sons remained Cleveland's only active brewer, one of a shrinking number of companies able to weather the increasingly hostile conditions within the American brewing industry.

Chapter Eleven

Carling: In Pursuit Of A National Market

As early as the 1870s, a few select brewers aspired to the dream of selling a single brand of beer to a national market. Certainly by no coincidence, it was largely those very same brewers who, more than a century later, topped the list of America's truly national beer-makers. Forward-thinking brewers like Anheuser-Busch, Pabst and Schlitz integrated the goal of coast-to-coast/border-to-border sales into their business philosophies at a very early date. And, indeed, each had come surprisingly close to achieving a true national market by the time National Prohibition brought the whole endeavor to an abrupt end.

That notwithstanding, brewers with national aspirations faced a number of significant obstacles before prohibition. Many of the hindrances stemmed from the simple fact that scientific achievements in brewing had not yet allowed for exact duplication of a brewer's product in two different breweries. Shipping beer from a single plant was the only viable system. But hauling beer over long distances was expensive and extremely bothersome, and it often proved detrimental to the quality of the

beer. Indeed, far more than any other factor, the trials and tribulations of long-distance shipping hindered brewers' ability to capture a true national market before prohibition.

However, after repeal (and even more so after the end of World War II), many of the earlier constraints on the nationally-minded brewers had disappeared. The automobile and the beginnings of the interstate highway system offered more flexibility in transportation. Mass media advertising gave brewers an efficient tool to promote their products on a national basis.

Increasing costs of raw materials eroded small brewers' profitability, thus softening markets for the national brewers and easing their infiltration efforts. And, perhaps most important of all, the single-plant barrier was broken in 1936 when the St. Louis-based Falstaff Brewing Corporation successfully replicated its Falstaff Beer in an Omaha brewery.[1] Other brewers soon followed suit.

Thus, not long after the end of World War II, a handful of bona fide nationally-shipping brewers arose in America. Certainly the trio of Anheuser-Busch, Schlitz and Pabst dominated in the national arena for much of the post-repeal era. But there were also brewers like P. Ballantine & Sons of Newark, the F. & M. Schaefer Brewing Company of Brooklyn, the Miller Brewing Company of Milwaukee and many others who were challenging to join the big three in their national status. Then, of course, there was Carling – a relative newcomer to the American brewing industry, but nevertheless determined to rank among the nation's largest beer-makers. Created as the result of a struggling automaker's search for new fields of business, the Carling Brewing Company (initially called Brewing Corporation of America) ultimately came to represent one of the most fascinating stories in American brewing history.

The Carling saga began in 1934 in the converted auto plant of the Peerless Motor Car Company, where Carling spent most of its first fifteen years searching for the niche that would allow it to achieve its goal of national distribution. In 1955, a Carling historian wrote of those early years that, "It is doubtful if there are many companies with a history over the past two decades which more resembles a ride on a roller coaster."[2] After recovering from a couple of false steps in its scramble to capitalize on a booming post-World War II beer market, Carling embarked on a meteoric rise into the caste of brewing industry leaders like none seen before or after. The company's success in America peaked in 1964 when, after fifteen consecutive years of sales growth, an impressive 5,775,000 barrels of Carling beer were sold.[3]

But, more than the sheer volume of production, it was the *rapidity* with which Carling broke into the upper crust of the American brewing industry that makes the company's history so extraordinary. From its rank as the 62nd-largest-producing brewer in America in 1949, Carling engineered its way into the lofty 4th position by 1960, behind only Anheuser-Busch, Schlitz and Falstaff, respectively.[4] Driven by the simple objective of selling its beer in every locale in America, Carling management assembled an organization as formidable as any brewing company in the post-war era. With the

The "Mabel, Black Label" slogan was an important part of Carling's phenomenal growth during the 1950s, and it became a key symbol of the company's success.

Carling Black Label brand leading the way, the company fought hand-to-hand with many of the brewers who are still today the industry leaders.

A large part of the fascination of the Carling story is that, as quickly as was its ascent into prominence, its *descent* into obscurity was faster still. A variety of problems – ranging from production mistakes to brand strategy miscalculations – eroded Carling's ability to prevail over the increasingly competitive conditions in the U.S. brewing industry. By 1979, the Carling Brewing Company had become a little-mourned victim of industry cannibalism. A name which had once stood among the greatest names in American brewing now existed merely as an auxiliary brand produced by one of Carling's former competitors. Carling Black Label Beer retains that humble status today.

The Metamorphosis

The Peerless Motor Car Company was an institution in Cleveland. For more than thirty years, the luxury automaker turned out what *The Automobile* magazine called "the most costly touring cars in America."[5] Peerless was perhaps best known in the early 1900s for its "Green Dragon" automobile, made famous in auto races around the country with notorious racer Barney Oldfield behind the wheel.

However, Peerless' origins date back to 1869, when the Peerless Wringer Company of Cincinnati joined forces with the Mercantile Manufacturing Company of Cleveland in the production of washing machine wringers. After finding great success with its popular Peerless Bicycle throughout the 1890s, the company moved into the manufacture of automobiles in 1900 and soon found its place in the luxury car market. As America entered World War I, the Peerless Motor Car Company (so named in 1902) converted its operations to the manufacture of trucks for the war effort, sending some 14,000 vehicles to France over the course of the war. Production of luxury passenger cars resumed at war's end. However, after the stock market crash of 1929, the high-priced Peerless line quickly lost its appeal, and the company found itself facing a bleak future.[6]

James A. Bohannon

At the head of the Peerless Motor Car Company was James A. Bohannon, often described as a flamboyant "tycoon-like character."[7] Bohannon came to Peerless in 1929 from the Marmon Motor Car Company of Indianapolis, where he had been that company's vice president. The thirty-three-year-old Bohannon (who became the youngest chief executive of an American car company when he came to Peerless) was hired by the Cleveland automaker to help remedy its ailing sales. But the market for luxury cars like the Peerless had evaporated, and Bohannon recognized that competing with Detroit in the low-priced segment of the industry would represent a prohibitive challenge. Thus, after three years of dwindling sales, Peerless halted production of automobiles on November 4, 1931.[8] On behalf of the 2,500 Peerless stockholders, James A. Bohannon embarked on a search for new lines of business in which to engage his company.

Not surprisingly, Bohannon reasoned that Peerless would best be served by making a product less vulnerable to economic fluctuations than automobiles had been. It would have to be a product which, in the words of the company's executive committee, would "cost less then ten cents and was either consumed or thrown away."[9] The likelihood of prohibition's repeal was increasingly in the news, and the brewing of beer thus presented itself as a natural opportunity for Peerless. Of course, Bohannon understood that competition in beer-making would be fierce, particularly for a company with no background in brewing and no name recognition within the industry. Thus, Bohannon sought to enlist a partner who could overcome those shortcomings for Peerless.

Early in 1933, the telephone rang in the Toronto office of E. P. Taylor, head of Brewing Corporation of Canada. The conversation was later recounted by a Taylor biographer:

> 'This is James A. Bohannon of Cleveland,' said the caller who introduced himself in a firm, authoritative voice. He continued: 'I represent a financial group planning to enter the brewing field as soon as prohibition ends here in the United States. We would like to visit you in Toronto and discuss the possibility of securing the right to brew and sell your Carling beer here in the United States.[10]

Carling had a celebrated history in the Dominion. Old Thomas Carling brewed his first batch of beer on a 100-acre farm outside London, Ontario not long after settling there in 1818. The young farmer gave his homebrew as gifts to neighbors and friends, and to the discerning beer connoisseurs of a nearby regiment of British soldiers. At the urging of those grateful recipients, Carling threw down his farming implements in 1840 and entered the beer business, establishing a brewery in London, Ontario.[11] Thomas Carling's sons took over the enterprise after their father's death in 1845. A palatial new brewery was erected in 1878 in replacement of the original buildings, which had become over-taxed by the popularity of the Carling products. By the late 1920s, Carling's London facility was the largest brewery in Canada. Its Red Cap Ale, introduced in 1927, was among the Dominion's best selling brews. When a group of Canadian breweries joined together in 1930 to form the Brewing Corporation of Canada, Carling was among them.[12]

On July 12, 1933, three months after Congress legalized the sale of 3.2 percent beer in the U.S., James A. Bohannon announced to the Peerless stockholders that an agreement had been reached with Brewing Corporation of Canada. The Canadian firm would grant Peerless the rights to manufacture and sell Carling's Red Cap Ale and Black Label Beer in America, and would provide all necessary technical assistance in converting Peerless' former automobile plant into a brewery. In return, the Canadians would be paid 25,000 shares of Peerless stock and E. P. Taylor, head of the Canadian company, would serve on the Peerless board of directors. James A. Bohannon would be chairman of the board (and, later, president) of Peerless' new beer-making subsidiary, Brewing Corporation of America.[13]

The Peerless automobile factory was located on an eight-acre site on Quincy Avenue at East 93rd Street. The mammoth structure was built between 1906 and 1909, and was designed by noted local architect J. Milton Dyer, best known for his design of City Hall.[14] With its vast interior spaces, the building was peculiarly well-suited for conversion to brewing. Still, the task of transforming the idle facility into an operating brewery was monumental; it was the largest single construction project undertaken in Cleveland in 1933. More than $800,000 was spent to equip the plant with an initial annual brewing capacity of 200,000 barrels of beer and ale. Provisions were made for easy expansion of the brewing capacity to as much as one million barrels per year.[15]

The new brewery was ready for its grand unveiling by summer of 1934. On June 15th, more than 20,000 took part in the opening festivities at the brewery, sampling the company's inaugural brew and marveling at the results of the old plant's metamorphosis.[16] Its past life as an auto facility was evidenced by a number of unique architectural characteristics. One visitor commented that the cavernous Tiffany-tiled entry way resembled a hotel lobby far more than a brewery. And, undoubtedly, more than a few guests took note of the decorative concrete auto wheels which adorned the facade just above the brewery's main entrance. Nevertheless, at least one observer chose to focus on the building's new function:

> *Rising floor upon floor, five stories high, were ruddy copper brew kettles of great spreading girth, sweeping stacks that reached skyward toward the squatty mash tanks where cereals are churned and crunched in preparation for the brew, a great cooling pan that looked more like a copper swimming pool than like a brewery part, and storage vats in which the product bides its time.[17]*

It was said that Otto P. Rindelhardt, the Canadian brewmaster sent to Cleveland to oversee the initial brewing, wept with joy as he surveyed the finished plant.[18]

Conversion of the Peerless auto plant into a brewery was the single largest construction project in Cleveland in 1933.

Cleveland State University

The Strategy

When the Brewing Corporation of America threw open its doors in 1934, its perspective on the brewing business was very much different than that of the other brewers in Cleveland. After the repeal of prohibition, most of the city's brewers (and, indeed, most brewers everywhere) simply intended to pick up where they had left off thirteen years earlier, making a local product for a primarily local beer-consuming public. The Peerless management, however, did not have its roots in brewing, but in automobiles. Shipping products to distant regions was second nature to the team of individuals which headed the new brewing concern. And, anyway, James A. Bohannon was simply not the type of businessman who would be satisfied with a merely local

221

market. Thus, it was apparent from the very beginning that the pursuit of ever-expanding territories for Carling's brew would be aggressive and unrelenting.

But the strategy which Bohannon employed to achieve his goal of national distribution was, at best, a precarious one. At some point early in the process of educating himself about the brewing industry, Bohannon was struck by the fact that America had no widely-consumed premium brand of *ale*. In this observation, Bohannon perceived a tremendous opportunity. And so, with the fine name of Carling's Red Cap Ale in hand, Bohannon elected to put nearly the brewery's entire resources behind ale – and not just regular ale, but a *premium-priced* ale.

When Red Cap made its debut in June, 1934, the brand was priced at a hefty 20¢ per bottle, compared to other local brands selling at 10¢ and national brands like Budweiser and Schlitz at 15¢.[19] In essence, Bohannon sought to create an entirely new *product category* with his premium ale – a category aligned more closely with champagne and caviar than with beer and pretzels.

With America in the very throes of the Great Depression, Bohannon's strategy was risky. Indeed, early sales of Red Cap Ale were consistently disappointing. Already in 1935, the company's financial condition was deteriorating rapidly. (Adding to the troubles was a strike in 1935 by the local brewery workers' union, which resulted in a number of boycotts of Cleveland-brewed products in cities such as Pittsburgh, Akron, Toledo and Cincinnati.) Realizing that drastic measures had become necessary, the brewery scaled back production of Red Cap Ale. In its place, two sister brands, Carling's Black Label Beer and Carling's Amber Creme Ale, were put forth at severely discounted prices.[20] The maneuver was a clear statement that the company had retrenched both from its initial allegiance solely to ale, and from its almost exclusive focus on the premium price market.

In 1936, after just one short year under the new policy, the Brewing Corporation of America had made a decidedly abrupt recovery, recording its

Advertisements for Red Cap Ale invariably depicted upper class social settings, and appeared in upscale publications such as *The New Yorker*, *Cue* and *Newsweek*.

The little man who's always there

People who insist two plus two always equals four aren't ever going to see the friendly little fellow under the red cap.

But he's there for those with a song in the heart, imagination in the brain-pan and a zest for living.

To them we say:

Down with dullness,
Caps off to Carling's.

CARLING'S ALE
BREWING CORPORATION OF AMERICA, CLEVELAND, OHIO

222

first profitable year since brewing began in 1934.[21] Sales of both Black Label Beer and Amber Creme Ale were strong, reflecting the positive impact of the brewery's decision to compete in lower price categories. With the early financial struggle behind him, Bohannon was finally free to pursue a nationwide market for the Carling products. Once begun, the pace was fast and furious. As early as 1939, Brewing Corporation's distribution area reached east to the Atlantic coast, west to the Mississippi River, and south to "the northern section of Dixie." The brewery's output soared from 152,166 barrels in 1936 to more than 400,000 barrels in 1939, necessitating near continual expansion of the plant.[22]

Achieving A National Market

Fueled largely by a strong war-time economy, Brewing Corporation of America's good fortunes continued into the 1940s. While 150,000 cases of Red Cap Ale were being shipped every week to troops overseas, Black Label Beer constituted the bulk of the company's sales at home. Aggressive advertising paved the way for a widening area of distribution. In 1945 alone, five new states were added to the Carling territory, which then comprised a total of twenty-two states. James A. Bohannon proudly declared the brewery to be "among the leading dozen producers" of beer and ale in America.[23]

War-time shortages of not only grains for brewing, but also all types of construction materials necessary for plant expansion challenged Brewing Corporation of America's ability to

As the majority of Red Cap Ale was sent to troops overseas during World War II, Black Label was Brewing Corporation of America's leading seller at home.

Mike Sapienza Collection

supply its growing markets with ample quantities of Carling beer and ale. Thus, the company, as did many, sought the acquisition of additional breweries to take over their grain quotas and production facilities. In July of 1944, the Forest City Brewery, Inc. and the Tip Top Brewing Company (both of Cleveland) were acquired by Brewing Corporation of America. At the time of the takeovers, James A. Bohannon was quoted as saying, "One of our original objectives was to make Cleveland an important national factor in the brewing industry. I think it is not excessive to say that we are well on our way to achieving that objective."[24]

The Forest City brewery, the larger of the two plants, was put to work handling production overflow from the main brewery on Quincy Avenue, thus boosting company-wide brewing capacity to more than 1,000,000 barrels annually. The Tip Top brewery was closed and its grain rations merged with that of Brewing Corporation of America. Carling's, Inc., a wholly-owned subsidiary, was set up to operate the Forest City facility and any future acquisitions.[25] (Incidentally, Carling's, Inc. was also in charge of the company's war-time food manufacturing division, which recycled used brewing grains to make "foods for human creatures." The food division was headed by former banker and local industrialist Charles A. Otis.[26])

James A. Bohannon also looked to regions outside of Cleveland for potential brewery acquisitions. Detroit was a significant

Non-returnable bottles and cans were a critical factor to the success of nationally-shipping brewers because they eliminated the high cost of transporting empties back to the brewery. Brewing Corporation of America was among the largest users of throw-away bottles in the brewing industry

market for the Carling products, and Bohannon made no secret of his investigations into a possible brewery takeover in that city, although no purchase was ever made there.[27] Parts of New England were also strong for Carling. Thus, Brewing Corporation of America began acquiring stock in the Harvard Brewing Company of Lowell, Massachusetts during the war. By 1945, more than 119,000 shares of Harvard stock had been purchased by Brewing Corporation.[28] The company undoubtedly intended to take over the Massachusetts brewery and convert it to production of Carling beer and ale. But, again, nothing to this end ever developed. Although a multi-plant strategy would later become a key aspect of the company's growth, it was not until 1954 that the Carling products would first be brewed in a plant outside of Cleveland.

Nevertheless, shipping beer from a single locale did not slow Brewing Corporation of America's quest for national distribution. In 1946, James A. Bohannon took great pleasure in announcing that, "This year, for the first time, our product has been sold in all of the 48 United States...a goal that has been thirteen years in attainment."[29] A massive advertising campaign was launched during the year in more than twenty national magazines. The heavy promotional efforts continued into 1947, when the company spent $1.25 million for advertising in publications such as *Collier's, Time, Life, Newsweek, The New Yorker* and a host of others.[30] Indeed, Brewing Corporation of America could finally fulfill the promise of its name.

While Black Label Beer had been the company's dominant brand throughout much of the war, it was instead the premium-priced Red Cap Ale which lead the way to expansion into all forty-eight states. Despite the company's failure in earlier years to find success exclusively with a premium-priced ale, Bohannon never lost confidence in the potential rewards of such a strategy. Thus, as World War II came to an end, he felt that the time had arrived for a return to the Red Cap strategy. After all, each of the dominant national brands of beer in America was premium-priced as well, and for good reason. It was considered economically unfeasible to ship a product to all parts of the country without pricing it in such a way as to recoup some of the costs of transportation. In effect, a national brand was, by definition, a premium-priced brand.

However, even the established national shippers recognized that a second-tier brand – a "popular-priced" brand – was a necessary component to help build sales volume in regions where shipping costs were not a significant factor. Anheuser-Busch, for example, had its low-priced Busch Bavarian brand; Schlitz had its Old Milwaukee Beer; and Pabst had its Red, White & Blue brand.[31] Although Black Label Beer had certainly proven itself to be a strong popular-priced offering during the war, Brewing Corporation of America placed little importance on the brand. In fact, when tightening federal restrictions on grain forced the closing of the old Forest City plant in 1946, Black Label was eliminated entirely. Bohannon explained that the brand was discontinued "to safeguard the supply and distribution of our premium product, Carling's Red Cap Ale, and to extend its distribution into markets scheduled for development."[32] Just as he had done many years earlier, Bohannon sought to build his foundation of national distribution entirely upon Red Cap Ale. It was a move which, just as before, would not bring good results.

The use of celebrities in beer advertising was common. Over the years, Carling beer and ale was promoted by such celebrities as Phil Silvers, Ethel Merman, Hugh Downs, Robert Cummings, David Niven, Randolph Scott and, of course, Lucille Ball.

War Crimes

In November of 1946, James A. Bohannon confidently told his stockholders that "the future holds great opportunities" for Brewing Corporation of America.[33] What he did not know is that the company was about to encounter a sudden and severe reversal of the momentum which it had sustained throughout the war. Within a year, the company would be teetering on the brink of collapse. Sales of Carling products would plummet by a remarkable *forty* percent between 1947 and 1949.[34] Premature initiation of a $5 million post-war plant expansion program would leave the company cash broke, and would ultimately result in Bohannon's ejection from management. While brewers across the nation were basking in the prosperity of the post-war era, Brewing Corporation of America was facing almost certain death.

Somewhat ironically, the failure lay mainly in the company's over-ambitious charge for national distribution during World War II. Little attention had been paid to the importance of building strong and reliable relationships with distributors. Instead, Brewing Corporation of America indiscriminately recruited wholesalers in as many regions as possible, and supplied them with only the minimum quantities of product necessary to retain their business. Bohannon and his cohorts felt that establishing inroads into all parts of the country during the war would spur a massive demand for the Carling products once war-time constraints on beer production were lifted. However, after grain restrictions were eased early in 1947 and the flow of beer increased, Bohannon soon learned that his corps of distributors had developed no real loyalty to the Carling products.[35] Their patronage during the war had been motivated largely by the shortages of beer. In sum, Brewing Corporation had simply spread itself too thin with its limited war-time beer production and found itself unable to maintain many of its wholesalers once other brands of beer became available.*

For many wholesalers, a major cause of their disenchantment with Brewing Corporation of America was the discontinuance of Black Label Beer in 1946. Despite James A. Bohannon's determination to make Red Cap Ale a leading national product, most wholesalers had little confidence in the ability of any brand of *ale* to succeed in the premium-price category. The popular-priced Black Label Beer, on the other hand, had sold well throughout the war. When the brand was abruptly terminated, many already-struggling wholesalers were left with one fewer product to sell. Moreover, when Black Label returned to the market in 1947, its price was raised to that of premium brands. One disgruntled observer commented, "That didn't fool anybody. Everyone had known it as a good popular-priced brand."[37]

Then too, there was the issue of the throw-away bottle. Convinced that home-consumption was the wave of the future, Bohannon discontinued production of draught beer in 1945. Returnable long-neck "bar bottles" were also phased out as the brewery committed itself exclusively to the throw-away bottles. Throw-aways were attractive to brewers who shipped over long distances because they eliminated the cost of sending empties back to the brewery. Bohannon had enjoyed good success with disposable bottles before the war, but only as a supplement to returnable bottles. Despite the admitted convenience of throw-aways, their acceptance both by household consumers and by tavern owners was sluggish, at best.[38] Thus, many Carling wholesalers felt that the

---

*Just how thin the company's beer production was stretched is revealed by the fact that while Brewing Corporation of America's total output dropped by 8.5 percent between 1945 and 1946 (due to raw material shortages), its number of distributors grew from 143 to 217 during the same period.[36]

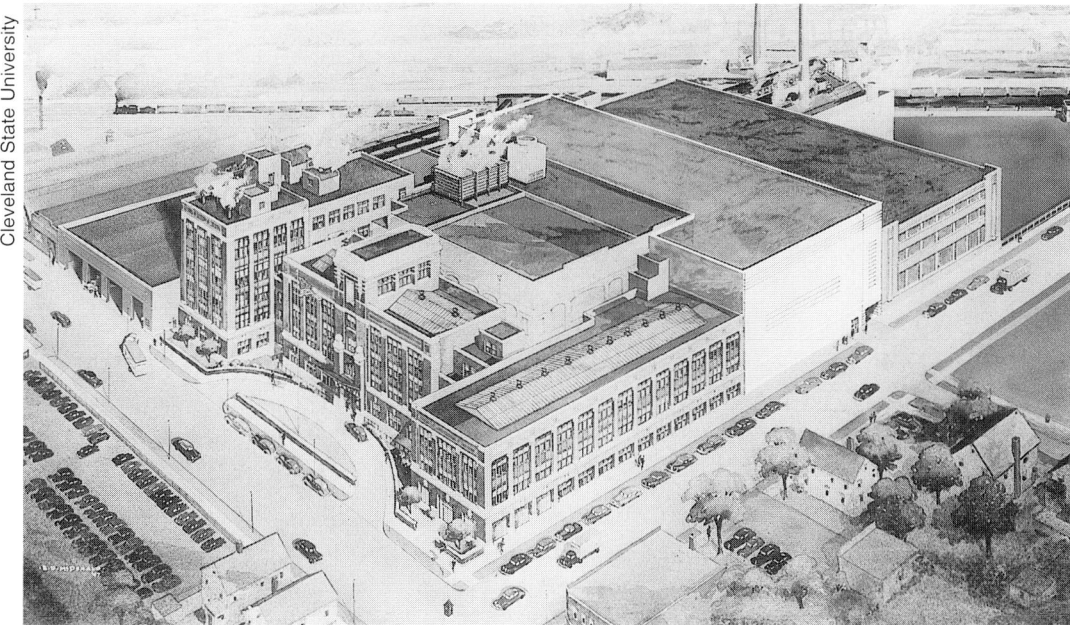

The plant of Brewing Corporation of America was enlarged significantly just after World War II. The enormous expenditures helped propel the company into crisis.

company's exclusive use of throw-aways handicapped sales of the Carling brands. It was, indeed, one more reason for a wholesaler to look elsewhere for his supplies of beer. (Both draught beer and returnable bottles were later reinstated.)

While wholesalers outside of Northeast Ohio became essentially indifferent to the Carling products after the war, those *inside* the Cleveland area were downright indignant. During the period of constrained beer production, Brewing Corporation of America made no special allocation for local distributors or retailers. On the contrary, in its efforts to supply an ever-increasing number of new customers abroad, the company sharply curtailed beer supplies to Cleveland-area outlets throughout the war, causing the failure of many a livelihood. When it was announced that Brewing Corporation had acquired both the Forest City brewery and the Tip Top brewery in 1944, many believed that local supplies of the Carling brands would subsequently increase. In reality, the takeovers only added to the animosity, as Brewing Corporation refused to service any of the some 700 former customers of the two purchased breweries.[39] The local trade, after all, would have to be treated the same as any other if the company was to achieve a true national presence.

The local hostilities toward Brewing Corporation of America were deep-seated and long-lasting. The following newspaper advertisement, placed by an angry beverage store owner in 1946, typified the sentiments of many retailers:

No Carling's Beer or Ale Today.

May God bless the Cleveland consumers, the dealers, the salesmen drivers and the personnel of Carling's. May they live long and well remember what the Carling's Brewing Company did to them....In April, 1945 our allotment [of Carling's Beer and Ale] was 410 cases, for April, 1946 our share was 148 cases. Yes, the government has cut the production of beer 30%, but Carling's has cut us 73%....Are Carling's taking on new accounts in different states at the expense of loyal Clevelanders? So you see, don't ask us for Carling's Beer or Ale.[40]

For decades after the war, Carling salesmen contended with what they called "bitter accounts" – retailers who refused to sell Carling brands because of the company's war-time policies. One salesman recalled that a particular tavern owner would not sell Carling products because the tavern had been bequeathed to him by his late father, who mandated *in his will* that Carling products never be permitted on the premises.[41] Indeed, for the remainder of the company's history, its brands suffered from mediocre sales in Cleveland as the local retail trade never entirely forgot how it had been sacrificed for far-away markets.

After wholesalers had abandoned Brewing Corporation of America en masse both locally and elsewhere, the company found itself in serious financial trouble by November of 1947. Plunging sales, coupled with the enormous amounts of money which had been committed for plant expansion, sent the company into a tailspin. Realizing the severity of the situation, Bohannon reluctantly summoned the aid of Canadian Breweries Limited (successor to Brewing Corporation of Canada). Within hours, E. P. Taylor and a small entourage arrived in Cleveland to assess the company's position. What they found astonished them. Cash reserves had been almost entirely depleted, and the company's distribution network was in virtual ruins. By the end of 1948, an entirely new management team composed primarily of executives from Canadian Breweries had been put in place at Brewing Corporation of America.[42]

The Takeover

Since 1945, Canadian Breweries Limited held the majority ownership in Brewing Corporation of America after James A. Bohannon agreed to exchange his interest in the U.S. company for $5 million in Canadian Breweries stock. In addition, Bohannon was granted a ten-year contract to serve as general manager of Brewing Corporation. But the deal did not come easily. In what was termed "a battle of the titans," Bohannon and E. P. Taylor faced-off over Taylor's admitted attempts to gain control of Brewing Corporation through covert purchases of the company's stock on the open market. When Taylor's activities were discovered, Bohannon reportedly "made no effort to hide his displeasure," and a melee ensued.[43] Egos may have been bruised, but the issue was satisfactorily resolved by the new arrangement.

At the time the agreement was adopted, no one could have foreseen the dismal condition in which the company would find itself by 1948. Once the decision was made to replace Brewing Corporation of America's entire management team with members of the Canadian parent, James A. Bohannon remained involved with the brewery in name only. Publicly, it was reported that he had been elevated from president to chairman of the board. In reality, Bohannon was effectively stripped of his authority and set aside. In 1949, Bohannon officially retired and was never again associated with the company he had founded sixteen years earlier. He spent the remainder of his years living at his Greystone Farm in Mentor, Ohio and, later, at Daisy Hill, the Hunting Valley estate first built and occupied by local real estate tycoons Oris P. & Mantis J. Van Sweringen. Bohannon died in 1968 while vacationing in Palm Beach, Florida. He was seventy-four years old.[44]

E. P. Taylor had taken over as president of Brewing Corporation of America in July of 1948. However, it was instead two of Taylor's henchmen, George M. Black, Jr. and Ian R. Dowie, to whom would fall the task of saving the "stumbling giant" from total collapse. Black had served for a number of years as assistant to the president of Canadian Breweries Limited. In his new post as vice president and general manager at Brewing Corporation of America, Black recognized that the fundamental problem facing the company was its crumbling sales network. Thus, he recruited Ian

228

R. Dowie, vice president of sales at Canadian Breweries, to come to Cleveland and rebuild the sales and marketing program.[45]

Breathing new life into the faltering Brewing Corporation of America represented a formidable challenge for the new management. From a record-high profit of just over $2 million in 1946, Brewing Corporation nose-dived to a net loss of more than $900,000 in 1948.[46] In his 1948 report to stockholders, E. P. Taylor attributed the massive loss to Bohannon's excessive post-war plant expansion program, to the large expenditures made to convert the brewery for exclusive use of throw-away bottles, and to "keen competitive conditions."[47] Indeed, the situation was nothing short of bleak, and the company's hopes for survival were slim.

Consequently, when representatives of the Falstaff Brewing Corporation approached Brewing Corporation of America in 1949 with a purchase proposal, the Canadian parent was eager to negotiate. Falstaff was reportedly interested in acquisition of the Red Cap Ale brand. Despite the recent financial woes of its maker, Red Cap had, indeed, achieved brief distribution into all forty-eight states. It was an accomplishment not to be taken lightly, and Red Cap's widespread name-recognition was a valuable asset regardless of whatever problems the company possessed. Nevertheless, with the buyout all but consummated, Falstaff retracted its offer at the last moment for reasons which were never revealed.[48] With no other prospective buyer in sight, Black and Dowie set about the enormous task of rehabilitating Brewing Corporation of America.

Ian R. Dowie joined Brewing Corporation of America in 1949 and spent the next thirteen years building the company into one of the most formidable beer-makers in America.

"Premium Beer at the Popular Price"

E. P. Taylor and his new management team had one thing in common with James A. Bohannon: The vision of nationwide sales for the Carling products in the United States. Once efforts to revive Brewing Corporation of America were under way, Taylor and his cohorts would not be satisfied until the company could compete on a national scale. It was no surprise, therefore, that Ian R. Dowie was chosen to head the company's sales function. During his time as vice president of sales at Canadian Breweries Limited, Dowie built an impressive record. Under his management, sales of the Canadian brewing firm climbed dramatically, thrusting the company into first place in beer sales in the Dominion.[49] Now in Cleveland, Dowie was called upon to perform his magic on behalf of the struggling U.S. brewer.

Dowie's first job was to evaluate Brewing Corporation of America's product strategy. Since the end of World War II, James A. Bohannon had poured the bulk of his resources into establishing Red Cap Ale in the premium price category. Despite the limited success, Dowie was reluctant to completely abandon the headway already achieved with the Red Cap brand, and so its production was maintained. But, at the same time, it was clear that Red Cap would not be an effective competitor against the well-established national brews. Thus, Carling Black Label Beer, which enjoyed a good degree of success during the war, would have to assume the role of Brewing Corporation's lead product.

With that decision made, Dowie and Black hit upon a simple but unique maneuver which, in little more than a few months, would halt the company's downward trend and put it in prime condition to pursue its goal of national distribution. Black Label's premium price (instituted by Bohannon in 1947) would be dropped to match that of the local brews in each of its markets. The brand would continue, however, to be promoted as a premium-quality brew, thus becoming the first brand to compete in the premium category at a discount price. Lead by the simple slogan "Premium Beer At The Popular Price," Black Label's reintroduction was launched in January of 1950. By the end of the year, sales were up an encouraging twenty-eight percent over 1949. The following year saw another increase of twenty-five percent, and Brewing Corporation of America had found a path to recovery.[50]

By 1952, sales of Carling Black Label had risen dramatically.

Of course, in reducing Black Label's price, profit margins were compromised somewhat. But re-establishing good sales volume was an utter necessity for survival, and the price-cut was the quickest and most effective means of building volume. In the years to come, Black Label's low profit margin (in relation to that of its national competitors) would cause serious problems for the company. However, in the meantime, Brewing Corporation of America watched as Carling Black Label Beer enjoyed one of the most dramatic periods of growth of any brand of beer in the post-war era.

Several factors beyond the price reduction played a role in Carling Black Label's phenomenal rise during the early

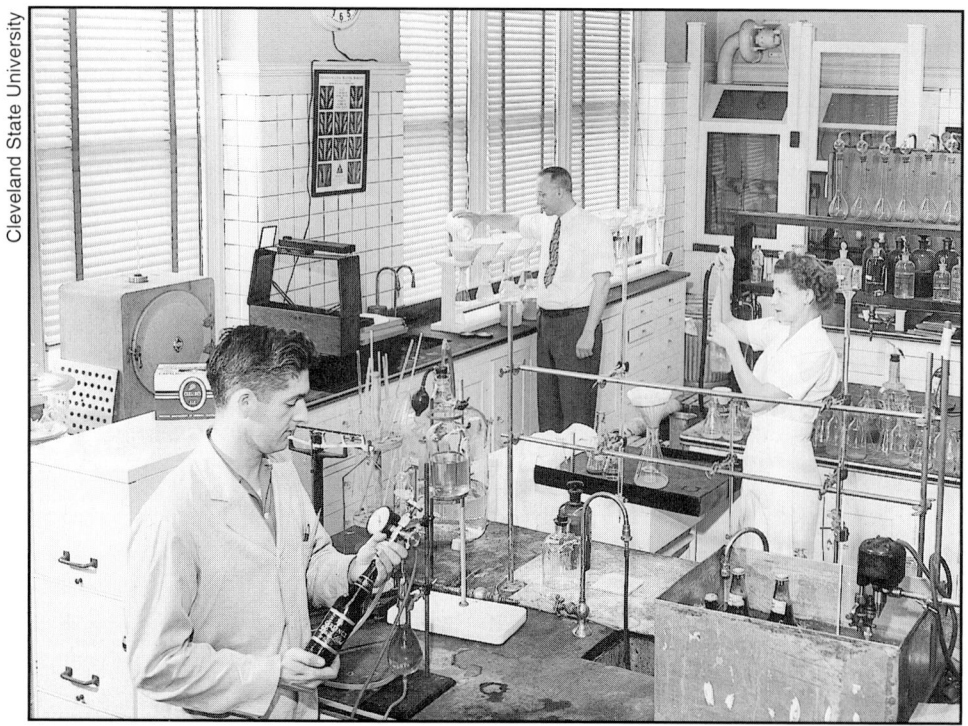

The Carling laboratory. Every batch of Carling beer and ale was said to undergo nine separate tests by Carling's chemists. In addition, a sample of all raw ingredients arriving at the brewery was sent to the laboratory for inspection prior to their use in brewing.

1950s. Ian R. Dowie's emphasis on forging strong alliances with wholesalers was certainly key. Also important was the fact that rising production costs throughout the industry were beginning to cripple many small brewers, thus creating new opportunities for large regional companies like Brewing Corporation of America. In addition, cash infusions from Canadian Breweries Limited allowed for a disproportionate amount of Black Label advertising.[51] But there was one very important element in Carling Black Label's coming-of-age which was far more visible than all the others: the simple rhyme "Mabel, Black Label." The now-historic slogan was first used in a 1949 radio commercial and quickly gained notoriety.[52] As Brewing Corporation of America moved more of its advertising dollars into television, Mabel followed in the form of an attractive young waitress. Her genial wink, which she tendered at the close of nearly all Black Label television commercials, became Mabel's trademark. For more than fifteen years, the "Mabel, Black Label" slogan was virtually the guiding icon of the company.

"Market segmentation" emerged in the 1950s and advertisers began tailoring their message to specific demographic groups.

On January 4, 1954, the Brewing Corporation of America was renamed the Carling Brewing Company in order to become more closely identified with its products.[53] The brewery had just finished a landmark year. With sales of 1,096,025 barrels for 1953, Carling became the first Cleveland brewer ever to reach the one million barrel mark in a single year. The plant expansion program which had been suspended five years earlier was resumed, thus boosting capacity of the Cleveland brewery to 1.8 million barrels annually. And Ian R. Dowie, who was elected Carling president in 1951, announced plans to build the company's first brewery outside of Ohio.[54] The successes of 1953 soon proved to be just the beginning. Throughout the next decade, the Carling Brewing Company was a rising star in the U.S. brewing industry, and Carling Black Label Beer would proudly claim the title of "America's Fastest Growing Beer."

"Divided We Stand"

The Carling Brewing Company was rarely timid in its efforts to expand into new territories. Between 1954 and 1961, Carling spent an astonishing $70 million building or acquiring new brewing plants around the country.[60] By 1965, a total of *nine* Carling breweries were in operation in the U.S., and the tenth was on the drawing board. But Carling was not the only American brewing company to employ a multi-plant strategy. In fact, throughout the 1950s, virtually all national brewers built additional plants strategically located to eliminate the high expense of shipping beer over long distances. For Carling, however, the economies of the multi-brewery concept were particularly crucial. The tremendous success of Black Label had been built

231

The Carling Darling

In the annals of advertising history, there are a select handful of product slogans which – through their memorability, catchiness or sometimes just plain indefinable qualities – have achieved virtual pop-culture status. Ad agencies everywhere dream of creating such slogans, but only rarely do. The phrase "Mabel, Black Label" is among those elite few which continues to hold a prominent place in the collective memory of the American consumer decades after its use in advertising has ended.

Despite the eventual success of "Mabel, Black Label," the slogan did not make its debut with any particular promise of future greatness. Nor was it launched with any special splash or fanfare. Rather, the first use of the phrase came in the form of a simple lyric in a series of radio commercials. The Cleveland firm of Lang, Fisher & Stashower – long-time ad agency for Black Label – had commissioned New York songwriters Phil Davis & Associates to compose music and lyrics for a group of radio commercials for a 1949 ad campaign. And it was in this batch of radio spots that the yet-to-be-famous line was born.[55] Not long after the commercials began airing, it was reported from the field that Carling salesmen and deliverymen were being greeted by their customers with a hearty "Hey Mabel!" Within a matter of months, virtually every piece of advertising for Black Label was exploiting the growing popularity of the slogan, and Carling officials soon declared it "the biggest thing in beer promotion this area has ever seen."[56]

Although the facts surrounding the creation of "Mabel, Black Label" are undisputed by those who were closest to its development, there are nevertheless a variety of somewhat colorful tales concerning the origins of the phrase. Perhaps the most often told of those stories involves a young copywriter at Lang, Fisher & Stashower. As the story goes, the recently-hired copywriter returned from lunch one afternoon and, having been discovered by his superiors to be in a decidedly drunken condition, was summarily dismissed. It was only after the copywriter had collected his belongings and departed that the phrase "Mabel, Black Label" was supposedly found typed on a piece of paper still sitting in the young man's typewriter. Of course, the simple genius of the slogan was recognized immediately, although the unfortunate copywriter was never seen or heard from again.

Another dubious account claims that Carling management initially saw little merit in the "Mabel, Black Label" slogan, and therefore rejected it before it was used in any advertising. According to legend, Al Fisher, co-founder of Lang, Fisher & Stashower, felt so strongly about the potential impact of the slogan that he developed a radio commercial using "Mabel, Black Label" and, without the permission of his client, aired the spot in a small Ohio town to gauge its

Actress and model Jeanne Goodspeed adorned Black Label ads for more than a decade as Mabel. She is shown here striking her familiar pose on the set of a 1951 television commercial.

performance. In the end, an enormous surge in beers sales in that particular small Ohio town proved the slogan's value, and Carling officials happily agreed to adopt it.

These and other equally mythical accounts notwithstanding, it is clear that the slogan "Mabel, Black Label" was a crucial element in the explosive growth of the Black Label brand during the 1950s. Exactly what it is about the slogan that made it so popular is a multi-faceted question. The simple fact that it was used for more than twenty years in virtually every Black Label ad – magazine, newspaper, radio or television – is certainly key. But mere repetition was only one of Mabel's ingredients. Signing-off every commercial with her charming and genial wink, the glamorous yet wholesome Mabel won the hearts of many a Black Label drinker. As one observer put it, "Her friendly smile and knowing wink would compel any man to leave home – to fetch a carton of Carling's, that is."[57]

Above: Jeanne Goodspeed with fellow Carling spokesman Phil Silvers. Left: Goodspeed performing her famous wink. She is being ogled by Carling executives (left to right) Henry Russell, Ian Dowie and Bob Thomas.

Over the years, many different actresses had the honor of playing the Mabel role. Lucille Schroeder, a receptionist at Cleveland television station WXEL, was likely the first to appear on television as Mabel. Throughout 1950, she appeared on nightly live broadcasts of the "Carling Sports Final" with host John Fitzgerald, who delivered the day's sports news from a bar stool while Mabel stood at the ready with a cold Black Label. However, it was New York actress and model Jeanne Goodspeed who was recognized by beer drinkers coast-to-coast as the Mabel of Mabels. An "Alabama belle" at heart, Jeanne Goodspeed was first recruited to play Mabel in 1951. Over the next fifteen years, she appeared in dozens of Black Label television commercials and print ads. Despite her long career as the "Carling Darling," it was a minor source of embarrassment when Cleveland newspapers noted in 1960 that Goodspeed's first visit to a Carling brewery did not occur until nearly a decade after her initiation as Mabel.[58]

In 1965, New York-based Tinker & Associates was hired as Carling's new national advertising agency, and Mabel abruptly disappeared from all Black Label ads. Mabel's absence, however, proved to be a mere respite. After enduring fledgling sales throughout the latter part of the 1960s, Carling looked to Mabel to help turn the tide. On December 2, 1970, at a meeting of beer wholesalers in Washington, D.C., Mabel's surprise return was announced in grand fashion as a young, blond model burst through a paper bullseye and was presented with a bouquet of roses by Carling executive Bob Thomas. The new Mabel had arrived. One historian deftly summarized the circumstances of Mabel's comeback: "In late 1950, she'd saved the company; Carling was hoping she could do it again."[59]

Unfortunately, Carling's troubles were too great for even Mabel to cure. She soon disappeared from television sets and magazine ads, never again to deliver her famous wink.

By 1965, the Carling Brewing Company operated nine plants around the country.

entirely upon the brand's competitive price. Thus, keeping transportation costs to a minimum was more than just good business; it was *integral* to the continued growth of Black Label.

It was perhaps this fact which caused the Carling Brewing Company to approach the multi-plant system in a somewhat different manner than did other brewers. Carling management felt very strongly that its products needed to be good competitors not just against the national brands, but also against the local brands in each of its marketing regions. Therefore, a policy of "regional autonomy" prevailed among the various Carling breweries. Although Carling headquarters in Cleveland maintained ultimate authority, each of the company's plants strived to cultivate a distinctly local character. Each employed its own advertising agency and public relations firm in order to be in closer touch with individual market conditions. And each brewery was headed by an individual chosen for his good reputation in the local community. After all, Carling management fully recognized that achieving a national market would have to come largely at the expense of the small regional brewers. Ian R. Dowie aptly summarized the Carling strategy with the phrase "Divided We Stand."[61]

The Carling Brewing Company's first move toward a multi-regional structure was a bold one. In 1954, Carling purchased the Griesedieck Western Brewery Company – an organization larger than Carling itself – for $10 million in cash. The acquisition included breweries in St. Louis and Belleville, Illinois and rights to the company's Stag Beer, a long-time leading seller in its eleven-state territory.[62] With a brewery in St. Louis, Carling now intruded on the turf of powerhouse brewers Anheuser-Busch and Falstaff. Indeed, many interpreted the Griesedieck Western purchase as an outright declaration of war, manifesting Carling's intention to compete for a top position in the U.S. beer market. And although the St. Louis brewery was closed in 1957 due to its age and inefficiency, Carling routinely expanded the Belleville plant. For many years, it remained the company's largest brewery outside of Cleveland.

But the crown jewel of Carling's mid-1950s expansion program was its brand new plant in Natick, Massachusetts – eighteen miles west of Boston. It was the first new brewery built in New England in forty years, and local residents welcomed Carling with open arms. The 1954 groundbreaking ceremonies were a harbinger of good things to come. The event was presided over by Massachusetts Governor Christian Herter, who presented Ian R. Dowie with a wood gavel carved from the historical oak tree under which colonial minister John Eliot preached to the Algonquian Indians and converted them to Christianity. From behind the controls of a steam shovel, Dowie then broke ground before a crowd of more than 5,000, all donning red crepe paper hats in honor of Red Cap Ale. As construction of the new brewery got under way, local enthusiasm over the project mounted. Consequently, Carling established the tongue-in-cheek "Brotherhood of Sidewalk Superintendents," designed to keep the community informed of the brewery's progress. Some 7,000 residents received membership cards in the club and were mailed periodic construction updates.[63]

Ian R. Dowie (right) with George F. Gund II, whose father ran the Gund Brewing Company in Cleveland before prohibition.

The first shipment of Carling beer left the Natick plant in April of 1956. The new brewery employed 300 and was capable of producing 600,000 barrels of beer annually. The facility's total price tag was about $12 million, a relatively low figure, and one with which industry insiders were quite impressed.* Henry E. Russell was named regional vice president and general manager of the Natick brewery. A former Harvard University football star, Russell had worked for a New York advertising agency and for New England Mutual Life Insurance before joining Carling in 1954.[64] Russell's ties to the New England region made him the perfect choice to head the Natick plant, as Carling pursued its policy of cultivating a strong local character for each of its breweries.

---

*While attending an industry gathering, Dowie was allegedly approached by the president of a rival national brewer who questioned Carling's honesty about the actual cost of the Natick plant. When Dowie confirmed the low cost, the competitor reportedly turned to his vice president and barked, "Why the hell do we have to build everything out of gold!?"[65]

By 1966, the Natick brewery had played host to more than 75,000 visitors who came to tour the popular brewery and sample its products. When Carling decided to hold a celebration in honor of its tenth anniversary in Natick, the company planned for a crowd of about 5,000; in the end, some 31,500 people turned out for the festivities. The celebration was called "the largest and most successful single community relations event ever conducted by any brewery anywhere."[66] Indeed, Carling had clearly become a cherished part of its New England community.

In dramatic contrast to its red carpet treatment in Natick, the Carling Brewing Company was utterly vilified when it announced plans to build a new brewery in Baltimore in 1956. The local Maryland brewers fought tooth and nail to block governmental permission for the new plant. They called Carling a "ruthless cartel" bent on causing the "economic ruin and possible total destruction" of the state's local breweries. The Maryland legislature agreed. Pointing to the fact that Carling was Canadian-owned, the legislature refused to grant permission for construction of the new brewery. The decision enraged not only the people of Maryland, but also the Canadian Parliament. The issue quickly escalated into one with the potential for "international repercussions." Acting under what was rumored to have been pressure from Washington officials, the governor of Maryland vetoed the state legislature's action.[67] After just about a year of conflict, Carling was finally welcomed into Maryland.

Carling's Atlanta brewery opened in 1958. When it closed in 1973, it was sold to the Coca-Cola Company.

Although the Baltimore plant did eventually come to fruition (opening in 1961), Carling was forced to look elsewhere for new brewing capacity while the Maryland problems were being sorted out. In 1956, Ian R. Dowie announced that arrangements had been made with International Breweries, Inc. to purchase its Frankenmuth, Michigan brewery for approximately $3 million.[68] Dowie explained that the acquisition was necessary to fill the ever-growing demand for Carling Black Label Beer and Red Cap Ale. Meanwhile, in service to that same goal, ground had already been broken for a brand new Carling plant in Atlanta. Opened in 1958, the brewery was under the supervision of retired Lieutenant General A. R. Bolling, a Georgian well known for his long command of Fort McPherson in Atlanta.[69] It was, of course, another example of Carling's efforts to be perceived as a locally-oriented company in each of its host communities.

On January 1, 1959, Carling took possession of the Heidelberg Brewing Company of Tacoma, Washington. Although a Carling sales office had been maintained on the west coast since 1949, the Heidelberg purchase represented the company's first large-scale infiltration into western markets. Carling officials called the acquisition "essential to the development of our plans for complete national distribution of the Carling brands."[70] Capable of brewing 650,000 barrels of beer annually, the Tacoma plant brought Carling's total brewing capacity up to an impressive 5.5 million barrels per year. Production of Black Label and Red Cap, of course, began immediately at the Tacoma brewery. However, the popular Heidelberg brand, with roots dating back to 1901, was kept alive by Carling as well. For many years to come, Heidelberg would remain a strong seller for Carling in the Pacific Northwest, and would ultimately be introduced into eastern markets.

236

The Carling Brewing Company encountered a minor setback in its new western territories when Washington state authorities banned the broadcast of Black Label television commercials featuring Mabel. The problem centered around Mabel's trademark wink, which signed-off virtually every commercial for Black Label. State authorities determined the wink to be "lascivious" and, thus, inappropriate for public broadcast.[71] Carling was left with no choice but to eliminate the wink from commercials airing in Washington, but compliance was reluctant. After all, Mabel and her beloved wink had been the cornerstone of Carling's advertising for years.

Reaching the Apex

The Carling Brewing Company entered the decade of the 1960s in prime condition. Although achieving true national distribution of the Carling products was still a few years away, the company's phenomenal growth over the previous decade gave rise to a new, more ambitious objective: To attain the leading sales position among American brewers. Carling had moved into the fourth position by 1960 (behind Anheuser-Busch, Schlitz and Falstaff) and the company had every intention of continuing the upward climb.[72] However, the Pabst Brewing Company of Milwaukee was in close striking distance in the fifth position, and Carling would spend the next several years jockeying between fourth and fifth place despite its steady rise in sales volume. In 1964, the Carling Brewing Company experienced its best year ever as sales reached 5,775,000 barrels.[73] It was also during 1964 that the Carling brands were first sold in all fifty states.

After fifteen consecutive years of sales increases, the Carling Brewing Company was finally officially among the ranks of the national brewers. Like its peers, Carling would have to be increasingly aggressive in its marketing efforts in order to maintain its place in the industry as competition intensified throughout the 1960s. Advertising, of course, was a fundamental weapon, and the Carling Brewing Company was not shy in wielding it. E. P. Taylor was once quoted as saying that Carling was "never afraid to spend a dollar to make a dollar."[74] Indeed, in 1966 alone, the company spent nearly $9 million on advertising, compared with just $2 million in 1954. The great majority – about seventy-five percent – was spent on television. Black Label advertisements also made regular appearances in national magazines like *Life, Look, Saturday Evening Post* and *Ebony.*[75] Newspapers, radio,

The Carling Brewing Company was among the best in the industry at developing strong relationships with its distributor network. *The Carling News*, a monthly publication for Carling wholesalers and retailers, had a circulation of more than 7,000.

Ian Dowie (right) out in the field.

outdoor billboards and point-of-purchase displays were also used in great abundance.

The bulk of Carling's advertising was associated with sports-related programs. For years, Carling was the sole beer sponsor of telecasts of both the Cleveland Indians and Cleveland Browns games. And well beyond Cleveland, Black Label Beer and Red Cap Ale hosted scores of sporting events – everything from the Flying Dutchman Yachting Competition in Nantucket, Rhode Island to the Carling Black Label Fishing Tournament in St. Louis.[76] But the pillar of Carling's sports promotions was its annual Carling Open International Golf Tournament. The event was started in Cleveland in 1953 with a purse of $15,000. By 1965, the purse had swelled to $200,000 and the Carling Open became the Carling World Golf Championship. The event ranked as the company's largest single promotional endeavor of the year and drew professional golfers from around the globe.[77]

Advertising, of course, was not the only key to maintaining a national market in the brewing industry. A strong and loyal network of wholesalers/distributors was crucial as well. About 700 wholesalers were handling the Carling products by the early 1960s. The Carling management was particularly adept at building good relationships with its wholesalers and motivating them to boost sales of Black Label and Red Cap. The Carling Distributor Management Services was created to provide sales, marketing and management assistance to all of its wholesalers. Traveling seminars were given by Carling on virtually every aspect of the beer distribution business. Frequent sales contests were held in which distributors were awarded cash prizes for good sales performance. And some 7,000 wholesalers and retailers nationwide received the *Carling News*, a monthly publication issued by the Carling Trade Relations Department.[78]

Technological innovation was another important facet of staying competitive in the modern brewing industry. Carling's most noteworthy technological development was the "Continuous Brewing Method." Ever in search of ways to cut costs and speed up

"Mabel Black Label"

CARLING
Black Label
BEER

People Like It

CARLING BREWING CO., INC. · CLEVELAND, OHIO

Black Label BEER

Black Label BEER

RED CAP Ale

RED CAP Ale

In 1959, Hollywood actor and comedian Phil Silvers was hired as a Carling spokesman. The company used Silvers as the centerpiece of what one Carling official called "the most elaborate and fully integrated advertising and sales promotion campaign ever put to work for...Carling." In addition to starring in four feature television programs sponsored by Carling, Silvers appeared in dozens of Black Label television commercials, print ads and point-of-purchase display items. To herald the new ad campaign, Carling salesmen visited their customers wearing black-rimmed glasses and badges reading "Glad To See Ya," Silvers' trademark greeting.

238

production, Carling chemists sought to develop a process whereby beer could be produced essentially in a constant stream, as opposed to the traditional batch method. The trick, of course, was to achieve that goal without compromising the quality and consistency of the finished product. After three years of experimentation at the Cleveland brewery, Carling announced in 1962 that it had perfected its Continuous Brewing Method. A brand new Carling brewery was to be built in Fort Worth, Texas and would become the first continuous brewing plant in the world. Though fully confident in the new technology, Ian R. Dowie admitted, "There will be a few raised eyebrows around the world over this innovation."[79]

The new Fort Worth brewery was significant not only because of its pioneering technology, but also because it represented Carling's bid to become the first national brewer to take command of the growing southwestern markets. Anheuser-Busch and Schlitz were eager to infiltrate the Southwest as well, and both announced plans to build breweries in Texas in the early 1960s. "It's apparent," wrote one industry analyst, "that some thorny marketing problems will develop in Texas in 1964 and 1965."[80] Carling management understood that gaining a foothold in Texas and surrounding states – and doing it in advance of its national rivals – could prove crucial to its quest to become the nation's largest brewer. Thus, when completion of the Fort Worth brewery encountered delays, Carling hastily acquired the plant of the Arizona Brewing Company in Phoenix in 1964 and began to supply the region with Black Label Beer and Red Cap Ale brewed at the Phoenix plant. In addition, Carling retained the Arizona Brewing Company's primary brand, A-1 Beer.[81]

Delays in the opening of Carling's Fort Worth brewery were partly the result of unexpected and, initially, unexplainable problems with the consistency of the beer produced at the new plant. Several months passed before the source of the trouble (a simple piece of stainless steel pipe) was finally pinpointed. In the meantime, the brewery suffered poor publicity as many observers erroneously attributed the problems to failure of the Continuous Brewing Process. Carling officials had hoped to herald the new plant as "the world's most modern brewery." Instead, the Fort Worth facility opened in May of 1965 amidst strong industry skepticism and lukewarm public interest.[82]

However, it was only a short time before Carling was facing far larger difficulties. Sales of the Carling products both from Phoenix and from Fort Worth were embarrassingly poor throughout 1965. Some attributed the failure to the strong foundations of the incumbent brewers in the Southwest. Others felt that Carling had been over anxious in its attempt to conquer the region, and had not properly "seated" a demand for its products before establishing breweries there. Whatever the case, just months after its opening, the Fort Worth brewery was shut down, never again to brew Carling beer and ale.* Likewise, the Phoenix brewery was sold in 1966 to the National Brewing Company of Baltimore.[83] In addition, plans for a new Carling brewery in San Francisco were halted. Carling's retreat from the West and Southwest marked the beginning of the company's demise. Throughout the ensuing decade, the Carling Brewing Company would fight valiantly for its survival. Unfortunately, it would ultimately lose the battle.

The Long Descent

Concurrently with his duties as president of Carling Brewing Company, Ian R. Dowie had served as president of the parent Canadian Breweries Limited since 1958, dividing his time between the U.S. and Canada. With Carling in seemingly sound condition, Dowie felt that it was time for him to return to Canada on a full time basis in 1962. Henry E. Russell, who had been in charge of Carling's highly successful New England territory, was named as the new president of Carling Brewing Company.[85] The job would not be an easy one. Over the course of the next four tumultuous years, Russell watched as Carling experienced both its highest peak of success and its lowest level of retrenchment.

In 1965, for the first time in fifteen years, Carling recorded a decline in sales from the previous year.[86] The drop-off, coupled with the debacles in the Southwest, conspired to make 1965 a "year of crisis" for Carling. Though acknowledging the magnitude of the challenges ahead, Henry E. Russell was nevertheless confident about Carling's ability to rebound in 1966:

> *Last year's experience has put us back to work – and hard. An enormous amount of work remains to be done. It may be that we had been lulled into thinking we could do no wrong, perhaps we were too content with the way things were going. As far as past history is concerned – let's just say "that's that." We're capable of doing what we want to do. We have been cool and calculating in our appraisal of ourselves. We're ready to make our big move on the consumer and from all indications 1966 will be the most exciting year in our history.*[87]

However, after Carling's sales continued to decline through 1966, Russell was somewhat less optimistic:

> *It is obvious that the severe competitive pressures will persist and probably intensify. So long as there is excess capacity in the industry this sometimes vicious, even voracious competitive climate will continue to breed economically unsound gyrations in the market-place.*[88]

It was, indeed, competitive pressures from other national brewers upon which the Carling Brewing Company could justifiably blame its woes. With its popular-priced Black Label brand,

---

*The Fort Worth plant was later sold to the Miller Brewing Company of Milwaukee. The first thing Miller did upon acquisition of the brewery was remove all of the Continuous Brewing Method equipment and donate it to a medical research facility. Miller officially re-opened the plant in 1969 and continues to operate it today.[84]

The Carling "Keg Bottle" helped bring rebounding sales in 1968 and 1969.

Carling had always positioned itself to be a formidable competitor against the small, local brewers in any given region. By the mid-1960s, however, the great majority of those local brewers had been driven from the market (due in no small part to Carling itself). Thus, the company was increasingly forced to do battle with the far more competitive national brewers for market share. It was a confrontation which Carling was simply ill-equipped to win. Without a well-performing premium-priced brand to compete against Budweiser, Pabst Blue Ribbon, Miller High Life and other premium beers, the Carling Brewing Company was at a tremendous disadvantage. Profit margins on the low-priced Black Label were much smaller than those enjoyed by Carling's competitors. In short, the very strategy which had saved Carling from bankruptcy in the 1950s was now contributing to the company's rapid decay.

Henry E. Russell

Carling management was not unaware of its need to compete in the premium price category. Of course, raising Black Label's price was not the answer, as such a move would surely have only accelerated the sales decline. Instead, in 1962, efforts were made to revitalize sales of the premium-priced Red Cap Ale.[89] A new formula was devised to make Red Cap more akin to the popular Canadian ales. And a new label design, "contemporary in spirit," was prepared by noted industrial designer Raymond Loewy. The strategy was certainly not without merit. Because of its premium price, Red Cap Ale could yield as much as $14 per barrel more in income than the lower-priced Black Label.[90] However, history might have predicted the failure of Red Cap Ale to achieve the hoped-for sales. Consumer indifference to the Red Cap brand had been a problem virtually since the company's founding in 1934. The new formula and new package did not turn the tide. For the remainder of its years, the Carling Brewing Company would struggle with its lack of a strong premium-priced product.

After a three-year sales decline, the Carling Brewing Company experienced a brief recovery in 1968 and 1969, showing sales increases in both years.[91] The reversal was caused by a number of factors, prominent among them a labor strike and subsequent work stoppages at both Anheuser-Busch and the Pabst Brewing Company. However, Carling preferred to credit the rebounding sales to one of its new marketing initiatives: the Keg Bottle – a unique keg-shaped bottle designed especially for Carling. The Keg Bottle was launched nationwide in 1968 after its initial release in Tacoma indicated great promise for the new package. "Our research found that people couldn't

E. P. Taylor was the millionaire mastermind behind formation of Canadian Breweries Limited, the Carling parent. With thirty-one breweries around the globe producing more than forty different brands of beer, Canadian Breweries boasted the title of "the largest brewing organization in the world" by 1964. Just as it had been in the U.S., Black Label Beer was a prodigy worldwide for Canadian Breweries. The brand was brewed in Canada, England, Scotland and Ireland and was sold in more than fifty countries. Nevertheless, the Carling Brewing Company in the U.S. was, by a wide margin, the largest single entity under the Canadian Breweries umbrella until the mid-1970s.

Taylor, however, relinquished his interest in Canadian Breweries in 1968 when a majority of the company's stock was acquired by Rothmans of Pall Mall, a South African-owned tobacco manufacturer. Many believed that the Rothmans takeover was a major factor in Carling's decline in the U.S. during the 1970s. Rothmans' lack of experience both in brewing and in American business practices was, according to some, the "nail in Carling's coffin."

keep their hands off the bottle," recalled a Carling marketing executive. "It had a very tactile quality that enhanced the consuming experience." Another executive predicted in 1968 that, "For us, this may well be the year of the Keg Bottle."[92]

Indeed, Carling management placed a great deal of hope in the Keg Bottle's ability to help fuel a complete turn-around for the company. Perhaps nothing was more indicative of that fact than the celebration which accompanied the Keg Bottle's introduction in the Cleveland brewery on May 22, 1968. The day was officially christened "K-Day" at the Quincy Avenue facility when, at 6:50 a.m., bottle shop superintendent Frank Kostrab pressed the ceremonial button which activated the plant's bottling lines. Carling managers, followed by a four-piece marching band, boisterously paraded through the entire brewery singing and waving banners which heralded K-Day. At the end of the workday, every employee was sent home with two six-packs of Black Label in the Keg Bottle – one for themselves and one for a neighbor. Had there previously been any doubt as to the company's hopes for the success of the Keg Bottle, all question was erased on that celebratory day.[93]

Almost exactly three years later, the mood at Carling's Cleveland plant was not so festive. On May 9, 1971, the Cleveland brewery was closed due to what Carling officials coldly described as the plant's "serious physical deficiencies which result in excessive operating costs."[94] Carling's annual sales had dropped by more than one million barrels since 1969, and the company desperately needed to shed its excess brewing capacity to remain solvent. As the Cleveland brewery was deemed the least modern and least efficient of the seven Carling plants, it was selected for disposal.

Many in Cleveland were not convinced that the brewery's "physical deficiencies" were the sole cause of its closure. Anthony Sapienza, president of the local Brewery and Soft Drink Workers Union, blamed the plant shutdown on poor acceptance of Carling products in Cleveland:

I just can't begin to comprehend how a company that has bent over backward to fill its civic responsibilities doesn't have the support of the people. I just can't believe that the people of Cleveland haven't seen fit to purchase Carling's products. Are we driving industry out of Cleveland? We're certainly not doing much to help it.[95]

Others berated Carling, charging that mismanagement was at the root of the plant closing. The Cleveland brewery, argued some, had been continually modernized over the years, and was thus not the "Rube Goldberg plant" which Carling had painted it to be. In fact, in 1969 and again in 1970, *Modern Brewery Age* featured pictorial articles reporting on the progress of a multi-million dollar modernization program taking place at Carling's Cleveland brewery.[96] The project, of course, was never completed.

The Carling Brewing Company moved its headquarters to Waltham, Massachusetts (near the Natick brewery) one month after brewing ceased at the Cleveland plant. Just weeks later, Henry E. Russell resigned as Carling president and was replaced by Canadian Breweries vice-president E. Norris Davis.[97] However, a dynamic Canadian Breweries marketing executive named Wilmat Tennyson took over as president of Carling in 1972 and embarked on an aggressive campaign to resuscitate the struggling U.S. brewer. In his trademark brassy demeanor, Tennyson vowed to rid the company of what he called the "gin and tonic club" style of management which he insisted had been the cause of Carling's troubles. "Carling," thundered Tennyson, "is going to fight like hell for its share of the U.S. beer market."[98]

In its on-going quest to establish itself in the premium-price category, Carling introduced Black Label Malt Liquor in 1971. The brand was discontinued a few years later.

Tennyson's promises were big, but his results were, as one analyst generously described it, "mixed." Mild sales increases were noted in some regions, but on the whole, Carling was sinking rapidly. In 1975, after showing a loss on operations of nearly $10 million in a single twelve-month period, the Carling Brewing Company announced that it was discussing a possible merger with the National Brewing Company of Baltimore. National operated three breweries (including the Phoenix brewery purchased from Carling in 1966) and was ranked as the sixteenth largest brewer in America. Both Carling and National were in dire need of added sales volume. Carling was highly attracted to National's top-selling Colt 45 Malt Liquor, a premium-priced brand sold in all fifty states. National sought to strengthen its presence in the Pacific Northwest and was thus enticed by the consistently good sales performance of Carling's Tacoma brewery. Late in 1975, the deal was consummated and Carling National Breweries, Inc. was formed. Managements were consolidated; breweries were eliminated; and, in its first full year of operation, the new company sold an encouraging 4,311,767 barrels of beer and ale.[99]

Despite a promising start, success was brief for Carling National Breweries. Between 1977 and 1978, sales declined by about twenty percent.[100] After a proposed merger with the Pabst Brewing Company was blocked by the U.S. Justice Department in 1978, Carling National sought a buyer. Early the following year, it found one. For the sum of $35,250,000 in cash, the G. Heileman Brewing Company of La Crosse, Wisconsin took possession of Carling National Breweries and its assets in March of 1979.[101] Heileman continued to produce many of the former Carling National brands, including Black Label Beer, until 1996 when the Stroh Brewery Company of Detroit purchased Heileman. Stroh inherited the rights to the Black Label brand and continues to market it today.[102]

A New Tenant at Quincy Avenue

When the Carling Brewing Company left Cleveland in 1971, few expected that the old brewery on Quincy Avenue would ever again produce beer. After all, its owners had publicly condemned the plant as an outdated and inefficient relic before abandoning it. The Greater Cleveland Growth Association and the Black Economic Union zealously searched for a brewer who might be interested in taking up production in the defunct plant. The president of the Peoples Brewing Company of Oshkosh, Wisconsin spent four days in 1971 looking over the brewery with thoughts of purchasing it, but finally concluded that the monolith was far too big for his needs.[103] Six months after Carling's departure from Cleveland, the future looked bleak for the historic brewery.

Thus, it came as a great surprise to everyone when Cleveland's sole remaining brewer – C. Schmidt & Sons on Train Avenue – announced in November of 1971 that it had negotiated the purchase of the Quincy Avenue brewery. The Philadelphia-based C. Schmidt & Sons came to Cleveland in 1964, taking over the Schaefer (formerly Standard) brewery on the city's west side. Schmidt enjoyed steady sales growth throughout the 1960s and was the nation's twelfth largest brewer by 1971. While

The majestic old auto plant-turned-brewery was taken over by C. Schmidt & Sons in 1971.

Carling had consistently quoted an asking price of $7 million for its Cleveland plant, Schmidt paid only $2.5 million. The acquisition was made in anticipation of Schmidt's need for more brewing capacity in the coming years. Capable of producing 1.5 million barrels annually, the Quincy Avenue brewery was twice the size of Schmidt's plant on Train Avenue.[104]

Schmidt was comfortably settled in its new facility by the spring of 1972, and production at the Train Avenue brewery was phased out.* The company's first few years in its new Cleveland home were palmy ones. In a shrewd marketing move, Schmidt purchased the brand names of the Duquesne Brewing Company when the Pittsburgh brewer announced its closing in 1972. Prominent among the acquired labels was Duke Beer, the third largest selling brand of beer in Cleveland (behind Budweiser and Stroh's).[105] Also important in the deal was the venerable P.O.C. Beer, which had been part of Duquesne's purchase of the Pilsener Brewing Company in 1963.

C. Schmidt & Sons paid tribute to its Cleveland market with this 1982 commemorative beer can.

Schmidt, of course, would enjoy an incumbent popularity for the P.O.C. brand in Cleveland.

Already in 1973, C. Schmidt & Sons was operating its new Cleveland brewery at near capacity. An unusually hot summer was causing shortages of beer as breweries throughout the Midwest were unable keep pace with soaring demand. Schmidt's employees were increased from 200 to 325 at the Cleveland brewery, and the plant was operating twenty-four hours a day to meet its orders for beer.[106]

The following year, however, brought disappointment as C. Schmidt & Sons suffered its first sales decline in fifteen years. The company's financial losses in 1974 were estimated at $4 million. Rumors abounded to the affect that, after more than a century of ownership by the Schmidt family, the brewing company was on the auction block. The G. Heileman Brewing Company was the first to confirm those rumors when it was granted permission from the U.S. Justice Department to pursue a Schmidt buyout. After lengthy negotiations, Heileman finally retracted its offer of $16 million dollars in 1975. In 1976, Schmidt was sold to William H. Pflaumer & Sons, a large Philadelphia beer distributor.[107] Philadelphians and Clevelanders alike were happy to see Schmidt acquired by an entity other than a rival brewing company because it meant continued operation of both plants. A takeover by another brewer would surely have resulted in consolidation of brewing facilities.

Schmidt's new owners entered the beer-making business with great ambition, and their initial results were good. Beer sales in Ohio alone were boosted thirty percent in 1976. Company-wide sales over the next several years were strong.[108] Schmidt took over the brands of the Erie Brewing Company (Erie, Pennsylvania) in 1978, brewing most of them in Cleveland. But, by the early 1980s, decline had set in at C. Schmidt & Sons. Competitive strains and rising costs of

---

*Schmidt later sold the Train Avenue plant to the Miller Brewing Company, which extracted the brewing equipment and shipped it to Fort Worth, Texas for use in the brewery which Miller had purchased from Carling in 1966.

operation made it increasingly difficult for large regional brewers like Schmidt to operate profitably. Amidst shrinking sales, Schmidt closed its Cleveland brewery in 1984 and transferred production to Philadelphia. Two years later, C. Schmidt & Sons ceased business altogether, selling its brand line to its earlier courter, the G. Heileman Brewing Company.[109]

The old Quincy Avenue brewery, Cleveland's last, was once again idle. This time, however, no surprise buyers would come to its rescue. In 1985, Pittsburgh interests acquired the plant with the intention of converting it for production of industrial alcohol, but the plan never developed. Instead, the once majestic structure stood empty, abandoned and heavily vandalized until its demolition in 1994. But the old brewery continued to be in the news as city officials battled the property's owners over the alleged numerous hazardous materials which littered the grounds. In 1997, Mayor Michael R. White declared the former brewery site "the worst environmental hazard in the city" and called in the EPA to help remedy the situation.[110]

Chapter Twelve

Coming Full Circle

George E. Condon, venerable newspaper man and biographer of Cleveland, wrote, "Once there were breweries all over the city, and the pungent smell of malt and hops wafted high on the breeze, putting a dreamy look on the faces of all who had strength enough to inhale."[1] Indeed, from the prosperous 1870s when the number of Cleveland's breweries peaked at nearly *thirty*, to the palmy late 1940s when a booming post-war economy spurred record beer sales, Cleveland was a beer town through and through. When C. Schmidt & Sons closed its brewery on Quincy Avenue in 1984, it was the first time in more than 150 years that Cleveland was without a brewery. A rich and colorful chapter in Cleveland's history had quietly come to an end.

It was, however, only a short time before Cleveland was again adding new history to its brewing heritage. Just when it seemed that the industry giants had all but eradicated the small,

local brewery in America, there came a sort of rebirth in beer-making. During the 1980s, a handful of brewers-turned-entrepreneurs sought to bring a sense of *craft* back to their ancient art, giving rise to a new era in American brewing. From the mere twenty-nine "craft brewers" operating in America in 1986, the figure has skyrocketed to more than 1,200 doing business in all but a few states in 1997. And the near-astronomical number of different types and styles of beer on the market today continues to grow. Though their collective share of the total beer consumption in America is no more than three percent, most craft brewers nevertheless enjoy great success with their relatively small niche markets. Indeed, in 1997, Cleveland alone boasted *six* craft brewers, each reporting healthy beer sales and growing numbers of customers.

The similarities between Cleveland's craft brewers and

their ancestral counterparts are profound, particularly as concerns the style of beer that each brewed and the methods employed to brew it. Both instilled in their beer the same sort of pride and care that an artist imbues in his work. Both strived for uniqueness – a special character or refinement in the flavor of their beer which was distinctly and undeniably their own. Both brewed in small, manageable batches and often served their beer exclusively on the brewery premises. And both refused to employ additives and adjuncts to lengthen shelf-life, create an artificial head, or otherwise stimulate an unnatural characteristic in their beer.

Like their predecessors, Cleveland's contemporary brewers recognize that fraternity, rather than rivalry, is mutually beneficial. In testament to that belief, the brewers of Cleveland formed the Northern Ohio Craft Brewer's Association (NOCBA) in 1995 for the purpose of "representing the industry in the marketplace, increasing the awareness of locally brewed beer, and educating the Ohio community about the many facets of beer and brewing."[2] In April of 1997, the NOCBA held its first annual "Midwest BrewFest" at the Powerhouse complex in the Flats. Hosted by more than a dozen craft brewers from all over the Midwest, the BrewFest was an opportunity for local beer drinkers to sample, side-by-side, the wide variety of new brews on the market. The event harkened back to an era when local brewers shared a distinct camaraderie and joined together to promote the advancement of their industry. "We're like an unofficial union," says Josh Breckel, assistant brewer at Cleveland's Rock Bottom brewery. "Most of the brewers in town are good friends. We help each other by trading ideas, finding jobs for out-of-work brewers, keeping the quality of the product strong."[3]

But if there is one thing that many of Cleveland's craft brewers share with the beer-makers of yesteryear more than anything else, it is their manifestly *local* character. Bygone brand names such as Clevelander Beer and Forest City Pilsner have been replaced with monikers like North Coast Gold Ale, Eliot Ness Lager and Lake Effect Winter Ale. Today, just as a century ago, the vast majority – if not the entirety – of Cleveland-brewed beer is consumed within its home region. And the city's brewers, both past and present, were more than content with that fact. Herbert F. Leisy, whose family brewed beer in Cleveland for three generations, once commented that "In the old days they used to say that any brewery that could see a large proportion of its market from the top of its own chimney was in good shape."[4] Echoing that notion was Gavin Smith of the Western Reserve Brewing Company, established in 1997, who summarized: "We are Clevelanders and we want to make beer for Cleveland."[5] The brewing industry has, indeed, come full circle.

The Modern Pioneers

When the craft brewing "phenomenon" made its start in America in the mid-1980s, Cleveland offered a fertile market for such entrepreneurial ventures. The city was in the midst of a pronounced renaissance as whole areas of downtown were being refurbished; the Flats was fast becoming the entertainment mecca of Northern Ohio; and plans were on the drawing board for a brand new baseball stadium and basketball arena. Cleveland was hungry for hometown pride, and icons of the city's "comeback," both big and small, were devoured with great enthusiasm by Clevelanders celebrating the revival of their city.

It was in this environment that Cleveland welcomed its first craft brewery – the first, in fact, in all of Ohio. Brothers Patrick and Daniel Conway opened the doors of their Great Lakes Brewing Company brewpub on September 6, 1988, thus reawakening Cleveland's proud brewing tradition. They chose Ohio City as the site for their brewery, in part due to the rich German beer-making heritage of the neighborhood. Just a few blocks in any direction once stood breweries which, like Great Lakes, catered exclusively to the residents of the charming west side neighborhood. The new brewery is housed in a century-plus-old red brick building on Market Street, opposite the West Side Market. The structure was originally home to the Market Street Exchange, a popular tavern and restaurant as far back as the mid-1800s.* Its well-preserved, almost majestic mahogany bar is a befitting artifact for the new brewery. One might guess that virtually all of Cleveland's past brews, at one time or another, were served over that very bar.

Patrick Conway, a former school teacher, first hatched the idea of opening a brewery while traveling in Germany and enjoying the wide variety of beers in each of the cities he visited. Brother Daniel Conway, a banker, joined the venture as financial manager while Patrick set about devising a formula for Great Lakes' first brew. He enlisted the expertise of Thaine Johnson, former brewmaster at the C. Schmidt & Sons brewery. When Schmidt closed its Cleveland plant in 1984, Johnson retired, ending a forty-year career in brewing. But, compelled by the spirit of the craft brew movement, Johnson came out of retirement to help the Conways establish their brewery, serving as Great Lakes brewmaster, a role which he continues to fill today.

Brothers Patrick (left) and Daniel Conway established the Great Lakes Brewing Company in 1988.

The cornerstone brew at the Great Lakes Brewing Company was its first product – a German-style lager named Dortmunder Gold which remains the brewery's best seller. It was originally titled The Heisman after football great Johnny Heisman, who grew up near the brewery. But objections from Heisman Trophy authorities forced a name change.[6]

In addition to the flagship Dortmunder Gold, Great Lakes' other brews include: Eliot Ness Lager, named in honor of the famous Cleveland Safety Director and one time Cleveland mayoral candidate; Burning River Pale Ale, in memory of the historic day when the Cuyahoga River caught fire; Edmund Fitzgerald Porter, commemorating the 1975 sinking of the iron ore vessel on Lake Erie; and Moon Dog Ale, titled after Alan Freed's legendary Cleveland rock & roll radio program of the 1950s.

Inside the Great Lakes brewpub.

---

*Surviving on an outer wall of the brewery is a painted advertisement for the old Market Street Exchange. The advertisement notes that the brews of Lloyd & Keys' Cleveland City Brewery were on draught at the tavern "for family and medicinal purposes."

In the tradition of the city's very earliest beer-makers, the Great Lakes Brewing Company initially served its beer only on the brewery premises and only on draught. But, as the popularity of the Great Lakes brews spread, bottling capabilities were added and off-premises sales began. In 1994, additional brewing facilities were added in the old Fries & Schuele

Great Lakes Brewing Company will begin brewing beer in its new $7 million brewery in early 1998. The plant is housed in former buildings of the L. Schlather Brewing Company.

building just down the block from the brewpub. By 1997, Great Lakes beer was being sold at approximately 1,000 locations throughout Ohio, and major expansion of the brewery was in progress. The Conway brothers took over the nearby remnants of the L. Schlather Brewing Company stables and bottle shop and started construction on a $7 million dedicated brewery. Capable of brewing 30,000 barrels annually when completed, the new facility is scheduled to turn out its first beer in March of 1998.[7]

Named "1994 Microbrewery Of The Year" by the Beverage Tasting Institute, the Great Lakes Brewing Company has cultivated a decidedly estimable reputation. The historic ambiance of its brewpub, the quaintness of its Ohio City neighborhood, and, of course, the quality of its award-winning brews have earned it a prominent place in Cleveland's brewing history.

The Brewpubs

Brewers who sell their product exclusively on the brewery premises (commonly called "brewpubs") comprise the majority of today's beer-makers, and for good reason. For the small brewer, getting beer into the hands of the consumer has always been a challenging task. In the old days, these challenges centered around the expense and difficulties of transportation and the perishability and fragility of the beer. In more recent times, the dominance of national brewers has made it increasingly difficult to secure retail shelf space and bar taps. Thus, rather than bringing their beer to the consumer, a great number of today's craft brewers have opted instead to bring the *consumer* to their *beer*. Many of today's breweries, therefore, are much more than breweries alone. On-premises brewpubs invariably include such enticements as restaurants, gift shops, live entertainment, brewery tours, beer seminars, special events, and, of course, a continual rotation of unique brews to keep patrons coming back to try something new.

The Diamondback Brewery on Prospect Avenue is one of Cleveland's new brewpubs. In the shadows of Gund Arena and Jacob's Field, Diamondback has attracted a loyal clientele since opening in June of 1996. Along with its eclectic dining menu, Diamondback offers a variety of year-round brews: Black Diamond Pale Ale, Steelcut Oatmeal Stout, Rattler Red Vienna Lager and White Diamond Pilsener. Among the approximately twenty different seasonal brews made at Diamondback are Whole Wheat Hefe-Weizen ("with a subtle banana and clove character"), and Gueuze Lambic. Brewers Bill Morgan and Dan Maerzluft are especially proud of the latter, which is fermented and aged in real oak casks. Several hogsheads of the brew have been set aside for multi-year aging, not to be tapped until reaching their peak flavor.[8] In 1997, the Diamondback Brewery completed a major expansion program and began providing its brews to off-site retailers.

The Rock Bottom Brewery & Restaurant, housed in the grand old Powerhouse complex in the Flats, has become a favorite in Cleveland. Opened in September of 1995, Rock Bottom is part of a Denver-based chain of brewpubs of the same name. Despite the twenty-one locations across the country, each Rock Bottom brewery formulates and brews its own unique beers according to the tastes of the region and the style of the brewmaster. During its first year, the Cleveland Rock Bottom brewery sold 77,500 gallons of beer, all consumed on-premises.[9] Featured brews at Rock Bottom include Cleveland American Light Ale, Northcoast Golden Ale, Riverbend Ale, Buzzard Brown Ale, and Terminal Stout – all brewed at the hand of head brewmaster Marc Anievas.

Like Rock Bottom, John Harvard's Brew House in the nineteenth century Customs House building on Old River Road is part of a brewpub chain. Based in Boston, John Harvard's opened its Cleveland brewpub – thirteenth in the chain – in September of 1997. Cleveland brewers Brian O'Reilly and David Sutula offer an ever-changing lineup of brews at John Harvard's. Among the mainstays are Pilgrim's Porter, Old Willy India Pale Ale and Big Bad Bock.[10]

John Harvard's Brew House borrows its title from Harvard University's namesake, a champion and connoisseur of good beer. As the story goes, John Harvard, who met his demise in 1638, bequeathed half of his estate to the college of New Towne, Massachusetts – now Harvard University. However, per Harvard's will, the funds were to be used in a very specific manner:

> *Whereas I have observed the beneficent effects of the consumption of beere in moderation upon all classes of our human society, and whereas I am resolved to build a juster and more rational society in the great land of America, now therefore, I, John Harvard, being of sound mind, do bequeath one half of my worldly goods to the establishment of a college of brewing sciences in New Towne, confident that it will aid in the establishment of a better regulated and nobler commonwealth than has hitherto blessed this earth.*[11]

For reasons which history fails to yield, John Harvard's wishes were never fulfilled. In fact, it was not until the recent discovery of Harvard's will that his quest to employ beer as means to "a juster and more rational society" became known.

On A Grand Scale

In early America, the evolution of the typical brewer's establishment was fairly predictable. He often started as a tavernkeeper, brewing only enough beer to supply his patrons. As the reputation of his brew slowly began to move beyond the confines of his tavern, a demand for the product developed within the community. In time, overtaken by growing demand, the brewer was compelled to give up his tavern and dedicate himself entirely to the making of beer.

In modern times, however, demand does not wait for evolution. As the market for craft-brewed beers began to blossom during the 1980s and early 1990s, a number of new brewers elected to bypass the traditional brewpub beginnings. Instead, they sought to compete on store shelves and bar tops right alongside century-old giants like Anheuser-Busch, Stroh and Coors.

The first of these daring entrepreneurs in Cleveland were David Lowman and Craig Chaitoff, both of whom left corporate lives in 1988 to establish the Cleveland Brewing Company. In contrast to the novelty of their venture, a familiar name from the past – Erin Brew Beer – was resurrected as their product. (Fittingly, Congressman Edward F. Feighan, grandson of Erin Brew founder John T. Feighan, was a major backer of the new brewing company.) "People say Cleveland's been experiencing a renaissance," said co-founder Craig Chaitoff. "But something was missing, and that was the beer."[12] That oversight was corrected in May of 1988 when the new Erin Brew made its debut. The beer, brewed under contract in Pittsburgh and shipped to Cleveland, enjoyed good initial reception in the Cleveland area, and distribution was soon extended into Akron, Canton and Columbus.

However, by 1990, the craft brew market in Cleveland was not the wide-open field it had been just two years earlier. Dozens of competing craft brews had invaded Cleveland, and their number was increasing steadily. Sales of Erin Brew began to drop off as a result.[13] By 1994, production of Erin Brew had ceased, and the Cleveland Brewing Company's Lakeside Avenue office and warehouse was closed. Just as it had done so many years earlier, competition from outside brewers caused the passing of Erin Brew Beer.

Strong competition did not dissuade other local entrepreneurs from picking up where the Cleveland Brewing Company had left off. In August of 1994, brewmaster Stephan Danckers and partner Stuart Sheridan christened their Settlers Ale, the first of four year-round brews to be marketed by their Crooked River Brewing Company (named, of course, in honor of the winding Cuyahoga River).[14] The venture was a long-time ambition of Danckers, whose training and background in brewing are extensive. After receiving a Master's degree in Brewing Science from the University of California at Davis, Danckers traveled to Germany where he studied on a Fullbright Scholarship at the University of Munich Brewing and Science School at Weihenstephan. The brewery at Weihenstephan is purported to be the world's

Inside the Crooked River Brewing Company plant.

WITH EVERYTHING GREAT GOING UP IN CLEVELAND, HERE'S SOMETHING GREAT GOING DOWN.

oldest, dating back to the year 1040. Upon his return to America, Danckers worked as a brewer for the Stroh Brewery Company at plants in Minnesota and California. In 1989, the twenty-eight-year-old brewer turned down a job offer from Anheuser-Busch to take a brewmaster's position at Melbourne's Brewing Company (now the Mad Crab Restaurant & Microbrewery) in Strongsville, Ohio.[15]

Brewing began early in 1994 at Crooked River's gleaming new $1.5 million brewery at 1101 Center Street in the Flats. Initial brewing capacity of the dedicated brewery was approximately 6,000 barrels annually. Since business began, however, about $1 million has been spent to improve and enlarge the facility, now capable of producing 12,000 barrels per year.[16] Among the more significant additions to the brewery was a cold-filtering system making it possible for Crooked River Beer to be sold *warm* without being pasteurized. Unlike most of the national brewers, virtually all craft brewers refuse to pasteurize because of the flavor-damaging nature of the process. Distributors and retailers who handle craft beer are thus plagued by the beer's need for constant refrigeration. Crooked River's cold-filtering system allows the brewery to side-step the problem entirely, representing a significant competitive advantage for its products.

The Crooked River Brewing Company bottles and kegs four different year-round brews: Settlers Ale, Black Forest Lager, Lighthouse Gold, and Cool Mule Porter. The brewery also offers a number of seasonal and holiday beers, among them Yuletide Ale (Christmas), Irish Red (winter), Doppelbock (spring), and the popular Erie Nights Pumpkin Brew (Halloween). Throughout Cleveland's Bicentennial celebration in 1996, the brewery marketed a limited-run beer called Crooked River Bicentennial, a German-style wheat beer.[17] The Crooked River brewery also makes exclusive brews for both Jacob's Field and Gund Arena. Ballpark Draft made its debut at the

Black Forest Lager, the brewery's largest seller, is named in tribute to the Black Forest Beer produced for many years by the Cleveland Home Brewing Company.

Erie Nights is a popular Halloween brew made using real pumpkins.

Suburban Affairs

Unlike their nineteenth-century counterparts, the new American craft brewers have not limited themselves to urban and semi-urban locales. In fact, brewpubs and microbreweries are becoming an increasingly *suburban* phenomenon. Cleveland, like most major cities, has seen a number of craft brewers spring up in its outlaying regions.

The Firehouse Brewery in Cleveland Heights was among the first. Housed in a historic, well-preserved firehouse, the brewery's feature brew is titled, likely enough, Backdraft Stout.

Wallaby's Grille & Brewpub in Westlake offers an "Aussie-style" motif both in its dining menu and its brews. In 1997, Wallaby's began construction on a full-scale dedicated brewery near its brewpub, and plans to market its beers throughout Northeast Ohio.

In Strongsville, the Mad Crab Restaurant & Brewery opened in 1996, replacing former occupant Melbourne's Brewing Company.

Just down the road from Mad Crab is the Brew Kettle and Ringneck Brewing Company. The Brew Kettle is Ohio's first "personal microbrewery," where weekend dabblers can brew their own beer using the equipment and facilities of the Brew Kettle. The adjoining Ringneck Brewing Company makes specialty beers on a contract basis for local restaurants and bars.

And the Willoughby Brewing Company of Willoughby, Ohio is soon to open its new brewpub in a century-old building which once housed the repair shop of the Cleveland, Painesville & Eastern Railroad Company.

Cleveland Indians 1995 home opener, and has remained a strong seller each season. Likewise, Arena Draft is popular during home games of the Cleveland Cavaliers.

By 1997, the Crooked River Brewing Company had firmly entrenched itself in the Northeast Ohio beer market. The brewery's products were carried by about 1,000 outlets in Greater Cleveland and select parts of Central Ohio. Between January and April of 1997 alone, five new distributors were brought into the Crooked River network. In April, the brewery signed a three-year agreement to be the exclusive craft beer sponsor of the annual Medic Drug Grand Prix race (formerly the Budweiser Grand Prix) at Lakefront Airport.[18] The deal sent a clear message that the Crooked River Brewing Company was intent on competing aggressively for an ever-greater share of the market. Late in 1997, Crooked River showed no signs of slowing down.

Among the newcomers with which Crooked River will have to compete is the Western Reserve Brewing Company, which began operations in Cleveland in July of 1997.[19] The company turns out three year-round varieties – American Wheat, Amber Ale and Nut Brown Ale – from its brewery at 4130 Commerce Avenue on the city's near east side. Its first seasonal brew, Lake Effect Winter Ale, came on the market late in 1997. Western Reserve, which handles all of its own distribution, sells its beer to about forty retailers in Cuyahoga County, and the number grows each week. Founders Andrew Craze and Gavin Smith pride themselves on the quality and uniqueness of their products, and urge customers to exercise special care: "Treat our beer like the family dog – keep it comfortable and out of extreme heat or cold, except when taking it out to play."[20]

On The Horizon

There is little doubt that the rebirth of Cleveland's brewing industry will continue in earnest over the next several years. At this writing, a handful of new Cleveland breweries are already in the planning, and more are likely to follow. What *is* in question, however, is what the long-term future will hold for the city's brewers. History certainly provides a few general prognostications. Just as did the beer makers of a 150 years ago, Cleveland's new generation of brewers will have to change and evolve in response to an ever-shifting beer market. Competition will undoubtedly continue to intensify; consumers' tastes will alter with time; and a variety of less-predictable factors will create continual challenges. Only those brewers who have succeeded in combining a superior product with savvy marketing skills will survive over the long haul. In the meantime, each will find its own unique place in Cleveland's long and proud brewing heritage.

Brief Histories of Selected Cleveland Breweries

William Aenis. Around 1877, William Aenis began brewing beer on Columbus Street in partnership with Charles Metzger. The latter was replaced in 1879 by John F. Froelich.[1] By the following year, Aenis had moved his works to Pearl (West 25th) Street near Vega Avenue, and was doing business as William Aenis & Company. After a brief partnership with Martin Haller, Aenis turned over management of the brewery to George Denbert in 1884. During the same year, the brewery passed into the hands of Mrs. Mary Angel. Not long afterward, old partner John F. Froelich was back in the business. In 1886, he sold the brewery to Bohemian immigrant Wenzl Medlin, who formed the Medlin Bohemian Brewing Company. Medlin sold the brewery in 1889 to employee Simon Fishel.[2] When Fishel sold out to the Cleveland & Sandusky Brewing Company in 1897, the brewery was shut down and its production transferred to the Barrett brewery on Riverbed Road.

John Bishop. Bavarian immigrant John A. Bishop commenced the brewing of lager beer in 1852 on Broadway Avenue near Pittsburgh Avenue. Throughout the following thirty years, the brewery seems to have operated basically unchanged, undergoing only minimal expansion. As late as 1879, Bishop's brewery was turning out a relatively small 1,200 barrels annually.[3] Lager beer not having brought the anticipated success, the brewery was producing only ale when it was sold to the firm of Lezius & Kaenzig in 1882. Within a year, Christian Kaenzig was alone in the business, partner Louis Lezius having left to pursue a brewery just two blocks down Pittsburgh Avenue (see Appendix I, "Lezius & Uehlein"). Christian Kaenzig's wife, Elizabeth Kaenzig, had taken over management of the brewery by 1887. By 1889, former partner Louis Lezius was back in control of the business. Two years later, production ceased at the brewery.[4]

August Burckhardt. In 1868, August Burckhardt established a brewery at the corner of Pearl (West 25th) Street and Monroe Avenue and began the brewing of lager beer. The brewery was later operated by Anton Kopp & Rudolph Mueller who brewed about 2,500 barrels per year. In 1878, Rudolph Mueller, cousin of Cleveland brewer Ernst W. Mueller, became sole proprietor. However, when the brewery closed in 1880, it was instead under the management of William Schneider & Company.[5]

City Brewery. In 1841, the firm of Blackwell, Lloyd & Company was operating the City Brewery near the Ohio Canal. By 1843, the brewery was under new management, as noted in the *Cleveland Herald*: "The undersigned would respectfully inform the lovers of Good Ale & Strong Beer, that the city Brewery has a plenty on board, and is now under full sail, with S. C. Ives, Master."[6] The brewery remained in operation under the direction of Samuel C. Ives and Henry Lloyd until its demise in 1847. (Ives then purchased the Cleveland Brewery on Canal Road, while Henry Lloyd later established the Cleveland City Brewery on St. Clair Avenue.)

Eagle Brewery. The Eagle Brewery on Michigan Street near Seneca (West 3rd) Street was a fixture in the city for many years. Originally established in the early 1840s by George W. Hamilton, the brewery was completely leveled by fire in 1845, just a few days before Christmas. Hamilton was sick in bed at the time of the fire, but was "within hearing of the crackling of the destroying element."[7] The *Cleveland Herald* reported the value of the brewery as being about $2,000, said to have represented Hamilton's life savings. Although no insurance covered the loss, a collection was organized for Hamilton's benefit, and rebuilding of the Eagle Brewery was soon under way. English-born brewer John Tutbury joined the business as Hamilton's partner around 1848. However, by 1856, Hamilton had left the partnership to pursue another brewing venture locally, and the Eagle Brewery was doing business under the control of J. Tutbury & Company.[8] After Tutbury's death in 1857, management of the brewery fell into the hands of John Quinn, a brewer who had been employed at the works. Under his direction, the Eagle Brewery continued in operation until its doors closed around 1869.[9]

Patrick Gavagan. In 1880, Patrick Gavagan and John Sterling purchased the old Briggs Street Brewery at Briggs (East 22nd) and Davenport Avenue. The brewery had passed through the hands of no less than *seven* different owners or partial owners since its founding in 1863, to wit: Martin Stumpf, Joseph Koestle, John Davies, Venewel D. Hammond, Ernst Weisgerber, Clark Hodge, and W. R. Ogden.[10] After Sterling departed from the business in 1882, the brewery remained in the proprietorship of Patrick Gavagan for the next thirty-two years. One observer wrote in 1893, "Gavagan's ale and porter are tonics and refreshing beverages, and owing to their purity, are highly recommended by physicians."[11] In 1914, the partnership of Gavagan & Oppmann was formed when family members of the late Cleveland brewer Andrew W. Oppmann joined Gavagan in the small ale brewery. Joseph Segal later took over Gavagan's interest in the firm. The brewery, which never grew beyond a marginal level of production, closed in 1916.[12]

Henry Hoffman. The Hoffman & Paschen brewery was established in 1871 when Henry Hoffman and William Paschen bought a former clock factory at the corner of Fulton Road and Walton Avenue and began brewing lager beer there.[13] After a falling out between the partners, Hoffman ran the brewery with the help of his son, William Hoffman. In 1878, the brewery was capable of brewing 8,000 barrels of lager beer annually, although actual sales during that year amounted to just over 2,000 barrels.[14] The brewery closed shortly after Henry Hoffman's death in 1881.

Lezius & Uehlein. The brewery on Pittsburgh Avenue opposite Jackson (East 25th) Street began operating as early as 1856, when a local newspaper informed its readers that the "Jones & Lloyd Star Brewery, Pittsburgh street, has constantly on hand pale ale, amber ale, and porter."[15] Throughout the 1860s and 70s, the brewery changed hands on a regular basis. Among the proprietors over the years were J. Gromlich, Charles Yahraus, Carl Seyler, and Louis Chormann.[16] In 1885, the brewery came into the possession of Louis Lezius and August Uehlein, both of whom had previously been associated with A. W. Oppmann's brewery on the west side (Lezius as a partial owner and Uehlein as a bookkeeper). The partnership of Lezius & Uehlein, however, ended after only three years, when Lezius sold his share in the brewery to Anthony J. Diebolt for $3,300, reportedly due to failed expectations of the business.[17] By 1891, Diebolt was alone in the business. The brewery remained in operation, doing busimess as the Diebolt Brewing Company, until 1919 when statewide prohibition went into effect.

Lloyd & Keys, Cleveland City Brewery. The H. Lloyd & Company's Cleveland City Brewery commenced the manufacture of ale in 1859 on the St. Clair Avenue hill between West 9th and West 10th Streets. At the head of the concern was Welsh immigrant Henry Lloyd, who had spent several years involved in the old City Brewery near the canal. In 1860, Daniel H. Keys left his clerk's position of twelve years at Samuel C. Ives' Cleveland Brewery to join Lloyd in the new Cleveland City Brewery.[18] Together, the partners built a brewing enterprise which was undeniably one of the city's most enduring. By the mid-1870s, the brewery's original output of 1,500 barrels per year had increased more than four-fold. Indeed, business was at its peak in 1875 when Henry Lloyd passed away. Son William Lloyd took over his father's place in the partnership with Daniel H. Keys, and the firm finished out the decade amidst a downtrend in sales. Production amounted to just 3,629 barrels in 1878, a figure which dropped again the following year to 2,781 barrels.[19] Nevertheless, the 1880s brought increased sales to the Cleveland City Brewery. Production had rebounded significantly by 1888, when the brewery employed as many as fifteen men. A local publication noted during that year that Lloyd & Keys' full line of ale, porter, and brown stout were being enjoyed not only throughout Ohio, but in Michigan and Indiana as well.[20] After William Lloyd's death in 1895, Daniel H. Keys assumed sole proprietorship of the brewery. As the competitive environment intensified throughout the 1890s and early 1900s, the Cleveland City Brewery quietly maintained its trade, though rapidly becoming outsized by nearly all of its competitors. Finally, in 1909, the brewery was sold and production ceased. Daniel H. Keys, who had spent more than *sixty* years involved in ale brewing locally, cited his "advanced age and poor health" as the reason for his sale of the brewery.[21]

Thomas Newman. Thomas Newman was engaged in the brewing of ale on Irving (East 25th) Street near Pittsburgh Avenue beginning around 1850. William H. Rogers (brother of brewer Charles C. Rogers) joined Newman as partner during the mid-1860s, but later departed to inherit management of his brother's brewery.[22] Interestingly, for much of its existence, Newman's brewery operated as the Forest City Brewery, the same name already claimed by Charles C. Rogers for his brewery. Whatever disputes inevitably arose over use of the Forest City name, Rogers appears to have prevailed. Newman's operation ultimately discontinued use of the name. Upon Newman's retirement in 1872, the business was taken over by Daniel Fovargue and James Dangerfield, the former having learned the brewing trade as Newman's apprentice. Alone in the business by 1875, Fovargue apparently recognized the increasingly lucrative market for lager beer. By 1878, fully two-thirds of the brewery's annual capacity of 9,000 barrels was devoted to the production of lager beer. After 1881, the brewery was under the management of Fovargue & Newman, a partnership between Creasey Fovargue and Thomas Newman, Jr.[23] For whatever reason, the business had failed by the mid-1880s.

Charles C. Rogers, Forest City Brewery. Irishman Charles C. Rogers came to Cleveland in 1839 and established the Forest City Brewery on Canal Road at the foot of Seneca (West 3rd) Street.[24] There is little indication that the business grew much beyond its original size during the first decade. In 1850, Rogers obtained permission of the City Council to "conduct the springs on Seneca st. into a reservoir," presumably in the interest of his brewery and possibly to accommodate increasing production.[25] But it was not until 1858 that business was clearly on the upswing. The *Cleveland Leader* published the following in December of that year:

> *A large addition to the brewery of Mr. C. C. Rogers has lately been completed. It is located on the canal, near the foot of Seneca street, where Mr. R. commenced, in a small way, and has carried on business for the past nineteen years. The size of this new building is forty by sixty feet, and three stories high. It has a stone basement, the foundations of which extend seven feet below the surface of the ground, and are five feet in thickness. The basement is of cut stone, so that if the projected cutting down of the street is ever effected, the looks of the building will be improved. The water used is brought from a cluster of springs a short distance, and is of the utmost purity. Mr. Rogers is engaged mostly in the manufacture of stock ale, which he sells at one and two years of age. The reputation of Mr. Roger's old ale is such that he finds it difficult to supply the demand.[26]*

After more than three decades of brewing ale in Cleveland, Charles C. Rogers had retired by 1871, passing management of the Forest City Brewery on to his younger brother, William H. Rogers.[27] In partnership with Robert Beggs, and later with Hazen Hughes (brother of noted Cleveland brewer John M. Hughes), the younger Rogers continued in the business – brewing as much as 6,500 barrels of ale per year – until its sale around 1878 to John P. Haley, a former Cleveland policeman. By 1880, Carling & Company of London, Ontario had bought the plant, had renamed it the London Brewery, and had begun making its ale, porter and stout there, thus marking the start of the Carling name's long presence in Cleveland.[28]

Christian Schneider. Around 1870, Bohemian immigrant Joseph Zika established a brewery at the corner of Train Avenue and Ash (West 47th) Street, soon afterward selling out to the firm of Braun & Deitz. Christian Schneider, a local cooper and maltster, gained control of the brewery in 1872 and continued to operate it for the next several years, brewing about 4,000 barrels per year. The authors of *Industries of Cleveland* reviewed Schneider's brewery in 1878:

> *Among the many manufacturing industries of Cleveland none have made more rapid strides in amount of product manufactured and quality, than the manufacture of lager beer, and while many are interested in brewing, none make a better, and but few as good beer as may be found at the brewery of C. Schneider, on the corner of Ash and Train streets. Mr. Schneider started the brewing of beer September 12th, 1872; and in order that nothing be left undone to make the best, employed Mr. Anton Kopp, formerly....of G. Muth & Sons brewery, as foreman, and it is a fact that none are more generally acknowledged to be first, as brewer, than is Anton. The brewery is a building thirty by seventy feet with three cellars, two of twenty-four by thirty feet arched and one*

twenty-four by sixty, lined with galvanized iron, one ice-house twenty-four by forty feet, now in course of being finished. Their ice houses have a capacity of 2,500 tons of ice. The capacity of the brewery is something in excess of 11,000 barrels, and Mr. Schneider confidently looks to the time when he will have to use it to its utmost capacity.* The cellars of this brewery are worthy of special mention, as it is safe to say they are the best of any in Cleveland; and to be convinced of this fact, it is only necessary to take a walk through them with Mr. Kopp, and the assertion here made will be fully sustained. Mr. Schneider was born in Bavaria in 1824, on February 26th. He emigrated to America in 1840, and came directly to Cleveland, where, with little exception, he has continued to reside. Mr. Schneider is a gentleman too well known and highly respected to require any further notice from us. His son, Mr. John H. Schneider, is a lawyer of our city, of some prominence, who studied in the office of Judge Ranney, the widely known jurist of our city, spending two and a half years at Ann Harbor University, and was admitted to the bar of this State three years ago, and to the United States bar about one and a half years ago. Although but twenty-three years of age, he is well read and extensively known as a lawyer of ability.[29]

Despite his law career, John H. Schneider joined his father as partner in the brewery in 1880. When Christian Schneider retired from the business in 1889, John purchased his father's share and remained in the brewery as sole owner.

In May of 1891, Schneider's brewery was completely leveled by a somewhat unusual act of nature. During a severe thunderstorm, lightning struck the brewery's elevator shaft, sending an electrical charge down through the center of the building and igniting flames in as many as a dozen spots. By the time fire crews arrived, the brewery was completely engulfed, and salvaging any part of the structure had become hopeless. Ironically, the United States Brewers Association was holding its annual convention in Cleveland that week, and – at the very time the brewery was falling victim to the flames – John H. Schneider was addressing convention attendees at the closing night banquet at the Hollenden Hotel. Relevant or not, the subject of Schneider's speech was "The Ladies," in which he spoke of "man's perennial admiration for women, and his love for her charming shortcomings." One attendee called the speech, "a fine tribute to women, eloquent as well as sympathetic."[31]

The brewery's destruction represented a loss to John H. Schneider of about $125,000, only a portion of which was recovered by insurance. Nevertheless, rebuilding of the works began almost immediately, and brewing was commenced in the new plant the following year. But the business never fully recovered from the financial devastation caused by the loss of its original facility, and the company quickly fell into arrears. By the end of 1893, after a poor economy contributed to the firm's woes, Schneider's brewery was seized and slated for Sheriff's sale. Interestingly, virtually all of the brewery's debt was owed to founder Christian Schneider.[32]

In 1895, the brewery was sold to a group of investors who incorporated as the Union Brewing Company. Among those involved in the new company were James Storer and George Myers, two of Christian Schneider's sons-in-law.[33] By 1897, the brewery was producing less than 5,000 barrels annually, placing it among the city's smallest-producing breweries. The following year, it was sold to the Cleveland & Sandusky Brewing Company, which closed the plant in 1902.

---

*The brewery's actual output for the year 1878 was 3,916 barrels.[30]

Jacob Wagner. Jacob Wagner operated a brewery at 332 St. Clair Street during the 1860s and early 1870s. In 1871, when Wagner unsuccessfully attempted to sell the brewery at public auction, it was valued at $9,500.[34]

Frederick Weidenkopf. Around 1857, long-time Cleveland resident Frederick Weidenkopf set up a brewery on Canal Street for the production of lager beer. Weidenkopf and his family had operated the popular Weidenkopf's German Tavern on Seneca (West 3rd) Street for a number of years, and it is supposed that the brewery may have been set up initially to provide a reliable source of lager beer to the tavern. That notwithstanding, the brewery had developed an extensive outside trade by 1859. In June of that year, advertisements appeared in the *Plain Dealer* seeking a partner for Weidenkopf's brewery. The advertisements noted that the brewery was "doing business to the amount of $15,000 to $20,000 per year."[35] And, indeed, a partner was soon found. The firm of Hamilton & Weidenkopf was established when George W. Hamilton – who had operated the old Eagle Brewery for a number of years – joined the business. By the end of 1859, however, Weidenkopf left the partnership and Hamilton took over sole control of the brewery.[36]

Hamilton's success in the business was short-lived. In 1861, the entire contents of the brewery were sold at public auction, the result of an unpaid debt to a local maltster. Among the contents were 328 lager beer kegs, 64 wooden casks, 8 tubs, 1 copper kettle, 1 pump, 1 wash tub and cooler, 1 malt mill, and 1 delivery wagon. By 1864, the brewery was under the management of brewer John Whitlock, who operated the plant until his death in 1874.[37]

References

"Adv." indicates a newspaper or magazine advertisement as source.
"n.p." indicates a source with no page numbers.

Chapter One

1. Baron, pp. 44-47.
2. Apps, p. 19.
3. 100 Years of Brewing, p. 86.
4. 100 Years of Brewing, p. 59.
5. 100 Years of Brewing, p. 79.
6. 100 Years of Brewing, p. 91.
7. 100 Years of Brewing, pp. 102-103.
8. Van Tassel and Grabowski, p. 156; Rose, p. 49.
9. Adv., *Cleveland Herald,* May 14, 1829.
10. Annals of the Early Settlers' Association of Cuyahoga County, Ohio, vol. V, no. IV, p. 352.
11. Cuyahoga County Land Deeds.
12. Wickham, vol. I, pp. 266-269.
13. Rose, p. 99.
14. Rose, pp. 92, 97, 99; Cleveland Newspaper Digest (1821) p. 104.
15. Van Tassel and Grabowski, p. xix.
16. Cleveland Newspaper Digest (1819) p. 737; Rose p. 88.
17. Van Tassel and Grabowski, p. xxi.
18. Condon, pp. 43-44.
19. Van Tassel and Grabowski, p. xxi.
20. Adv., *Cleveland Herald,* May 29, 1832.
21. Adv., *Plain Dealer,* Sep. 7, 1863.
22. Wickham, vol. II, p. 381; Van Tassel and Grabowski, pp. 182-183.
23. Adv., *Cleveland Herald,* Feb. 4, 1833.
24. Adv., *Cleveland Herald,* April 5, 1834.
25. Adv., *Daily Herald & Gazette,* June 1, 1837; Adv., *Cleveland Daily Herald,* March 26, 1840; Avery, Vol. I, p. 209.
26. Adv., *Cleveland Daily Herald,* Dec. 10, 1840; Cleveland Newspaper Digest (1839) p. 110.
27. Adv., *Cleveland Herald,* Sep. 25, 1843; Adv., *Cleveland Herald,* July 1, 1845.
28. "Child's Brewery," *Plain Dealer,* Oct. 19, 1847; "Ives' Brewery," *Plain Dealer,* Oct. 20, 1847; "Ives' Brewery," *Cleveland Leader,* March 5, 1863.
29. Adv., *Cleveland Herald,* Oct. 25, 1842; Adv., *Cleveland Herald,* Feb. 6, 1843; Peet (1846-47), p. 145; "Ives' Brewery," *Plain Dealer,* Oct. 20, 1847.
30. "Ives' Brewery," *Cleveland Leader,* March 5, 1863.
31. Cuyahoga County Death Records, Cuyahoga County Archives.
32. Last Will & Testament of Samuel C. Ives, Cuyahoga County Archives.
33. Annals of Cleveland Court Records, p. 287.
34. Spear, Denison & Co.'s Cleveland City Directory for 1856,p. 74; Adv., *Cleveland Leader,* May 27, 1857.
35. Adv., *Plain Dealer,* Aug. 26, 1862.
36. "Ives' Brewery," *Cleveland Leader,* March 5, 1863.
37. Alburn, vol. II, p. 745; "Great Conflagration," *Cleveland Leader,* Jan. 2, 1865.
38. "Great Conflagration," *Cleveland Leader,* Jan. 2, 1865.
39. "Personal," *Cleveland Leader,* June 21, 1865.
40. "Cleveland Manufactures," *Cleveland Leader,* Dec. 22, 1858.
41. The Cleveland Herald's First Annual Statement of the Trade and Commerce of Cleveland for 1858, p. 15.
42. Annual Statement of the Trade, Commerce and Manufactures of the City of Cleveland For the Year 1867, pp. 7, 10, 13, 30.
43. "Cleveland Manufactures," *Cleveland Leader,* Dec. 22, 1858; Industries of Cleveland (1888) p. 179; The Cleveland Directory for the Year Ending July, 1885, p. 109.
44. Industries of Cleveland (1888), p. 164.
45. Industries of Cleveland (1888), p. 112; "Brewery For Sale," *Western Brewer,* May, 1907, p. 283; "New Breweries," *Western Brewer,* June, 1909, p. 349.
46. "The Late John M. Hughes," *Plain Dealer,* May 29, 1871; Cuyahoga County Land Deeds.
47. Peet (1846-47) p. 70; Cuyahoga County Land Deeds; "After Great Suffering," *Plain Dealer,* March 6, 1893; 100 Years of Brewing, p. 321.
48. *Daily True Democrat,* Oct. 9, 1850; "Fire," *Plain Dealer,* Oct. 9, 1850.
49. Adv., *Daily True Democrat,* Aug. 11, 1853.
50. *Cleveland Leader,* July 25, 1857; "A Model Brewery," *Cleveland Leader,* Jan. 18, 1858.
51. "A Model Brewery," *Cleveland Leader,* Jan. 18, 1858; Schade, p. 137; "Arrival of Artemus Ward," *Plain Dealer,* August 22, 1861.
52. "A Disastrous Fall," *Cleveland Leader,* Dec. 21, 1868.
53. "Present Use," *Cleveland Leader,* Sep. 10, 1862.
54. "Hughes' Ale," *Plain Dealer,* Nov. 14, 1859.

55. J. H. Williston's Directory for the City of Cleveland for 1861-62, p. 78; Van Tassel and Grabowski, p. 1035; Boyd's Cleveland Directory and Cuyahoga County Business Directory, p. 143.
56. "Aid The Orphans," *Plain Dealer*, Jan. 22, 1862.
57. "In Memorium," *Cleveland Leader*, June 3, 1871.
58. Bailey (1872-73), p. 243.
59. The Cleveland Directory for the Year Ending July, 1885, pp. 80 and 298.
60. Articles of Incorporation, The Hughes Brewing Company, Ohio Secretary of State's Office; The Cleveland Directory for the Year Ending July, 1889, p. 365.
61. The Cleveland Directory for the Year Ending July, 1892, pp. 449, 492; "Death of Arthur Hughes," *Plain Dealer*, May 9, 1890.
62. The Cleveland Directory for the Year Ending July, 1889, p. 365.
63. *Western Brewer*, Oct. 15, 1894, p. 2006; Sanborn Fire Insurance Maps, 1874 and 1894.
64. Schade, p. 137; Salem, p. 242; Friedrich and Bull, p. 214.
65. *Western Brewer*, Aug. 15, 1894, p. 1590; The Cleveland Directory for the Year Ending July, 1897, p. 660.
66. The Cleveland Directory for the Year Ending July, 1900, p. 1034; *Western Brewer*, Feb. 15, 1899, p. 50; *Western Brewer*, June, 1901, p. 168.

Chapter Two

1. 100 Years of Brewing, p. 99.
2. Arnold and Penman, p. 62.
3. Arnold and Penman, pp. 92-95.
4. 100 Years of Brewing, p. 207; Schlüter, pp. 52-53.
5. Levine, p. 15.
6. Mueller and Gardiner, p. 57.
7. Green, n.p.; Van Tassel and Grabowski, p. 447.
8. Rose, p. 367; "The Policeman's Puzzle," *Plain Dealer*, March 20, 1874; Duis, p. 7.
9. Baron, p. 180.
10. Mueller, p. 171.
11. Berry, pp. 17, 62.
12. Sanborn Fire Insurance Maps, 1874; Cuyahoga County Atlas, 1874.
13. Sanborn Fire Insurance Maps, 1874.
14. Van Tassel and Grabowski, p. 483.
15. Sanborn Fire Insurance Maps, 1874; Cleveland und Sein Deutschthum (1897) pp. 465-466; Industries of Cleveland, (1878) p. 166; Cleveland Necrology File, Cleveland Public Library.
16. Cleveland und Sein Deutschthum (1897) pp. 462; Cleveland Newspaper Digest (1873) p. 108.
17. "St. Clair Street Railroad," *Cleveland Leader*, September 21, 1868.
18. *Wächter und Anzeiger*, August 9, 1902, p. 114.
19. "Lager Beer," *Cleveland Leader*, June 8, 1858.
20. Van Tassel and Grabowski, p. 483.
21. Annual Statement of the Trade, Commerce and Manufactures of the City of Cleveland for the Year 1870, p. 38.
22. Figures estimated using output levels published in Schade, pp. 137-137; Salem, pp. 242-243.
23. "Cleveland's Brauereien," *Wächter Und Anzeiger*, August 9, 1902, p. 35.
24. 100 Years of Brewing, p. 30.
25. Cleveland und sein Deutschthum (1897), pp. 375-376.
26. Salem, pp. 242-243.
27. 100 Years of Brewing, p. 478.
28. "Cleveland's Brauereien," *Wächter und Anzeiger*, Aug. 9, 1902, p. 35; Brewers' Handbook for 1898, pp. 19 and 99.
29. *Western Brewer*, Feb., 1901, p. 62; *Western Brewer*, Feb., 1906, p. 78; The Cleveland Directory for the Year Ending August, 1907, p. 125.
30. Brewers' Handbook for 1906, p. 103; The Cleveland Directory for the Year Ending August, 1906, p. 1583.
31. *Western Brewer*, May, 1905, p. 203; Sanborn Fire Insurance Maps 1912-13; *Western Brewer*, Aug., 1914, p. 465.
32. The Cleveland Directory for the Year Ending August, 1902, p. 823; The Cleveland Directory for the Year Ending August, 1904, p. 739; The Cleveland Directory for the Year Ending July, 1900, p. 152.
33. Peet, (1845-46), p. 93; "Martin Stumpf," Naturalization Index, Cuyahoga County Archives; Cuyahoga County Court of Common Pleas, Execution Docket, Vol. 19, p. 172.
34. Although Cuyahoga County Land Deeds show that Michael did not legally own the Lake street property until 1853, the U.S. Census for 1850 (City of Cleveland, p. 223) lists Michael Stumpf's value of real estate as $400 – the same sale price of the land officially deeded to Michael in 1853. It seems certain, therefore, that Michael purchased the Lake street land under mortgage prior to 1850, but did not hold legal title until completion of the mortgage in 1853.
35. Cuyahoga County Court of Common Pleas, Execution Docket, Vol. 19, p. 172 [Document refers to the business as the "late firm of M. Stumpf & Co." as of March of 1850].
36. "Fire," *Plain Dealer*, Feb. 2, 1857; U. S. Census for 1860, City of Cleveland, p. 445.
37. Robison, Savage & Co.'s Annual Cleveland Directory

for the Year Ending July 6, 1877, p. 596; Bailey (1873-74), p. 512.

38. Schade, p. 136; Salem, p. 243.

39. The Cleveland Directory for the Year Ending July, 1886, p. 594; "Deaths," *Plain Dealer*, Sep. 19, 1886; Information from Virginia Stief Sords, descendant of Michael Stumpf.

40. Cuyahoga County Land Deeds; Knight & Parsons' Business Directory of the City of Cleveland, p. 258 [Note: Hamilton street was formerly known as York street]; City Atlas of Cleveland, Ohio, 1881.

41. Arnold and Penman, p. 61.

42. Cuyahoga County Land Deeds.

43. Cleveland und Sein Deutschthum (1897) p. 252; Loomis & Talbott's Cleveland City Directory for 1861, p. 144.

44. 100 Years of Brewing, p. 291.

45. "C.W. Schmidt," *Plain Dealer*, March 30, 1887.

46. Atlas of Cuyahoga County, Ohio, 1874; Sanborn Fire Insurance Maps, 1887.

47. 100 Years of Brewing, p. 291; Salem, p. 243.

48. Industries of Cleveland (1878), p. 126.

49. "An Old Citizen Gone," *Cleveland Leader*, March 28, 1882; *Western Brewer*, April 15, 1884, p. 634; "Cleveland's Brauereien," *Wächter und Anzeiger*, August 9, 1902; U. S. Census for 1870, City of Cleveland, p. 431, and City of East Cleveland, p. 288; Industries of Cleveland (1878) p. 126; "C.W. Schmidt," *Plain Dealer*, March 30, 1887.

50. The Cleveland Directory for the Year Ending July, 1893, p. 169.

51. Mueller and Gardiner, p. 115.

52. Letter from Ernst Mueller to Rudolph Mueller, September 1, 1887, Curt Muller Collection.

53. "Cleveland's Brauereien," *Wächter Und Anzeiger*, Aug. 9, 1902, p. 35; Brewers Handbook for 1897, p. 105.

54. The Cleveland Directory for the Year Ending July, 1893, p. 169; The Cleveland Directory for the Year Ending July, 1897, p. 195.

55. *Western Brewer*, June, 1898, p. 1010.

56. "Brewery Closes. First In City To Meet Dry Law," *Cleveland Press*, Sep. 23, 1919; *Western Brewer*, Oct., 1919, p. 120.

57. Industries of Cleveland (1878) p. 160.

58. Peet (1845-46), p. 99.

59. "Cleveland's Brauereien," *Wächter Und Anzeiger*, Aug. 9, 1902, p. 35; Boyd (1857) p. 52; Cuyahoga County Land Deeds; U. S. Census for 1860, Brooklyn Township, p. 386.

60. "After Great Suffering," *Plain Dealer*, March 6, 1893.

61. "A Model Brewery," *Cleveland Leader*, Jan., 18,1858.

62. Industries of Cleveland (1878) p. 101; Baker's Cleveland Directory, 1864-65, p. 68; "After Great

Suffering," *Plain Dealer*, March 6, 1893; Gehring Family Diary, Don Gehring Collection.

63. Industries of Cleveland (1878) p. 101; Salem, p. 242.

64. Gehring Family Diary, Don Gehring Collection.

65. The Cleveland Directory for the Year Ending July, 1889, p. 225; Cleveland und Sein Deutschthum (1897), pp. 242-248.

66. Cleveland und Sein Deutschthum (1897), p. 242; "Brewing Interests", The City of Cleveland and its Resources, A Souvenir of the Plain Dealer, 1889.

67. Gehring Family Diary.

68. "After Great Suffering," Plain Dealer, March 6, 1893; Program of the Thirteenth Annual Brewers' Congress, pp. 4, 56.

69. Cleveland und Sein Deutschthum (1897) p. 160; Annual Report of the City of Cleveland, 1875, p. 554, and 1876, pp. 219-220; "Winsor French," *Cleveland Press*, May 12, 1956.

70. *Western Brewer*, April, 1893, p. 822; "After Great Suffering," *Plain Dealer*, March 6, 1893.

71. Gehring Family Diary, Don Gehring Collection; *Western Brewer*, June, 1898, p. 1010.

72. Gehring Family Diary, Don Gehring Collection.

73. "Cleveland's Brauereien," *Wächter und Anzeiger*, Aug. 9, 1902, p. 35.

74. "Fire Destroys Brewery Built 60 Years Ago," *Cleveland Press*, March 4, 1927.

75. "Brewing Interests of Cleveland," *Plain Dealer*, May 22, 1902; "Beer – But Our City's Old Brewers Are Gone," *Press*, April 15, 1933; "After Great Suffering," *Plain Dealer*, March 6, 1893.

76. Downs, p. 67; Coates, vol. III, p. 23.

77. The Cleveland Directory for the Year Ending July, 1897, p. 908.

78. Coates, vol. III, p. 23; The Industries of Cleveland (1888), p. 70.

79. Downs, p. 67; J. H. Williston & Co.'s Directory for the City of Cleveland for 1859-60, p. 157; Sanborn Fire Insurance Maps, 1874; J. H. Williston's Directory for the City of Cleveland for 1861-62, p. 135; Cuyahoga County Land Deeds; "Cleveland's Brauereien," *Wächter und Anzeiger*, Aug. 19, 1902, p. 35; Alburn, Vol. III, p. 204.

80. *Western Brewer*, March, 1880, p. 251; *Western Brewer*, Sep., 1880, p. 924.

81. Leading Manufacturers and Merchants of the City of Cleveland and Environs. A Half Century's Progress. 1836-1886, p. 142; "Cleveland's Six Lager Beer Brewing Enterprises," *Cleveland Press*, Aug. 23, 1898.

82. Industries of Cleveland (1878), p. 127; Salem, pp. 242-243; Sanborn Fire Insurance Maps, various editions; Van Tassel and Grabowski, p. 930.

83. *Cleveland Leader*, Aug. 29, 1874.

84. Downs, p. 68; Van Tassel and Grabowski, p. 626.

85. Cuyahoga County Land Deeds; Downs, p. 68.
86. Documents contained in "Schlather Estate," Vertical File, Rocky River Public Library.
87. Unidentified clipping on file at the Rocky River Public Library.
88. Records at the Rocky River Public Library.
89. "Cleveland's Brauereien," *Wächter und Anzeiger*, Aug. 22, 1902, p. 35; "Cleveland's Six Lager Beer Brewing Enterprises," *Cleveland Press*, Aug. 23, 1898; "Brewing Interests," City of Cleveland And Its Resources, A Souvenir of the Plain Dealer, p. 91.
90. Brewers' Handbook for 1897, p. 107; History of the Cleveland Fire Department, p. 24; History of the Cleveland Police Department, p. 16;"John Schneider, Deceased," *Western Brewer*, May 1914, p. 207.
91. "Cleveland's Six Lager Beer Brewing Enterprises," *Cleveland Press*, Aug. 23, 1898.
92. "Trust Secures Big Brewery," *Plain Dealer*, April 25, 1902; *Western Brewer*, March 1903, p. 121.
93. Rose, p. 498; "Cleveland Past," *Plain Dealer*, June 20, 1978; Adv., *Wächter und Angzeiger*, Aug. 9, 1902, p. 35.
94. Alburn, vol. III, pp. 203-209; Cleveland Newspaper Digest (1867) p. 761; "Schlather, Brewer In City For 65 Years, Is Dead," *Cleveland Press*, April 20, 1918.

Chapter Three

1. Davison, p. 126.
2. Boyd's Cleveland Directory (1863), p. 211; Annual Statement of Trade (1865), p. 21; Shade, pp. 136-137.
3. 100 Years of Brewing, p. 539.
4. *Cleveland Leader,* October 29, 1862.
5. 100 Years of Brewing, p. 539.
6. "Records of Religious Societies," manuscript, Cuyahoga County Archives, p. 402.
7. *Leader,* June 8, 1874.
8. Chidsey, p. 11.
9. Sinclair, p. 37; Peet (1845-46), p. 116.
10. Baron, p. 198.
11. Van Tassel and Grabowski, p. 959.
12. *Leader,* April 13, 1863.
13. Peet (1845-46), p. 116; Peet (1846-47), p. 32.
14. *Leader*, August 22, 1854.
15. Rose, p. 396; Chidsey, pp. 27-29.
16. Rose, p. 460.
17. Program of the Thirteenth Annual Brewers Congress, p. 4.
18. Baron, p. 225.
19. "Cleveland's Brauereien," *Wächter und Anzeiger*, Aug. 9, 1902, p. 35.
20. "Cleveland's Brauereien," *Wächter und Anzeiger*, Aug. 9, 1902, p. 35.
21. "The Beer Brewers Association," *Leader*, July 21, 1873; "Brewers' Picnic," *Plain Dealer*, July 21, 1873.
22. Golden Jubilee, n.p.
23. Schlüter, p. 169.
24. "No Brewers' Strike Probable," *Plain Dealer*, May 1, 1888; Golden Jubilee, n.p.; *Western Brewer*, May, 1893, p. 1062.
25. Golden Jubilee, n.p.
26. "Cleveland's Beer Barons," *The Sun & Voice*, Dec. 13, 1891.
27. Leisy, p. 25.
28. Leading Manufacturers, p. 78.
29. Cuyahoga County Land Deeds.
30. Leisy, pp. 6-7; Industries of Cleveland (1878), p. 103.
31. Leisy, pp. 6-7.
32. Cuyahoga County Land Deeds.
33. *Plain Dealer,* July 3, 1873; Annals of Cleveland Court Records, vol. 10, p. 103.
34. Mueller and Gardiner, pp. 171-172.
35. Leisy, p. 13; Industries of Cleveland (1878), p. 103.
36. Industries of Cleveland (1878), p. 103.
37. Leisy, pp. 18-19.
38. Leisy, p. 30.
39. Unidentified newspaper clipping at Cleveland Public Library.
40. Sanborn Fire Insurance Maps, 1952.
41. *Cleveland Press,* May 17, 1934.
42. "Leisy Brewing Company," manuscript, Western Reserve Historical Society; *Cleveland News*, August 10, 1933; *Plain Dealer,* March 2, 1914.
43. Leisy, p. 19.
44. Cleveland und Sein Deutschthum (1897), pp. 377-386.
45. *Plain Cealer,* July 12, 1892.
46. *Plain Dealer,* Feb. 19, 1899.
47. Brewers Handbook (1898), p. 101; "Leisy Brewing Company," mansucript, Western Reserve Historical Society.
48. Tarr, n.p.; Leisy, p. 62.
49. Leisy, pp. 53-56.
50. *Western Brewer,* Sep. 1909, p. 494.
51. Leisy, pp. 56-57.
52. "Otto I. Leisy Dies On Day Of His Gift," *Plain Dealer*, March 2, 1914; "Death Summons Otto I. Leisy," *Press*, March 2, 1914.
53. *Brewers Journal,* July, 1916, p. 373; Leisy, p. 61.
54. "Leisy Brewing Company," mansucript, Western Reserve Historical Society.
55. Adv., *Plain Dealer*, July 7, 1917.
56. Adv., *Plain Dealer*, Jan. 16, 1934.

57. "Wets Boots in $300,000 Worth of Honest Beer," *Plain Dealer*, Oct. 6, 1923.
58. Leisy, p. 33.
59. Coates, pp. 121-123.
60. Cleveland und Sein Deutschthum (1897), p. 459.
61. Cleveland und Sein Deutschthum (1897), p. 459.
62. Cleveland und Sein Deutschthum (1897), p. 459.
63. *Western Brewer*, Jan., 1892, p. 110.
64. Adv., *Cleveland Town Topics*, July 21, 1894; "Noted Woman Called By Death," *Leader*, March 31, 1909; Coates, pp. 121-123.

Chapter Four

1. Weeks, n.p.
2. 100 Years of Brewing, p. 121.
3. Baron, p. 229.
4. Zverina, p. 12; Leading Manufacturers, p. 142.
5. Cochran, pp. 162-163.
6. Hurt, pp. 41, 46.
7. Annual Statement of Trade (1867), pp. 7, 30.
8. Cleveland Directory for the Year Ending July, 1897, p. 1192; Sanborn Fire Insurance Maps, 1896.
9. *Wächter und Anzeiger*, Aug. 9, 1902, pp. 60 and 124.
10. Cleveland Directory for the Year Ending July, 1892, p. 237; Adv., *Wächter und Anzeiger*, June 23, 1910.
11. *Milwaukee Sentinel*, March 18, 1883 and April 15, 1883, as quoted in a letter from Mike Reilly to Carl H. Miller dated January 16, 1995; Cleveland Directory for the Year Ending July, 1885, p. 537.
12. Cleveland Directory for the Year Ending July, 1889, p. 646.
13. Cleveland Illustrated, p. 78.
14. "Engine Crashes Into Brewery," *Plain Dealer*, July 8, 1907.
15. *Western Brewer*, Dec., 1896, p. 2308.
16. "Cleveland's Brauereien," *Wächter und Anzeiger*, Aug. 19, 1902, p. 35.
17. Industries of Cleveland (1888), p. 179.
18. Illustrated Baltimore: The Monumental City, p. 149.
19. *Western Brewer*, Jan., 1884.
20. Industries of Cleveland (1888), p. 179.
21. *Western Brewer*, July, 1891; *Western Brewer*, Aug., 1891, p. 1853; Cleveland Illustrated, p. 202.
22. *Western Brewer*, May, 1893, p. 1038.
23. Van Tassel and Grabowski, pp. 851-852
24. *Leader*, Sep., 13, 1869.
25. Baron, p. 288.
26. *Western Brewer*, Feb., 1914, p. 68.
27. Mueller & Gardiner, p. 69.
28. Leisy, p. 33.
29. Alburn, vol. II, p. 205.
30. Wing's Brewers' Hand-Book, pp. 99-101.
31. Annual Report of the Cleveland Board of Trade (1884), pp. 219-220.
32. Cleveland und Sein Deutschthum (1897), pp. 466-469.
33. Cuyahoga County Land Deeds.
34. Wing's Brewers' Hand-Book, pp. 99-101.
35. *Wächter und Anzeiger*, Aug. 9, 1902, p. 151.
36. "Law and Liquor," *Leader*, April 15, 1874.
37. Cleveland und Sein Deutschthum (1897), pp. 466-469.
38. *Western Brewer*, Dec., 1877, p. 518.
39. Articles of Incorporation, Anhaeusser Co-Operative Bottling Company, Secretary of State's Office, Columbus, Ohio; Cleveland Directory for the Year Ending July 1890, pp. 85, 436, 563; Cleveland Directory for the Year Ending July 1893, p. 41.
40. Sanborn Insurance Maps, 1886; Sanborn Insurance Maps, 1896; Cleveland Directory for the Year Ending July, 1890, p. 39.
41. "Manufacturers Record," manuscript, Cuyahoga County Archives, vol. 2, pp. 316-318.
42. "A Beer Brewery Fire," *Plain Dealer*, July 5, 1889.
43. "The Brewery Fire," *Plain Dealer*, July 7, 1889.
44. "Manufacturers Record," manuscript, Cuyahoga County Archives, vol. 2, pp. 316-318.
45. Brewers' Handbook for 1897, p. 107.
46. *Western Brewer*, March, 1908, p. 171.
47. "A.W. Oppmann, Deceased," *Western Brewer*, July, 1910, pp. 335-336.
48. "Death Puts Halt To Life's Mission," *Plain Dealer*, June 28, 1910.
49. Cleveland Leader Annual City Directory for 1868-69, p. 265.
50. Annals of Cleveland Court Records, pp. 70-71.
51. Annals of Cleveland Court Records, pp. 70-71.
52. "Another Suicide," *Leader*, July 22, 1871.
53. Cleveland und Sein Deutschthum (1897), pp. 262-264.
54. *Western Brewer*, April, 1896, p. 687.
55. Brewers' Handbook for 1898, p. 101.
56. "George V. Muth Dead," *Plain Dealer*, Oct. 18, 1899.
57. Industries of Cleveland (1878), p. 158.
58. "Manufacturers Record," manuscript, Cuyahoga County Archives, vol. 1, pp. 206-207.
59. Annals of Cleveland Court Records, vol. 10, pp. 173-174.
60. Cleveland Directory for the Year Ending July, 1886, p. 590; *Western Brewer*, Aug., 1883, p. 1417.
61. *Western Brewer*, Sep., 1888, pp. 2006, 2017A.
62. *Western Brewer*, May, 1891, p. 1130.
63. *Western Brewer*, Nov., 1891, p. 2588; Van Tassel and Grabowski, p. 582.

64. <u>Brewers' Handbook for 1898</u>, p. 99.

Chapter Five

1. Green, Appendix A.
2. Duis, p. 59.
3. Baron, p. 270.
4. "A Beer Trust," *Press*, Aug. 29, 1895; *Western Brewer*, Oct., 1896, p. 1898.
5. Baron, p. 293.
6. "Bitter," *Press* June 28, 1898.
7. "One Dollar," *Press*, June 14, 1898; "Threat," *Press*, June 16, 1898; "Beer War," *Press*, June 17, 1898.
8. "Bitter," June 28, 1898; "Smaller," *Press*, July 15, 1898; "Beer War," *Press*, July 23, 1898.
9. Baron, p. 293.
10. Baron, 294.
11. *Western Brewer*, Feb., 1890, p. 345; Baron, p. 269.
12. *Western Brewer*, Aug., 1892, p. 1772.
13. "A Beer Brewery Fire," *Plain Dealer*, July 5, 1889; "The Brewery Fire," *Plain Dealer*, July 7, 1889; *Western Brewer*, Feb., 1890, p. 345.
14. "A Beer Trust," *Press*, Aug. 29, 1895.
15. "A Syndicate," *Press*, Dec. 9, 1897; Articles of Incorporation, Cleveland & Sandusky Brewing Company, Ohio Secretary of State's Office; "Brewery Deal Is Closed," *Sandusky Register*, May 28, 1898.
16. *Western Brewer*, June, 1898, p. 1010.
17. Articles of Incorporation, Cleveland & Sandusky Brewing Company, Ohio Secretary of State's Office.
18. *Western Brewer*, Nov., 1904, p. 482; "New Brewery is Opened," *Lorain Times-Herald*, Oct. 27, 1904.
19. <u>Sanborn Insurance Maps</u>, 1900, 1905.
20. *Western Brewer*, June, 1898, p. 1058g; *Western Brewer*, March, 1898, p. 482; *Western Brewer*, July, 1898, p. 1221.
21. Articles of Incorporation, Cleveland & Sandusky Brewing Company, Ohio Secretary of State's Office.
22. "An Important Statement," *Plain Dealer*, June 29, 1902.
23. "Beer War May Result," *Plain Dealer*, Feb. 18, 1899.
24. "Beer War May Result," *Plain Dealer*, Feb. 18, 1899.
25. "Monnett After The Breweries," *Plain Dealer*, July 4, 1899; "Fight Against Beer Trust," *Press*, July 4, 1899; "Breweries," *Sandusky Daily Register*, July 5, 1899.
26. "All Ohio," *Press*, June 3, 1898; "Gobbling," *Press*, Sep. 20, 1898.
27. "Into One Big Beer Trust," *Cleveland Leader*, Aug. 24, 1902.
28. "Trust Secures Big Brewery," *Plain Dealer*, April 25, 1902.
29. "Investigation of Cudell-Schmidt Charges,"
manuscript, Glen Kuebeler Collection, p. 253.
30. "Investigation of Cudell-Schmidt Charges," manuscript, Glan Kuebeler Collection, p. 253.
31. "Not In It Says Leisy," *Press*, March 6, 1907; *Western Brewer*, March, 1905, p. 106.
32. Bottle label, Bill Carlisle Collection.
33. "Not In It Says Leisy," *Press* March 6, 1907; "Investigation of Cudell-Schmidt Charges," manuscript, Glen Kuebeler Collection, p. 76.
34. "Claim Beer Deal Was In Open," *Plain Dealer*, March 5, 1907.
35. "Row Grows Out Of Beer Merger," *Plain Dealer*, March 3, 1907.
36. "Claim Beer Deal Was In Open," *Plain Dealer*, March 5, 1907.
37. "Beer War Now Seems Certain," *Plain Dealer*, March 6, 1907.
38. "Sets Forth Inside Of Brewery Deal," *Leader*, March 5, 1907.
39. <u>United States Brewers Association Year Book</u>, 1911, p. 306.
40. "Beer War Nows Seems Certain," *Plain Dealer*, March 6, 1907.
41. "War of Brewers Is In Prospect," *Leader*, March 7, 1907.
42. "Mueller Seeks Peace in Beer," *Plain Dealer*, April 23, 1907.
43. "Investigation of Cudell-Schmidt Charges," manuscript, Glen Kuebeler Collection.
44. "Big Brewery To Tackle ComBine," *Plain Dealer*, March 8, 1907; "Not In It Says Leisy," *Press*, March 6, 1907.
45. *Western Brewer*, March, 1910, p. 119; *Western Brewer*, Dec., 1908, p. 636; *Western Brewer*, Jan., 1909, p. 20.
46. "Simon Fishel, Deceased," *Western Brewer*, Feb., 1917, p. 41.
47. *Western Brewer*, March, 1905, p. 120.
48. *Western Brewer*, Jan., 1915, p. 14.
49. *Western Brewer*, Aug., 1918, p. 35.
50. *Western Brewer*, March, 1898, p. 482.
51. "Brewery War Threatened by Trust Deal," *Cleveland News*, March 6, 1907.
52. "The Brewing Interests of Cleveland," *Plain Dealer*, May 22, 1902.
53. Mlachak, Norman, "Soon the Demolition Crews Will Come," *Press*, April 30, 1979.
54. "Anthony Diebolt Rites Saturday," *Plain Dealer*, Feb. 29, 1940; Buffalo City Directories; Miller, William, "Beer — But Our City's Old Brewers Are Gone," *Press*, April 15, 1933; <u>One Hundred Years of Brewing</u>, p. 484.
55. Cuyahoga County Land Deeds; Buffalo City Directories.

56. One Hundred Years of Brewing, pp. 301-302.
57. Friedrich and Bull, p. 213; Brewers' Handbook for 1898, p. 101; "Brewery War Threatened by Trust Deal," *Cleveland News*, March 6, 1907.
58. "The Brewing Interests of Cleveland," *Plain Dealer*, May 22, 1902; Adv., *Plain Dealer*, July 2, 1915; Adv., *Plain Dealer*, July 16, 1915.
59. Sanborn Fire Insurance Maps, 1912-1913; *Brewers Journal*, Oct. 1, 1911, p. 565.
60. *Brewers Journal*, Jan. 1, 1916, p. 128; *Western Brewer*, Jan., 1916, p. 11.
61. One Hundred Years of Brewing, pp. 301-302; *Western Brewer*, Aug., 1918, p. 38.
62. "Cleveland's Six Lager Beer Brewing Enterprises," *Press*, Aug. 23, 1898.
63. Cleveland und Sein Deutschthum (1897), p. 252.
64. "George F. Gund," *American Brewers' Review*, April, 1916, p. 132.
65. Cleveland und Sein Deutschthum (1897), p. 249.
66. Adv., *Plain Dealer*, Jan. 1, 1904.
67. 100 Years of Brewing, p. 304-305.
68. Cleveland und Sein Deutschthum (1907), p. 140.
69. Adv., *Plain Dealer*, Jan. 4, 1912.
70. Evans, Christopher, "Waiting For George," *Plain Dealer, Sunday Magazine*, January 26, 1997, p. 11.
71. "George F. Gund," *American Brewers' Review*, April, 1916, p. 132.
72. "George F. Gund," *American Brewers' Review*, April, 1916, p. 132.
73. Evans, Christopher, "Waiting For George," *Plain Dealer, Sunday Magazine*, January 26, 1997, p. 11.
74. *Brewers Journal*, Oct., 1916, p. 499; Bottle label, Bob Kay Collection.
75. *Western Brewer*, July, 1919, p. 22.
76. 100 Years of Brewing, p. 484;
77. Cleveland Directory for the Year Ending July, 1895, p. 646.
78. *Western Brewer*, Aug. 15, 1894, p. 1616; *Western Brewer*, Dec. 15, 1894, p. 2424.
79. *Western Brewer*, Dec. 15, 1894, p. 2214.
80. "Cleveland's Six Lager Beer Brewing Enterprises," *Press*, Aug. 23, 1898.
81. Post card, Carl Miller Collection.
82. Adv., *Plain Dealer*, July 16, 1914.
83. "Educational Campaign to Make Friends for the Brewer," *Western Brewer*, Aug. 15, 1915, p. 39.
84. "Reception at New Offices of Pilsener Brewing Co., Cleveland, Ohio," *Brewers Journal*, Jan. 1, 1917, p. 137.
85. Audio recording, Carl Miller Collection.
86. Cleveland Directory for the Year Ending July, 1919, p. 1410.
87. Adv., *Plain Dealer*, Aug. 1, 1914.
88. Van Tassel and Grabowski, pp. 110, 338.
89. Miller, William, "Beer! Brewers Here to Spend $1,500,000," *Press*, July 14, 1932.
90. *Wächter und Anzeiger*, June 28, 1912; Miller, William, "Beer — But Our City's Old Brewers Are Gone," *Press*, April 15, 1933.

Chapter Six

1. Duis, p. 56.
2. Duis, pp. 153-154.
3. Duis, pp. 22-23.
4. Duis, p. 25-26.
5. Leisy, p. 42.
6. Duis, p. 26-27.
7. Tarr (unpublished), n.p.
8. "An Important Statement," *Plain Dealer*, June 29, 1902.
9. Chidsey, p. 59; Turner, p. 538.
10. Duis, p. 23.
11. *Western Brewer*, Jan., 1898, p. 109.
12. "Beer War May Result," *Plain Dealer*, Feb. 18, 1899.
13. "2,360 Saloons In County," *Plain Dealer*, July 2, 1904.
14. "Few Saloons Are In Danger," *Plain Dealer*, May 22, 1904.
15. "Ohio Will Regulate Saloons," *Western Brewer*, March, 1909, p. 151.
16. "Brief Survey of Excise and License Legislation in Ohio," *Western Brewer*, March, 1911, p. 133.
17. "Licenses in Ohio Cities Under New Law," *Western Brewer*, Dec., 1913, p. 285
18. "Proprietors Like Limit To Saloons," *Plain Dealer*, Feb. 4, 1911.
19. *Western Brewer*, Dec., 1907, p. 677.
20. *Western Brewer*, Feb., 1905, p. 53.
21. Turner, pp. 528-533.
22. *Western Brewer*, Jan., 1902, p. 21; *Western Brewer*, March, 1902, p. 99.
23. *Western Brewer*, June, 1901, p. 267.
24. Articles of Incorporation, Standard Brewing Company, Ohio Secretary of State's Office.
25. Cleveland und Sein Deutschthum (1907), p. 151.
26. Cleveland, Ohio, Pictorial & Biographical, pp. 243-244.
27. Interview with John T. Feighan, Jr., Feb. 13, 1992.
28. "Standard Brewery of Cleveland Outgrows Its Plant While Sticking to its Natural Home Market," *Brewers Journal*, May 15, 1939, p. 52.
29. Cleveland Directory for the Year Ending August, 1905, p. 1323.
30. "To the Future Progress of Our City, We Great You," brochure, Standard Brewing Company, 1911.

31. "Brewery War Threatened By Trust Deal," *Cleveland News,* March 6, 1907; *Western Brewer,* Jan., 1911, p. 29.

32. "Investigation of Cudell-Schmidt Charges," manuscript, Glan Kuebeler Collection, p. 253; *Western Brewer,* Nov., 1906, p. 562; *Western Brewer,* Dec., 1906, p. 595.

33. "To the Future Progress of Our City, We Great You," brochure, Standard Brewing Company, 1911.

34. Post card, Gregg Grossman Collection.

35. "To the Future Progress of Our City, We Great You," brochure, Standard Brewing Company, 1911.

36. Cleveland, Ohio, Pictorial & Biographical, p. 244; Sanborn Insurance Maps, 1903 corrected to 1911.

37. "40 Years A Banker," *Cleveland Trust Magazine,* Nov/Dec., 1935, p. 11.

38. "New Brewmaster Says Cleveland-Sandusky 'Can't Miss,'" *Ohio Tavern News,* April 25, 1949.

39. Weeks, n.p.

40. Baron, pp. 245-246.

41. Turner, p. 528-543.

42. "Mueller Seeks Peace in Beer," *Plain Dealer,* April 23, 1907.

43. Mueller and Gardiner, p. 121.

44. Cleveland Directory for the Year Ending August, 1908, p. 284.

45. Advertising trade cards, Carl Miller Collection.

46. Adv., The Hermits in Vienna (1914), p. 162.

47. "Say Trust Holds None of Stock," *Press,* March 9, 1904.

48. Cleveland Directory for the Year Ending August, 1905, p.1407; *Western Brewer,* April, 1916 p. 124.

49. *Western Brewer,* March, 1904, p. 131; *Western Brewer,* April, 1904, p. 181; *Western Brewer,* June, 1904, p. 244.

50. *Western Brewer,* May, 1909, p. 248.

51. Cleveland und Sein Deutschthum (1907), pp. 152-153.

52. Cleveland und Sein Deutschthum (1907), pp. 152-153.

53. *Western Brewer,* Feb., 1917, p. 56.

Chapter Seven

1. Chidsey, p. 71.
2. Chidsey, p. 72.
3. Chidsey, p. 57.
4. Baron, p. 297-298.
5. Chidsey, p. 63-64.
6. Chidsey, p. 66-67.
7. Chidsey, p. 69.
8. Baron, p. 312.

9. "C.&S. Starts Stang Plant on 'Near Beer,'" *Sandusky Register*, March 21, 1919.

10. Baron, p. 302.

11. Chidsey, p. 65.

12. Baron, p. 284.

13. "Drys Will Ignore One Wet Proposal," *Plain Dealer,* April 20, 1918.

14. Sinclair, p. 120.

15. Sinclair, p. 120.

16. Baron, p. 303.

17. *Western Brewer,* Nov., 1918, p. 140.

18. *Western Brewer,* Nov., 1917, p. 176.

19. *Western Brewer,* Dec., 1917, pp. 209-210.

20. *Western Brewer,* Dec., 1917, pp.. 209-210; *Western Brewer,* Oct., 1916, p. 132

21. Brewer's Almanac, 1986, p. 76.

22. Siebel and Schwarz, p. 175.

23. Weeks, n.p.

24. Adv., *Plain Dealer,* July 4, 1917.

25. "Wets Boots in $300,000 Worth of Honest Beer," *Plain Dealer,* Oct., 6, 1923.

26. *Western Brewer,* Oct., 1919, p. 128; *Beverage Journal,* Aug., 1923, p. 74.

27. *Brewer & Maltster,* May 15, 1919, p. 45.

28. Adv., *Plain Dealer,* July 1, 1920; Adv., *Plain Dealer,* July 22, 1920.

29. "C.&S. Starts Stang Plant on 'Near Beer,'" *Sandusky Register*, March 21, 1919.

30. Unidentified advertisement dated Aug. 25, 1926, Bill Carlisle Collection.

31. Cleveland Directory for the Year Ending August, 1917, p. 444.

32. Cleveland City Directory, 1921, p. 236.

33. "Breweries Here Set For Beer O.K.," *Press,* Oct., 16, 1930.

34. Cleveland City Directory, 1921, p. 234.

35. "Certificate of Amendment to the Articles of Incorporation of the Standard Brewing Company," Dec. 28, 1922, Ohio Secretary of State's Office; "Certificate of Increase of Capital Stock of the Standard Brewing Company," Dec. 21, 1922, Ohio Secretary of State's Office.

36. *Western Brewer,* Dec., 1917, p. 207; Cleveland City Directory, 1921, p. 951.

37. Bottle label, Bob Kay Collection; Cleveland City Directory, 1921, p. 235.

38. Golden Jubilee, n.p.

39. Adv., *Plain Dealer,* July 6, 1920.

40. Cleveland City Directory, 1921, p. 236.

41. Cleveland City Directory, 1919, p. 1425.

42. Unidentified manuscript, Cuyahoga County Archives.

43. Cochran, p. 334; Sinclair, p. 191.

44. "Anthony Diebolt Rights Saturday," *Plain Dealer,*

Feb. 29, 1940; *Plain Dealer* (picture page), Aug. 12, 1928.

45. "1,705,305 Listed as Diebolt Estate," *Plain Dealer*, Oct. 20, 1934.

46. Will of Joseph A. Diebolt, Cuyahoga County Archives.

47. Cleveland City Directory, 1923, p. 1257.

48. Evans, Christopher, "Waiting for George," *Plain Dealer*, Jan. 26, 1997.

49. Cleveland City Directory, 1921, p. 309; Cleveland City Directory, 1922, p. 1467.

50. Levy, Paul, "Gund Funds: Giving It Away," *Plain Dealer*, Feb. 10, 1991.

51. Evans, Christopher, "Waiting for George," *Plain Dealer*, Jan. 26, 1997.

52. Van Tassel and Grabowski, p. 445.

53. Evans, Christopher, "Waiting for George," *Plain Dealer*, Jan. 26, 1997.

Chapter Eight

1. Sinclair, p. 338.

2. Baron, p. 315.

3. Van Tassel and Grabowski, p. 800.

4. Porrello, p. 28.

5. Van Tassel and Grabowski., pp. 800-801; Porrello, p. 29.

6. Baron, p. 321.

7. Anderson (Beer USA), p. 53.

8. Loveland, Roelif, "State Ready to Give Beer Permits Here," *Plain Dealer*, April 6, 1933.

9. Ranney, Omar, "City Thousands Cheer for Beer," *Press*, April 1, 1933.

10. Adv., *Press,* April 5, 1933.

11. "State Ready to Give Beer Permits Here," *Plain Dealer*, April 6, 1933; "City Waits For Trucks And Planes," *Plain Dealer*, April 7, 1933.

12. "Thousands Crowd For Drink of Honest Brew," *Plain Dealer*, April 8, 1933.

13. Corporate Record, "The Pilsener Ice, Fuel & Beverage Company," May 1933, manuscript, Cuyahoga County Archives; "Dark Pilsener Ready Today," *Plain Dealer*, July 31, 1933.

14. "Cleveland Brewery Uses An Old Bavarian Formula," *Cleveland News*, May 12, 1933.

15. Adv., *Press*, October 25, 1933.

16. "4 Breweries Here Start Amber Flow," *Press*, May 26, 1933; "Beer Increases Spending," *Plain Dealer*, April 10, 1933.

17. "Eilert Brewery Will Offer Stock," *Plain Dealer*, Dec. 16, 1932; Adv., *Plain Dealer*, Dec. 17, 1932.

18. "Sue to Halt Brewery," *Plain Dealer*, April 4, 1933;

19. Adv., *Plain Dealer*, June 10, 1933.

20. Letter to Stockholders, May 13, 1933, Glen Kuebler Collection.

21. Adv., *Press*, July 13, 1933.

22. Cochran, pp. 366-367.

23. Computed from information in McGahan, p. 254.

24. Computed from information in Weeks, n.p.

25. McGahan, p. 258.

26. "City Brewers Slash Prices To $12 On Keg," *Press*, Sep. 22, 1933.

27. "Brew Workers Of City Go On Strike," *Plain Dealer*, April 19, 1935.

28. "Union to Bar Outside Beer," *Press*, Aug. 13, 1935; "Fights Boycott of City's Beer," *Press*, Aug. 14, 1935.

29. White, Lloyd, "Brewery Union Truce Returns 350 to Work," *Press*, Nov. 15, 1935.

30. McGahan, p. 230.

31. "Forest City Brewery Will Spend $400,000," *Plain Dealer*, March 25, 1933.

32. Downard, p. 134; Van Wieren, p. 271.

33. *Western Brewer*, July, 1933, p. 76; *Western Brewer*, Aug., 1933, p. 78.

34. "Forest City Brewery Will Spend $400,000," *Plain Dealer*, March 25, 1933; "Cleveland Pilsener On Sale Next Week," *Plain Dealer,* April 26, 1933.

35. "Waldorf," brochure, Forest City Brewing Company, Bill Carlisle Collection.

36. Golden Jubilee, n.p.

37. "Brewery Files Petition For Reorganization," *Press*, July 13, 1939; *Brewers Journal*, Oct., 1938, p. 85.

38. "Brewery Reorganized," *Plain Dealer*, June 26, 1940; "Brewery Creditors Move to Reopen Bankruptcy Case," *Press*, Sep. 28, 1944; "Win Reopening of Brewery Estate," *Plain Dealer*, Oct. 10, 1945; "Brewery Creditors Select a Trustee," *Plain Dealer*, Oct. 20, 1945.

39. "Brewery Creditors Select a Trustee," *Plain Dealer*, Oct. 20, 1945.

40. "Starts Brewing Here," *Plain Dealer*, July 23, 1933.

41. Adv., *Plain Dealer*, Aug. 23, 1933; "Brewery Gives Party," *Plain Dealer*, Aug. 23, 1933; *Brewers Journal*, June 29, 1933, p. 7.

42. Adv., *Press*, Jan. 18, 1934.

43. "Tax Evasion Charges Denied by Brewery," *Plain Dealer*, Dec. 19, 1934; "Brewery Plant Seizure Looms," *Press*, Jan. 24, 1935; "Brewing Halted, Sunrise is Probed," *Plain Dealer*, Jan. 24, 1935; "Sunrise Brewery Seized by U.S. Aids in Libel Action," *Press*, Feb. 8, 1935; "U.S. Sues Sunrise Brewery on Tax," *Plain Dealer*, Feb. 9, 1935; "Orders Sale of Brewery for Fines, Taxes," *Press*, Feb. 19, 1935.

44. Unidentified memo, Cleveland Press Collection, Cleveland State University.

45. *Modern Brewer*, June, 1938, pp. 32-33, 66.
46. Messick, p. 183.
47. *Western Brewer*, May 1933, p. 70; Porello, p. 158.
48. 20 Years of American Beers, p. 38; Beer Cans Unlimited, p. 90.
49. Cleveland City Directory 1935, p. 923; Cleveland City Directory 1937, pp. 39 and 712.
50. Messick, pp. 183-184.
51. Widder, Milton, "Brewing Corp. Buys Tip-Top," *Press*, July 1, 1944.
52. "Four Fireman Hurt in Blaze in Warehouse," *Plain Dealer*, June 28, 1954; "Thieves Perk Coffee, Swipe $600 in Wine," *Press*, Feb. 7, 1962.
53. Porrello, p. 203.
54. Miller, William, "Beer—But Our City's Old Brewers Are Gone," *Press*, April 15, 1933.
55. "Leisy Stirs the Curiosity and Whets the Appetites," *Western Brewer*, March, 1934, p. 51.
56. "Punchy Advertising Puts Leisy Back In Spotlight," *Brewers News,* June 28, 1934, p. 16.
57. Adv., *Plain Dealer*, May 15, 1934.
58. "Brewery Whistle Blows Again," *Cleveland News*, May 15, 1934; Scott, M. M., "Leisy's Is Back," *Brewery Age*, Oct., 1934, p. 71; "Punchy Advertising Puts Leisy Back In Spotlight," *Brewers News*, June 28, 1934.
59. Adv., *Press*, May 14, 1934.
60. Scott, M. M., "Leisy's Is Back," *Brewery Age*, Oct., 1934, p. 71.
61. Ranney, Omar, "Happy Days Here Again As Leisy's Whistle Sounds," *Press*, May 17, 1934.
62. Scott, M. M., "Leisy's Is Back," *Brewery Age*, Oct., 1934, p. 74.
63. "Punchy Advertising Puts Leisy Back In Spotlight," *Brewers News,* June 28, 1934, p. 16.
64. "Carling Made Ale Flows for 20,000," *Plain Dealer*, June 16, 1934.
65. "The Red Caps Are Coming," brochure, Brewing Corporation of America, 1947.
66. Shea, p. 14.

Chapter Nine

1. Weeks, n.p.
2. Brewer's Almanac, 1959, p. 17.
3. Scott, M. M., "Leisy's Is Back," *Brewery Age*, Oct. 1934, pp. 72-74; *Brewers Journal*, June 1934, p. 78.
4. Baron, p. 327; "Waldorf," brochure, Forest City Brewery, Inc.
5. Anderson (The Beer Book), pp. 56-57.
6. "Waldorf," brochure, Forest City Brewery, Inc.
7. "Leisy Dramatizes New Offering," *Modern Brewer*, Oct., 1935, pp. 96-97; "Stubby Used in Cleveland," *Brewers Technical Review*, Oct., 1935, p. 356.
8. "The Red Caps Are Coming," brochure, Brewing Corporation of America.
9. Nekvasil, p. 30.
10. Lewis, pp. 229 and 231.
11. "Standard Brewery of Cleveland," *Brewers Journal*, May, 1939, p. 56; "Beer Advertising Over the Airwaves," *Modern Brewery Age*, Jan., 1946, p. 106.
12. "Sunrise Broadcasted Bike Races," *Modern Brewer*, Feb., 1937, p. 50.
13. Adv., *Plain Dealer*, Aug. 2, 1935.
14. Adv., *Ohio Tavern News*, July 25, 1949; "Gold Bond Bock Beer Orders Hit All Time High," *Ohio Tavern News*, May 10, 1950.
15. Interview with disc jockey Norman Knight, Aug., 19, 1997.
16. "Starts Third Year On Air For Leisy Brewery," *Modern Brewer*, Jan., 1937, p. 57.
17. "Standard Brewing Company of Cleveland to Sponsor Indains Baseball Broadcasts," *Brewers Journal*, May, 1949, p. 24; Van Tassel and Grabowski, p. 816.
18. "Erin Brew's Ace Representatives," *Ohio Tavern News*, Feb., 10, 1951.
19. "Beer Advertising Over The Airwaves," *Modern Brewery Age*, May, 1944.
20. Kiczek, Gene, pp. 41, 56, 84, and 110.
21. "P.O.C. Takes To The Air," Cleveland Arena Hockey Program 1949-50, pp. 5 and 73.
22. Adv., Cleveland Arena Program 1937-38 and 1941-42.
23. Baron, p. 331.
24. Chesler, H. A., "The Idea Back of 'King Kole' Beer and its National Aspect," *Brewers Journal*, July, 1934, pp. 58-59.
25. "Asks King's Brewery Be Declared Bankrupt," *Plain Dealer*, Jan. 7, 1941; *Modern Brewery Age*, July, 1941, p. 77; Death Notices, *Press*, March 22, 1952.
26. McGahan, pp. 262-263; Baron, p. 334.
27. Baron, p. 335.
28. "Pilsener Brewing Company of Cleveland Initiates Successful Used Bottle Cap Program," *Brewers Journal*, June, 1942, p. 44.
29. "Carling's Earns Flag," *Modern Brewery Age*, Dec., 1942, p. 60.
30. *Modern Brewery Age*, Feb., 1942, p. 65.
31. "Cleveland Brewers Ship 1,000,000 Bottles Weekly To Armed Service," *Ohio Tavern News*, Aug. 25, 1944.
32. Baron, p. 339.
33. Annual Report, Brewing Corporation of America, 1948.
34. "Strictly Business," *Cleveland News*, April 19, 1951.

35. Annual Report, City Ice & Fuel Company, 1935.

36. Cleary, Jack, "Strictly Business," *Cleveland News*, April 19, 1951; *Modern Brewery Age*, March, 1948, p. 84.

37. "No Beer? Here's Why–Not How," *Press*, Aug., 14, 1946.

38. *Modern Brewery Age*, Dec., 1948, p. 89; "Standard Brewing Opens New Plant," *Cleveland News*, April 13, 1950.

39. *Modern Brewery Age*, May, 1950; *Modern Brewery Age*, Sep., 1950; "Erin Brew Flows From New Plant," *Plain Dealer*, April 21, 1950.

40. "Standard Brewery of Cleveland," *Brewers Journal*, May 15, 1939, p. 50; Van Tassel and Grabowski, p. 921.

41. Official Directory & Log of the National Air Races (1939), p. 62.

42. "Carl Faller, 83, Brewmaster, Dies," *Plain Dealer*, Dec. 25, 1939.

43. *Brewers Journal*, Sep., 1937, p. 43; *Brewers Journal*, Nov. 15, 1940, p. 69; "C.&S. Declines Offer," *Plain Dealer*, Oct. 12, 1940.

44. "Cleveland-Sandusky Brewing Elects Marshman President," *Press*, Nov. 11, 1948; "Frank P. van de Westelaken," *Modern Brewer*, Sep., 1936, p. 51.

45. "Cleveland-Sandusky Co. Celebrating 100th Year," *Cleveland News*, May 11, 1944.

46. Adv., *Buckeye Tavern*, 1947, p. 7.

47. *Brewers Journal*, Feb., 1947, p. 54.

48. "Famous Gold Bond Label To Come Back," *Ohio Tavern News*, Feb., 25, 1950.

49. Annual Report, City Ice & Fuel, 1939; Cleveland Arena Program, 1941-42.

50. *Modern Brewery Age*, Nov., 29, 1976, p. 28.

51. "Effective Outdoor Advertising of Black Forest Beer," *Brewers Journal*, Sep., 1936.

52. "Men Whom You Know," *Modern Brewer*, June, 1937, p. 40.

53. Van Tassel and Grabowski, p. 240; "Omar E. Mueller Dies Suddenly," *Brewers Journal*, Aug., 1946, p. 44.

54. "Brewmaster Who Began Practicing His Trade in 1891 Recalls Day When His Word Was Law at Brewery," *Ohio Tavern News*, Oct. 25, 1947.

55. Mueller and Gardiner, p. 197.

56. *Modern Brewery Age*, Blue Book Issue, March, 1951, p. 133; Van Tassel and Grabowski, p. 240; *Modern Brewery Age*, Feb., 1952, p. 88; *Brewers Journal*, March, 1952, p. 53.

57. "Brewery Trade Names Go At $500," *Press*, March 26, 1952.

58. "Bidding Is Spirited as Old Brewery Is Flowing Away," *Plain Dealer*, March 27, 1952.

Chapter Ten

1. McGahan, p. 267; Horowitz, pp. 5, 19.

2. McGahan, pp. 267-268; Baron, pp. 337-338.

3. Baron, p.346; Adv. (United States Brewers Foundation), unidentified, Carl Miller Collection.

4. *Brewers Journal*, March, 1951, p. 11; *Modern Brewery Age*, March, 1961, pp. 28, 31.

5. Seltzer, Robert, "3 Cleveland Breweries, Hit by Mounting Costs, Hike Prices," *Press*, Feb., 8, 1956.

6. Seltzer, Robert, "3 Cleveland Breweries, Hit by Mounting Costs, Hike Prices," *Press*, Feb., 8, 1956.

7. Baron, p. 345.

8. "TV And Radio Expenditures Were Greater Than Newspaper Outlays," *Modern Brewery Age*, June, 1959, p. 34.

9. Adv., *Plain Dealer*, January 5, 1952; Video tape of Leisy Premiere Theatre, Carl Miller Collection.

10. Adv., *Ohio Tavern News*, May 14, 1957.

11. Adv., *Cleveland Gazette*, March, 1954, p. 11.

12. Anderson, Stan, "See-Hear," *Cleveland Press*, April 20, 1949; Condon, George E., "Games in Stadium To Be Televised," *Plain Dealer*, April 20, 1949.

13. Anderson, Stan, "See-Hear," *Cleveland Press*, April 27, 1949.

14. "Homer Marshman, Was Lawyer, Businessman," *Plain Dealer*, Nov., 16, 1989; Van Tassel and Grabowski., p. 727; Adv., *Plain Dealer*, Sep., 4, 1954.

15. "Pilsener Televises Sports Show," *Buckeye Tavern*, May, 1950, p. 14.

16. "Bob Hope Guest on Pilsener Show," *Modern Brewery Age*, Aug., 1955, p. 42.

17. "Carter Stuck When Kovacs Goes West With 1951 P.O.C. Professional Tennis Championship Trophy," *Ohio Tavern News*, May 25, 1952.

18. *Modern Brewery Age*, Feb., 1953, p. 70.

19. Cleary, Jack, "Pilsener $5 Million Modernization, Expansion Boosts Capacity 35 Pct.," *Cleveland News*, April 19, 1951.

20. "Three Year Increase in Sales And Distribution Of P.O.C.," *Ohio Tavern News*, Aug. 26, 1954.

21. "Erin Brew Distributors Meet in Cleveland," *Buckeye Tavern*, June, 1953, p. 28.

22. Adv., *Plain Dealer*, May 19, 1953.

23. Adv., *Plain Dealer*, May 22, 1953.

24. Anderson (Beer USA), p. 142.

25. "Leisy's to Toast 90 Years of Brewing Beer," *Press*, March 14, 1952.

26. Television script dated Dec. 5, 1952, Carl Miller Collection.

27. "The Leisy Brewing Company," mansucript, Western

References

Reserve Historical Society.

28. Leisy, p. 92.

29. Peck, L. Doyle, "New Beer For A New Market," *American Brewer*, Aug., 1955, p. 33.

30. Peck, L. Doyle, "New Beer For A New Market," *American Brewer*, Aug., 1955, p. 67.

31. Unidentified promotional item at Cleveland Public Library.

32. Unidentified promotional item at Cleveland Public Library.

33. "Leisy Expands," *Plain Dealer*, Jan. 30, 1958.

34. Bryan, John E., "Carter Returns to Leisy's Helm," *Plain Dealer*, June 22, 1958.

35. Bryan, John E., "Carter Returns to Leisy's Helm," *Plain Dealer*, June 22, 1958.

36. Bryan, John E., "Carter Returns to Leisy's Helm," *Plain Dealer*, June 22, 1958.

37. Adv., *Press*, Dec. 10, 1958.

38. Christiansen, Harry, "Leisy Plant Shuts Down Brewing," *Cleveland News*, Oct. 30, 1959.

39. "Verband Dortmunder Bierbauer vs. The Leisy Brewing Co., Inc.," Civil Docket, U.S. District Court, Northern District of Ohio, Eastern Division.

40. "Ship Leisy Brewery to Greece," *Press*, May 12, 1961; Leisy, p. 96.

41. Van Wieren, p. 78; Records from Cleveland Trust Bank, Bill Viancourt Collection.

42. Letter to Shareholders, Cleveland-Sandusky Brewing Corp., May 26, 1946, Glenn Kuebeler Collection.

43. *Brewers Journal*, Feb., 1949, p. 28; *Modern Brewery Age,* Blue Book Issue, March, 1951, p. 146.

44. "Brewing Corp. Names Pavlik As Brewmaster," *Buckeye Tavern*, May 1949, p. 28; "New Brewmaster Says Cleveland-Sandusky 'Can't Miss,'" *Ohio Tavern News*, April 4, 1949; Warfel, Jack, "Creates New Lager To Celebrate 35th Anniversay as Brew-Master," *Press*, March 25, 1938; "Jaro H. Pavlik," *Modern Brewery Age*, November 1955, p. 94.

45. Seltzer, Robert, "Finds Big Near Beer Market in States' Dry Territories," *Press*, March 16, 1955.

46. Seltzer, Robert, "Finds Big Near Beer Market in States' Dry Territories," *Press*, March 16, 1955.

47. "Bilsky of Cleveland-Sandusky Shows How A Small Brewery Can Make A Big Comeback," *Modern Brewery Age*, Nov., 1958, pp. 62-63, 82.

48. "Bilsky of Cleveland-Sandusky Shows How A Small Brewery Can Make A Big Comeback," *Modern Brewery Age*, Nov., 1958, pp. 62-63, 82.

49. "Cleveland-Sandusky Puts on Big Campaign for Gold Bond Beer," *Brewers Journal*, July, 1956, p. 36.

50. "Modernized Plant Undergoing Vast Expansion to Double Production," *Ohio Tavern News*, May 14, 1957; *Modern Brewery Age*, Feb., 1959, p. 43; "Bilsky of Cleveland-Sandusky Shows How A Small Brewery

Can Make A Big Comeback," *Modern Brewery Age*, Nov., 1958, pp. 62-63, 82.

51. "Cleveland-Sandusky Buys Star-Peerless Equipment," *Modern Brewery Age*, Feb., 1959, p. 31.

52. Metcalfe, John, "Cleveland-Sandusky's Sales Up; Adds Wine," *Plain Dealer*, Jan. 21, 1961.

53. "Detroit Brewery to Make G-B Beer," *Press*, Sep. 20, 1962; "International to Produce Cleveland-Sandusky Products," *Buckeye Tavern*, Oct., 1962, p. 9.

54. "P.O.C.'s Brewery – Goin', Goin', Gone," *Press*, Aug. 28, 1963.

55. "City Products Corp. Acquires Controlling Interest in Ohio Firm," *Buckeye Tavern*, Nov., 1952, p. 30.

56. "Pilsener Expands," *Brewers Journal*, Dec., 1954, p. 52.

57. Cleary, Jack, "Pilsener Plans to Double or Triple Beer Capacity," *Cleveland News*, July 11, 1956.

58. Annual Report, Brewing Corporation of America, 1945.

59. "Carter Resigns Post as President of Pilsener," *Plain Dealer*, May 4, 1958.

60. Annual Report, City Products Corporation, 1962.

61. Van Wieren, p. 61.

62. Annual Report, City Products Corporation, 1962; "P.O.C.'s Brewery – Goin', Goin', Gone," *Press*, Aug. 28, 1963.

63. Gerdel, Thomas W., "Last Call For Pilsener On Call Beer," *Plain Dealer*, date unknown.

64. "John T. Feighan," *Modern Brewery Age*, Sep., 1953, p. 103.

65. "40 Years A Banker," *Cleveland Trust Magazine*, Nov-Dec., 1935, p. 11.

66. "40 Years A Banker," *Cleveland Trust Magazine*, Nov-Dec., 1935, p. 11.

67. "Standard Brewing Company," *Buckeye Tavern*, Aug., 1956, p. 8.

68. "John Feighan Elected Head of Standard," *Press*, June 27, 1960.

69. Feighan Jr., John T., "Standard Brewing Co. In Cleveland Operated Successfully For 55 Years," *Ohio Tavern News*, Dec. 10, 1957.

70. Braham, Jim, "Standard Sells 28-Bottle Beer Case," *Press*, March 20, 1961.

71. Adv., *Ohio Tavern News*, May 9, 1961.

72. Braham, Jim, "Standard Sells 28-Bottle Beer Case," *Press*, March 20, 1961.

73. "Schaefer Beer Firm in N.Y. Buys Standard Brewing Co.," *Plain Dealer*, June 21, 1961; "Schaefer Beer Due Here Soon," *Press*, May 26, 1961.

74. "Carling Says Schaefer Is Infringing," *The Brewing World*, Sep., 1961, p. 14.

75. "Schaefer, Carling End Label Battle," *Plain Dealer*, Sep., 26, 1961.

76. "Schaefer Beer Firm in N.Y. Buys Standard Brewing

Co.," *Plain Dealer*, June 21, 1961
77. Nekvasil, p. 90.
78. *Modern Brewery Age*, March, 1965, p. 21.
79. Glueck, Robert, "Schaefer Brewery to Quit in Cleveland," *Plain Dealer*, Jan., 8, 1964.
80. "Schaefer's Brewery Sold, Jobs Retained," *Plain Dealer*, March 6, 1964; *Modern Brewery Age*, March, 1965, p. 21.

Chapter Eleven

1. McGahan, p. 243.
2. Shea, p. 66.
3. *Modern Brewery Age*, March, 1965, p. 21.
4. *Modern Brewery Age*, March, 1961, p. 28.
5. Wager, p. 72.
6. Wager, pp. 71, 85-86; Shea, p. 66; "The Saga of Carling's," *Beer Distributor*, July, 1938.
7. Interview with David L. Stashower.
8. Wager, pp. 83-86.
9. Wager, p. 86.
10. Shea, p. 65.
11. "This Is Carling," brochure, Carling Brewing Company, circa 1965 edition.
12. Bowering, pp. 62-63; Shea, pp. 13-17.
13. Nekvasil, p. 6; Rockwell, Guy T. "Peerless Plans Sale Of Stock To Produce Ale," *Plain Dealer*, Sep., 14, 1933.
14. Van Tassel and Grabowski, pp. 153 and 352.
15. Special Advertising Insert, *Plain Dealer*, June 17, 1934, p. 1; "Peerless Plant Changes Over To Ale Making," *Press*, June 29, 1933; "The Saga Of Carling's," *Beer Distributor*, July, 1938.
16. "Carling Made Ale Flows For 20,000," *Plain Dealer*, June 16, 1934.
17. "Carling Made Ale Flows For 20,000," *Plain Dealer*, June 16, 1934.
18. Special Advertising Insert, *Plain Dealer*, June 17, 1934, p. 1
19. Nekvasil, p. 8.
20. Shea, p. 67; "The Saga Of Carling's," *Beer Distributor*, July, 1938.
21. "Peerless Corp.'s Sales In 1936 More Than Twice Those of 1935," *Wall Street Journal*, Feb., 15, 1937.
22. "Packie Goes Into The Beer Market," *Modern Brewery Age*, April, 1939, p. 48; Rockwell, Guy T., "Peerless Earns 84 Cents in Year," *Plain Dealer*, Dec. 28, 1937; Nekvasil, p. 11.
23. Press Release (undated), Cleveland Press Collection, Cleveland State University; Annual Report, Brewing Corporation of America, 1945.
24. "Carling's To Handle Tip Top - Forest City Operations," undated newspaper clipping in Cleveland Press Collection, Cleveland State University; Widder, Milton, "Brewing Corp. Buys Tip Top," *Press*, July 1, 1944.
25. "Confirms Sale Of Breweries," *Cleveland News*, July 5, 1944.
26. Lerch, Walter, "Waste From Yeast To Be Used As Food," *Press*, Dec. 26, 1944; Rockwell, Guy T., "Brewing Corp. To Develop Food Products Department," *Plain Dealer*, Dec. 26, 1944.
27. *Modern Brewery Age*, Sep., 1944, p. 78.
28. *Modern Brewery Age*, Jan., 1945, p. 81.
29. Annual Report, Brewing Corporation of America, 1946.
30. Archival materials at Liggett-Stashower, Inc.; "The Red Caps Are Coming," brochure, Brewing Corporation of America.
31. Cochran, p. 390.
32. Annual Report, Brewing Corporation of America, 1946.
33. Annual Report, Brewing Corporation of America, 1946.
34. Nekvasil, p. 135.
35. Interview with Ian R. Dowie, May 31, 1997; Shea, pp. 68-69.
36. Annual Report, Brewing Corporation of America, 1946.
37. Interview with Ian R. Dowie, May 31, 1997.
38. Shea, p. 69.
39. "Charge Beer Supply Stopped By Carlings," unidentified newspaper clipping at Cleveland Press Collection, Cleveland State University.
40. Adv., *The Shaker Guide*, April 11, 1946.
41. Nekvasil, p. 18.
42. Shea, pp. 68-69.
43. Shea, p. 68.
44. "Bohannon Up At Carling's; Canadian Named President," *Plain Dealer*, May 27, 1948; "Bohannon Retires As Board Chairman of Brewing Corp.," *Press*, July 2, 1949; "Industrialist Bohannon Is Dead at 74," *Plain Dealer*, Sep. 2, 1968.
45. Shea, p. 70.
46. Annual Report, Brewing Corporation of America, 1946.; Annual Report, Brewing Corporation of America, 1948.
47. Annual Report, Brewing Corporation of America, 1948.
48. Interview with Ian R. Dowie, May 31, 1997.
49. "Ian R. Dowie Made Vice President of Brewing Corporation of America," *Brewers Journal*, Feb., 1949, p. 27.
50. Interview with Ian R. Dowie, May 31, 1997; Nekvasil, pp. 37 and 135; *Brewers Journal*, March, 1951, p. 11; *Brewers Journal*, March, 1952, p. 11.

References

51. Interview with Ian R. Dowie, May 31, 1997.
52. "The Fable Of Mabel," *Brewing World*, May, 1963, p. 5.
53. "Approve Name Change to Carling Brewing Co.," *Press*, Dec. 29, 1953; "Brewing Corp. Shifts Name To Carling," *Cleveland News*, Dec. 29, 1953.
54. *Modern Brewery Age*, March, 1954, p. 26; "Brewing Corp. Sets New Sales Record," *Cleveland News*, Dec. 11, 1953; Cleary, Jack, "Brewing Corp. to Add $3 Million Plant, Increase Capacity 50 Pct.," *Cleveland News*, May 7, 1953.
55. Interview with David L. Stashower.
56. *Buckeye Tavern,* March 1951, p. 11.
57. "Carling's Sports Final," brochure, WXEL.
58. Mellow, Jan, "Mother of 3 Is Warm To City's Whistlers," *Plain Dealer*, February 19, 1960.
59. Nekvasil, pp. 126-127.
60. "This Is Carling," brochure, Carling Brewing Company, circa 1961 edition.
61. Interview with Ian R. Dowie, May 31, 1997; Dowie, Ian R., "How The Carling Brewery Developed Its Formula For Marketing Success," *Modern Brewery Age*, Sep., 1959, pp. 106-110.
62. "Carling Buys Griesedieck For $10 Million," *Cleveland News*, Sep. 24, 1954; *Plain Dealer*, Sep. 24, 1954.
63. Seltzer, Robert, "Entire Town Turns Out As Carling's Breaks Ground For New Brewery," *Press*, Oct. 18, 1954; "Carling Brewing Company's Natick Plant," *Suburban Press & Recorder*, July 14, 1966.
64. "Carling Brewery Officially Opens At Ceremony On Tuesday," *Natick Bulletin*, May 17, 1956.
65. Nekvasil, p. 56.
66. "Carling Brewing Company's Natick Plant," *Suburban Press & Recorder*, July 14, 1966; "Carling's County Fair At Natick," *Modern Brewery Age*, Aug., 1966, p. 30.
67. Nekvasil, pp. 60-65, "Maryland Governor Vetoes Anti-Carling Bill; Other Legislative, Regulatory Developments," *Modern Brewery Age*, March, 1956, p. 38; "Carlings and the Public Both Won in Maryland," *Press*, Jan. 7, 1957.
68. "Carling Takes Possession of Frankenmuth," *Brewers Journal*, Dec., 1956, p. 39.
69. "Carling Breaks Ground In Atlanta," *Brewers Journal*, Aug., 1956, p. 36; "Lt. Gen. A. R. Bolling, U.S.A. Made V.P. of Carling," *Brewers Journal*, Sep., 1956, p. 53; "New Carling Brewing Company Plant Is Now In Operation," *Brewers Journal*, April, 1958, p. 34.
70. "Carling Buys Out Tacoma Brewery For $3,500,000," *Plain Dealer*, undated, Corporation File, Cleveland Public Library; "Carling Plans To Purchase Heidelberg Brewing Co.," *Brewers Journal*, Dec., 1958, p. 24; *Modern Brewery Age*, Sep., 1949,

p. 91.
71. Nekvasil, p. 80.
72. *Modern Brewery Age*, March, 1961, p. 28.
73. *Modern Brewery Age*, March, 1965, p. 21.
74. Silver, Don, "Predicts 25% Sales Gain for Carling Parent," *Press*, April 7, 1955.
75. *Modern Brewery Age*, Aug., 1967, pp. 18-19; "Carling of Cleveland Reports on Plans," June, 1954, p. 49; "Theme And Variations in Flavor," *Modern Brewery Age*, Aug., 1965, pp. 34-35.
76. "This Is Carling," brochure, Carling Brewing Company, circa 1961 edition; *Modern Brewery Age*, Aug., 1955, p. 42.
77. "Carling's to Sponsor Golf Tournament in 1954," *Brewers Journal*, Jan., 1954, p. 54; "Theme and Variations on Flavor," *Modern Brewery Age*, Aug., 1965, p. 34.
78. "This Is Carling," brochure, Carling Brewing Company, circa 1961 edition; *Modern Brewery Age*, May, 1951, p. 60; *Brewing World*, May, 1963, pp. 9 and 11.
79. Dowie, Ian R., "The State Of The Industry," *Modern Brewery Age*, July, 1964, pp. 18-19 and 51;
80. *Modern Brewery Age*, March, 1964, p. 45.
81. "Carling Buys Arizona Brewing Co." *Plain Dealer*, Oct. 9, 1964.
82. Interview with Ian R. Dowie, May 31, 1997; "On Stream With Carling in Fort Worth, Texas," *Modern Brewery Age*, July, 1965, pp. 30-32 and 58.
83. Van Wieren, p. 14.
84. *Modern Brewery Age*, Oct., 1969, pp. 24-25.
85. "Henry E. Russell New Head of Carling," *Plain Dealer*, Nov. 14, 1962.
86. *Modern Brewery Age*, March, 1966, p. 18.
87. Nekvasil, p. 111.
88. *Modern Brewery Age*, March, 1967, p. 19.
89. "Carling's Red Cap Gets New Treatment," *Modern Brewery Age*, April, 1962, p. 45.
90. Nekvasil, p. 72.
91. *Modern Brewery Age*, March, 1970, p. 5.
92. Annual Report, Canadian Breweries Limited, 1970, p. 5; Nekvasil, p. 122 and 126; "Landreth Hails Heidelberg Success, Looks For Black Label Comeback," *Carling News*, June, 1968, p. 3.
93. "K Day," *Carling News*, June, 1968, pp. 4-5.
94. Kovac, Carl, "Carling To Close Here," *Plain Dealer*, April 9, 1971.
95. Kovac, Carl, "Carling To Close Here," *Plain Dealer*, April 9, 1971.
96. Mlachak, Norman, "Future Is Uncertain for 385 at Carling's," *Press*, April 15, 1971; "Carling's Modernization Program for the Cleveland Brewery," *Modern Brewery Age*, June, 1969, pp. 42-43; "Second Progress Report on Carling's Continuing Plant

Modernizations," *Modern Brewery Age*, April, 1970, pp. 42-45.

97. Coyne, John P., "Carling's HQ to Leave City; 150 Employees to be Affected," unidentified newspaper clipping dated June 5, 1971, Corporation File, Cleveland Public Library.

98. "Tennyson and the Carling Revolution," *Modern Brewery Age*, Oct. 14, 1974, pp. MS46-MS51.

99. "Carling and National May Work Out a Unique Brewing Organization," *Modern Brewery Age*, Oct. 13, 1975, p. MS18-MS20; *Modern Brewery Age*, Feb. 14, 1977, p. MS10.

100. *Modern Brewery Age*, April 9, 1979, p. MS15.

101. Marshall, Christy, "Analysts Assail Gov't Move To Halt Pabst, Carling Deal," *Advertising Age*, July 3, 1978, p. 46; Marshall, Christy, "Heileman Gets Carling," *Advertising Age*, April 2, 1979, p. 4.

102. Preddy, Melissa, "Stroh Taps Heileman In Big Brewery Deal," *Detroit News*, March 1, 1996.

103. Miller, William F., "Carling Plant Auction Is Planned This Week," *Plain Dealer*, Sep. 1, 1971.

104. Mlachak, Norman, "Why Would Schmidt's Buy That 'Old' Carling Brewery?," *Press*, Nov. 11, 1971; Miller, William F., "Schmidt Brewing at Quincy Plant," *Plain Dealer*, March 29, 1972.

105. Sabath, Donald, "Duke Brewer Will Fold, Sell Label to Schmidt," *Plain Dealer*, Oct. 25, 1972.

106. Barth, Larry, "Hot Days Put Steam Into Beer Makers' Production," *Press*, Sep. 5, 1973.

107. "Uneasy Days Ahead For Brewery Workers," *Press*, Aug. 7, 1975; Mlachak, Norman, "Schmidt's May Be Swallowed By Competitors, Union Fears," *Press*, June 19, 1975; "Schmidt's, Cleveland's Last Brewery, Is Again Up for Sale," *Press*, March 10, 1976; Hals, Tom, "Plan for Schmidt Brewery May Be Flat," *Philadelphia Business Journal*, Jan. 27, 1997.

108. "Expansion Of Brewery Postponed By Schmidt," *Plain Dealer*, May 6, 1977

109. Gleisser, Marcus, "City's Last Brewery May Close," *Plain Dealer*, June 7, 1984; "Andrzejewski, Thomas S., "Search For New Jobs Begins For 250 Workers At Schmidt's," *Plain Dealer,* June 21, 1984; Hals, Tom, "Plan for Schmidt Brewery May Be Flat," *Philadelphia Business Journal*, Jan. 27, 1997; Van Wieren, p. 327.

110. "Old Schmidt Brewery To Make Gas Additive," *Plain Dealer*, Dec. 14, 1985; Vickers, Robert J., "City Hopes Action Will Prod Cleanup Of Site," *Plain Dealer*, March 1, 1997.

Chapter Twelve

1. Condon, George E., "The End Of A Peerless Era," *Plain Dealer*, April 16, 1971.

2. "Northern Ohio Craft Brewer's Association," brochure.

3. McCarty, James F., "Microbrews Are Tapping Into A Trend," *Plain Dealer*, Oct. 2, 1996.

4. Leisy, pp. 13, 16.

5. Interview with Gavin Smith.

6. "What's In A Name," *Plain Dealer*, April 30, 1992.

7. Interview with Pat Conway, Dec. 4, 1997.

8. Interview with Bill Morgan, Dec. 8, 1997; *Great Lakes Brewing News*, Aug-Sep., 1997, p. 17.

9. Interview with Marc Anievas.

10. Heltzell, Melissa, "John Harvard's Brew House," *Downtown Tab*, Nov. 3-16, 1997, p. 15.

11. "Who Was John Harvard?," brochure, John Harvard's Brew House.

12. Hill, Miriam, "Cleveland To Regain Its Own Beer," *Plain Dealer*, May 19, 1988; Brunton, David, "Entrepreneurs Raise Their Steins," *Plain Dealer*, Nov. 1, 1988.

13. Mooney, Barbara, "'Micro-brewers' Staging A Specialty Beer Invasion," *Crain's Cleveland Business*, May 22, 1989.

14. Gaw, Jonathan, "Brewing Home-town Taste Is Major Effort," *Plain Dealer*, Aug. 16, 1994.

15. Sutula, Don, "Something's Brewing In The Cleveland Flats," *Brew Review*, May 1994, p. 1; Crooked River Brewing Company Web Site.

16. Gaw, Jonathan, "Brewing Home-town Taste Is Major Effort," *Plain Dealer*, Aug. 16, 1994; Johnson, Terrence L., "Ready To Brew Up A National Storm," *Plain Dealer*, April 5, 1997.

17. Melilli, Denise, "Bottom's Up," *Plain Dealer*, March 17, 1996.

18. Interview with Stephan Danckers, Dec. 4, 1997.

19. Interview with Gavin Smith.

20. "Western Reserve Brewing Company," brochure.

Appendix

1. *Western Brewer*, April 15, 1879, p. 301.

2. *Western Brewer*, March 15, 1884, p. 454; *Western Brewer*, Aug. 15, 1884, p. 1360; *Western Brewer*, Dec. 15, 1886, p. 2628; *Western Brewer*, Aug. 15, 1889, p. 1742; 100 Years of Brewing, pp. 293-294.

3. Industries of Cleveland (1878) p. 160; Salem, p. 242.

4. Tovey's, p. 83; Cleveland Directory for the Year

References

Ending July, 1883, p. 345; _Cleveland Directory for the Year Ending July, 1884_, p. 325; _Cleveland Directory for the Year Ending July, 1888_, p. 354; _Cleveland Directory for the Year Ending July, 1890_, p. 460.

5. _Industries of Cleveland_ (1878), p. 167; Salem, p. 242; _Cleveland Directory for the Year Ending June, 1881_, p. 590.

6. _Cleveland Herald_, Dec. 4, 1841; _Cleveland Herald_, Feb. 6, 1843.

7. "Fire," _Cleveland Herald_, Dec. 23, 1845.

8. Stephenson, p. 220 [Note: the listing erroneously refers to Hamilton & Tutbury's brewery as the "City brewery, Champlain st." The Smead & Cowles directory for 1850 correctly lists the brewery as "Hamilton & Tutberry [sic], Eagle Brewery, Michigan st.," on page 196.]; _Spear, Denison & Co.'s Cleveland City Directory for 1856_, p. 123.

9. William H. Boyd, _Boyd's Cleveland City Directory_, p. 227; _Spear, Denison & Co.'s Cleveland City Directory for 1856_, p. 98; _J. H. Williston & Co.'s Directory for the City of Cleveland for 1859-60_, p. 148; _Cleveland Leader Annual City Directory for 1869-70_, p. 243.

10. _Western Brewer_, Aug., 1879, p. 679; _Western Brewer_, March, 1880; _Western Brewer_, June, 1881, p. 696; _Cleveland: Its Aim: Progress, Perseverance and Public Spirit_, p. 137; _100 Years of Brewing_, p. 307.

11. _Cleveland Illustrated_, p. 179.

12. _Brewers Journal_, Sep. 1, 1914, p. 522; _Brewers Journal_, Jan. 1, 1915, p. 114; _Brewers Journal_, June 1, 1916, p. 338.

13. _Annals of Cleveland Court Records_, p. 171.

14. _Industries of Cleveland_ (1878), p. 149; Salem, p. 242.

15. _Plain Dealer_, Feb. 7, 1856.

16. _Cuyahoga County Atlas_, 1874 ; _Tovey's_, p. 83.

17. Cuyahoga County Land Deeds; Orth, vol. III, pp. 462, 465.

18. _Industries of Cleveland_ (1888), p. 112; _Cleveland Newspaper Digest_ (1841) p. 92; Peet (1846-47), p. 145.

19. _100 Years of Brewing_, p. 301; Schade, p. 136; Cleveland Necrology File, Cleveland Public Library; _Robison, Savage & Co.'s Annual Cleveland Directory for the Year Ending July 6, 1877_, p. 375; Salem, p. 242.

20. _Industries of Cleveland_ (1888), p. 112;

21. Cleveland Necrology File, Cleveland Public Library; _Western Brewer_, Jan. 15, 1896, p. 81; "Brewery For Sale," _Western Brewer_, May, 1907, p. 283; _Western Brewer_, June, 1909, p. 349.

22. _Industries of Cleveland_ (1888) p. 164; _Baker's Cleveland Directory, 1864-65_, pp. 202 and 214.

23. _Industries of Cleveland_ (1888) p. 164; _The Cleveland Directory for the Year Ending June, 1882_, p. 191.

24. _Annals of the Early Settlers' Association of Cuyahoga County, Ohio_, vol. III, no. VI, p. 987; "Cleveland Manufactures," _Cleveland Leader_, Dec. 22, 1858.

25. "City Council," _Daily True Democrat_, Nov. 21, 1850.

26. "Cleveland Manufactures," _Cleveland Leader_, Dec. 22, 1858.

27. Bailey (1871-72), pp. 359 and 467.

28. Bailey (1873-74), p. 443; Schade, p. 136; _Industries of Cleveland_ (1888), p. 179.

29. _Industries of Cleveland_ (1878), p. 143.

30. Salem, p. 243.

31. _Western Brewer_, June, 1891, p. 1354, 1386; "Burnt Beer," _Plain Dealer_, May 22, 1891.

32. _Western Brewer_, Jan. 1894, p. 99.

33. Articles of Incorporation, Union Brewing Company, Ohio Secretary of State's Office.

34. "Fire," _Cleveland Leader_, Jan. 9, 1865; _Annals of Cleveland Court Records_, p. 74.

35. Advertisement, _Plain Dealer_, June 22, 1859.

36. Advertisement, _Plain Dealer_, Dec. 2, 1859.

37. "Mortgages," _Plain Dealer_, May 2, 1861; _Baker's Cleveland Directory, 1864-65_, pp. 236, 247; Cleveland Necrology File, Cleveland Public Library; _W. S. Robison & Co.'s Cleveland Directory for the Year Ending April, 1875_, p. 666.

Selected
Bibliography

100 Years of Brewing. Chicago & New York: H. S. Rich & Co., 1903.

Alburn, W. H.. This Cleveland of Ours, vol. II. Cleveland: S. J. Clarke Publishing Co., 1933.

Anderson, Will. Beer, USA. Dobbs Ferry, New York: Morgan & Morgan, 1986.

Anderson, Will. The Beer Book. Princeton: The Pyne Press, 1973.

Annals of Cleveland Court Records. Publisher unknown. Date unknown.

Annals of the Early Settlers' Association of Cuyahoga County, Ohio, vol. III, no. VI. Cleveland: Cleveland Publishing Co., 1907.

Annals of the Early Settlers' Association of Cuyahoga County, Ohio, vol. V, no. IV. Publisher unknown, 1907.

Annual Report of the Cleveland Board of Trade for the Year Ending December 31st, 1884.

Annual Statement of the Trade, Commerce and Manufactures of the City of Cleveland For the Year 1865. Cleveland: Fairbanks, Benedict & Co., 1866.

Annual Statement of the Trade, Commerce and Manufactures of the City of Cleveland For the Year 1867. Cleveland: Fairbanks, Benedict & Co., 1868.

Annual Statement of the Trade, Commerce and Manufactures of the City of Cleveland for the Year 1870. Cleveland: Fairbanks, Benedict & Co., 1871.

Apps, Jerry. Breweries of Wisconsin. Madison, Wisconsin: University of Wisconsin, 1992.

Arnold, John P., and Frank Penman. History of the Brewing Industry and Brewing Science in America. Chicago: Publisher unknown, 1933.

Avery, Elroy McKendree. A History of Cleveland And Its Environs, vol. I. Chicago and New York: Lewis Publishing Co., 1918.

Bailey, A. W. S. Robison & Co.'s Cleveland Directory, 1871-72. Cleveland: W. S. Robison & Co., 1871.

Bailey, A. G. Robison & Co.'s Cleveland Directory, 1872-73. Cleveland: W. S. Robison & Co., 1872.

Bibliography

Bailey, A. W. S. Robison & Co.'s Cleveland Directory, 1873-74. Cleveland: W. S. Robison & Co., 1873.

Baker's Cleveland Directory, 1864-65. Cleveland: Fairbanks, Benedict & Co., 1864.

Baron, Stanley. Brewed In America. A History of Beer and Ale in the United States. Boston: Little, Brown & Co., 1962.

Beer & Ale in Cleveland. Cleveland: The Cleveland Press, 1952.

Berry, Marriott & Bartlett. The Complete Business Directory of the City of Cleveland for 1857-58. Cleveland: J. H. Williston & Co., 1857.

Bowering, Ian. The Art & Mystery Of Brewing In Ontario. Ontario: General Store Publishing House, 1988.

Boyd, William H. Boyd's Cleveland City Directory. New York: William H. Boyd, 1857.

Boyd's Cleveland Directory and Cuyahoga County Business Directory. Cleveland: Fairbanks, Benedict & Co., 1863.

Brewers' Handbook for 1897. Supplement to the Western Brewer. Chicago and New York: H. S. Rich & Co., 1897.

Brewers' Handbook for 1898. Supplement to the Western Brewer. Chicago and New York: H. S. Rich & Co., 1898.

Brewers' Handbook for 1906. Supplement to the Western Brewer. Chicago and New York: H. S. Rich & Co., 1906.

"Brewing Interests," The City of Cleveland and its Resources, A Souvenir of the Plain Dealer, 1889.

"Brewing Interests of Cleveland," Plain Dealer, May 22, 1902.

Chidsey, Donald Barr. On And Off the Wagon. New York: Cowles Book Co., 1969.

Cleveland As It Is. Cleveland: J. Wiggins & Company, 1871.

Cleveland City Directory. Cleveland: Cleveland Directory Co., multiple editions.

Cleveland Herald's First Annual Statement of the Trade and Commerce of Cleveland for 1858. Cleveland: Fairbanks, Benedict & Co., 1859.

Cleveland Illustrated. Cleveland: Consolidated Illustrating Co., 1893.

Cleveland. Its Aim: Progress, Perseverance and Public Spirit. Cleveland: Mercantile Advancement Co., 1897.

Cleveland Leader Annual City Directory for 1868-69. Cleveland: Cleveland Leader Printing Co., 1868.

Cleveland Leader Annual City Directory for 1869-70. Cleveland: Cleveland Leader Printing Co., 1869.

Cleveland, Ohio, Pictorial & Biographical, vol. 2. Chicago and Cleveland: S. J. Clarke Publishing Co., 1910.

Cleveland und Sein Deutschthum. Cleveland: Deutsch-Amerikanische Historisch-Biographische Gesellschaft, 1897. (Note: There are at least 3 different versions of this volume. Not all versions contain all of the same biographical entries, and no indication of these differences appears on any of the books' title pages.)

Cleveland und Sein Deutschthum. Cleveland: Deutsch-Amerikanische Historisch-Biographische Gesellschaft, 1907.

"Cleveland's Brauereien," Wächter und Anzeiger, Aug. 9, 1902, p. 35.

"Cleveland's Six Lager Beer Brewing Enterprises," Cleveland Press, Aug. 23, 1898.

Coates, William R. A History of Cuyahoga County and the City of Cleveland. Chicago and New York: American Historical Society, 1924.

Cochran, Thomas C. The Pabst Brewing Company. The History of an American Business. New York: New York University Press, 1948.

Condon, George E. Cleveland. The Best Kept Secret. Garden City, New York: Doubleday & Co., 1967.

Davison, Kenneth E. Cleveland During the Civil War. Columbus: Ohio State University Press, 1962.

Downard, William L. Cincinnati Brewing Industry. Columbus: Ohio University Press, 1973.

Downs, Winfield S. Encyclopedia of American Biography. New York: American Historical Society, 1923.

Duis, Perry R. The Saloon: Public Drinking in Chicago and Boston 1880-1920. Urbana and Chicago: University of Illinois, 1983.

Friedrich, Manfred, and Donald Bull. The Register of United States Breweries 1876-1976, vol. I. Stamford, Connecticut: Holly Press, 1976.

Golden Jubilee 1886-1936. Brewery Workers Union No. 17, Cleveland, O. Cleveland: Central Lithography Co., 1936.

Green, David E. The Invasion of Cleveland By Europeans. Cleveland: Cleveland Pastor's Union and Young Peoples' Organizations, 1906.

History of the Cleveland Fire Department. Cleveland: Firemen's Relief Association, 1897.

History of the Cleveland Police Department. Publisher unkown, 1898.

Horowitz, Ann and Ira. "Profiles of the Future: The Beer Industry," Business Horizons, Fall 1967.

Hurt, R. Douglas. "Cold Comfort. Harvesting Natural Ice." Timeline. February-March 1986.

Industries of Cleveland. Trade, Commerce and Manufactures for the Year 1878. Cleveland: Richard Edwards, 1879.

Industries of Cleveland. A Resume of the Mercantile and Manufacturing Progress of the Forest City. Cleveland: Elstner Publishing Co., 1888.

Kiczek, Gene. Forgotten Glory. The Story of Cleveland Barons Hockey. Cleveland: Blue Line Publications, 1994.

Bibliography

Knight & Parsons' Business Directory of the City of Cleveland. Cleveland: E. G. Knight & Co. and Parsons & Co., 1853.

Leading Manufacturers and Merchants of the City of Cleveland and Environs. A Half Century's Progress. 1836-1886. New York: International Publishing Co., 1886.

Leisy, Bruce R. A History of the Leisy Brewing Companies. North Newton, Kansas: Mennonite Press, 1975.

Levine, Bruce. The Spirit of 1848. Urbana and Chicago: Univeristy of Illinois Press, 1992.

Lewis, Thomas S. W. Empire Of The Air. The Men Who Made Radio. New York: Edward Burlingame Books, 1991.

Loomis & Talbott's Cleveland City Directory for 1861. Cleveland: Cleveland Herald Press, 1861.

McGahan, A. M. "The Emergence of the National Brewing Oligopoly: Competition in the American Market, 1933-1958." Business History Review, Summer 1991, pp. 229-284.

Messick, Hank. The Silent Syndicate. New York: MacMillan Company, 1967.

Miller, William, "Beer — But Our City's Old Brewers Are Gone," Press, April 15, 1933.

Mueller, Jacob. Memories of a Forty-Eighter. Sketches from the German-American Period of Storm and Stress in the 1850s. Cleveland: Rudolph Schmidt Printing Co., 1896. (Translated and reprinted by Western Reserve Historical Society, 1996.)

Mueller, Werner Diebolt, and Duncan Buchanan Gardiner. To Cleveland And Away. Of Muellers, Reids, and Others. Novelty, Ohio: Werner Diebolt Mueller, 1993.

Nekvasil, Glen. Murdered by Mabel: The Rise and Fall of Carling. Unpublished, 1996.

Official Roster of the Soldiers of the State of Ohio. Akron: Werner Printing & Manufacturing Co., 1887.

Orth, Samuel P. A History of Cleveland, Ohio, vol. III. Cleveland: S.J. Clarke Publishing Company, 1910.

Peet, Elijah. Peet's General Business Directory of the Cities of Cleveland & Ohio for the Years 1845-46. Cleveland: Sanford & Hayward, 1845.

Peet, Elijah. Peet's Business Directory of the City of Cleveland for 1846-47. Cleveland: Smead & Cowles, 1846.

Porrello, Rick. The Rise and Fall of the Cleveland Mafia. New York: Barricade Books, 1995.

Program of the Thirteenth Annual Brewers' Congress. Publisher unknown, 1873.

Robison & Co.'s Cleveland Directory for the Year Ending April, 1875. Cleveland: Robison & Co., 1874.

Robison, Savage & Co.'s Annual Cleveland Directory for the Year Ending July 6, 1877. Cleveland: Robison, Savage & Co., 1876.

Rose, William Ganson. Cleveland. The Making of A City. Cleveland: World Publishing Co., 1950.

Salem, F. W. Beer, Its History and its Economic Value As A National Beverage. Hartford, Connecticut: F. W. Salem & Co., 1880.

Schade, Louis. Brewers' Handbook for 1876. Washington: Office of the Washington Sentinel, 1876.

Schlüter, Hermann. The Brewing Industry and the Brewery Workers' Movement in America. Cincinnatti: S. Rosenthal & Co., 1910.

Shea, Albert A. Vision In Action. The Story of Canadian Breweries Limited from 1930 to 1955. Toronto: Canadian Breweries Limited, 1955.

Siebel, Dr. John E., and Anton Schwarz. History of the Brewing Industry and Brewing Science in America. Chicago: Publisher unknown, 1933.

Sinclair, Andrew. Prohibition: The Era of Excess. Boston: Little, Brown & Co., 1962.

Spear, Denison & Co.'s Cleveland City Directory for 1856. Cleveland: Spear, Denison & Co., 1856.

Stephenson, William. Smead & Cowles' General Business Directory of the City of Cleveland for 1848-49. Cleveland: Smead & Cowles, 1850.

Tarr, David B. History of the Pontiac Improvement Company. Unpublished, 1967.

Tovey's Official Brewers' and Maltsters' Directory of the United States and Canada, 1882. New York: A. E. J. Tovey, 1882.

Turner, George Kibb, "Beer And The City Liquor Problem." McClure's. vol. 33, p. 528-543, (1909).

Van Tassel, David D., and John J. Grabowski, eds. Encyclopedia of Cleveland History. Bloomington & Indianapolis: Indiana University, 1987.

Van Wieren, Dale P. American Breweries II. West Point, Pennsylvania: Eastern Coast Breweriana Association, 1995.

Wager, Richard. Golden Wheels: The Story of the Automobiles Made in Cleveland and Northeastern Ohio, 1892-1932. Cleveland: John T. Zubal, Inc., 1986.

Weeks, Morris, Jr. Beer And Brewing In America. New York: Publisher unknown, 1949.

Wickham, Gertrude Van Rensselaer. Pioneer Families of Cleveland, vol. I. Evangelical Publishing House, 1914.

Williston & Co.'s Directory for the City of Cleveland for 1859-60. Cleveland: Williston & Co., 1859.

Williston's Directory for the City of Cleveland for 1861-62. Cleveland: Ben Franklin Print, 1861.

Wing's Brewers' Hand-Book of the United States and Canada, 1884. Chicago and New York: J. M. Wing & Company, 1884.

Zverina, Frances S. The Story of the Anton Mitermiler and Rose Zverina Families. Cleveland: Robert J. Liederbach Company, 1980.

Index

Ackerman Bill, 159

Ackerman, Joseph N., 159-160

Adams, Mathias, Lager Beer Hall, 34

advertising, beer, 182-185, 197-200

Aenis, William, 120, 257

Akron, Ohio, 160-161, 167, 222, 252

Alaska, 119

Albany, New York, 20, 27, 215

Albl, Frank E., 151

Albl, Michael, 140

ale, description of, 15

Alexandria, Virginia, 98

"All Outdoors," 199

Alten, Nicholas, 98

Altenheim home, 49, 54

Altoona, Pennsylvania, 50

Amber Ale, 254

American Federation of Labor, 167

American House, 29

American Trust Building, 107, 149

American Wheat, 254

Anders, Carl, 124

Anders, Fred J., 161

Andorn, Sydney, 183

Angel, Mary, 257

"Angle" (neighborhood), 46, 135, 213

Anhaeusser Co-Operative Bottling Co., 93

Anhaeusser Malt Tonic, 92

Anhaeusser, Herman, 93

Anheuser-Busch, Inc., 84, 85, 212, 217, 218, 225, 234, 237, 239, 252, 253

anti-German sentiment, 146

Anti-Saloon League, 130, 143-144, 146, 147, 158

architecture, brewery, 70, 72, 83, 94

Arctic Ice Machine Co., 10

Arena Draft, 254

Arizona Brewing Co. (Phoenix), 239-240

artificial refrigeration, 65, 81-82, 84

Ashtabula Worsted Mills, 75

Ashtabula, Ohio, 121, 150, 185

Association Against the Prohibition Amendment, 157

Atlanta, Georgia, 236

Atlas Brewing Co. (Chicago), 161

Backdraft Stout, 254

Backus, Jim, 183

Baehr brewery, 77-80, 83, 95, 104, 107

Baehr, Emil, 80

Baehr, Herman C., 78-80, 107, 110

Baehr, Jacob, 68, 77-78, 89

Baehr, Magdalena, 78-80

Baehr-Phoenix brewery, 80, 95, 113

Baker, Newton D., 76

Ball, Lucille, 225

Ballantine, P., & Sons, 218

Ballpark Draft, 253

Baltimore, Maryland, 87, 104, 190, 215, 236, 240

Barcher, Henry, Wine and Lager Beer Saloon, 34

Barnett, James, 80

Barrett & Barrett, 87

Barrett Brewing Co., 86-87, 104, 105, 114, 257

Barrett, Charles R., 87

Barrett, William H., 87

Battlecreak, Michigan, 155

Bavarian Benevolent Society, 92

Bavarian National Association of North America, 92

Bayerischer Unterstuetzungsverein, 92

Beer Brewers Aid Society, 64

beer gardens, 10, 34-37, 47, 48

Beggs, Robert, 260

Belle View brewery, see Stoppel brewery

Belleville, Illinois, 234-235

Beltz brewery, 38-39, 112, 138

Beltz, Carl E., 39

Beltz, John J., 39, 89, 139

Beltz, Joseph, 38-39, 89

Beltz, Lawrence C., 38

Beltz, Otto W., 151, 161, 192

Ben Franklin variety stores, 212

Bennett, Robert, 21-22

Bevera, 76-77, 148-149, 152

Beverage Bureau of Louisville, Kentucky, 169

Beverage Distributors, Inc., 161

Beverage Tasting Institute, 250

Bierbrauer Unterstutzungsverein, 64

Big Bad Bock, 251

Bilsky Baking Co., 208

Bilsky, Marvin 207-210

Bishop, John A., 45, 257

Black Dallas Malt Liquor, 203-204

Black Diamond Pale Ale, 251

Black Economic Union, 244
Black Forest Beer, 161-162, 180, 192-194
Black Forest Lager, 253
Black, George F., Jr., 228-229
Blackwell, Lloyd & Co., 258
bock beer, 37, 203
Boehmke, Henry, 93, 107
Bohannon, Benton P., 214
Bohannon, James A., 177-178, 182, 187, 214, 219-228
Bohemian Brewing Co., 87, 104, 107, 110, 113, 115, 120, 121
Bohemian National Hall, 124
Bola, 149, 150
Bolling, A. R., 236
bootlegging, 157-158
Boston, 33, 156, 235, 251
bottled beer, 14, 69, 70, 75, 76, 83, 92-93, 116, 138, 179-182
bottles, disposable, 181-182, 226
Bowlsby, Cornelia A., 30
Brannock Law, 133
Braun & Dietz, 260
Breckel, Josh, 248
Brew Kettle, 254
Brewer, John C., 23
breweries, Cleveland,
    first, 19;
    number of, 10, 37-38, 58, 66, 90;
Brewing Corporation of America, 86, 170, 172, 177-178, 182, 186, 187, 190, 208, 218-230
Brewing Corporation of Canada, 177, 220, 228
brewing process, 16-18
Brewmaster's Special, 190-191
brewpubs, 11, 247-251
Briggs Street Brewery, 258
Bringman, Henry, 129
British syndicates, 104
Broadway Savings & Trust Co., 119
Brooklyn Township, Ohio, 67
Brooklyn, New York, 214, 218
Brotherhood of Teamsters, 166-167
Brown-Graves Co., 165
Buckes, Catherine, 54
Buckeye Weiss Beer Co., 39
Budweiser Beer, 11, 68, 85, 189, 222, 241
Budweiser Grand Prix, 254
Buffalo, 20, 33, 109, 115, 116, 120, 170, 190, 204
Burckhardt, August, 35, 257
Burning River Pale Ale, 249
Busch Bavarian Beer, 225
Buzzard Brown Ale, 251
C. Schmidt & Sons, 212-213, 215-216, 244-246, 247, 249
California Seals, 156

California, 91, 210
Cameron, Rod, 197
Camp Van Dorn, 186
Canadian Ace Brewing Co. (Chicago), 206
Canadian Breweries Ltd., 177, 228-244, 242
Canadian Parliament, 236
Canandaigua, New York, 30
canned beer, 180-182, 189
Canton, Ohio, 185, 252
Capone, Al, 171-172
Carling & Co., 27, 86-87, 114, 260
Carling Ale, 114
Carling Brewing Co., 86, 207, 214, 216, 218-219,
Carling Distributor Management Services, 238
Carling National Breweries, Inc., 243-244
Carling News, 237-238
Carling Open, 238
"Carling Sports Final," 233
Carling Trade Relations, 238
Carling World Golf Championship, 238
Carling's Amber Creme Ale, 222-223
Carling's Black Label Beer, 170, 178, 186, 218-244
Carling's Red Cap Ale, 170, 177, 187, 218-244
Carling's, Inc., 224
Carling, Col. J. Innes, 177
Carling, Sir John, 86-87
Carling, Thomas, 220
Carter, George S., 199-201, 205, 210-211
Carter, Lorenzo, 18-19
Casino Cafe, 56
Cedar Point, 106
Chaitoff, Craig, 252
Chapman, William H., 105, 107, 108, 113
Charles, Ray, 203
Cheerio Ale, 171
Chicago World's Fair of 1893, 87
Chicago, Illinois, 27, 33, 87, 91, 104, 116, 120, 141, 155, 161, 171, 172, 185, 190, 206, 208
Childs, Herrick, 22
Chormann, Louis, 259
Christopher, L. E., 160
Cincinnati, Ohio, 11, 14, 20, 64, 84, 91, 109, 117, 167, 168, 219, 222
City Brewery, 23, 258
City Council, Cleveland, 49, 61, 193, 260
City Ice & Fuel Co., 187-188
City Products Corp., 188, 200, 210, 212
Civil War, 10, 57-58, 62, 67, 81, 195
Claussen, H. J., 117
Claussen-Sweeney Brewing Co. (Seattle), 117
Cleaveland, Moses, 120
Cleveland & Sandusky Brewing Co., 45, 49, 55, 56, 73, 80, 87, 95, 98, 100, 104-114, 130, 132, 136, 138, 145, 149-150, 160, 163, 257, 261

Cleveland-Sandusky Brewing Corp., 164, 167, 184, 186, 190-191, 197, 198-199, 201, 207-210
Cleveland-Sandusky Co., 149, 152-153
Cleveland Airport, 161
Cleveland American Light Ale, 251
Cleveland Arena, 185
Cleveland Barons, 156, 184-185
Cleveland Board of Health, 21
Cleveland Board of Park Commissioners, 71
Cleveland Brauer Verein, 59
Cleveland Brewers Assoc., 59, 63, 102, 104, 165, 191
Cleveland Brewers Board of Trade, 112, 133
Cleveland Brewery (1832-1865), 19-26, 259
Cleveland Brewing & Malting Co., 106
Cleveland Brewing Co. (1852-1919), 44-45, 83, 104, 105, 107
Cleveland Brewing Co. (1988-1994), 252
Cleveland Browns, 198-199, 215, 238
Cleveland Cavaliers, 156, 254
Cleveland Chamber of Commerce, 56, 90
Cleveland City Brewery, 26, 249, 258, 259
Cleveland Co-Operative Brewing Co., 134
Cleveland Day Nursery, 54
Cleveland Federation of Labor, 167
Cleveland Foundation, 156
Cleveland Gesangverein, 87, 88
Cleveland Heights, Ohio, 89, 117, 254
Cleveland Home Brewing Co., 108, 138-139, 151, 154, 160, 161, 165, 191-194, 208, 253
Cleveland Hygeia Ice Co., 116, 152
Cleveland Indians, 184, 198, 238, 254
Cleveland Life Insurance Co., 119
Cleveland Local #17 (union), 64-66, 167, 242 (see also labor; see also strikes)
Cleveland Museum of Art, 156
Cleveland Orchestra, 54
Cleveland, Painesville & Eastern Railroad Co., 254
Cleveland Philharmonic Orchestra, 35
Cleveland Police Commissioner, 49
Cleveland Protestant Orphan Asylum, 29
Cleveland Railway Co., 75
Cleveland Rams, 199
Cleveland Realization Co., 119
Cleveland Trust Co., 120, 137, 156, 213
Clevelander Beer, 120, 161, 192
Clicco-Brew Beer, 114
Colorado River, 95
Colt 45 Malt Liquor, 243
Columbia Brewing Co., 100, 104, 105, 107, 114
Columbus, Ohio, 109, 188, 211, 252
"Column of the Air," 183
competition, brewery, 11, 101-102, 127, 195-196
Con Edison, 156
Condon, George E., 247

Congress, U.S., 95, 143, 144, 146, 157-159
consolidations, brewery, 103-104
"Continuous Brewing Method," 238-239
Conway, Daniel, 248-250
Conway, Patrick, 248-250
Cooke, Thomas Hawley, 22
Cool Mule Porter, 253
Coors, Adolph, Co., 252
Coral Gables, Florida, 172
Corcoran's Saloon, 61
Corlett, Amanda, 76
costs of operating a brewery, 196
craft brewers, 11, 247-255
Craze, Andrew, 254
Creadon's Ginger Ale, 152
Creadon, George E., 213, 214
Creadon, Stephen S., 109-110, 134-138, 152
Crooked River Brewing Co., 252-254
Crown Cork & Seal Co., 181
Crusaders, 158
Crystal Rock Beer, 106, 107, 113, 150, 163, 186, 191, 208
Crystal Rock Products Co. 150
Cuddell, Frank E., 113
Cullen Bill, 159
Cummings, Robert 225
Customs House building, 251
Cuyahoga County Republicans, 193
Cuyahoga County, 19, 132, 254
Cuyahoga River, 20, 252
Daisy Hill estate, 228
Danckers, Stephan, 252-253
Dangeleisen, John, 37, 46
Dangerfield, James, 259
Davies, John, 258
Davis, E. Norris, 243
Davis, Harry, 175
Davis, Phil, & Assoc., 232
Dayton, Ohio, 109
Dean Law, 133
"Defense Tax," 185
DeMaioribus, Alessandro "Sonny," 191-194
DeMaioribus, Dr. Anthony D., 193
Dempsey, Jack, 184
Denbert, George, 257
Denver, Colorado, 251
Dertinger, William, 47
Detroit Avenue Savings & Trust Co., 213
Detroit, Michigan, 19, 85, 104, 140, 177, 210, 219, 224, 244
DeWitt Beer & Ale, 169
DeWitt Hotels, 169
Diamondback Brewery, 251
Diebolt & Ruble brewery, 129

Diebolt brewery, 83, 109, 114, 115-117, 141, 148-149, 152, 154-155, 259
Diebolt, Andrew, 117
Diebolt, Anthony J., 108, 115-117, 155, 259
Diebolt, Frank, 116
Diebolt, Joseph A., 88, 116, 155
Diebolt, Mathias L., 116, 155
Diebolt's Perlex, 148-149
Diemer, Frank E., 85
distillers, 20, 87, 99, 146
Doan Brook, 42
Doan's Corners, 42
Doppelbock, 253
Dortmunder Beer, 190, 206
Dortmunder Gold, 249
Dowie, Ian R., 228-240
Downer, Truman, 27, 46
Downs, Hugh, 225
Dr. Swett's Root Beer, 152
Dudley, Jimmy, 184
Duke Beer, 245
Duquesne Brewing Co. (Pittsburgh), 210, 212, 245
Dyer, J. Milton, 220
Eagle Brewery, 27, 46, 258
East Cleveland Township, 42
EBCO Cola, 152
Edd's Place, 127
Edgewater Park, 88
Edmund Fitzgerald Porter, 249
Edwards, William, Co., 85
Ehle, Frederick, 39
Ehrlich, Joseph G., 169-170
Eighteenth Amendment to Constitution (see National Prohibition)
Eilert Beverage Co., 150-151, 152, 163
Eilert Brewing Co., 160, 163, 185
Eilert, Henry F., 150-151, 163, 185
Eilert's Clev-Ale, 151
Eilert's Pep, 152
Eilert's Supreme Lager, 163
Eliot Ness Lager, 249
Eliot, John, 235
Elk, Severin, 95, 98
Elyria, Ohio, 185
equipment, brewing, 17
Ereshe, John, 165
Erie Brewing Co. (Erie, Pennsylvania), 245
Erie Canal, 20
Erie Nights Pumpkin Brew, 253
Erie Sales Co., 170
Erie, Pennsylvania, 182
Erin Brew Beer, 9, 135, 137, 163, 184, 197, 201, 208, 210, 213-216, 252
Erlanger, Joseph, 100

Excelsior Brewing Co., 138, 141-142, 150
Extra Pilsener Beer, 121
Fairview General Hospital, 49
Faller, Carl, 174, 190
Falstaff Brewing Corp. (St. Louis), 218, 229, 234, 237
Fay, George, Philadelphia Lager Beer Saloon, 34
Feighan, Edward F., 252
Feighan, John T. Jr., 213
Feighan, John T., 135, 137, 213
Fifty-Fifty, 150
Firehouse Brewery, 254
fires, brewery, 22, 25, 27, 40, 93-94
Fishel Brewing Co., 110-111, 114, 138, 149, 163
Fishel, Oscar J., 113, 149, 190
Fishel, Simon, 105, 107, 110-114, 120, 257
Fishel, Theodore, 113, 149
Fishel's Kulmbacher Beer, 114
Fisher & Schafer's Lager Beer Hall, 34
Fisher, Al, 232
Fitzgerald, John, 233
Flats, 19, 20, 27, 28, 248, 253
Florida, 172, 228
Flying Dutchman Yachting Competition, 238
Food Control Law 146
Forest City Bank, 49
Forest City Brewery (1850-1880), 26-27, 86, 259, 260
Forest City Brewery, Inc., (1933-1944), 160, 168-170, 180, 181, 224, 225, 227
Forest City Brewing Co. (1904-1919), 138, 140-141, 151
Forest City Ice Co., 32
Forest City Malthouse, 25
Forest City New Process Co., 151
Forest City Railway Co., 75
Forest City Savings & Trust Co., 213
Forest City Savings Bank, 135
"Formula Ten-O-Two," 197, 201
Fort Leavenworth, Kansas, 91
Fort McPherson (Atlanta), 236
Fort Worth, Texas, 239-240, 245
Fovargue, Creasey, 259
Fovargue, Daniel, 259
Frankel, David, 170
Frankel, Harry, 170
Frankenmuth, Michigan, 236
Franklin Brewing Co. (Columbus, Ohio), 211
Freed Alan, 184, 249
Frieden Beer, 114
Fries & Schuele Building, 250
Froelich, John F., 257
Fromm, Carl, 188, 205
Full Weight Tonic, 137, 151
Fuller & Smith & Ross, 173
Fulton Manufacturing Co., 72
Gaensslen, Philip, 93

Gambrinus Assembly of Knights of Labor, 64
Gambrinus, King, ("patron saint of beer"), 54, 64, 70, 94
Gavagan & Oppmann, 258
Gavagan, Patrick, 85, 258
Gay Nineties Rathskeller, 175, 203
GB Beer, 210
Gehring brewery, 46-49, 83, 84, 104, 104, 105, 107, 114
Gehring, Albert, 48, 88, 89
Gehring, Carl Ernst Jr., 47
Gehring, Carl Ernst, 9, 46-49, 59, 62, 63, 88, 89
Gehring, F.W., 48-49, 107, 108
Gehring, John A., 48
General Foods, 156
General Motors, 157
"Genuine 51 Flavor," 200-201, 205
George F. Stein Brewery (Buffalo), 204
George Gund Foundation, 156
George J. Meyer Malt & Grain Corp., 169-170
Georgetown University, 213
German Hospital, 49
German immigration, 10, 30, 31, 33, 101
German-American Alliance, 146
Gesangverein, see Cleveland Gesangverein
Giunta, John, 209
Gold Bond Beer, 9, 111, 113, 149-150, 163, 186, 191, 199, 201, 207-210
Gold Bond Building, 149
"Gold Bond Polka Party," 184
"Gold Bond Walking Six-Pack," 209
"golden age" of brewing, 13
Golden Dawn Lager Beer, 170
Golden Seal Beer, 141, 151
Goodfellow's Hall, 141
Goodspeed, Jeanne, 232-233
government regulation of brewing industry, 164
grain, government restriction of, 146, 172, 186, 226
Grand Canyon, 95
Graney, Jack, 184
Granite City, Illinois, 188
Great Lakes Brewing Co., 248-250
Greater Cleveland Brewing Co., 134
Greater Cleveland Growth Assoc., 244
"Green Dragon" (automobile), 219
Greystone Farm, 228
Griesedieck Western Brewery Co., 234-235
Gromlich, J., 259
Grossvater Lager, 161
growlers, 14-15, 103, 125
Guarantee Trust Co., 105, 107
Gueuze Lambic, 251
Gund Arena, 251, 253
Gund brewery, 41, 109, 114, 117-120, 161, 170, 235
Gund Gold Mining Co., 119
Gund Realty Co., 155

Gund, Agnes, 156
Gund, Anna M., 155
Gund, Geofrey, 156
Gund, George F., 88, 108, 117-119
Gund, George F. II, 119, 155-156, 235
Gund, George F. III, 156
Gund, Gordon, 156
Gund, Graham, 156
Gund, Louise, 156
Gund's Clevelander Beer, 120
Gund's Crystal Lager, 118, 119
Gund's Finest Beer, 118-119
Haley, J. P., 260
Haller, Jacob F., 141-142, 150-151
Haller, Martin, 257
Haltnorth, Frederick, 35, 67, 69, 72, 90, 91
Haltnorth's Garden, 35, 37, 64, 67
Hamilton, George W., 27, 258, 262
Hamm Brewery (Baltimore), 215
Hammer, John J., 39
Hammond, Venewel D., 258
Hanna Building, 155
Hanna, Marcus, 80
Hanseatic League, 171
Hansky, Max, 141, 168
Harris, Jack H., 168-169
Harvard Brewing Co. (Lowell, Massachusetts), 224
Harvard Business School, 119
Harvard University, 48, 156, 235, 251
Harvard, John, 251
Hawley, Joseph, 22
Hawley, Richard, 22
Hawley, Thomas, 22
Hecht, Joseph, 170
Heidelberg Brewing Co. (Tacoma), 236
Heileman, G., Brewing Co. (LaCrosse, Wisconsin), 244, 245, 246
Heisman, Johnny, 249
Herrick, Myron, 144
Herter, Christian, 235
"Hochwald," 75, 89
Hodge, Clark, 258
Hofbrau House, 85
Hoffman & Paschen, 258
Hoffman, Henry, 258
Hoffman, William, 258
Hoffmann, Louis, 43-45
Hoffmann, Robert, 42-43, 87
Hollenden Hotel, 261
Hollywood, 119
Home Beer, 139
Homestead, Pennsylvania, 63
Hope, Bob, 199
Hotel Carter, 201

Hotel Statler, 191
House of Representatives, U.S., 144
Hubach's Tavern, 14
Huebner brewery (Toledo), 168
Hughes brewery, 27-30, 49, 50
Hughes, Arthur, 30
Hughes, Eliza, 29-30
Hughes, Hazen, 260
Hughes, John M., 27-30, 46, 260
Hughes' Ale, 28, 30
Humel, Adolph F., 161
Humel, Vaclav 121, 140
ice, 10, 32, 47, 65, 82, 84, 116, 152-153
Immigrant Protection Society, 56
Indiana, 259
Indianapolis, Indiana, 219
industry, Cleveland, 9-10, 57-58
International Breweries, Inc. (Detroit), 210, 236
International Union of United Brewery Workers, 167
Iowa, 26, 66, 67, 68, 73, 77, 119, 144
Irish population, Cleveland, 135
Irish Red, 253
Irr, Anthony J., 116
Irr, Joseph A., 116
Italian Swiss Colony Wine, 210
Ives' Cleveland Brewery, 22-26
Ives, Eliza, 24-26
Ives, Levi F., 29-30
Ives, Samuel C., 22-25, 29, 258, 259
Ives, Samuel C., Jr., 24
J. Kraus & Co., 99
Jacob Mall Brewing Co., 41, 114, 117-118
Jacob's Field, 251, 253
Jersey City, 120
John Gund Brewing Co. (Wisconsin), 117
John Harvard's Brew House, 251
Johnson, Earl L., 175
Johnson, Thaine, 249
Johnson, Tom L., 76, 80
Jones & Lloyd Star Brewery, 258
Jones Home for Friendless Children, 49
Joseph & Feiss, 100
Joseph, Emil, 100, 107
Joseph, Moritz, 100
Kaenzig, Christian, 257
Kaenzig, Elizabeth, 257
Kaercher, Gustav, 117
Kaffee Hag Corp., 155-156
Kalsen, Otto, 205
Kansas City Brewing Co., 95
Kansas City, 87
Kansas, 91
"Keg Bottle," 241-242
Keith Building, 155

Kellersaft Beer, 113-114
Kellogg Co., 155-156
Kellogg, W. K., 155-156
Kennedy, Bob, 184
Kentucky, 141
Keokuk, Iowa, 66, 68, 77, 202
Keys, Daniel H., 26, 27, 259
Kilbane, Johnny, 184
Kindsvater & Mall brewery, 41
Kindsvater, Paul, 36-37, 41, 117
Kindsvater's Billiard and Beer Saloon, 34
Kindsvater's Garden, 36-37
King Kole Beer, 185
King's Ale, 185
King's Brewery, Inc., 185
King, Frank "Pee Wee," 197
Kirkwood, John H., 30
Knopp, Frank, 124, 150, 161, 188
Koenig, Valentine, 38
Koepke, Charles J., 165
Koestle, Joseph, 258
Kopp, Anton, 64, 257, 260-261
Korean War, 185
Kostrab, Frank, 242
Kovacs, Frank, 199
Kratochvil, Frank, 124, 161
Kress Weiss Beer Co., 39, 134, 135
Kress, Andrew, 39, 135
Kuebeler brewery (Sandusky), 104-106, 114, 150
Kuebeler, Jacob, 105, 107
Kuebeler-Stang Brewing & Malting Co., 104-107
Kuebler, Gottfried, 89
Kuebler, Gotthold, 188-189
Kuebler, Gottlieb, 93
Kuebler's Malt Tonic, 149
L&C Cafe, 131
La Crosse, Wisconsin, 117
labor, brewery, 16, 29, 63-66, 166-167 (see also
      Cleveland Local #17; see also strikes; see also unions)
lager beer,
      cultural aspects of, 33;
      description of, 31-32;
      dominance of, 30, 31-34
"Lager Beer Riots," 34
Lake City Ice Co., 137
Lake Effect Winter Ale, 254
Lake Erie, 9-10, 21, 26, 41, 65, 77, 84, 182, 249
Lakefront Airport, 154
Lakewood Historical Society, 54
Lancaster, Pennsylvania, 46
Lang, Carl F., 168-169
Lang, Fisher & Stashower, 232
Lang, Gerhard, 115
Lang, Hascal C., 163

Laysy, Henry, 69
Laysy, J. & Co., 69
Laysy, Jacob, 69
Laysy, John, 69
Leicht, John M., 98, 105, 107, 113, 122
Leisy brewery, 66-77, 83, 84, 109, 112, 130, 148-149,
    152, 184, 187, 190, 197, 198, 200, 201, 202-207
"Leisy Growler," 180
Leisy Pilsner Beer, 205-206
"Leisy Premiere Theatre," 197
"Leisy Schooner," 181-182
"Leisy Sports Review," 184
Leisy, August, 67, 77
Leisy, Christine, 68
Leisy, Henry, 67, 69, 77, 89
Leisy, Herbert F., 173-176, 198, 202-207, 248
Leisy, Hugo, 76
Leisy, Isaac, 9, 46, 59, 66-73, 76, 77, 88-89, 104, 173,
    202
Leisy, John, 68, 77
Leisy, Otto, 71, 72, 73-76, 104, 107-108, 112, 173, 202
Leisy, Rudolph, 68
"Leisy's Billy Bock Contest," 203
Leisy's Dortmunder Beer, 190, 206
Leisy's Mello-Gold Beer, 202-203
Leisy's Old Fashion Root Beer, 152
Leisy's Saturday Night Singing Society, 175
Lemp, William J., 68
Lewis, Joe, 184
Lezius & Kaenzig brewery, 257
Lezius & Uehlein brewery, 116, 257, 259
Lezius, George, 193
Lezius, Louis, 116, 257, 259
Liberty Bonds, 146
Lied's Garden, 36
Lied, Balthasar, 36
light beer, 200, 202
Lighthouse Gold, 253
Lincoln Park, 72
Lincoln Savings & Banking Co., 75
Lincoln, Abraham, 29
Lion Brewery, 117
Lion Brewery, Inc. (Cincinnati), 168
Liquor Dealers' and Brewers' Assoc., 59
Liska, Joseph, 124
Lloyd & Keys Cleveland City Brewery, 26, 249, 259
Lloyd, Henry, 258, 259
Lloyd, William, 259
Local Association of Brewers of Cleveland, 48
Loew Manufacturing Co., 10
Loewy, Raymond, 241
Log Cabin Cafe, 128
London Brewery, 27, 86, 260
London, Ontario, 86, 114, 220, 260

Lorain brewery (Lorain, Ohio), 106, 114
Lorain, Ohio, 150
Love Me Dearie hair tonic, 158
low-alcohol beer, see near beer
Lowell, Massachusetts, 224
Lowman, David, 252
Lubeck Beer, 171
Lubeck Brewing Co. (Toledo), 171-172
Lubeck Distributing Co., 172
Lucas, H.G., 25
Lusitania, 75
"Mabel, Black Label," 218, 231, 232-233, 237
Macbeth, John S., 86-87
Mack, Mathias, 46
Mad Crab Brewery & Restaurant, 253, 254
Mader's Saloon, 60
Maerzluft, Dan, 251
"Maine Law," 60
Mall, Jacob (see also Jacob Mall Brewing Co.), 41, 83,
    117
Mall's Crystal Lager, 118
Malt Liquid (brand name), 139
maltsters, 27, 28, 43, 47, 72, 87
Manhattan Brewing Co. (Chicago), 171
Mankato, Minnesota, 208
Manning, Tom, 184
Market Street Exchange, 249
Marmon Motor Car Co., 219
Marshall, J. W., 85
Marshall, John W., 167
Marshman, Homer, 199, 207
Massachusetts, 22
Master Brewers' Association of America, 190
Mayfield Road Mob, 157
mayor, Cleveland, 19, 78-80, 159, 175, 246
McKechnie, J.&A., Brewing Company, 30
mechanization in breweries, 11, 81-82
Medic Drug Grand Prix, 254
Medlin Bohemian Brewery, 120, 257
Medlin Pilsener Brewing Co., 120 (see also Pilsener
    Brewing Co.)
Medlin, Wenzl, 39, 115, 120-121, 124, 257
Meister Brau, 139, 161
Melbourne's Brewing Co., 253, 254
Meldrum & Fewsmith, 200
Mentor, Ohio, 150, 228
Mercantile Manufacturing Co., 219
Merman, Ethel, 225
Metropolitan Opera, 88
Metzger, Charles, 257
Miami, Florida, 188, 212
Michel & McDonough's Saloon, 134
Michel, Alois, 134
Michigan, 189, 196, 209, 259

microbrewers, 11, 247-255
Midwest BrewFest, 248
Miller Brewing Co. (Milwaukee), 168-169, 218, 240, 245
Miller High Life Beer, 168, 241
Miller, Abraham, 170
Miller, Ray T., 159
Miller-Becker Bottling Co., 160
Million Dollar Hair Tonic Co., 158
Milwaukee, Wisconsin, 11, 68, 85, 120, 168, 173, 190, 218, 237, 240, 245
Minnesota North Stars, 156
Missippi River, 223
Missippi Valley, 20
Missippi, 186
Missouri, 68
Mitermiler, Andrew, 50, 53, 70, 83
Modell, Art, 215
Moderation League, 158
Monnett, Frank S., 108
Moon Dog Ale, 249
"Moon Dog Show," 184
Morgan, Bill, 251
"Morgan's Musical Inn," 184
Morlein, Christian, 117
Mueller & Mildner (architects), 140
Mueller Brothers Brewery (Chicago), 91
Mueller, Ernst W., 43-45, 89, 105, 107, 108, 110, 111-113, 138-139, 151, 192, 193, 257
Mueller, Hermann, 45, 89
Mueller, Irma, 89
Mueller, Jacob, 46, 67
Mueller, Julius, 45
Mueller, Omar E., 108, 151, 192-193
Mueller, Peter, & Co., maltsers, 43
Mueller, Rudolph, 45, 139, 257
Mueller, Werner D., 192
Muenchner Double Brew, 151
Muth, George V., 83, 95-98
Muth, George, 95-98, 260
Muth, Matthias, 98
Myers, George, 261
Nantucket, Rhode Island, 238
Nashville, Tennessee, 207
Natick, Massachusetts, 235-236
Nation, Carrie, 131
National Bank of Commerce, 119
National Brewing Co. (Baltimore), 240, 243-244
National Prohibition, 9, 11, 62, 76, 86, 143-147, 157-159, 187
National Union of the Brewery Workmen of the United States, 64-65
National Woolen Mills, 75
national brewers, 11, 85-86, 196, 197
Neal, Bob, 198

near beer, 114, 147-152
Ness, Eliot, 249
Nevada, 119
New Beer's Day, 160-161
New Beer's Eve, 159-160
New England Mutual Life Insurance Co., 235
New England, 211, 224, 235-236
New Orleans, 20, 188, 212
New Philadelphia brewery (New Philadelphia, Ohio), 168, 169
New Towne, Massachusetts, 251
New York, 11, 27, 47, 91, 189, 196, 211
New York City, 11, 20, 27, 33, 58, 64, 77, 105, 155, 173, 190, 233
New York Special Brew, 150, 207
Newark, 190, 218
Newman, George L., 25
Newman, Thomas, 27, 259
Newman, Thomas, Jr., 259
Night Cap Coffee, 155
Nivens, David, 225
Northcoast Golden Ale, 251
Northern Ohio Craft Brewer's Assoc., 248
Nut Brown Ale, 254
O'Reilly, Brian, 251
Oberlin, Ohio, 143
Ogden, W. R., 258
Ohio Attorney General's Office, 108
Ohio Brewers Assoc., 101, 119, 133
Ohio Brewery, Inc. (Columbus), 188
Ohio Canal, 20-21, 28
Ohio City, 248
Ohio License Code, 133
Ohio River, 20-21, 130
Ohio Senate, 159
Ohio Stone Co., 30
Old Bee's Wing Ale, 23
Old Bohemian Style Pilsener Beer, 169
Old German Lager Beer, 170
Old Milwaukee Beer, 225
Old Tavern Ale, 165
Old Tavern Brewing Co., 165
Old Timer's Ale, 163, 191, 199, 207-210
Old Willy India Pale Ale, 251
Oldfield, Barney, 219
Omaha, Nebraska, 218
Ontario, Canada, 27, 86, 87, 220
Oppmann brewery, 83, 90-95, 129, 259
Oppmann Terrace, 95
Oppmann, Andrew W., 9, 90-95, 104, 258
Oregon, 188
organized crime, 157-158, 171-172
Oshkosh, Wisconsin, 244
Otis, Charles A., 224

Otto Moser's, 161
Owens, Jesse, 184
Pabst Beer, 11, 172, 189, 241
Pabst Brewing Company, 85, 217, 218, 225, 237, 244
packaged beer, 179-182
Palace Theatre, 163
Palm Beach, Florida, 228
Paniesville, Ohio, 24
Parfay Cola, 152
Paschen, William, 258
Pavlik, Jaro H., 124, 137, 170-171, 208
Payer, Frank, 37
Pearl Harbor, 185
Pearl Street Savings & Trust Co., 75
Peerless Bicycle, 219
Peerless Motor Car Co., 177, 218, 219-220
Peerless Wringer Co., 219
Pennsylvania, 11, 13, 47, 57, 105, 189, 209, 211
People's Brewing Co. (Oshkosh, Wisconsin), 244
People's Savings Bank, 56
Peoria, Illinois, 87
Persch, John P., 104-105, 107
Pflaumer, William H., & Sons, 245
Philadelphia, Pennsylvania, 11, 13, 33, 145, 212-213, 215-216, 244-246
Phoenix Brewing Co., 93, 95, 104, 105, 107
Phoeniz, Arizona, 239-240
Pilgrim's Porter, 251
"Pilseneers," 184
Pilsener Brewing Co., 83, 114, 120-124, 140, 150, 151, 154, 155, 160, 161, 162, 165, 170, 184-185, 187, 191, 199-201, 205, 208, 210-213, 245
"Pilsener Cellars," 185
Pilsener Ice, Fuel & Beverage Co., 154
Pilsener Pete, 200
Pilsener Square, 120, 122
Pittsburgh, Pennsylvania, 10, 14, 34, 50, 69, 84, 92, 109, 161, 167, 222, 245
P.O.C. Beer, 9, 120-124, 150, 161, 188, 199-201, 205, 210-213, 245
P.O.C. Ginger Ale, 152
P.O.C. Hockey Network, 184-185
P.O.C. Products Co., 152
"P.O.C. Saturday Night Sports Club," 199
"P.O.C. Trophy," 199
Polizzi, Alfred "Big Al," 171-172
Pontiac Improvement Co., 75
population, Cleveland, 20, 57
porter, decsription of, 15
premium beer, 189-190
price wars, beer, 11, 86, 101-102, 107-108, 128, 165-166
prices, beer, 86, 101-102, 103, 164-165, 196, 222, 241
Prince, Hiram, 144
production of Cleveland breweries, total, 26, 58

Prohibition Bureau, 157
prohibition in Ohio, 45, 60, 62, 100, 114, 146-147 (see also National Prohibition)
Public Square, 9, 29, 56, 85, 107, 159-160, 215
Puget Sound National Bank, 119
Quinn, John, 27, 258
radio advertising, 183-185
Rambler-Caribou Mining Co., 119
"Ranch Ten-O-Two," 197
Rathbone, Basil, 197
Rattler Red Vienna Lager, 251
Realty & Rental Co., 119
Red Cross, 187
Red Label Beer, 214
Red Velvet Ale, 214
Red, White & Blue Beer, 225
Reindl, Gottfried, 95
Renner brewery (Akron), 160-161
Richter, William, 34
Rindelhardt, Otto P., 221
Ringneck Brewing Co., 254
Riverbend Ale, 251
Robert Portner Brewing Co. (Alexandria, West Virginia), 98
Rochotte, Henry, 37
Rock Bottom Brewery & Restaurant, 248, 251
rock & roll, 184
Rockefeller, John D., 55
Rocky River Public Library, 54
Rocky River, Ohio, 50, 54
Roether, Louis F., 155
Rogers & Hughes Forest City Brewery, 86
Rogers, Charles C., 27, 259, 260
Rogers, William H., 259, 260
Roosevelt, Franklin D., 158
Rosa, Nathan, 160
Rose Law, 133
Rothmans of Pall Mall, 242
Rowe, Francis, 25
Ruble, Edward, 116
Russell, Henry E., 233, 235, 240-243
Saengerfest, 88
saloons, Cleveland, 125-134;
    and "free lunch," 125-126;
    brewery control of, 75, 102, 127-134;
    conflict with brewers, 102-103;
    legislation of, 132-134;
    number of, 34, 131-133, 157;
    social aspects of, 126-127;
    under attack, 130-134, 143-144;
    vice in, 132
Salvation Army, 156
San Francisco, 69, 91
San Jose Sharks, 156

Index

Sandusky, Ohio, 45, 104, 105, 106, 163, 167, 182, 185, 190
Sanka, 156
Sapienza, Anthony, 242-243
Schaefer Brewing Co. of Ohio, Inc., 215
Schaefer, F. & M., Brewing Co., 214-216, 218, 244
Schaefer, Rudolph J. II, 215
Schaefer, Rudolph J. III, 215
Schiller and Goethe monument, 88
Schlather brewery, 49-56, 83, 84, 104, 105, 109, 114, 127, 129, 130, 149, 250
Schlather, Anna Catherine Sohpia, 54
Schlather, Christian, 50
Schlather, Frederick, 50
Schlather, Leonard, 9, 46, 49-56, 59, 88, 89, 109
Schlitz Beer, 11, 85, 123, 189, 200, 222
Schlitz, John, 85
Schlitz, Jos., Brewing Co., 85, 217, 218, 225, 237, 239
Schmidt & Hoffmann brewery, 12, 42-46, 87, 108, 117
Schmidt brewery (C. Schmidt & Sons), 212-213, 215-216, 244-246, 247, 249
Schmidt, C. W., 42-43, 87, 88
Schmidt, Carl F., 43, 113
Schmidt, Charles, 43
Schmidt, Herman 151
Schmidtbauer, Johann, 95
Schneider, Christian, 260-261
Schneider, John H., 83, 261
Schneider, John, 55, 84
Schneider, William, & Co., 257
Schroeder, Carl F., 139
Schroeder, Lucille, 233
Schumann, Adam, 90, 92
Scott, Randolph, 225
Seattle Brewing & Malting Co., 117, 118
Seattle National Bank, 119
Seattle, Washington, 119
Segal, Joseph, 258
Select Pilsner Beer, 141
Senate, Ohio State, 159
Senate, U.S. 146
Settlers Ale, 252-253
Seyler, Carl, 259
Sheridan, Stuart, 252
Sheriff Street Market House, 56
shipping of beer, 21, 26, 81, 83-84, 196
Silhavy, John, 141
Silvers, Phil, 225, 233, 238
Sixteenth Amendment to Constitution, 146
Slavic Village, 140
Smith, Gavin, 248, 254
Smith, John B., 27, 28
Snajdr, Vaclav, 124
Society for Savings, 56

soft drinks, 152-154
Sonny's Premium Beer, 191
Spanish-American War, 102, 103, 138
speakeasies, 157
Speaker, Tris, 184, 198
Spencer Brewing Co., 30
Spencer, Hugh, 30, 86
Spietschka, Vinzenz, 124
Spring Street Brewery, 27, 46
Squire, Sanders & Dempsey, 107
St, Paul, Minnesota, 87
St. Clair Street Railroad, 37
St. Louis, Missouri, 33, 68, 84, 85, 91, 104, 141, 173, 218, 234-235, 238
Standard Brewing Co., 83, 109-110, 111, 134-138, 151, 152, 154, 160, 163, 170, 183, 184, 186, 188-189, 197, 201, 208, 213-216
Standard Food Products Co., 151
Standard Oil Co., 157
Standard Old Bohemian Style Beer, 137, 151, 208
Standard Premium Beer, 213-214
Standard Special Beer, 151
Stang brewery (Sandusky), 104, 105, 106, 114, 150, 163, 167, 190
Stang, Frank, 107
Stang, John E. 145, 150
Stanton, Edward C., 171
Star Brewing Co., 98, 104, 105, 107, 113
Star-Peerless Brewing Co. (Belleville, Illinois), 209
Starlight Beer, 109, 114, 150
"State Trooper," 197
steam power, 82
Steelcut Oatmeal Stout, 251
Sterling, John, 258
Stone, Frank D., 25-26
Stop-N-Shop Supermarkets, 209
Stoppel brewery, 83, 99-100, 104
Stoppel, Alphonso, 99-100
Stoppel, Joseph, 99-100
Stoppel, Omar, 99-100
Storer, James, 261
stout, description of, 15
Strangmann, Carl A., 98
strikes, brewery labor, 166-167, 222 (see also labor; see also unions)
Stroh Brewery Co., 85, 244, 252, 253
Stroh's Beer, 85
Strongsville, Ohio 253, 254
Stumpf, Louis, 40
Stumpf, Martin, 38-41, 42, 117, 258
Stumpf, Michael, 38-41, 42
Stumpf, William, 40
Success Beer, 141
Sullivan, Frank B., 184, 187